AUTOCAD 200

NO EXPERIENCE REQUIRE

AUTOCAD® 2002
NO EXPERIENCE REQUIRED®

David Frey

SYBEX®

San Francisco • Paris • Düsseldorf • Soest • London

Associate Publisher: Cheryl Applewood
Acquisitions and Developmental Editor: Kathy Yankton
Editor: William Rodarmor
Production Editor: Mae Lum
Technical Editor: Sam Sol Matzkin
Book Designer: Franz Baumhackl
Electronic Publishing Specialist: Franz Baumhackl
Proofreaders: Laurie O'Connell, Nancy Riddiough, Laura
Schattschneider, Yariv Rabinovitch, Mae Lum
Indexer: Ted Laux
Cover Designer: Design Site
Cover Illustrator/Photographer: Jack D. Myers

Library of Congress Card Number: 2001091745
ISBN: 0-7821-4016-5

Manufactured in the United States of America

10 9 8 7 6 5 4 3 2 1

*To my siblings—Jeanne, Virginia,
and Bill—and their families,
and to their sister-in-law and auntie,
my lovely wife Esther.*

ACKNOWLEDGMENTS

There are many people who deserve acknowledgment and gratitude for their contribution to the development and publication of this book.

Many thanks to the folks at Sybex who were involved in this project. Kristine O'Callaghan and Darlene M. Zandanel of the Contracts and Licensing team helped me finalize the contract. Thanks also to Cheryl Applewood, associate publisher, and Raquel Baker, for their efforts to gain support for the publication of this book. Acquisitions and Developmental Editor Kathy Yankton helped me get started. I appreciate the very professional efforts of William Rodarmor, who served as editor; he has been a pleasure to work with. Mae Lum served as production editor and has done wonders to coordinate everything, keep me very well informed, catch numerous errors, and make sure the book got done on time. Also, thanks to Sam Sol Matzkin, who served as the technical editor; his edits and intelligent suggestions have added to the quality of the book.

I also want to mention the production team at Sybex: Electronic Publishing Specialist Franz Baumhackl; Proofreaders Laurie O'Connell, Nancy Riddiough, Laura Schattschneider, and Yariv Rabinovitch; and Indexer Ted Laux. They've been successful in maintaining the standards of high quality that Sybex is known for, and I appreciate their ability and effort in putting together such a good-looking book.

Finally, much thanks to Ron Kappe of Kappe Architects for contributing his designs, drawings, photographs, and time to the color insert. I am very grateful as well to the members of his staff who helped prepare the materials in the color insert for publication: Jason Baggs, David Cookman, and Tylor Bohlman. It's been a pleasure to work with them.

CONTENTS AT A GLANCE

CONTENTS

CHAPTER 14   Printing an AutoCAD Drawing   501

CHAPTER 15   Making the Internet Work With AutoCAD   537

INTRODUCTION

This book was born of the need for a simple yet engaging tutorial that would help beginners step into the world of AutoCAD without feeling intimidated. That tutorial has evolved over the years into a full introduction to the way in which architects and civil and structural engineers use AutoCAD to increase their efficiency and ability to produce state-of-the-art computerized production drawings and designs.

This book is directed toward AutoCAD novices—users who know how to use a computer and do basic file-managing tasks, such as creating new folders and saving and moving files, but who know nothing or very little about AutoCAD. If you are new to the construction and design professions, this book will be an excellent companion as you're learning AutoCAD. If you're already practicing in those fields, you'll immediately be able to apply the skills you'll pick up from this book to real-world projects. The exercises included have been successfully used to train architects, engineers, and contractors, as well as college and high school students, in the basics of AutoCAD.

What Will You Learn from This Book?

Learning AutoCAD, like learning any complex computer program, requires a significant commitment of time and attention, and, to some extent, tolerance for repetition. There are new concepts you must understand to operate the program and to appreciate its potential as a drafting and design tool. But to become proficient at AutoCAD, you must also use the commands enough times to gain an intuitive sense of how they work and how parts of a drawing are constructed.

At the end of most chapters, you will find one or more additional exercises and a checklist of the tools you have learned (or should have learned!). The steps in the tutorial have a degree of repetition built into them that allows you to work through new commands several times and build up confidence before you move on to the next chapter.

Progressing through the book, the chapters fall into four general areas of study:

▶ Chapters 1 through 3 will familiarize you with the organization of the screen, go over a few of the most basic commands, and equip you with the tools necessary to set up a new drawing.

▶ Chapters 4 and 5 develop drawing strategies that will help you use commands efficiently.

- ► Chapters 6 through 11 work with AutoCAD's major features.
- ► Chapters 12 through 15 and Appendices A and B examine intermediate and advanced AutoCAD features.

In the process of exploring these elements, you will follow the steps involved in laying out the floor plan of a small, three-room cabin. Then you will learn how to generate elevations from the floor plan and, eventually, how to set up a title block and print out your drawing. Along the way, you will also learn how to:

- ► Use the basic drawing and modifying commands in a strategic manner
- ► Set up layers
- ► Put color into your drawing
- ► Define and insert blocks
- ► Generate elevation views
- ► Place hatch patterns and fills on building components
- ► Use text in your drawing
- ► Dimension the floor plan

Chapters in the last part of the book touch on more advanced features of AutoCAD, including:

- ► Drawing a site plan
- ► Using external references
- ► Setting up a drawing for printing with Layouts
- ► Making a print of your drawing
- ► Connecting to the Internet through AutoCAD
- ► Working in three dimensions
- ► Defining attributes and extracting data from the drawing

All of these features are taught using the cabin as a continuing project. As a result, you will build up a set of drawings that document your progress through the project and that can be used as reference material later if you find that you need to refresh yourself with material in a specific skill. If you are already somewhat familiar with

AutoCAD and reading only some of the chapters included, you can pull accompanying files for this book from Sybex's Web page, at www.sybex.com.

At the end of the book, there is a glossary of terms that are used in the book and are related to AutoCAD and building design, followed by an index.

Hints for Success

Because this book is essentially a step-by-step tutorial, it has a side effect in common with any tutorial of this type. After you finish a chapter and see that you have progressed further through the cabin project, you may have no idea how you got there and are sure you couldn't do it again without the help of the step-by-step instructions. This feeling is a natural result of this kind of learning tool, and there are a couple of things you can do to get past it. You can do the chapter over again. This may seem tedious, but it has a great advantage. You gain speed in drawing. You'll accomplish the same task in half the time it took you the first time. If you repeat a chapter a third time, you'll halve your time again. Each time you repeat a chapter, you can skip more and more of the explicit instructions and eventually you'll be able to execute the commands and finish the chapter by just looking at the figures and glancing at the text. In many ways this is just like learning a musical instrument. You must go slow at first, but over time and through practice, your pace picks up.

Another suggestion for honing your skills is to follow the course of the book, but apply the steps to a different project. You might draw your own living space, or design a new one. If you have a real-life design project that isn't too complex, that's even better. Your success of learning AutoCAD, or any computer program, is greatly increased when you are highly motivated, and a real project of an appropriate size can be the perfect motivator.

Ready, Set...

When I started learning AutoCAD about 14 years ago, I was at first surprised how long I could sit at a workstation and be unaware of time passing. Then, shortly afterwards, I experienced a level of frustration that I never thought I was capable of feeling. When I finally "got over the hump" and began feeling that I could successfully draw with this program after all, I told myself that I would someday figure out a way to help others get over the hump. That was the primary motivating force for writing this book. I hope it works for you and that you too get some enjoyment while learning AutoCAD. As the title says, "No experience is required," only an interest in the subject and a willingness to learn!

Getting to Know AutoCAD

- ▶ Opening a new drawing
- ▶ Getting familiar with the AutoCAD Graphics window
- ▶ Modifying the display
- ▶ Calling up and arranging toolbars

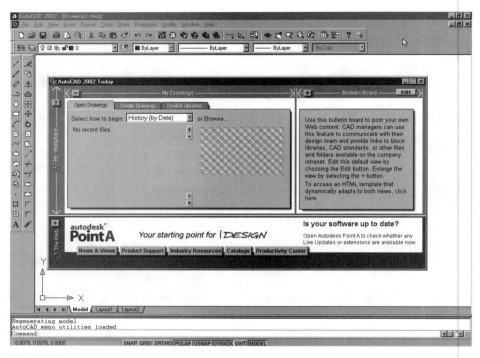

FIGURE 1.2: The AutoCAD Today window

1. Move the cursor to the upper-right corner of the Today window.

2. Click the Close button. The Today window disappears and you see the full AutoCAD Graphics window.

N O T E   Until we get to Chapter 15, we will assume you will be using the Startup dialog box setup option.

CHAPTER 1

Getting to Know AutoCAD

- ▶ Opening a new drawing
- ▶ Getting familiar with the AutoCAD Graphics window
- ▶ Modifying the display
- ▶ Calling up and arranging toolbars

Your introduction to AutoCAD begins with a tour of the features of the AutoCAD screen. In this chapter, you will also learn some tools to help you control the screen's appearance, and how to find and start commands. Starting up AutoCAD is the first task at hand.

Starting Up AutoCAD

If you have installed AutoCAD using the default settings for the location of the program files, start AutoCAD by selecting Programs ➤ AutoCAD 2002 ➤ Auto-CAD 2002 from the Start menu. If you have customized your installation, find and select the AutoCAD 2002 icon to start the program.

The Startup dialog box has four buttons in the upper-left corner. The first two let you set up a new drawing and choose an existing drawing to revise or update. The second two use templates and wizards to initiate advanced setup routines.

The Startup Dialog Box

Dialog Boxes with various combinations of buttons and text boxes are used extensively in AutoCAD. You will learn their many functions as you progress through the book.

If AutoCAD has opened with the Startup dialog box sitting in front of the Auto-CAD Graphics window, your screen will look like Figure 1.1.

The Startup dialog box has four buttons in the upper-left corner. The first two let you set up a new drawing and choose an existing drawing to revise or update. The second two use templates and wizards to initiate advanced setup routines. The middle portion of the dialog box changes depending on which of the four buttons you choose. By beginning a new drawing, we can get past this dialog box to the AutoCAD Graphics window.

1. Click the Start from Scratch button, the second button from the left.

2. Select the English (feet and inches) radio button in the rectangular area titled Default Settings.

Radio buttons are round, and come in a list or a group. Only one item can be activated at a time.

3. Click OK. The dialog box disappears, and your monitor displays the AutoCAD Graphics window, sometimes called the Graphical User Interface or GUI (look ahead to Figure 1.3).

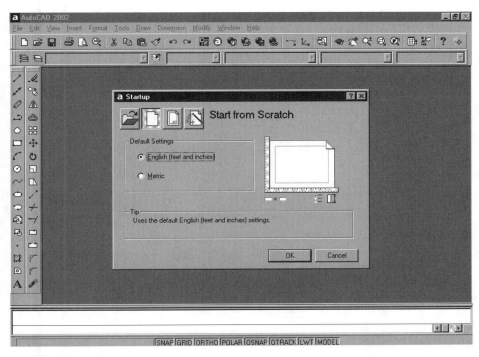

FIGURE 1.1: The Startup dialog box

The AutoCAD Today Window

If AutoCAD has opened with the AutoCAD Today window displayed, your screen will look like Figure 1.2. AutoCAD Today is a window interface that includes the options provided by the Startup dialog box, and also houses features for using AutoCAD with the Internet or an intra-office network. We'll look more closely at this feature in Chapter 15, *Making the Internet Work for AutoCAD.* For now we just need to get past it to view the AutoCAD Graphics window.

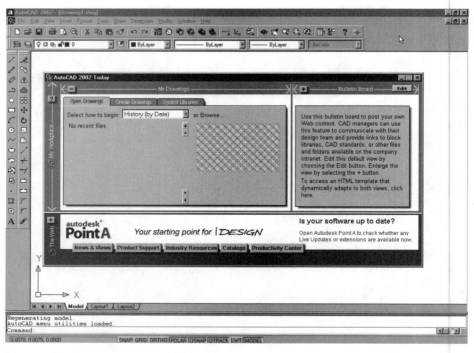

FIGURE 1.2: The AutoCAD Today window

1. Move the cursor to the upper-right corner of the Today window.

2. Click the Close button. The Today window disappears and you see the full AutoCAD Graphics window.

 N O T E   Until we get to Chapter 15, we will assume you will be using the Startup dialog box setup option.

Title bar   Menu bar   Drawing area   Standard toolbar   Object Properties toolbar

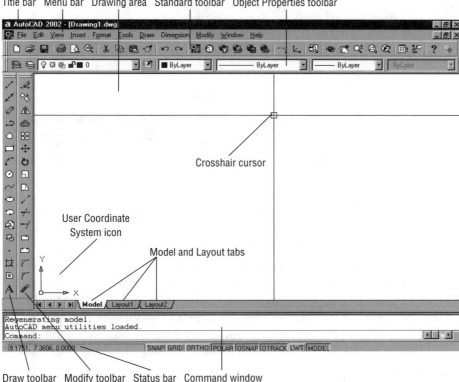

Crosshair cursor

User Coordinate
System icon

Model and Layout tabs

Draw toolbar   Modify toolbar   Status bar   Command window

FIGURE 1.3: The AutoCAD Graphics window

CONTROLLING THE WAY AUTOCAD STARTS UP

You can set AutoCAD to start up in any of three ways.

1. On the Menu bar click Tools ➤ Options.

2. In the Options dialog box, click the System tab to bring it forward.

3. Go to the General Options area and open the Startup drop-down list.

▶ If you want the Today window, click Show Today Startup Dialog.

▶ If you want the Startup dialog box, click Show Traditional Startup Dialog.

▶ If you want just the AutoCAD Graphics window to come up by itself, click Do Not Show a Startup Dialog.

4. Click Apply, and then click OK.

The next time you start up AutoCAD, your preference will be used.

Introduction to the AutoCAD Graphics Window

At the top of the Graphics window sits the title bar, the menu bar, and two toolbars.

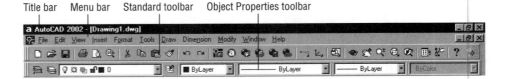

Title bar   Menu bar   Standard toolbar   Object Properties toolbar

The title bar is analogous to the title bar on any Windows program. It contains the program name (AutoCAD) and the title of the current drawing with its *path*. Below the title bar is the menu bar, where you will see the drop-down menus. Among the drop-down menus, the first two on the left and the last one on the right are Microsoft menus (meaning that they appear on most Windows applications). These Microsoft menus also contain a few commands specific to AutoCAD. The rest of the menus are AutoCAD menus. Below these menus is the *Standard toolbar*, which contains 30 command buttons. Several of these buttons will be familiar to Windows users; the rest are AutoCAD commands. Just below this toolbar is the *Object Properties toolbar*, which contains three command buttons and five drop-down lists.

The blank middle section of the screen is called the *drawing area*. Notice the movable *crosshair cursor*.

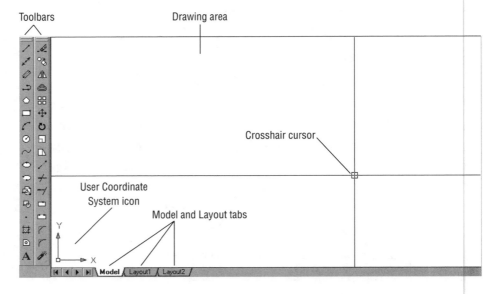

Toolbars

Drawing area

Crosshair cursor

User Coordinate System icon

Model and Layout tabs

Notice the little box at the intersection of the two crosshair lines. This is one of several forms of the AutoCAD cursor. When you move the cursor off the drawing area, it changes to the standard Windows pointing arrow. As you begin using commands, it will take on other forms, depending on which step of a command you are in. There is also an icon with a double arrow in the lower-left corner of the drawing area. This is called the *User Coordinate System icon* and is used to indicate the positive direction for x and y coordinates. You won't need it for most of the chapters in this book, so you'll learn how to make it invisible in Chapter 3, *Setting Up a Drawing*. At the bottom of the drawing area, there are three tabs: a Model tab and two Layout tabs. These are used for switching between viewing modes and will be discussed in Chapter 13, *Using Layouts to Set Up a Print*. Our example shows no toolbars floating in the drawing area, but there are two docked toolbars on the left of the drawing area. Your screen may or may not have them, or they may be in a different position. If the toolbars are within the drawing area, they will have a colored title bar. For more specifics, see the section titled "Toolbars" later in this chapter.

Below the drawing area is the *Command window*.

The Command window is where you tell the program what to do, and where the program tells you what's going on. It's an important area and you will need to learn about how it works in detail. There should be three lines of text visible. If your screen has fewer than three lines showing, you will need to make another line or two visible. You'll learn how to do this later in this skill in the section titled "The Command Window."

Below the Command window is the *Status bar*.

On the left end of the Status bar, you'll see a coordinate readout window. In the middle there are eight readout buttons that indicate various drawing modes. It is important to learn about the coordinate system and most of these drawing aids (Snap, Grid, Ortho, and Osnap) early on as you learn to draw in AutoCAD. They will help you create neat and accurate drawings. Polar and Otrack are advanced drawing tools and will be introduced in Chapter 5, "Gaining Drawing Strategies: Part 2." Lwt stands for Lineweight and will be discussed in Chapter 14, "Printing an AutoCAD Drawing," in the discussion on plotting. The Model button is an advanced aid that will be covered in Chapter 13.

This has been a quick introduction to the various parts of the Graphics window. There are a couple of items I didn't mention which may be visible on your screen. You may have scroll bars below and to the right of the drawing area. And you may have a menu on the right side of the drawing area. Both of these features can be useful, but they may also be a hindrance and can take up precious space in the drawing area. They won't be of any use while working your way through this book, so I suggest that you remove them for now.

To temporarily remove these features, follow these steps:

1. From the menu bar, click Tools ➤ Options. The Options dialog box appears (shown in Figure 1.4). It has nine tabs across the top that act like tabs on file folders.

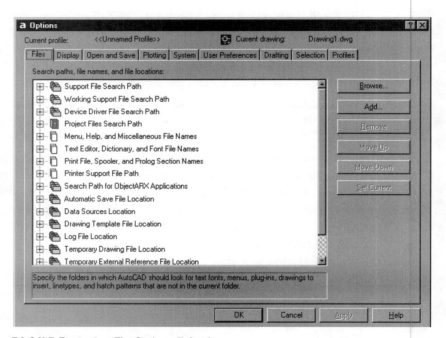

FIGURE 1.4: The Options dialog box

2. Click the Display tab. The display settings come up (Figure 1.5). Focus in on the rectangular area titled Window Elements. If you have scroll bars visible on the lower and right edges of the drawing area,

the first check box, Display Scroll Bars in Drawing Window, should be selected.

3. Click the check box to remove the checkmark, as you will not be using the scroll bars. This turns off the scroll bars. Do the same for the second check box, named Display Screen Menu, to turn off the screen menu. Don't click the OK button yet.

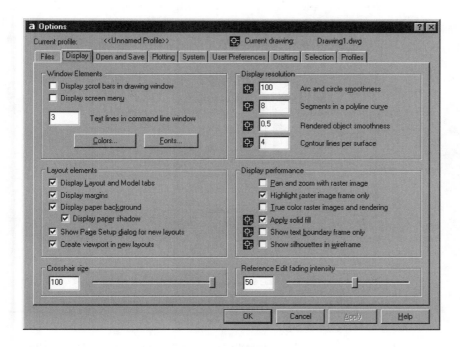

FIGURE 1.5: The Display tab of the Options dialog box

Another display setting that you may want to change at this point controls the color of the cursor and the drawing area background. The illustrations in this book show a white background and black crosshair cursor, but you may prefer to have the colors reversed. To do this, follow these steps:

1. Click the Colors button in the bottom of the Window Elements of the Display tab in the Options dialog box. The AutoCAD Color Options dialog box comes up (Figure 1.6). In the middle of the dialog box, in the drop-down list titled Window Element, Model tab background should be visible. If it's not, open the drop-down list and select it.

2. Move to the Color drop-down list, which is below the Window Element drop-down list. If your drawing area background is currently white, a square followed by White will be displayed. Open the Color drop-down list. Scroll to the color Black (or the background color you want) and select it. The drawing area will now have that color, and the cursor color will change to white, as shown in the Model Tab preview window in the upper-left corner of the dialog box.

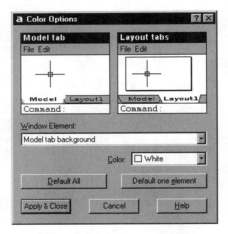

FIGURE 1.6: The AutoCAD Color Options dialog box

3. Click the Apply & Close button to close the AutoCAD Color Options dialog box.

4. Click OK to close the Options dialog box.

Your screen and crosshair cursor will take on their newly assigned colors.

 T I P   If you choose a color other than black as the Model tab background color, the color of the crosshair cursor remains the same as it was (black). To change the crosshair color, stay in the AutoCAD Color Options dialog box, open the Window Element drop-down list, and select Model tab pointer. Then select a color from the Color drop-down list.

The Command Window

Just below the drawing area is the Command window. This window is actually separate from the drawing area and behaves like a Microsoft Windows window; that is, you can drag it to a different place on the screen and resize it, although I don't recommend that you do this at first. If you currently have fewer than three lines of text in the window, you will need to increase its vertical size. To do this, move the cursor to the horizontal boundary between the drawing area and the Command window until it changes to an up-and-down arrow broken by two parallel horizontal lines.

Hold down the left mouse button and drag the cursor up by approximately the amount that one or two lines of text would take up, then release the mouse. You should get more lines of text showing, but you may have to try it a couple of times to get exactly three lines visible. When you close the program, the new settings will be saved, and it will be right the next time you start up AutoCAD.

 T I P   The number of lines of text in the Command window can also be set in the Options dialog box. Click Tools ➢ Options and activate the Display tab. In the Window Elements area, set the Text Lines in Command Line Window setting to 3. Then click the Apply button and the OK button.

The Command window is very important. It is here that you will give information to AutoCAD, and where AutoCAD will prompt you as to the next step in executing a command. It is a good practice to get into the habit of keeping one eye on it as you work on your drawing. Most errors are made from not watching it often enough.

Before you begin to draw, you should take a close look at the menus, toolbars, and keyboard controls.

 N O T E   In many cases, AutoCAD offers you a number of ways to start up commands: from drop-down menus, from the toolbars, or from the keyboard. When you get used to drawing with AutoCAD, you will learn some of the shortcuts available to start commands quickly, and you will find the way that is most comfortable for you.

Drop-Down Menus

The menu bar, just below the title bar (see Figure 1.2), consists of 11 words and an icon. Click any of these and you will find a drop-down menu. The icon on the left end, as the File and Edit options, are Microsoft menus that come with all Windows-compatible applications, although they are somewhat customized to work with AutoCAD. The menu associated with the icon contains commands to control the appearance and position of the drawing area. Commands in the File menu are for opening and saving new and existing drawing files, printing, exporting files to another application, choosing basic utility options, and exiting the application. The Edit menu contains the Undo and Redo commands, the Cut and Paste tools, and options for creating links between AutoCAD files and other files. The Help menu (the last menu on the right) works like all Windows help menus.

The other eight menus contain the most often-used AutoCAD commands. You will find that if you can master the logic of how the commands are organized by menu, it will be immensely helpful in finding the command you want. Here is a short description of each of the other AutoCAD drop-down menus:

View   Contains tools for controlling the display of your drawing file.

Insert   Has commands for placing drawings and images, or parts of them, inside other drawings.

Format   Is where you'll find commands for setting up the general parameters for a new drawing.

Tools   Contains special tools for use while you are working on the current drawing, such as those for finding how long a line is or for running a special macro.

Draw   Holds the commands for putting new objects (like lines or circles) on the screen.

Dimension   Is where you'll find commands for dimensioning a drawing.

Modify   Has the commands for making changes to objects already existing in the drawing.

Window   Has options for displaying currently open windows and lists currently open drawing files.

Toolbars

Just below the drop-down menus is the most extensive of the toolbars—the Standard toolbar.

The 30 icons don't appear as buttons until you put the pointer arrow on them, and then they are highlighted. They are arranged into 10 logical groups. The icons on the left half of the Standard toolbar are for commands used in all Windows-compatible applications, so you may be familiar with them. The icons on the right half of the Standard toolbar are AutoCAD commands that you will use during your regular drawing activities for a variety of tasks. These commands can do a number of things, including:

▶ Link up and communicate with other AutoCAD users through the Internet.

▶ Change the view or orientation of the drawing on the screen.

▶ Change the properties of an object, such as color or linetype.

▶ Borrow parts of a drawing to use in your current drawing.

▶ Force a line you are drawing to meet another line or geometric feature at specified points.

Toolbar Flyouts

Notice that a few icons on the Standard toolbar have a little triangular arrow in the lower-right corner. These arrows indicate that more than one command can be found through these icons. Follow the next six steps to see how these special icons work.

1. Move the cursor up to the Standard toolbar and place the arrow on the icon that has a magnifying glass with a rectangle in it.

2. Rest the arrow on the button for a moment without clicking. A small window opens just below it, revealing what command the button represents. In this case, the window should say "Zoom Window." This is a tool tip—all buttons have them. Notice the small arrow in the lower-right corner of the icon. This is the multiple-command arrow mentioned before.

3. Place the arrow cursor on the button and hold down the left mouse button. As you hold the mouse button down, a column of eight buttons drops down vertically below the original button. The top button in the column is a duplicate of the button you clicked. This column of buttons is called a *toolbar flyout*.

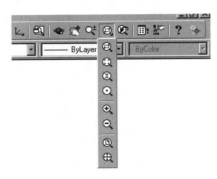

The Zoom All command changes the view of your drawing to include special pre-set parameters. We'll look at it in Chapter 3.

4. While still holding the mouse button down, drag the arrow down over each button until you get to the one that has a magnifying glass with a piece of white paper on it. Hold the arrow there until you see the tool tip. It should say "Zoom All." Now release the mouse button. The flyout disappears and AutoCAD executes the Zoom All command. Look in the Command window at the bottom of the screen.

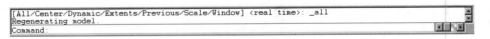

At the end of the top line of text, it says "_all." This tells you that you have used the All option of the Zoom command. This flyout is called the Zoom flyout because it contains tools for changing views of the drawing, or "zooming around in the drawing."

5. Look at the Standard toolbar where the Zoom Window button was previously located. Notice that it's been replaced by the Zoom All button.

T I P On a toolbar flyout, the button you select replaces the button that was on the toolbar. This is handy if you are going to be using the same command several times, because now the button for the command is readily available and you don't have to open the flyout to select it again. The order of the flyout buttons remains the same, so when you open the Zoom flyout again, the Zoom Window button will be at the top of the list. You will need to become familiar with any flyout buttons you use, because the last one used becomes the representative button on the home toolbar.

6. Press Esc to cancel the List command.

By taking a look at the Zoom flyout on the Standard toolbar, you have been introduced to the mechanisms that govern the behavior of flyouts in general.

N O T E Whenever you start up AutoCAD for a new drawing session, the toolbars will be reset and contain the flyout buttons that were originally there.

The toolbar flyouts are actually regular toolbars that have been attached to another toolbar. There are 26 toolbars in all, and only four are flyouts. These are all attached to the Standard toolbar. Any of these flyouts can be called up as a regular toolbar, independent from the Standard toolbar.

Calling Up and Arranging Toolbars

We'll use the Zoom toolbar as an example of some ways in which toolbars can be controlled and manipulated.

1. Right-click on any toolbar button that is on the screen. The Toolbars menu comes up (Figure 1.7).

FIGURE 1.7: The Toolbars menu

2. Find Zoom on the menu on the list and click it. The Zoom toolbar will appear in the form of a floating box in the drawing area.

3. Notice that the Zoom toolbar now has a title bar. Toolbars that are positioned on the drawing area have title bars. By putting the cursor on the title bar and holding down the left mouse button, you can drag the toolbar around on the screen. Try this with the Zoom toolbar.

4. Click and drag the Zoom toolbar to the right side of the screen. You will notice that as you drag it, the toolbar stays put and you are dragging a rectangle of the same size as the toolbar (see Figure 1.8). As you drag the rectangle to the right of the drawing area and begin to move it off the drawing area onto the right side of the screen, the rectangle changes size to become taller and thinner.

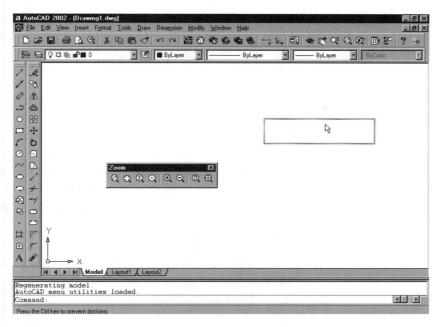

FIGURE 1.8: Dragging the Zoom toolbar

5. Release the left mouse button once the toolbar is out of the drawing area. The rectangle changes to the Zoom toolbar, which is now positioned off the drawing area without its title bar.

This procedure is called *docking* a toolbar. Notice how the Standard and Object Properties toolbars have no title bars—they are docked.

6. Move the cursor arrow to the left end of the Standard toolbar so the point of the arrow is on the two vertical grab bars.

7. Hold down the left mouse button while on the grab bars and drag the Standard toolbar onto the drawing area. Release the mouse button. The Standard toolbar now has a title bar, and the space it was occupying at the top of the screen has been filled in, making the drawing area a little larger, as you will see in Figure 1.9. The Standard toolbar is now a *floating* toolbar and can be moved around the drawing area.

Floating toolbars don't affect the size of the drawing area, but they cover your drawing. Each docked toolbar takes up a little space that would otherwise be drawing area. You have to decide how many docked and floating toolbars you need on the screen at a time. A good way to start out is to leave the Standard and Object Properties toolbars docked at the top of the screen, and the Draw and Modify toolbars docked on the left side of the screen, as in Figure 1.2.

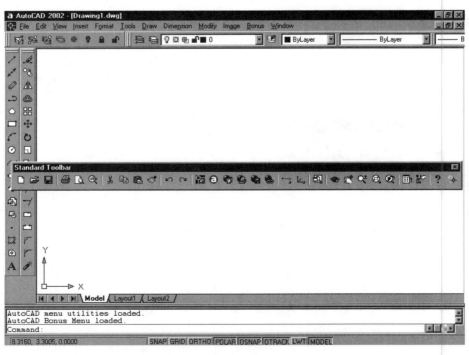

FIGURE 1.9: The Standard toolbar on the drawing area

To put the Standard toolbar back where it was and delete the Zoom toolbar, follow these steps:

1. Drag the Standard toolbar up to its former position above the Object Properties toolbar.

2. Drag the Zoom toolbar back onto the drawing area, using the grab bars. You can easily change the shape of any floating toolbar by dragging its edge. Let's change the shape of this toolbar.

3. Move the cursor to the far-right edge of the Zoom toolbar until the crosshair cursor changes into a two-way arrow.

   Then hold down the left mouse button with the cursor on the right edge of the toolbar and drag the arrow to the left until the rectangle changes shape. Then release the mouse button.

   Each floating toolbar can be reshaped and repositioned to fit on the drawing area just how you like it. You won't need the Zoom toolbar just now, so remove it.

4. Move the cursor up to the title bar and click the box with an × in it. The Zoom toolbar disappears.

If your Draw and Modify toolbars are positioned on the left side of the drawing area as in Figure 1.2, go on to the next section. If these toolbars are in another location on the drawing area, try out the steps you have used in this section to dock them on the left side. If the toolbars are not visible, right-click any visible toolbar button, then click Draw on the Toolbar menu. Drag the Draw toolbar to the left side of the drawing area and dock it. Do the same with the Modify toolbar, positioning it next to the Draw toolbar.

This arrangement of the toolbars will be convenient because commands on these four toolbars are used often. When you need other toolbars temporarily, you can use the Toolbars menu to bring them onto the drawing area and let them float.

Custom Toolbars

Each toolbar can be customized and you can build your own custom toolbars with only the command buttons you need for your drawing. You can even design your own buttons for commands that aren't already represented by buttons on the toolbars. These activities are for more advanced users, however, and are not covered in this book. To find out more about how to work with toolbars, see *Mastering AutoCAD 2002,* by George Omura (Sybex, 2001).

Profiles

As you become accustomed to working with AutoCAD, you will develop your own preferences for the layout of the AutoCAD Graphics window, including:

 ▶ Which toolbars are docked and where

 ▶ The shape of the crosshair cursor

 ▶ The background color of the drawing area

These features can be controlled from the Options dialog box. If you share your workstation with others, you will find it convenient to set up a profile and save it. That way, if someone changes the organization of your Graphics window, you can quickly restore your preferences. Here's how to do this:

1. Click Tools ➤ Options, then click the Profiles Tab to make it active (Figure 1.10).

2. Click the Add to List button. The Add Profile dialog box comes up (Figure 1.11).

3. Type in the name of your profile. You also have the option of entering a description below the name.

4. Click Apply & Close. Your new profile appears in the list of Available Profiles. It is a copy of whatever profile was current when you added yours.

5. Click the Display tab and make any changes you want, then click OK to close the Options dialog box.

6. Make any changes to the toolbars. These settings will be saved as your profile.

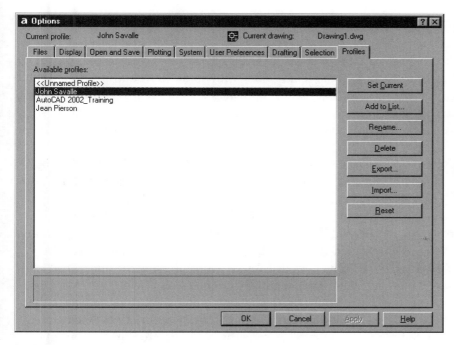

FIGURE 1 . 1 0 : The Profiles tab in the Options dialog box

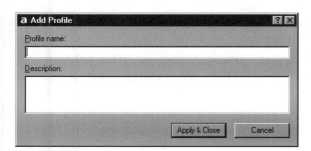

FIGURE 1 . 1 1 : The Add Profile dialog box

The next time you start up AutoCAD, if the Graphics window is not set up the way you want:

1. Click Tools ➢ Options and click the Profiles tab.

2. Highlight your profile and click the Set Current button.

3. Click OK. The Graphics window should now be set to your preferences.

The Keyboard

The keyboard is an important tool for entering data and commands. If you are a good typist, you can gain speed in working with AutoCAD by learning how to enter commands on the keyboard. AutoCAD provides what are called *alias keys*—single keys or key combinations that will start any of several often-used commands. You can add more or change the existing aliases as you get more familiar with the program.

In addition to the alias keys, several of the F keys (function keys) on the top of the keyboard can be used as two-way or three-way toggles (switches) to turn Auto-CAD functions on and off. Although there are buttons on the screen that duplicate these functions (Snap, Grid, etc.), it is sometimes faster to use the F keys.

Finally, you can activate commands on the pull-down menus from the keyboard, rather than using the mouse. Notice that each menu has an underlined letter, called a *hotkey*. By holding down the Alt key while pressing the underlined letter, the menu is activated. Each command on the menu also has a hotkey. Once you have activated the menu with the hotkey combination, you can type in the underlined letter of these commands without using the Alt key to execute them. For a few commands, this method can be the fastest way to start them up and select options.

While working in AutoCAD, you will need to key in a lot of data, such as dimensions and construction notes, answer questions with "yes" or "no," and use the arrow keys. The keyboard will be used constantly. It may help to get into the habit of keeping the left hand on the keyboard and the right hand on the mouse—if you are right-handed—or the other way around, if you are left-handed.

The Mouse

Your mouse will most likely have two or three buttons. (If it's an IntelliMouse, it will have two buttons with a wheel between them.) So far in this chapter, you have used the left mouse button for choosing menus, commands or command options, or for holding down the button and dragging a menu, toolbar, or window. The left mouse button is the one you will be using most often, but the right mouse button will also be used.

While drawing, the right mouse button will be used for the following three operations:

> ▶ To bring up a menu containing options relevant to the particular step you are in at the moment

▶ To use in combination with the Shift key to bring up a special menu called the Cursor menu (see Chapter 10, *Controlling Text in a Drawing*)

▶ To bring up a menu of toolbars when the pointer is on any icon of a toolbar that is presently open

If you have a three-button mouse, the middle button is usually programmed to bring up the Cursor menu mentioned above, instead of using the right button with the Shift key. If you have an IntelliMouse, the wheel can be used in several ways to control the view of your drawing. We'll cover those methods in subsequent chapters.

AutoCAD makes extensive use of toolbars and the right-click menu feature. This makes your mouse a very important input tool. The keyboard is necessary for inputting numerical data and text, and it has hotkeys and aliases that can speed up your work. But the mouse is the primary tool for starting commands, selecting options, and controlling toolbars.

The next chapter will familiarize you with a few basic commands that will enable you to draw a small diagram. If you are going to take a break and want to close down AutoCAD, click File ➤ Exit and choose not to save the drawing.

Are You Experienced?

Now you can...

☑ **open a new drawing using the Start Up dialog box**

☑ **recognize the elements of the AutoCAD Graphics window**

☑ **understand how the Command window works and why it's important**

☑ **use drop-down menus**

☑ **call up and control the positioning of toolbars**

CHAPTER 2

Basic Commands to Get Started

- ▶ Understanding coordinate systems
- ▶ Drawing your first figure
- ▶ Erasing, offsetting, filleting, extending, and trimming lines in a drawing

Now that you have taken a quick tour of the AutoCAD screen, you are ready to begin drawing. In this chapter you will be introduced to the most basic commands used in drawing with AutoCAD. To get you started, I will guide you through the process of drawing a box (Figure 2.1).

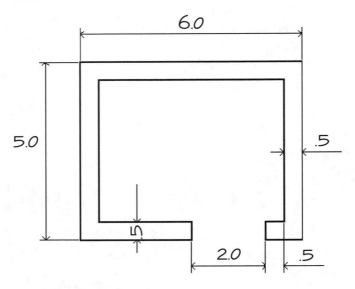

FIGURE 2.1: The box to be drawn

You only need to use five or six commands to draw the box. First, you'll become familiar with the Line command and how to make lines a specific length. Then you'll go over the strategy for completing the box.

The Line Command

In traditional architectural drafting, lines were often drawn to extend slightly past their endpoints (Figure 2.2). This is no longer done in CAD except for special effects.

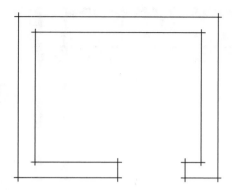

FIGURE 2.2: Box drawn with overlapping lines

The *Line command* draws a line between locations on existing lines, between geometric figures, or between two points that you can choose anywhere within the drawing area. These points can be designated by clicking them on the screen, by entering the x and y coordinates for each point in the Command window, or by entering distances and angles at the command line. After the first segment of a line is drawn, you have the option of ending the command or drawing another line segment from the end of the first one. You can continue to draw adjoining line segments for as long as you like. Let's see how it works.

1. Choose File ➤ New. In the Create New Drawing dialog box, be sure English is selected, then click the Start from Scratch button and click OK to start a new drawing.

2. Glance down at the Status bar at the bottom of your screen. All buttons except Model should be off—that is, in an unpushed state. If any are pushed, click them to turn them off.

3. Be sure that the Draw and Modify toolbars have been docked on the left side of the drawing area, as in Figure 2.3. Refer to Chapter 1, *Getting to Know AutoCAD*, if you need a reminder on how to bring up or move toolbars.

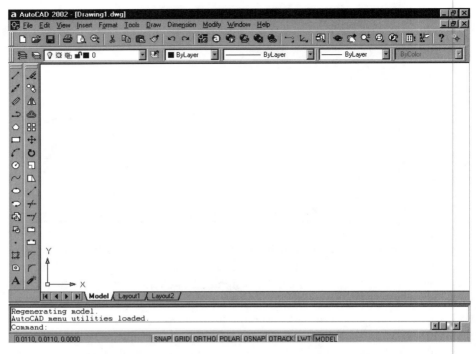

FIGURE 2.3: The Draw and Modify toolbars docked on the left side of the drawing area and all Status bar buttons except Model turned off

4. Click the Line button at the top of the Draw toolbar.

Look at the bottom of the Command window and see how the Command: prompt has changed.

The prompt now tells you that the Line command has been started (Command: _line) and that AutoCAD is waiting for you to designate the first point of the line (Specify first point:).

5. Move the cursor onto the drawing area and, using the left mouse button, click a random point to start a line.

6. Move the cursor away from the point you clicked and notice how a line segment appears which stretches like a rubber band from the

> The Line command can also be started by choosing Draw ➤ Line on the Menu bar, or by typing **L** and pressing the Enter key.

point you just picked to the cursor. The line changes length and direction as you move the cursor.

7. Look at the Command window again and notice that the prompt has changed.

It now is telling you that AutoCAD is waiting for you to designate the next point (Specify next point or [Undo]:).

8. Continue picking points and adding lines as you move the cursor around the screen (see Figure 2.4). After the third segment is drawn, the Command window repeats the Specify next point or [Close/Undo]: prompt each time you pick another point.

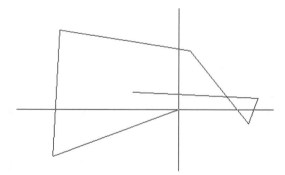

FIGURE 2.4: Drawing several line segments

9. When you've drawn six or seven line segments, press the Enter key to end the Line command. The cursor separates from the last drawn line segment. Look at the Command window once again.

The Command: prompt has returned to the bottom line. This tells you there is no command running.

In this exercise, you used the left mouse button to select the Line button from the Draw toolbar and also to pick several points in the drawing area to make the line segments. Then you pressed Enter (↵) on the keyboard to end the Line command.

N O T E   In the exercises that follow, the Enter symbol (↵) will be used. When I say to "type" or "enter" something, it means to type the data that follows the word *type* or *enter* and then to press the Enter key (↵).

Coordinates

Try using the Line command again, but instead of picking points in the drawing area with the mouse as you did before, this time enter x and y coordinates for each point from the keyboard. To see how, follow these steps:

First, you'll clear the screen using the Erase command.

1. Type erase ↵.

2. Type all ↵.

3. Press ↵.

Now start drawing lines again by following these steps:

1. Start the Line command again by clicking the Line button on the Draw toolbar.

2. Type 2,2 ↵.

3. Type 6,3 ↵.

4. Type 4,6 ↵.

5. Type 1,3 ↵.

6. Type 10,6 ↵.

7. Type 10,1 ↵.

8. Type 2,7 ↵.

9. Press ↵ again to end the command.

The lines will be similar to those you drew previously, but this time you know where each point is located relative to the 0,0 point. In the drawing area, every point has an absolute *x* and *y* coordinate. In steps 2–8 above, you entered the *x* and *y* coordinates for each point. For a new drawing, like this one, the origin (0,0 point) is in the lower-left corner of the drawing area and all points in the drawing area are positive (Figure 2.5).

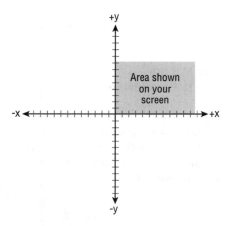

FIGURE 2.5: The *x* and *y* coordinates on the drawing area

Let's explore how the cursor is related to the coordinates in the drawing.

1. Move the cursor around and notice the left end of the Status bar at the bottom of the screen. This is the coordinate readout, and it displays the coordinates of the cursor's position.

2. Move the cursor as close to the lower-left corner of the drawing area as you can without it changing into an arrow. The coordinate readout should be close to 0.0000,0.0000,0.0000.

N O T E   You will see a readout for the *z* coordinate as well, but we can ignore it for now as you will be working only in two dimensions for the majority of this book. The *z* coordinate will always read as 0 until we work in three dimensions (see Appendix A, *A Look at Drawing in 3D*).

3. Move the cursor to the top-left corner of the drawing area. The read-out will change to something close to 0.0000,9.0000,0.0000, indicating that the top of the screen is nine units away from the bottom.

4. Move the cursor one more time to the upper-right corner of the drawing area. The readout will still have a y coordinate of approximately 9.0000 and the x coordinate will now have a value of somewhere between 12.0000 and 16.0000, depending on the size of your monitor and how the various parts of the AutoCAD Graphics window (see Skill 1 for a recap) are laid out on your screen.

The drawing area of a new drawing is preset to be 9 units high and 12–16 units wide, with the lower-left corner of the drawing at the coordinates 0,0.

N O T E   For the moment, it doesn't matter what measure of distance these units represent. Those decisions will be addressed in Chapter 3, *Setting Up a Drawing*. And don't worry about the four decimal places in the coordinate readout. The number of places is controlled by a setting you will learn about soon.

Relative Coordinates

Once you understand the coordinate system used by AutoCAD, you can draw lines to any length and in any direction you desire. Look at the box in Figure 2.1. Because you know the dimensions, you could calculate, by adding and subtracting, the absolute coordinates for each *vertex*—the connecting point between two line segments—and then use the Line command to draw the shape by entering these coordinates from the keyboard. But AutoCAD offers you several tools for drawing this box much more easily. Two of these tools are the relative Cartesian and the relative polar coordinate systems.

When drawing lines, these systems use a set of new points based on the last point designated, rather than the 0,0 point of the drawing area. They are called "relative" coordinate systems because the coordinates used are *relative* to the last point specified. If you have the first point of a line located at the coordinate 4,6 and you want the line to extend 8 units to the right, the coordinate that is relative to the first point is 8,0 (8 units in the positive x direction and 0 units in the positive y direction), while the actual—or *absolute*—coordinate of the second point would be 12,6.

The *relative Cartesian coordinate system* uses relative x and y coordinates in just the manner shown above, while the *relative polar coordinate system* relies on a distance and an angle relative to the last point specified. You will probably favor one system over the other, but you need to know both systems because there will be times when, due to what information you have at hand, you will be able to use only one of the two. A limitation of this nature will be illustrated in Chapter 4, *Gaining Drawing Strategies: Part 1*.

When entering the relative coordinates, you need to enter an "at" symbol (@) before the coordinates. In the above example, the relative Cartesian coordinates would be entered as @8,0. The @ symbol lets AutoCAD know that the numbers following that symbol represent coordinates that are relative to the last point designated.

Relative Cartesian Coordinates

The Cartesian system of coordinates, named after the philosopher René Descartes, who invented the x,y coordinate system in the 1600s, uses a horizontal (x) and vertical (y) component to locate a point relative to the 0,0 point. The relative Cartesian system uses the same components to locate the point relative to the last point picked, so it's a way of telling AutoCAD how far left or right and up or down to extend a line or move an object from the last point picked (Figure 2.6). If the direction is to the left, the x coordinate will be negative. Similarly, if the direction is down, the y coordinate will be negative. Use this system when you know the horizontal and vertical distances from point 1 to point 2. To enter data using this system, use this form: @x,y.

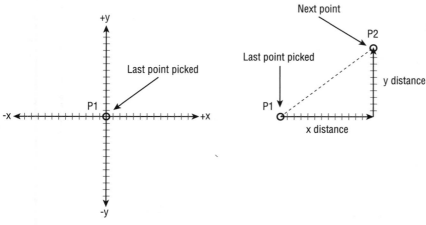

FIGURE 2.6: The relative Cartesian coordinate system

Relative Polar Coordinates

This system requires a known distance and direction from point 1 to point 2. Calculating the distance is pretty straightforward: It's always positive and is simply the distance away from point 1 that point 2 will be placed. The direction requires a convention for determining an angle. AutoCAD defines right (toward three o'clock) as the direction of the 0° angle. All other directions are determined from a counterclockwise rotation (Figure 2.7). On your screen, up is 90°, left is 180°, down is 270°, and a full circle is 360°. To let AutoCAD know that you are entering an angle and not a relative *y* coordinate, use the "less than" symbol (<) before the angle and after the distance. So in the example above, to designate a point 8 units to the right of the first point, you would enter @8<0.

 N O T E   Remember, use the relative polar coordinates method to draw a line from the first point when you know the distance and direction to its next point. Enter data using this form: **@distance<*angle***.

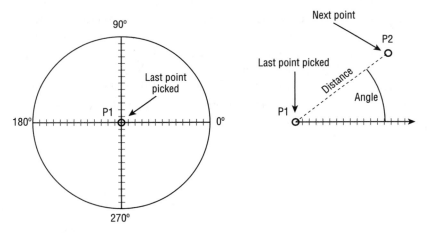

FIGURE 2.7: The relative polar coordinate system

Drawing the Box

Now that you have the basics down, the following exercises will take you through the steps to draw the four lines that form the outline of the box using both relative coordinate systems.

Using Relative Cartesian Coordinates

To begin drawing the box, we'll start with a new drawing.

1. Choose File ➤ Close. You will be prompted to save your last drawing: Click No.

2. Choose File ➤ New.

3. In the Create New Drawing dialog box, click Start from Scratch, select English, then click OK.

4. Select the Line button from the top of the Draw toolbar.

5. At the `Specify First point:` prompt in the Command window, type in 3,3 ↵. This is an absolute Cartesian coordinate and will be the first point.

6. Type @6,0 ↵.

7. Type @0,5 ↵.

8. Type @-6,0 ↵.

9. Type c ↵. The letter *c* stands for *close*. Entering this letter after drawing several lines closes the shape by making the next line segment extend from the last point specified to the first point (Figure 2.8). It also ends the Line command. Notice that in the Command window the prompt is `Command:`. This signifies that AutoCAD is ready for a new command.

Erasing Lines

To prepare to draw the box again, use the Erase command to erase the four lines you have just drawn.

1. Choose Modify ➤ Erase. Notice how the cursor changes from the crosshair to a little square. This is called the *pickbox*. When you see it on the screen, it's a sign that AutoCAD is ready for you to select objects on the screen. Also, notice the Command window. It is prompting you to select objects.

2. Place the pickbox on one of the lines and click. The line changes into a dashed line. This is called *ghosting* or *highlighting*.

3. Do the same thing with the rest of the lines.

4. Press ↵. The objects are erased and the Erase command ends.

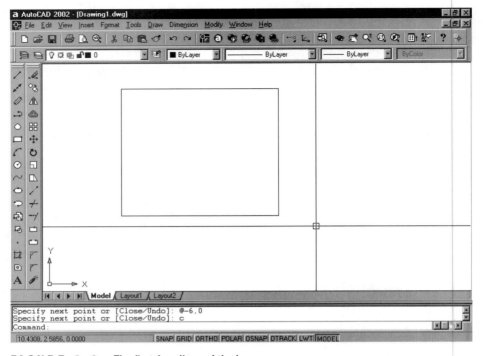

FIGURE 2.8: The first four lines of the box

Using Relative Polar Coordinates

Now draw the box again using the polar method by following these steps:

1. Start the Line command. (Choose the Line button from the Draw toolbar.)

2. Type 3,3 ↵ to start the box at the same point.

3. Type @6<0 ↵.

4. Type @5<90 ↵.

5. Type @6<180 ↵.

6. Type c ↵ to close the box and end the Line command. Your box will once again resemble the box in Figure 2.8.

You can see from this simple exercise that either method can be used to draw a simple shape. When the shapes you are drawing get more complex and the amount of available information about the shapes varies from segment to segment, there will be situations where one of the two relative coordinate systems will turn out to be more appropriate. As you start drawing the floor plan of the cabin in Chapters 3 and 4, you will get more practice using these systems.

There are additional tools that make the process of drawing simple, *orthogonal* lines like these, much easier. These tools will also be introduced in the following three chapters.

The Offset Command

The next task is to create the lines that represent the inside walls of the box. Because they are all equidistant from the lines you have already drawn, the *Offset command* is the appropriate command to use. You will offset the existing lines 0.5 units to the inside.

The Offset command has three steps:

► Setting the offset distance

► Picking the object to offset

► Indicating the offset direction

Here's how it works:

1. Be sure the prompt line in the Command window reads Command:. If it doesn't, press the Esc key until it does. Then click the Offset button on the Modify toolbar. The prompt changes to Specify offset distance or Through <1.0000>:. This is a confusing prompt, but it will become clear soon. For now, let's specify an offset distance through the keyboard.

You can also start the Offset command by choosing Modify ➤ Offset from the pull-down menus, or typing o ↵.

WARNING   As important as it is to keep an eye on the Command window, some of the prompts may not make sense to you until you get used to them.

2. Enter .5 ↵ for a distance. Now you move to the second stage of the command.

   Note that the cursor has changed to a pickbox, and the prompt changes to say Select object to offset or <exit>:.

3. Place the pickbox on one of the lines and click. The selected line ghosts (Figure 2.9), the cursor changes back to the crosshair, and the prompt changes to Specify point on side to offset:. AutoCAD is telling you that to determine the direction of the offset, you must

specify a point on one side of the line or the other. You make the choice by picking anywhere in the drawing area, on the side of the line where you want the offset to occur.

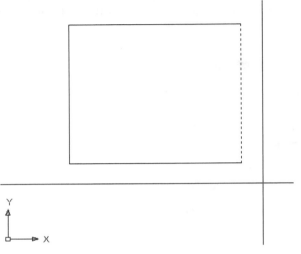

FIGURE 2.9: The first line to be offset is selected.

4. Pick a point somewhere inside the box. The offset takes place and the new line is exactly 0.5 units to the inside of the chosen line (Figure 2.10). Notice that the pickbox comes back on. The Offset command is still running and you can offset more lines the same distance.

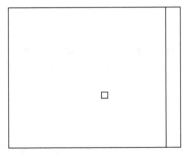

FIGURE 2.10: The first line is offset.

You have three more lines to offset.

5. Click another line, then click inside the box again. The second line is offset.

6. Click a third line, click inside the box, then click the fourth line and click again inside the box (Figure 2.11).

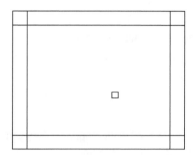

FIGURE 2.11: Four lines have been offset.

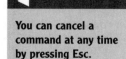
You can cancel a command at any time by pressing Esc.

NOTE The offset distance stays set at the last distance you specify—0.5, in this case—until you change it.

7. Press ↵ to end the Offset command.

This command is similar to the Line command in that it keeps running until it is stopped. With Offset, after the first offset, the prompts switch between Select object to offset or <exit>: and Specify point on side to offset: until you press ↵ to end the command.

The inside lines are now drawn, but to complete the box, you need to clean up the intersecting corners. To handle this task efficiently, we will use a new tool called the Fillet command.

Specifying Distances for the Offset Command

The prompt you see in the Command window after starting the Offset command is:

Specify offset distance or [Through] <1.0000>:

This prompt is actually describing several options for setting the offset distance.

▶ Enter a distance at the keyboard.

▶ Pick two points on the screen to establish the offset distance as the distance between those two points.

▶ Press ↵ to accept the offset distance that is displayed in the prompt in the angle brackets.

▶ Type **t** ↵ to use the Through option. When you select this option, you are prompted to select the line to offset. Then you are prompted to pick a point. The line will be offset to that point. When you pick the next line to offset, you then pick a new point to locate the position of the new line. The Through option allows each line to be offset a different distance.

As you get used to using Offset, you will find uses for each of these options.

The Fillet Command

The *Fillet command* allows you to round off a corner formed by two lines. You control the radius of the curve, so if you set the curve's radius to zero, the lines will form a sharp corner. In this way you can clean up corners like the ones formed by the lines inside the box.

You can also start the Fillet command by choosing Modify ➢ Fillet from the menu bar, or by typing f ↵.

1. At the Command: prompt, click the Fillet button on the Modify toolbar.

Notice the Command window:

```
Command: _fillet
Current settings: Mode = TRIM, Radius = 0.5000
Select first object or [Polyline/Radius/Trim]:
```

The default fillet radius is 0.5 units, but you want to use a radius of 0 units.

2. Type r ↲ 0 ↲ to change the radius to zero.

3. Move the cursor—now a pickbox—to the box and click two intersecting lines as shown in Figure 2.12. The intersecting lines will both be trimmed to make a sharp corner (Figure 2.13). The Fillet command automatically ends.

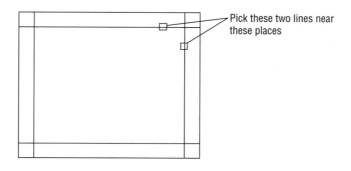

Pick these two lines near these places

FIGURE 2.12: Pick two lines to execute the Fillet command.

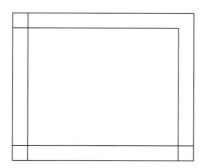

FIGURE 2.13: The first cleaned-up corner

Once a command has ended, you can restart it by pressing Enter, or by right-clicking and then picking the Repeat command option at the top of the short-cut menu that appears.

4. Press ↵ to restart the command and fillet two more lines in a similar fashion.

5. Continue restarting the command and filleting the lines for each corner until all corners are cleaned up (Figure 2.14).

FIGURE 2.14: The box with all corners cleaned up

N O T E   If you make a mistake and pick the wrong part of a line or the wrong line, press Esc to end the command and then type u ↵. This will undo the effect of the last command.

Used together like this, the Offset and Fillet commands are a powerful combination of tools to lay out walls on a floor plan drawing. Since these commands are so important, let's take a closer look at them to see how they work. Both commands are found on the Modify toolbar or drop-down menu, both have the option to enter a numerical value or accept the current value—for offset distance and fillet radius—and both hold that value as the default until it is changed. However, the Offset command keeps running until you stop it, and the Fillet command stops after each use and must be restarted for multiple fillets. These two commands are probably the most frequently used tools in AutoCAD. You will learn about more of their uses in later chapters.

Completing the Box

The final step in completing the box (Figure 2.1) is to make an opening in the bottom wall. From the diagram, you can see that the opening is 2 units wide and set off from the right inside corner by 0.5 units. To make this opening, you will use the Offset command twice, changing the offset distance for each offset, to create marks for the opening.

Offsetting Lines to Mark an Opening

Follow these steps to establish the precise position of the opening:

1. At the Command: prompt, start the Offset command, either from the Modify toolbar or the Modify menu. Notice the Command window. The default distance is now set at 0.5, the offset distance you previously set to offset the outside lines of the box to make the inside lines. You want to use this distance again. Press ⏎ to accept this preset distance.

2. Pick the inside vertical line on the right, and then pick a point to the left of this line. The line is offset to make a new line 0.5 units to its left (Figure 2.15).

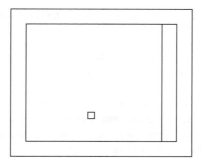

FIGURE 2.15: Offsetting the first line of the opening

3. Press ↵ to end the Offset command, then press it again to restart the command. This will allow you to reset the offset distance.

4. Enter 2 as the new offset distance and press ↵.

5. Click the new line, then pick a point to the left. Press ↵ to end the Offset command (Figure 2.16).

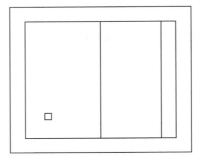

FIGURE 2.16: Offsetting the second line of the opening

You now have two new lines indicating where the opening will be. You can use these lines to form the opening using the Extend and Trim commands.

> **TIP**   The "buttons" you have been clicking in this skill are also referred to as "icons" and "tools." When they are in dialog boxes or on the Status Bar, they actually look like buttons to push that have icons on them. When they are on the toolbars, they look like icons, i.e., little pictures. But when you move the Pointer Arrow cursor onto one, it takes on the appearance of a button with an icon on it. All three terms—"button," "icon," and "tool"—will be used interchangeably in this book.

Extending Lines

The *Extend command* is used to lengthen (extend) lines to meet other lines or geometric figures (called *boundary edges*). The execution of the Extend command may be a little tricky at first until you see how it works. Once you understand it, however, it will become automatic. The command has two steps: First, you will pick the boundary edge or edges, and second, you will pick the lines you wish to extend to meet those boundary edges. After selecting the boundary edges, you must press ↵ before you begin selecting lines to extend.

1. To begin the Extend command, click the Extend button on the Modify toolbar. Notice the Command window.

```
Current settings: Projection=UCS Edge=None
Select boundary edges ...
Select objects:
```

You can also start the Extend command by selecting Extend from the Modify pull-down menu, or by typing ex ↵.

2. The bottom line says to "Select objects," but, in this case, you need to observe the bottom two lines of text in order to know that AutoCAD is prompting you to select boundary edges.

3. Pick the very bottom horizontal line (Figure 2.17) and press ↵.

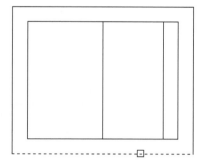

FIGURE 2.17: Selecting a line to be a boundary edge

TIP The Select Objects: prompt would be more useful if it said, "Select objects and press Enter when finished selecting objects." But it doesn't. You have to train yourself to press Enter when you are finished selecting objects in order to get out of selection mode and move on to the next step in the command.

4. Pick the two new vertical lines created by the Offset command. Be sure to place the pickbox somewhere on the lower halves of these lines, or AutoCAD will ignore your picks. The lines are extended to the boundary edge line. Press ↵ to end the Extend command (Figure 2.18).

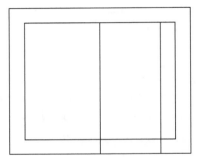

FIGURE 2.18: The lines are extended to the boundary edge.

Trimming Lines

The final step is to trim away the horizontal lines to complete the opening. To do this, you will use the *Trim command*. As with the Extend command, there are two steps to trimming. The first one is to select reference lines—in this case, they're called *cutting edges* because they determine the edge or edges to which a line is trimmed.

> You can also start the Trim command by picking Trim from the Modify pull-down menu, or by typing **tr** ↵.

1. Click the Trim button on the Modify toolbar to start the Trim command.

Notice the Command window. Similar to the Extend command, the bottom line prompts you to select objects, but the second line up tells you to select cutting edges.

2. Pick the two vertical offset lines that were just extended as your cutting edges. Then press ↵ (Figure 2.19).

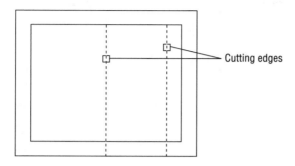

Cutting edges

FIGURE 2.19: Lines selected to be cutting edges

3. Pick the two horizontal lines across the opening somewhere between the cutting edge lines (Figure 2.20).

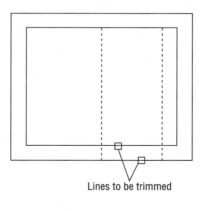

Lines to be trimmed

FIGURE 2.20: Lines selected to be trimmed

The opening is trimmed away (Figure 2.21).

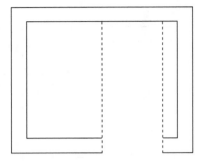

FIGURE 2.21: Wall lines are trimmed to make the opening.

N O T E   If you trim the wrong line or wrong part of a line, you can click the Undo button on the Standard toolbar. This will undo the last trim without canceling the Trim command, and you can try again.

Now let's remove the extra part of our trimming guide lines.

1. Press ↵ twice—once to end the Trim command and again to restart it. This will allow you to pick new cutting edges for another trim operation.

2. Pick the two upper horizontal lines in the lower wall as your cutting edges, shown in Figure 2.22, and press ↵.

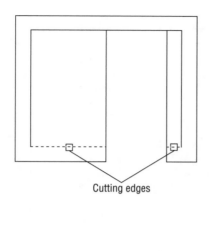

FIGURE 2.22: Lines picked to be cutting edges

3. Pick the two vertical lines that extend above the new opening. Be sure to pick them above the opening (Figure 2.23). The lines are trimmed away and the opening is complete. Press ↵ to end the Trim command (Figure 2.24).

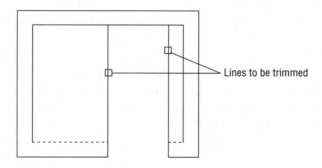

Lines to be trimmed

FIGURE 2.23: Lines picked to be trimmed

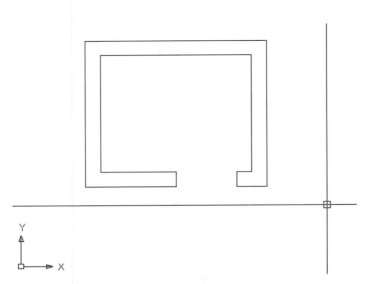

FIGURE 2.24: The completed trim

Congratulations! You have just completed the first drawing project in this book and have covered all the tools in this chapter. These skills will be very useful as you learn how to work on drawings for actual projects.

A valuable exercise at this time would be to draw this box two or three more times, until you can do it without the instructions. This will be a confidence-builder and will get you ready to take on new information in the next chapter, in which you will set up a drawing for a building.

The box you drew was 6 units by 5 units, but how big was it? You really don't know at this time, because the units could represent any actual distance: inches, feet, meters, miles, etc. Also, the box was positioned conveniently on the screen so you didn't have any problem viewing it. Consider the situation if you were drawing a building that was 200 feet long and 60 feet wide! In the next chapter, you will learn how to set up a drawing for a project of a specific size.

You can exit AutoCAD now without saving this drawing. To do this, choose File ➤ Exit. When the dialog box comes up asking if you want to save changes, click No. Or you can leave AutoCAD open and go on to the following practice section or the next chapter.

If You Would Like More Practice...

Draw the following object (Figure 2.25).

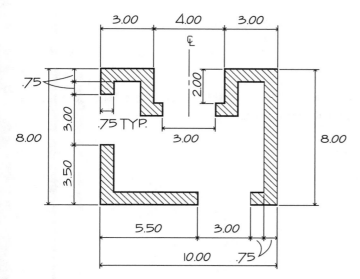

FIGURE 2.25: Practice drawing

You can use the same tools and strategy used to draw the box. Choose File ➤ New to start a new drawing and click the Start from Scratch button in the Create New Drawing dialog box. Here's a summary of the steps to follow:

▶ Ignore the three openings at first.

▶ Draw the outside edge of the shape.

▶ Offset the outside lines to create the inside wall.

▶ Fillet the corners to clean them up.

▶ Use Offset, Extend and Trim commands to create the three openings.

Are You Experienced?

Now you can...

- ☑ understand the basics of coordinates

- ☑ discern between the two relative coordinate systems used by AutoCAD

- ☑ use the Line, Erase, Offset, Fillet, Extend, and Trim commands to manipulate lines in a drawing

CHAPTER 3

Setting Up a Drawing

- ▶ Setting up drawing units
- ▶ Using a grid
- ▶ Zooming in and out of a drawing
- ▶ Naming and saving a file

I n Chapter 2, *Basic Commands to Get Started*, you explored the default draw-ing area that is set up when a new drawing is opened. It is probably 9 units high by 12 to 16 units wide, depending upon the size of your monitor. You drew the box within this area. If you drew the additional diagram offered as a supplemental exercise, the drawing area was set up the same way.

For most of the rest of this book, you will be developing drawings for a cabin with outside wall dimensions of 25' × 16'. In this chapter you will learn how to set up the drawing area to lay out the floor plan for a building of a specific size. The decimal units with which you have been drawing until now will be changed to feet and inches, and the drawing area will be transformed so that it can repre-sent an area large enough to display the floor plan of the cabin you will be draw-ing. You will be introduced to some new tools that will help you visualize the area your screen represents and allow you to draw lines to a specified incremen-tal distance, such as to the nearest foot. Finally, you will save this drawing to a floppy disk or to a special directory on your hard disk.

Drawing Units

When you draw lines of a precise length in AutoCAD, you will use one of five kinds of linear units. Angular units can also be one of five different types. You can select the type of units to use, or accept the default decimal units that you used in the last chapter.

When you start a new drawing using the Start from Scratch option, AutoCAD brings up a blank drawing called Drawing1.dwg with the linear and angular units set to decimal numbers. The units and other basic setup parameters applied to this new drawing are based on a prototype drawing, or drawing template, with default settings—including those for the units—that are stored with the drawing template file Acad.dwt. You can choose another template file as a prototype drawing, or you can create your own set of prototype drawings. This chapter will cover some of the tools for changing the basic parameters of a new drawing so you can tailor it to the cabin project. You will start by setting up new units.

1. Start up AutoCAD and, in the Startup dialog box, click the Start from Scratch button. Be sure English is selected and click OK. To get started with the steps in this chapter, check to be sure that, for now, all the Status bar buttons except Model are clicked to the Off posi-tion—that is, they will appear unpushed.

2. From the Format menu, select Units. The Drawing Units dialog box appears (Figure 3.1). In the Length area, Decimal is currently selected. Similarly, in the Angle area, Decimal Degrees is the default.

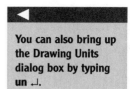

You can also bring up the Drawing Units dialog box by typing **un ↵**.

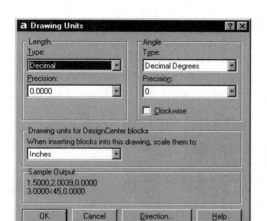

FIGURE 3.1:   The Drawing Units dialog box

3. In the Length area, click the arrow in the Type drop-down list and select Architectural. These units are feet and inches, which you will be using for the cabin project. Notice the two Precision drop-down lists at the bottom of the Length and Angle areas. When the linear units specification was changed from Decimal to Architectural, the number in the Precision drop-down list on the left changed from 0.0000 to 0'-0 ¹⁄₁₆". At this level of precision, linear distances will be displayed to the nearest ¹⁄₁₆".

4. Select some of the other Length unit types from the list and note the way the units appear in the Sample Output area at the bottom of the dialog box. Then select Architectural again.

N O T E   Drop-down lists are lists of choices with only the selected choice displayed. When you click the arrow, the list opens. When you make another selection, the list closes and your choice is displayed. Only one choice from the list can be made at a time.

5. Click the arrow in the Precision drop-down list in the Length area. The drop-down list appears, showing the choices of precision for Architectural units (Figure 3.2). This setting controls the degree of precision to which AutoCAD will display a linear distance. If set to $\frac{1}{16}$", this means that any line that is drawn more precisely—such as a line 6'-3 $\frac{1}{32}$" long—will be displayed to the nearest $\frac{1}{16}$" or, in the example, as 6'-3 $\frac{1}{16}$". But the line will still be 6'-3 $\frac{1}{32}$" long. If you change the precision setting to $\frac{1}{32}$" and then use the Distance command (explained in Chapter 7, *Grouping Objects into Blocks*) to measure the line, you will see that its length is 6'-3 $\frac{1}{32}$".

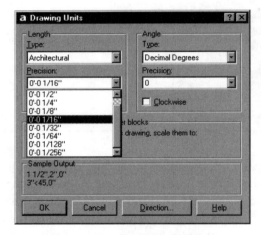

FIGURE 3.2: The Precision drop-down list for Architectural unitsx

6. Click 0'-0 $\frac{1}{16}$" to maintain the precision for display of linear units at $\frac{1}{16}$".

If you open the Type drop-down list in the Angle area, you can see that there is a choice between Decimal Degrees and Deg/Min/Sec, among others. Most drafters find the decimal angular units the most practical, but the default precision setting is to the nearest degree. This might not be accurate enough, so you should change that to the nearest hundredth of a degree.

1. Click the arrow in the Angle Precision drop-down list.

2. Click 0.00.

The Drawing Units dialog box will now indicate that, in your drawing, you plan to use Architectural units with a precision of ¹⁄₁₆", and Decimal angular units with a precision of 0.00 (Figure 3.3).

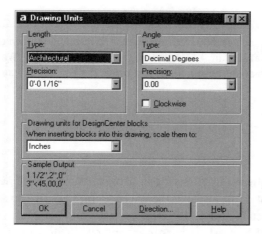

FIGURE 3.3: The Drawing Units dialog box after changes

The Direction button at the bottom of the dialog box takes you to another dialog box that has settings to control the direction of 0 degrees and the angular direction of rotation for positive angular displacement. By default, 0 degrees is to the right and positive angular displacement goes in the counterclockwise direction. (See Figure 2.7 in Chapter 2 for a figure that explains this.) These are the standard settings for most uses of CAD. There is no need to change these from the defaults; so, if you want to take a look, open the Direction Control dialog box, note the choices, and then click OK to close it. You won't have occasion in the course of this book to change any of those settings.

N O T E   You will have a chance to work with the Surveyor angular units later in the book, in Chapter 12, *Managing External References*, when you develop a site plan for the cabin.

3. Click OK in the Drawing Units dialog box to close it. Notice the coordinate readout in the lower-left corner of the screen. It now reads out in feet and inches.

This tour of the Drawing Units dialog box has introduced you to the choices you have for the type of units and the degree of precision for linear and angular measurement. The next step in setting up a drawing is learning how to determine the size of a drawing.

> **N O T E**   If you accidentally click the mouse with the cursor on a blank part of the drawing area, AutoCAD starts a rectangular window. We'll talk about these windows soon, but for now, just press the Esc key to cancel the window.

Drawing Size

As you discovered earlier, the default drawing area on the screen for a new drawing is 12 to 16 units wide and 9 units high. After changing the units to Architectural, the same drawing area is now 12 to 16 *inches* wide and 9 *inches* high. You can check this by moving the crosshair cursor around on the drawing area and looking at the coordinate readout, as you did in the previous chapter.

> **T I P**   When Decimal units are changed to Architectural units, one Decimal unit translates to one inch. Some industries use Decimal units to represent feet instead of inches. If the units in their drawings are switched to Architectural, a distance that was a foot now measures as an inch. To correct this, the entire drawing must be scaled up by a factor of 12.

The drawing area is defined as the part of the screen in which you draw. The distance across the drawing area can be made larger or smaller through a process known as zooming in or out. To see how this works, you'll learn about a tool called the grid that helps you to draw and to visualize the size of your drawing.

The Grid

The *grid* is a pattern of regularly spaced dots used as an aid to drawing. You can set the grid to be visible or invisible. The area covered by the grid depends on a setting called *drawing limits*. To learn how to manipulate the grid size, you'll make the grid visible, use the Zoom In and Zoom Out commands to vary the view of the grid and then change the area over which the grid extends by resetting the drawing limits. Before doing this, however, let's turn off the User Coordinate System icon that presently sits in the lower-left corner of the drawing area.

1. At the Command: prompt, type **ucsicon** ⏎, then type **off** ⏎. The icon will disappear.

2. At the Command: prompt, move the crosshair cursor to the status bar at the bottom of the screen and click the Grid button. The button will appear to have been pushed down and dots will appear on most of the drawing area (Figure 3.4). These dots are the grid. They are preset by default to be ½" apart, and they extend from the 0,0 point (the Origin), out to the right, and up to the coordinate point 1'-0",0'-9". Notice that rows of grid dots run right along the left edge, top, and bottom of the drawing area; but the dots don't extend all the way to the right side. The grid dot at the 0,0 point is positioned exactly at the lower-left corner of the screen, and the one at 1'-0",0'-9" is on the top edge, not too far from the upper-right corner.

> You can also control the visibility of the UCS icon by choosing View ➤ Display ➤ UCS Icon ➤ On. If On has a check mark, clicking it turns off the UCS icon. If it doesn't, clicking turns the icon back on.

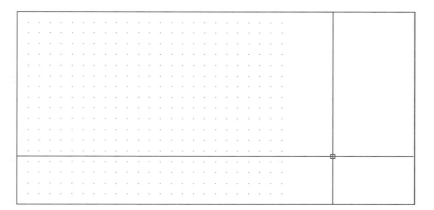

FIGURE 3.4: The AutoCAD default grid

3. For a better view of the entire grid, use the Zoom Out command. From the drop-down menus, select View ➤ Zoom ➤ Out. The view changes and the grid appears smaller (Figure 3.5). Move the crosshair cursor to the lower-left corner of the grid, then move it to the upper-right corner and note the coordinate readout in the lower left of your screen. These two points should read as approximately 0'-0",0'-0" and 1'-0",0'-9", respectively.

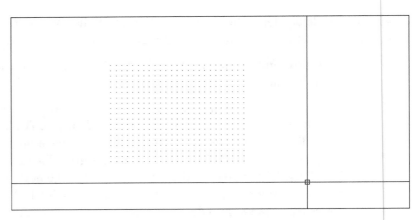

FIGURE 3.5: The grid after zooming out

4. On the status bar, next to the Grid button, click the Snap button, then move the cursor back onto the grid and look at the coordinate readout again. The cursor stops at each grid point and the readout is to the nearest half inch. Now when you place the crosshair cursor on the lower-left corner of the grid, the readout is exactly 0'-0",0'-0", and 1'-0",0'-9" for the upper-right corner. The Snap tool locks the cursor onto the grid dots, and even when the cursor is not on the grid but somewhere outside it on the drawing area, the cursor maintains the grid spacing.

5. Use the Zoom Out command a few more times. The first time, the grid gets even smaller. After the second or third use of the command, the grid may disappear, in which case you would get a message on the second line of the Command window that says, Grid too dense to display. Once the dots get too close together, AutoCAD lets you know that the monitor can't display them.

6. On the same menu, use the Zoom In tool enough times to bring the view of the grid back to the way it was in Figure 3.5. You are not changing the size of the grid, just the view of it. It's like switching from a normal to a telephoto lens on a camera.

The grid is more of a guide than an actual boundary of your drawing. You can change a setting to force lines to be drawn only in the area covered by the grid, but this is not ordinarily done. For most purposes, you can draw anywhere on the screen. The grid merely serves as a tool for visualizing how your drawing is going to be laid out.

Because it will serve as a layout tool for this project, you need to increase the area covered by the grid from its present size of 1' × 9" to 60' × 40'. Because the Drawing Limits setting controls the size of the grid, you need to change it.

Drawing Limits

The Drawing Limits setting records the coordinates of the lower-left and upper-right corners of the grid. The coordinates for the lower-left corner are 0,0 by default, and are usually left at that setting. You only need to change the coordinates for the upper-right corner.

1. At the Command: prompt, pick Format ≻ Drawing Limits from the drop-down menus. Notice the Command window:

    ```
    Command: '_limits
    Reset Model space limits:
    Specify lower left corner or [ON/OFF] <0'-0",0'-0">:
    ```

    The bottom command line tells you that the first step is to decide whether to change the default coordinates for the lower-left limits, which are presently set at 0',0". There is no need to change these.

2. Press ↵ to accept 0',0" for this corner. The bottom command line changes and is now allowing you to change the coordinates for the upper-right corner of the limits. This is the setting you want to change.

3. Type 60',40' ↵. Be sure to include the foot sign (').

 N O T E   AutoCAD requires that, when using Architectural units, you always indicate when a distance is feet by using the foot sign ('). You do not have to use the inch sign (") to indicate inches.

The grid now appears to extend to the top-right edge of the drawing area (Figure 3.6), but it actually extends way past the edges. It was one foot wide and now it's 60 times that, but the drawing area is only showing us the first foot or so. To bring the whole grid onto the screen, use the Zoom command again, but this time you will use the All option.

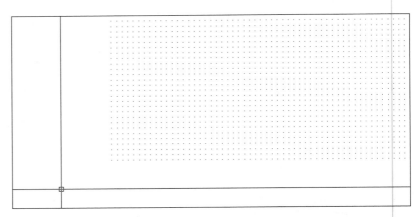

FIGURE 3.6: The same view with the grid extended to 60'×40'

4. Select View ➤ Zoom ➤ All. The grid disappears, and you get the `Grid Too Dense To Display` message in the Command window.

Remember that you found the grid spacing to be ½", by default. If the drawing area is giving us a view of a 60' × 40' grid with dots at ½", the grid is 1440 dots wide and 960 dots high. If the whole grid were to be shown on the screen, the dots would be so close together that they would only be about one pixel in size and would solidly fill the drawing area. So AutoCAD won't display them at this density. For this reason you need to change the spacing for the dots.

You need to change the spacing for two reasons: First, the spacing needs to be larger so that AutoCAD will display the dots; and second, for the drawing task ahead, it will be more useful to have the spacing set differently. Remember how we turned Snap on, and the cursor stopped at each dot? If you set the dot spacing to 12", you can use Grid and Snap modes to help you draw the outline of the cabin because the dimensions of the outside wall line are in whole feet: 25' × 16'. Here's how:

1. Right-click on the Grid button on the Status bar. Click Settings on the small menu that appears. The Drafting Settings dialog box appears and the Snap and Grid tab is active (Figure 3.7). The settings in both the Grid and Snap areas include *X* and *Y* Spacing settings. Notice that they are all set for a spacing of ½". The other settings in the dialog box don't concern us right now.

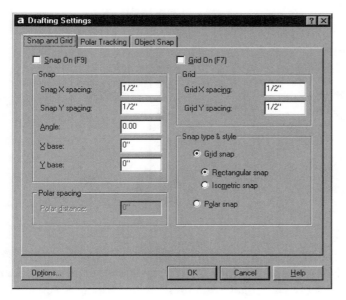

FIGURE 3.7: The Snap and Grid tab of the Drafting Settings dialog box

2. In the Grid section, click in the Grid X spacing text box and change it to 0. If you set the grid spacing to 0, it will then take on whatever spacing you set for the Snap X spacing text box. This is how you lock the two together. When the Grid X spacing reads 0, click the ½" in the Grid Y spacing text box. It changes to match the Grid X spacing.

3. In the Snap section, change the Snap X spacing to 12. The inch sign is not required. Then click the Snap Y spacing setting. It changes to automatically match the Snap X spacing.

4. In the Snap Type and Style area, be sure Grid Snap and Rectangular Snap are selected. The Snap On and Grid On check boxes at the top should be checked. If they aren't, check them.

5. Click OK. The grid is now visible (Figure 3.8). Move the cursor around on the grid—be sure Snap is on (Check the Snap button on the Status bar. It will be depressed when Snap is on.)—and notice the coordinate readout. It is displaying coordinates to the nearest foot to conform to the new grid and snap spacing.

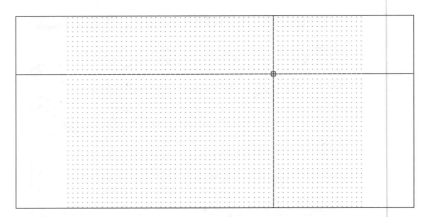

FIGURE 3.8: The new 60'×40' grid with 12" dot spacing

6. Move the crosshair cursor to the upper-right corner of the grid and check the coordinate readout. It should display 60'-0", 40'-0", 0'-0".

Drawing with Grid and Snap

Your drawing area now has the proper settings and is zoomed to a convenient magnification. You should be ready to draw the first lines of the cabin.

1. At the Command: prompt, start the Line command (Choose the Line button on the Draw toolbar.) and pick a point on the grid in the lower-left quadrant of the drawing area (Figure 3.9).

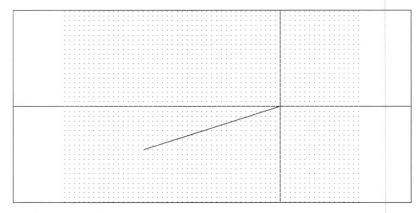

FIGURE 3.9: One point picked on the grid

2. Hold the crosshair cursor to the right of the point just picked and look at the coordinate readout. It may be displaying relative polar coordinates from the first point picked, but probably not. If it isn't, try clicking once on the coordinate readout. If that doesn't work, clicking one more time will do the job, as the coordinate readout is controlled by a three-way toggle.

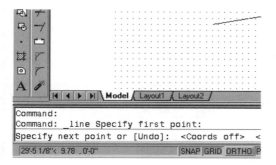

3. Now hold the crosshair cursor directly out to the right of the first point picked and look at the coordinate readout. It will be displaying a distance in whole feet and should have an angle of 0.00. (Ignore the extra *z* coordinate.)

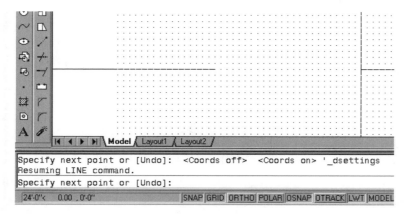

4. Continue moving the crosshair cursor left or right until the readout displays 25'-0"<0.00. At this point, click the left mouse button. The first line of the cabin wall is drawn (Figure 3.10).

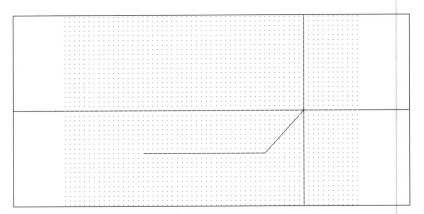

FIGURE 3.10: The first line of the cabin wall is drawn.

5. Move the crosshair cursor directly above the last point picked to a position such that the coordinate readout displays 16'-0"<90.00, and pick that point.

6. Move the crosshair cursor directly left of the last point picked until the coordinate readout displays 25'-0"<180.00, and pick that point (Figure 3.11).

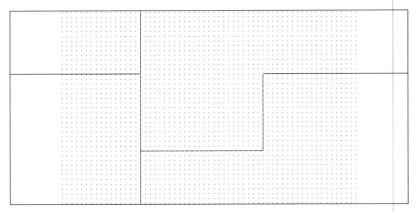

FIGURE 3.11: Drawing the second and third wall lines

7. Finally, type c ↵ to close the box. This tells AutoCAD to draw a line from the last point picked to the first point picked and, in effect, closes the box. Then AutoCAD automatically ends the Line command (Figure 3.12).

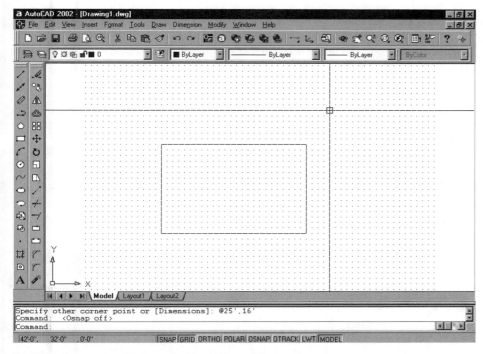

FIGURE 3.12: The completed outside wall lines

This method of laying out building lines by using Snap and Grid and the coordinate readout is quite useful if the dimensions all conform to a convenient rounded-off number, such as the nearest 6 inches, or as in this case, the nearest foot. It is not necessary to keep Snap and Grid set to the same spacing, as they were in this example, as long as the grid spacing is a whole multiple of the snap spacing. In this project, you could have kept the snap spacing at 1' and set the grid spacing to 4'. Then you wouldn't have so many dots on the screen, and Snap would still have forced the crosshair cursor to stop at quarter intervals (every 12") between the 4-foot–spaced grid dots. This would have been a slightly more elegant way to accomplish the same thing.

The key advantage to this method over just typing in the relative coordinates—as was done with the box in Chapter 2—is that you avoid having to type in the numbers. You should, however, assess whether the layout you need to draw has characteristics that lend themselves to using grid, snap, and the coordinate readout area, or whether just typing in the relative coordinates would be more efficient. As you get more comfortable with AutoCAD, you will see that this is the sort of question that comes up often: which way is the most efficient? This happy dilemma is inevitable in an application with enough tools to give you many strategic choices. In Chapters 4 and 5, *Gaining Drawing Strategies: Parts I & II,* you will learn about other techniques for drawing rectangles.

Saving Your Work

As with all Windows-compatible applications, when you save a file for the first time by choosing File ➤ Save, you are given the opportunity to designate a name for the file and a directory or folder to store it in. Normally you use Windows Explorer to designate file and directory information before you start a new drawing; but for the cabin project, you will do that now, after the drawing has been started.

I recommend that you create a special folder called something like Training Data, for storing the files you will generate as you work your way through the book. This will keep them separate from project work already on your computer, and you will always know where to save or find a training drawing. To save your drawing, follow these steps. While in AutoCAD:

1. Click the Save button on the Standard toolbar or select File ➤ Save. Because you haven't named this file yet, the Save Drawing As dialog box comes up.

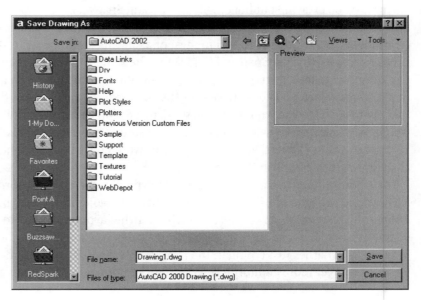

N O T E The actual directories and files may be different on your computer.

2. In the Save In drop-down list, designate the drive and folder where you wish to save the drawing. If you are saving it on the hard drive or server, navigate to the directory in which you want to place the new Training Data folder.

3. Click the Create New Folder button near the top-right corner of the dialog box.

4. Enter **Training Data** (or whatever name you wish to give the new folder) ↵.

5. Double-click the new folder to open it.

6. In the File Name box, change the name from the default name (Drawing1.dwg) to Cabin03. You're not required to enter the .dwg extension in this case.

N O T E From now on, when you are directed to save the drawing, you should save it as Cabinx, with *x* indicating the number of the chapter. This way, you will know where in the book to look for review, if necessary. Multiple saves within a chapter should be called Cabinxa, Cabinxb, etc.

7. Click Save. Notice that the Title bar now displays the new name of the file along with its path. It is now safe to exit AutoCAD.

8. If you want to shut AutoCAD down at this time, choose File ➤ Exit. Otherwise, keep your drawing up and read on.

The tools covered in this chapter will be your key to starting up a new drawing from scratch and getting it ready for a specific project.

USING THE WIZARD TO SET UP A NEW DRAWING

AutoCAD comes with two Setup Wizards, Quick and Advanced. Neither helps you set up the Grid and Snap, but they do help you with setting the Units and the Drawing Limits. Here is a summary of how the wizards work.

When you select Use a Wizard in the Startup dialog box, you are then prompted to choose Quick or Advanced.

The Quick Wizard

▶ *Units:* Select the Units, then Click the Next button.

▶ *Area:* Here you set the Drawing Limits by specifying the *x* and *y* coordinates of the upper-right corner. You do this by entering the *x* value for the Width, and the *y* value for the Length. So, for example, if the coordinates of the upper-right corner are 60', 40' as they are for the cabin drawing, enter 60' for the width and 40' for the length. Then click Next.

▶ AutoCAD then Zooms to All for you, but it doesn't set up the grid and snap. They stay at the default setting of ½" and both remain off. You have to set those on your own using the procedure shown in this chapter.

The Advanced Wizard

▶ *Units:* Select the Linear Units and the Precision. Then click Next.

▶ *Angle:* Select the Angular Units and the Precision. Then click Next.

▶ *Angle Measure:* Ignore this and click the Next button.

▶ *Angle Direction:* Ignore this and click the Next button.

▶ *Area:* Here you set the Drawing Limits by specifying the *x* and *y* coordinates of the upper-right corner. You do this by entering the *x* value for the Width, and the *y* value for the Length. So, for example, if the coordinates of the upper-right corner are 60', 40' as they are for the Cabin drawing, enter 60' for the Width and 40' for the Length. Then click Next.

▶ AutoCAD then Zooms to All for you, but it doesn't set up the grid and snap. They stay at the default setting of ½" and both remain off. You have to set those on your own, using the procedure shown in this chapter.

N O T E When we get to Chapter 10, *Controlling Text in a Drawing*, we will discuss the Use a Template option of the Startup dialog box.

The next chapter will focus on adding to the drawing and modifying commands you learned as part of Chapter 2 and will develop strategies for solving problems that occur in the development of a floor plan.

If You Would Like More Practice...

Set up a few more new drawings. Below are three practice setup challenges, and a summary of steps described in this skill. Use this procedure, or feel free to try the Use a Wizard options in the Startup dialog box.

Project 1:	Building size:	125' × 85'
	Units:	Architectural
	Drawing Limits:	200', 150'
	Grid/Snap Spacing:	5'
Project 2:	Building size:	87' × 60'
	Units:	Architectural
	Drawing Limits:	120', 90'
	Grid/Snap Spacing:	3'
Project 3:	Building size:	12'-6" × 14'-6"
	Units:	Architectural
	Drawing Limits:	16' × 20'
	Grid/Snap Spacing:	6"

Summary of procedure:

▶ Set the units.

▶ Set the drawing limits.

▶ Set Grid spacing to 0 and Snap spacing to the given distance.

▶ Turn on Grid and Snap.

▶ Zoom to all.

▶ Draw the rectangle.

Are You Experienced?

Now you can...

☑ set up linear and angular units for a new drawing

☑ make the grid visible and modify its coverage

☑ use the Zoom In and Zoom Out features

☑ activate the Snap mode and change the snap and grid spacings

☑ use the Zoom All function to fit the grid on the drawing area

☑ draw lines using Grid, Snap, and the coordinate readout

☑ create a new folder on your hard drive from within AutoCAD

☑ name and save your file

CHAPTER 4

Gaining Drawing Strategies: Part 1

- ▶ Making interior walls
- ▶ Zooming in on an area using various zoom tools
- ▶ Making doors and swings
- ▶ Using Object Snaps
- ▶ Using the Copy and Mirror commands

Assuming that you have worked your way through the first three chapters, you have now successfully drawn a box (Chapter 2, *Basic Commands to Get Started*) as well as the outer wall lines of the cabin (Chapter 3, *Setting Up a Drawing*). From here on, you will develop a floor plan for the cabin and, ultimately, elevations (views of the front, back, and sides of the building that show how the building will look if you're standing facing it). These will be drawn in Chapter 8, *Generating Elevations*. The focus in this chapter is on gaining a feel for the strategy of drawing in AutoCAD, and on how to solve drawing problems that may come up in the course of laying out the floor plan. As you work your way through this chapter, your activities will include making the walls, cutting doorway openings, and drawing the doors (Figure 4.1). In Chapter 5, *Gaining Drawing Strategies: Part 2*, you will add steps and a balcony, and place fixtures and appliances in the bathroom and kitchen.

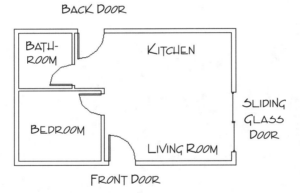

FIGURE 4.1: The basic floor plan of the cabin

Each of the exercises in this chapter will present you with opportunities to practice using commands you already know from previous chapters and to learn a few new ones. The most important goal is to begin to use strategic thinking as you develop methods for creating new elements of the floor plan.

Laying Out the Walls

For most floor plans, the walls come first. The first lesson of this chapter is to understand that you will not be putting very many new lines in the drawing, at least not as many as you might expect. Most new objects in this chapter will be created from items already in your drawing. In fact, no new lines will be drawn to make walls. All new walls will be generated from the four exterior wall lines you drew in the last chapter.

You will need to create an inside wall line for the exterior walls (because the wall has thickness) and then make the three new interior walls (Figure 4.2). The wall thickness will be 4" for interior walls and 6" for exterior walls, as exterior walls have an additional layer or two of weather protection, such as shingles or stucco. Finally, you will need to cut five openings in these walls (interior and exterior) for the doorways.

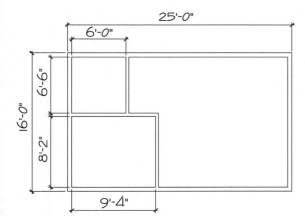

FIGURE 4.2: The wall dimensions

All the commands used for this exercise have been presented in Chapters 2 and 3, so feel free to glance back to these chapters if you find you need a refresher.

The Exterior Wall Lines

The first step is to offset the existing four wall lines to the inside to make the inside wall lines for the exterior walls. Then you will need to fillet them to clean up their corners, just like you did for the box in Chapter 2.

T I P   Buildings are usually—but not always—dimensioned to the outside edge of exterior walls and to the center line of interior walls. Wood frame buildings are dimensioned to the outside edges of their frames, and to the center lines of the interior walls.

1. If AutoCAD is already running, choose File ➤ Open. In the Select File dialog box, navigate to the folder you have designated as your training folder and select your cabin drawing. (You named it Cabin03 .dwg at the end of Chapter 3.)

Then click Open. If you are starting up AutoCAD, the Startup dialog box will appear. Be sure the Open a Drawing button is selected, then look for the Cabin03 drawing in the Select a File list box. This box keeps a list of the most recently opened .dwg files. Highlight your .dwg file and click OK. If you don't find your file in the list, click the Browse button. The Select File dialog box will open. Find and open your training folder, select your drawing file, and click Open. The drawing should consist of four lines making a rectangle (Figure 4.3).

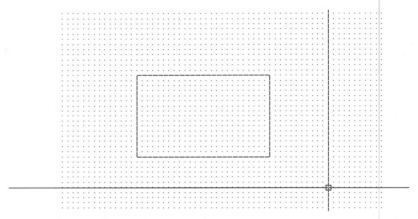

F I G U R E 4 . 3 : The cabin as you left it in Chapter 3

> **You can also start the Offset command by typing o ↵, or selecting Modify ➤ Offset from the drop-down menus.**

2. On the status bar, click the Grid and Snap buttons to turn them off. Then start the Offset command by clicking the Offset button on the Modify toolbar.

3. At the Offset distance: prompt, type 6 ↵.

N O T E Remember: You do not have to enter the inch sign ("), but you are required to enter the foot sign (').

4. At the Select object to offset: prompt, click one of the four lines.

5. Click in a blank area inside the rectangle. The first line is offset 6" to the inside (Figure 4.4). The Offset command is still running and the Select object to offset: prompt is still in effect.

FIGURE 4.4: The first line is offset.

6. Select another outside wall line and click in a blank area on the inside again. Continue doing this until you have offset all four outside wall lines to the inside at the set distance of 6". Then press ⏎ to end the Offset command (Figure 4.5). Now you will clean up the corners with the Fillet command.

FIGURE 4.5: All four lines are now offset 6" to the inside.

7. Start the Fillet command by clicking the Fillet button on the Modify toolbar.

8. Look at the Command window to see whether or not the radius is set to zero. If it is, go on to step 9. Otherwise, type r ⏎, then type 0 ⏎ to set the Fillet radius to zero.

9. Click any two lines that form an inside corner. Be sure to click the part of the lines you want to remain after the fillet is completed. (Refer to Chapter 2 to review how the Fillet command is used in a similar situation.) Both of the two lines will be trimmed to make an inside corner (Figure 4.6). The Fillet command automatically ends after each fillet.

FIGURE 4.6:   The first corner is filleted.

You can restart the most recently used command by pressing ↵ at the Command: prompt, or by right-clicking and selecting the top item on the shortcut menu that appears.

10. Press ↵ to restart the Fillet command.

11. Pick two more lines to fillet, then press ↵ to restart the Fillet command. Continue doing this until all four corners have been cleaned up (Figure 4.7). After the last fillet, the Fillet command will end automatically.

FIGURE 4.7:   The four inside corners have been cleaned up.

This procedure was identical to the one you performed in Chapter 2 on the box.

CHARACTERISTICS THAT OFFSET AND FILLET HAVE IN COMMON

Both are found on the Modify toolbar and on the Modify drop-down menu.

Both have a default distance setting—offset distance and fillet radius—which can be accepted or reset.

Both require you to select object(s).

CHARACTERISTICS THAT ARE DIFFERENT IN OFFSET AND FILLET

You select one object with Offset and two with Fillet.

Offset keeps running until you stop it. Fillet ends after each fillet operation, so Fillet needs to be restarted to be used again.

You will find several uses for Offset and Fillet in the subsequent sections of this chapter and throughout the book.

The Interior Walls

Create the interior wall lines by offsetting the exterior wall lines.

1. At the Command: prompt, start the Offset command by typing o ↵ (the letter o, not the number 0) or by selecting Offset from the Modify toolbar.

2. At the Offset distance: prompt, type 9'4 ↵. Leave no space between the foot sign (') and the 4.

N O T E AutoCAD requires that you enter a distance containing feet and inches in a particular format: no space between the foot sign (') and the inches, and a hyphen (-) between the inches and the fraction. So if you were entering a distance of 6'-4¾", you would type 6'4-3/4. The measurement will be displayed in the normal way, 6'-4¾", but it must be entered in the format that has no spaces.

3. Click the inside line of the left exterior wall (Figure 4.8).

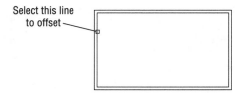

Select this line to offset

FIGURE 4.8: Selecting the wall line to offset

4. Click in a blank area to the right of the selected line. The line is offset 9'-4" to the right.

5. Press ↵ twice. The Offset command is now restarted, and you can reset the offset distance.

T I P In the Offset command, your opportunity to change the offset distance comes right after you start the command. So if the Offset command is already running, and you need to change the offset distance, you need to stop and then restart the command. This is easily done by pressing ↵ twice.

6. Type 4 ↵ to reset the offset distance.

7. Click the new line that was just offset, and then click in a blank area to the right of that line. You have created a vertical interior wall (Figure 4.9). Press ↵ twice to stop and restart the Offset command.

FIGURE 4.9: The first interior wall

8. Type 6.5'↵. This sets the distance for offsetting the next wall.

N O T E   With Architectural units set, you can still enter distances in decimal form for feet and inches, and AutoCAD will translate them into their appropriate form. So 6'-6" can be entered as 6.5 and 4½" can be entered as 4.5 without the inch sign. Remember, when entering figures, the inch sign (") can be left off, but the foot sign (') must be included.

9. Pick a point on the inside, upper exterior wall line (Figure 4.10).

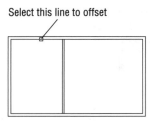

Select this line to offset

FIGURE 4.10: Selecting another wall line to offset

10. Click in a blank area below the line selected. The inside exterior wall line is offset to make a new interior wall line. Press ↵ twice to stop and restart the Offset command.

11. Type 4 ↵. Click the new line and click again below it. A second wall line is made, and you now have two interior walls. Press ↵ to end the Offset command.

These interior wall lines form the bedroom and one side of the bathroom. Their intersections with each other and with the exterior walls need to be cleaned up. If you take the time to do this now, it will be easier to make the last interior wall and thereby complete the bathroom. Refer back to Figures 4.1 and 4.2 to see where we're headed.

Cleaning Up Wall Lines

Earlier, you used the Fillet command to clean up the inside corners of the exterior walls. You can use that command again to clean up some of the interior walls, but you will have to use the Trim command to do the rest of them. You'll see why as you progress through the next set of steps.

1. It will be easier to pick the wall lines if the drawing is made larger on the screen. Type z ↵, then type e ↵. Press ↵, then type .6x ↵. The drawing is bigger. You've just used two options of the Zoom command: First, you zoomed to *Extents* to fill the screen with your drawing. Then you zoomed to a scale (.6x) to make the drawing 0.6 the size it had been after zooming to Extents. This is a change in magnification on the view only, as the building is still 25 feet long by 16 feet wide.

2. Click the Fillet button from the Modify toolbar to start the Fillet command and, after checking the Command window to be sure that the radius is still set to zero, click two of the wall lines as shown in Figure 4.11a. The lines will be filleted, and the results will look like Figure 4.11b.

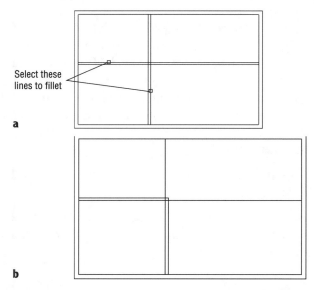

FIGURE 4.11: Selecting the first two lines to fillet (a), and the result of the fillet (b)

3. Press ⏎ to restart the Fillet command. Select the two lines as shown in Figure 4.12a. The results are shown in Figure 4.12b.

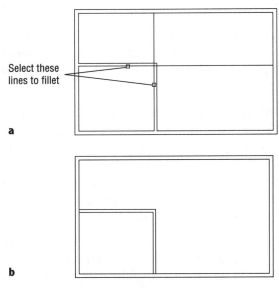

FIGURE 4.12: Selecting the second two lines to fillet (a), and the result of the second fillet (b)

The two new interior walls are now the right length, but you will have to clean up the area where they form T intersections with the exterior walls. The Fillet command won't work in T intersections because too much of one of the wall lines gets trimmed away. You'll have to use the Trim command in T intersection cases. The Fillet command does a specific kind of trim and is easy and quick to execute, but its uses are limited (for the most part) to single intersections between two lines.

Using the Zoom Command

To do this trim, you need to have a closer view of the T intersections. Use the Zoom command to get a better look.

1. Type z ⏎. Then move the crosshair cursor to a point slightly above and to the left of the upper T intersection (Figure 4.13) and click in a blank area outside the floor plan.

> The best rule for choosing between Fillet and Trim is the following: If you need to clean up a single intersection between two lines, use the Fillet command. For other cases, use the Trim command.

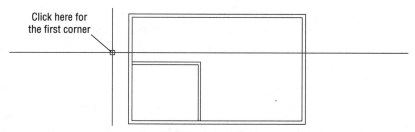

FIGURE 4.13: Positioning the cursor for the first click of the Zoom command

2. Move the cursor down and to the right, and notice a rectangle with solid lines being drawn. Keep moving the cursor down and to the right until the rectangle encloses the upper T intersection (Figure 4.14a). When the rectangle fully encloses the T intersection, click again. The view changes to a closer view of the intersection of the interior and exterior walls (Figure 4.14b). The rectangle you've just created is called a *zoom window*. The part of the drawing enclosed by the zoom window becomes the view on the screen. This is one of several zoom options for changing the magnification of the view. Other zoom options are introduced later in this chapter and throughout the book.

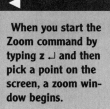

When you start the Zoom command by typing z ↵ and then pick a point on the screen, a zoom window begins.

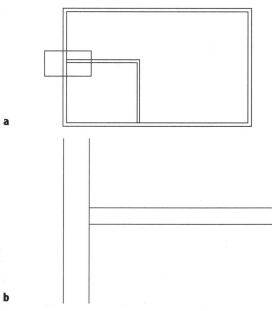

FIGURE 4.14: Using the Zoom Window option: positioning the rectangle (a), and the new view after the Zoom command (b)

3. On the Modify toolbar, click the Trim button. In the Command window, notice the second and third lines of text. You are being prompted to select cutting edges (objects to use as limits for the lines you want to trim).

4. Select the two interior wall lines and press ↵. The prompt changes, now asking you to select the lines to be trimmed.

5. Select the inside exterior wall line at the T intersection, between the two intersections with the interior wall lines that you have just picked as cutting edges (Figure 4.15a). The exterior wall line is trimmed at the T intersection (Figure 4.15b). Press ↵ to end the Trim command.

▶

In the Trim command, when picking lines to be trimmed, click the part of the line that needs to be trimmed away. In the Fillet command, select the part of the line that you want to keep.

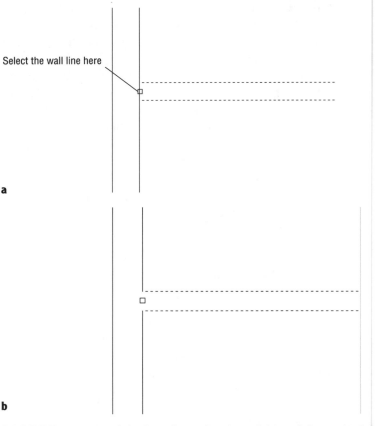

Select the wall line here

a

b

FIGURE 4.15: Selecting a line to be trimmed (a), and the result of the Trim command (b)

6. Return to a view of the whole drawing by typing **z** ↵, then **p** ↵. This is the Zoom command's Previous option, which restores the view that was active before the last use of the Zoom command (Figure 4.16).

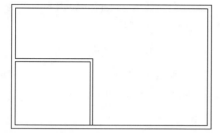

FIGURE 4.16: The result of the Zoom Previous command

7. Repeat this procedure to trim the lower T intersection. Follow these steps:

A. Type **z** ↵ and click two points to make a rectangular zoom window around the intersection.

B. Start the Trim command by choosing Modify ➤ Trim, select the interior walls as cutting edges, and press ↵.

C. Select the inside exterior wall line between the cutting edges.

D. Press ↵ to end the Trim command.

E. Zoom Previous by typing **z** ↵ **p** ↵.

Figure 4.17 shows the results.

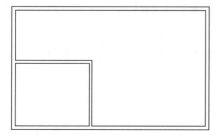

FIGURE 4.17: The second trim is completed.

You need to create one more interior wall to complete the bathroom.

Finishing the Interior Walls

You will use the same method to create the last bathroom wall that you used to make the first two interior walls. Briefly, this is how it's done:

1. Offset the upper-inside line of the left exterior wall 6' to the right, then offset this new line 4" to the right.

2. Use Zoom Window to zoom into the bathroom area.

3. Use the Trim command to trim away the short portion of the intersected wall lines between the two new wall lines.

4. Use Zoom Previous to restore the full view.

The results should look like Figure 4.18. You used Offset, Fillet, Trim, and a couple of zooms to create the interior walls. The next task is to create five doorway openings in these walls. If you need to end the drawing session before completing the chapter, click File ➤ Save As, then change the name of this drawing to Cabin04a.dwg and click Save. Then you can exit AutoCAD.

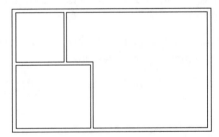

F I G U R E   4 . 1 8 : The completed interior walls

Cutting Openings in the Walls

Of the five doorway openings needed, two are on interior and three are on exterior walls (Figure 4.19). Four of them will be for swinging doors, and one will be for a sliding glass door.

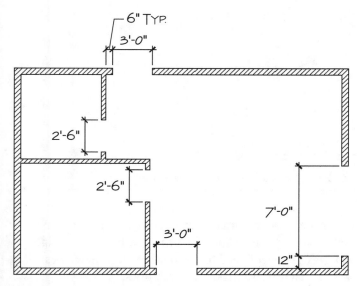

FIGURE 4.19: The drawing with doorway openings

The procedure used to make each doorway opening is the same one that you used to create the opening for the box in Chapter 2. First, you establish the location of the *jambs*, or sides, of an opening. One jamb for each swinging door opening will be located 6" away from an inside wall corner. This allows the door to be positioned next to a wall and out of the way when swung open. When the jambs are established, you will trim away the wall lines between the edges. The commands used in this exercise are Offset, Extend, and Trim. You'll make openings for the 3'-0" exterior doorways first.

The Exterior Openings

These openings are on the front and back walls of the cabin and have one side set 6" in from an inside corner.

1. Click the Offset button on the Modify toolbar to start the Offset command, then type 6 ↵ to set the distance.

2. Click one of the two lines indicated in Figure 4.20, then click in a blank area to the right of the line that you selected. Now do the same thing to the second wall line. You have to offset one line at a time because of the way that the Offset command works.

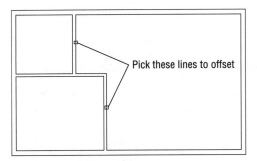

FIGURE 4.20: Lines to offset for 3'-0" openings

3. End and restart the Offset command by pressing ↵ twice, then type
3'↵ to set a new offset distance and offset the new lines to the right
(Figure 4.21). Next, you will need to extend these four new lines
through the external walls to make the jamb lines.

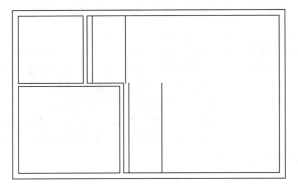

FIGURE 4.21: Offset lines for 3'-0" openings

4. Be sure to end the Offset command by pressing ↵, then type ex ↵
to start the Extend command. Extend is used here exactly as it was
used in Chapter 2. Select the upper and lower horizontal outside,

external wall lines as boundary edges for the Extend command, and press ↵.

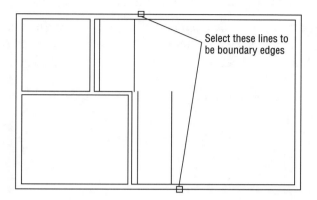

Select these lines to be boundary edges

5. Click the four lines to extend them. The lines are extended through the external walls to make the jambs (Figure 4.22). End the Extend command by pressing ↵.

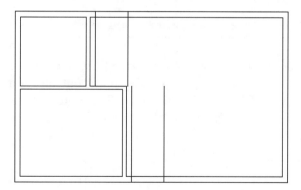

FIGURE 4.22: The lines after being extended through the external walls

 T I P   The lines to be extended must be picked on the half of them nearest the boundary's edge, or they will be extended to the opposite boundary edge.

To complete the openings, we will continue with steps 6 and 7. First, we'll trim away the excess part of the jamb lines and then, the wall

lines between the jamb lines. We'll use the Trim command the same way you used it in Chapter 2, but this time we'll do a *compound* trim to clean up the wall and jamb lines in one cycle of the command.

6. Type **tr** ↵ to start the Trim command and select the three lines at each opening as shown in Figure 4.23. Then press ↵ to tell AutoCAD you are finished selecting objects to serve as cutting edges.

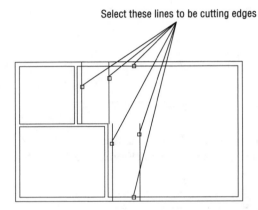

FIGURE 4.23: Selecting the cutting edges

7. Pick the four wall lines between the jamb lines, and then pick the jamb lines—the lines you just extended to the outside exterior walls. Each time you pick a line, it is trimmed. Press ↵ to end the command. Your drawing should look like Figure 4.24.

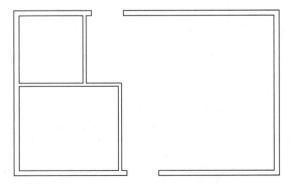

FIGURE 4.24: The finished 3'-0" openings

T I P　When picking lines to be trimmed, remember to pick the lines on the portion to be trimmed away.

The two interior openings can be constructed using the same procedure.

The Interior Openings

These doorways are 2'-6" wide and also have one jamb set in 6" from the nearest inside corner. Figure 4.25 shows the three stages of fabricating these openings. Refer to the previous section on making openings for step-by-step instructions.

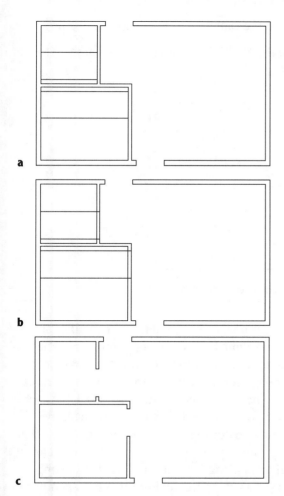

FIGURE 4.25: Creating the interior openings: the offset lines that locate the jamb lines (a), the extended lines that form the jamb lines (b), and the completed openings after trimming (c)

Construct the 7'-0" exterior opening using the same commands and technique.

The 7'-0" Opening

Notice the opening on the right side of the building has one jamb set 12" in from the inside corner. This will be the sliding glass door.

You've done this before, so here's a summary of the steps:

1. Offset a wall line 12".

2. Offset the new line 7'-0".

3. Extend both new lines through the wall.

4. Trim the new lines and the wall lines to complete the opening.

Save this drawing now as Cabin04b.dwg. This completes the openings. The results should look like Figure 4.26.

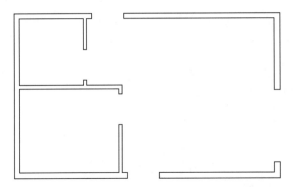

FIGURE 4.26: The completed doorway openings

As you gain more control over the commands you used here, you will be able to anticipate how much of a task can be done for each use of a command. Each opening required offsetting, extending, and trimming. You constructed these openings by drawing two at a time except for the last one, thereby using each of the three commands three times. It is possible to do all the openings using each command only once. In this way, you would do all the offsetting, then all the extending, and finally, all the trimming. In cutting these openings, however, the arrangement of the offset lines determined how many cycles of the Trim command were most efficient to use. If lines being trimmed and used as cutting edges cross each other, the trimming gets complicated. For these five openings, the most efficient procedure would be to use each command twice. In Chapter 8, when you draw the elevations, you'll get a chance to work with more complex multiple trims.

Now that the openings are complete, doors and door swings can be placed in their appropriate doorways. In doing this, you'll be introduced to two new objects and a few new commands, and there will be an opportunity to use the Offset and Trim commands in new, strategic ways.

WHAT TO DO WHEN YOU MAKE A MISTAKE

When you are Offsetting, Trimming, and Extending lines, it's easy to pick the wrong line. Here are some tips on how to correct these errors and get back on track:

▶ You can always cancel any command by pressing the Esc key until you see the Command: prompt in the Command window. Then click the Undo button on the Standard toolbar to undo the results of the last command.

▶ Errors made with the Offset command include setting the wrong distance, picking the wrong line to offset, or picking the wrong side to offset toward. If the distance is correct, you can continue offsetting, end the command when you have the results you want, then erase the lines that were offset wrong. Otherwise, press Esc and undo your previous offset.

▶ Errors made with the Trim and Extend commands can sometimes be corrected on the fly so you don't have to end the command, because each of these commands has an Undo option. If you pick a line and it doesn't trim or extend the right way, you can undo that last action without stopping the command, then continue trimming or extending. The Undo option used while the command is running can be activated in three ways: Click the Undo button on the Standard toolbar; type **u** ↵; or right-click and pick Undo from the shortcut menu that appears. Each of these will undo the last trim or extend, and you can try again without having to restart the command. Each time you activate the Undo option *from within the command*, another trim or extend is undone.

▶ The Line command also has the same Undo option as the Trim and Extend commands. You can undo the last segment drawn (or the last several segments) and redraw them.

Creating Doors

In a floor plan, a rectangle or a line for the door and an arc showing the path of the door swing usually indicates a door. The door's position varies, but it's most often shown at 90° from the closed position (Figure 4.27). The best rule I have come across is to display them in such a way that others working with your floor plan will be able to see how far, and in what direction, the door will swing open.

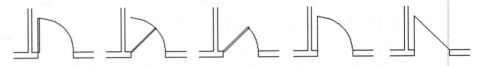

FIGURE 4.27: Possible ways to illustrate doors

The cabin has five openings. Four of them need swinging doors, which open 90°. The fifth is a sliding glass door. Drawing the sliding glass door will require a different approach.

Drawing Swinging Doors

The swinging doors are of two widths: 3' for exterior and 2'-6" for interior (refer to Figure 4.1). In general, doorway openings leading to the outside are wider than interior doors, with bathroom and closet doors usually being the narrowest. For the cabin, we'll use two sizes of swinging doors. You will draw one door of each size, and then copy these to the other openings as required. Start with the front door at the bottom of the floor plan. To get a closer view of the front door opening, use the Zoom Window command.

1. Before you start drawing, check the Status Bar at the bottom of the screen and make sure only the Model button at the far right is depressed. All other buttons should be in the Off position—that is, up. If any are depressed, click them once to turn them off.

2. Choose Tools ➤ Drafting Settings to bring up the Drafting Settings dialog. Then click the Object Snap tab to activate it, if it's not already on top.

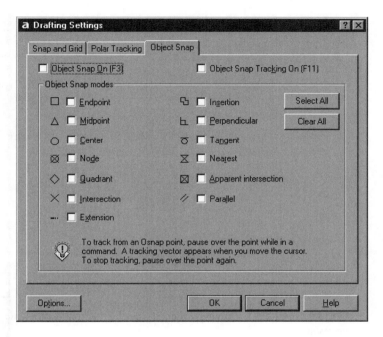

Be sure all check boxes are unchecked. If any boxes have check marks in them, click the Clear All button to uncheck them. Then click OK to close the dialog box.

3. At the Command: prompt, move the cursor to the Standard toolbar and click the Zoom Window button.

4. Pick two points to form a window around the front doorway opening, as shown in Figure 4.28a. The view changes, and you now have a close-up view of the opening (Figure 4.28b). You'll draw the door in a closed position and then rotate it open.

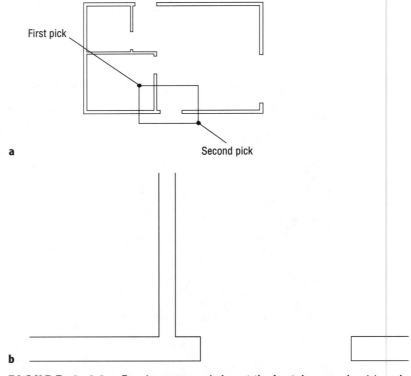

FIGURE 4.28: Forming a zoom window at the front door opening (a), and the result (b)

You can also start the Rectangle command by picking Rectangle from the Draw drop-down menu, or by typing rec ⏎ in the Command window.

"Osnap" is a nickname for Object Snap. The two terms are used interchangeably.

5. To draw the door, click the Rectangle button on the Draw toolbar.

Notice the Command window prompt. There are several options in brackets, but option `Specify first corner point` (before the brackets) is the default and is the one you want. The rectangle is formed like the zoom window—by picking two points to represent opposite corners of the rectangle. In its closed position, the door will fit exactly between the jambs, with its upper corners coinciding with the upper endpoints of the jambs. To make the first corner of the rectangle coincide with the upper endpoint of the left jamb exactly, you will use an Object Snap to assist you. *Object Snaps* (or *Osnaps*) allow you to pick specific points on objects such as endpoints, midpoints, the center of a circle, etc.

6. Move the cursor onto the Temporary Tracking Point button on the Standard toolbar and hold down the left mouse button. The Object Snap flyout opens and you see all the Object Snap tools (Figure 4.29).

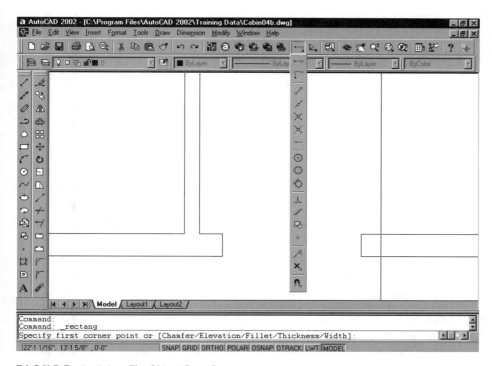

FIGURE 4.29: The Object Snap flyout

 7. Holding the left mouse button down, drag the cursor down the flyout to the Endpoint button, and release the mouse button. The prompt line now displays the addition of _endp of. This is a signal to you that the Endpoint Object Snap has been activated.

8. Move the cursor near the upper end of the left jamb line. When the cursor gets very close to a line, a colored square appears at the nearest endpoint. This shows you which endpoint in the drawing is closest to the position of the crosshair cursor at that moment.

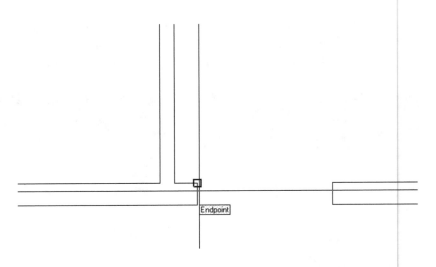

Endpoint

Because of the way
AutoCAD displays the
crosshair cursor,
when its lines coin-
cide with lines in the
drawing, both the
lines and the cross-
hair disappear. This
makes it difficult to
see the rectangle
being formed.

9. Move the cursor until the square is positioned on the upper end of the left jamb line, as shown above, and then click that point. The first corner of the rectangle now is located at that point. Move the cursor to the right and slightly down to see the rectangle being formed (Figure 4.30a). To locate the opposite corner, let's use the relative Cartesian coordinates discussed in Chapter 2.

10. When the Command window shows the Specify other corner point: prompt, type @3',-1.5 ↵ in the command line. The rectangle is drawn across the opening, creating a door in a closed position (Figure 4.30b). The door now needs to be rotated around its hinge point to an opened position.

N O T E   You could have used the Rectangle command to lay out the first four wall lines of the cabin in Chapter 3. Then you could have offset all four lines in one step to complete the exterior walls, and the corners would have been automatically filleted. It would have been faster than the method we used, but a rectangle's lines are all one object. In order to offset them to make the interior walls, they would have to be separated into individual lines using the Explode command.

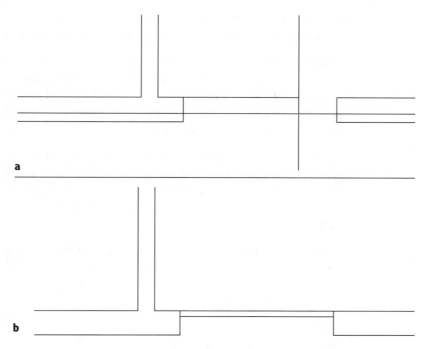

F I G U R E 4 . 3 0   The rectangle after picking the first corner (a), and the completed door in a closed position (b)

Rotating the Door

This rotation will be through an arc of 90° in the counterclockwise direction, making it a rotation of +90. By default, counterclockwise rotations are positive and clockwise rotations are negative. You'll use the Rotate command to rotate the door.

 1. Click the Rotate button from the Modify toolbar. You'll see a prompt to select objects. Click the door and press ↵.

You will be prompted for a base point. You need to indicate a point around which the door will be rotated. To keep the door placed correctly, pick the hinge point for the base point. The hinge point for this opening is the upper endpoint of the left jamb line.

 2. Return to the Standard toolbar and click the Endpoint Osnap button. Endpoint Osnap has replaced the Tracking button because it was the last Osnap button selected from the flyout toolbar.

The Rotate command can also be started by clicking Modify ↵ Rotate on the pulldown menus or by typing **ro** ↵.

Note that when you select the door, one pick selects all four lines. Rectangles are made of a special line called a *polyline* that connects all segments into one object. You will learn more about them in Chapter 10, *Controlling Text in a Drawing*.

3. Move the cursor near the upper-left corner of the door. When the colored square is displayed at that corner, left-click to locate the base point.

4. Check the status bar to be sure the Ortho button is not depressed. If it is, click it to turn Ortho off. When the Ortho button is on, the cursor is forced to move in a vertical or horizontal direction. This is very useful at times, but in this instance such a restriction would keep you from being able to see the door rotate.

5. Move the cursor away from the hinge point and see how the door rotates as the cursor moves (Figure 4.31a). If the door swings properly, you are reassured that you correctly selected the base point. The prompt reads Specify rotation angle or [reference], asking you to enter an angle.

6. Type 90 ↵. The door is rotated 90° to an open position (Figure 4.31b).

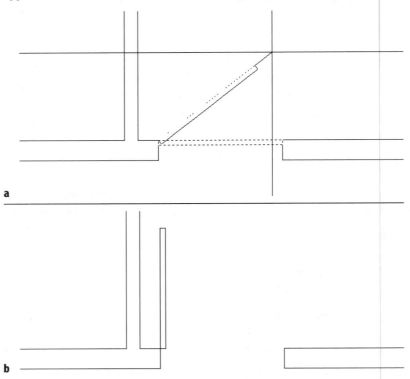

FIGURE 4.31 The door rotating with movement of the cursor (a), and the door after the 90° rotation (b)

To finish this door, you need to add the door's swing. You'll use the Arc command for this.

Drawing the Door Swing

The *swing* shows the path that the outer edge of a door takes when it swings from closed to fully open. Including a swing with the door in a floor plan helps to resolve clearance issues. The swings are drawn with the *Arc command*, in this case using the Endpoint Osnap.

Abbreviated versions of the Arc command can be started from the Draw toolbar, or by typing a ↵.

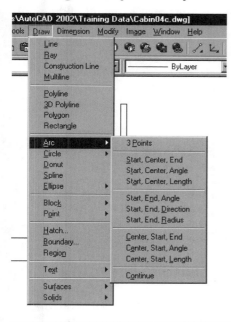

1. From the Draw menu, select Arc. The Arc menu is displayed. An arc for this door swing needs to be drawn from the upper end of the right jamb line through a rotation of 90°. So we know the start point of the arc, the center of rotation, and the angle through which the rotation occurs. The center point of the arc is the hinge point of the door.

THE OPTIONS OF THE ARC COMMAND

The position and size of an arc can be specified by a combination of its components, some of which are starting point, ending point, angle, center point, and radius. The Arc command gives you 11 options, each of which uses three components. With a little study of the geometric information available to you on the drawing, you can choose the option that best fits the situation.

When you use the Draw drop-down menu to select the Arc command, 10 options are displayed with their three components and an 11th option is used to continue the last arc drawn. For that reason, this is the best way to start the Arc command when you are first learning it.

When you start the Arc command by using the Arc button on the Draw toolbar or by typing **a** ↵, you get an abbreviated form of the command in the Command window. All 11 options of the command can be accessed through this prompt, but you have to select various options along the way.

2. From the Arc menu, select Start, Center, Angle. The command prompt now reads: arc Specify start point of arc or [Center]:. The default option is Specify start point of arc. There is also the option to start with the center point, but you would have to type c ⏎ before picking a point to be the center point.

3. Activate the Endpoint Osnap and pick the upper endpoint of the right jamb line.

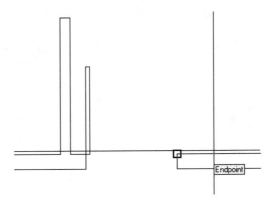

The prompt changes to read: Specify second point of arc or [Center/End]: _c Specify center point of arc.

This may be confusing at first. The prompt gives you three options: Second Point, Center, and End. (Center and End are in brackets.) Because you have previously chosen the Start, Center, Angle option, AutoCAD automatically chooses Center for you. That is the last part of the prompt.

4. Activate the Endpoint Osnap again and select the hinge point. The arc is now visible, and its endpoint follows the cursor's movement (Figure 4.32a). The prompt displays a different set of options, then ends with the Included angle option.

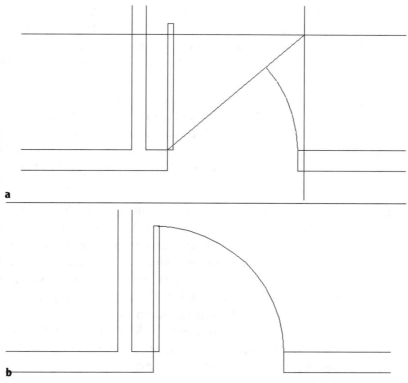

FIGURE 4.32: Drawing the arc: the ending point of the arc follows the cursor's movements (a), and the completed arc (b)

5. Type 90 ↵. The arc is completed and the Arc command ends (Figure 4.32b).

The front door is completed. Since the back door is the same size, you can save time by copying this door to the other opening. Let's see how to do that.

Copying Objects

The *Copy command* makes a copy of the objects you select. This copy can be located either by a point you pick or by relative coordinates that you enter from the keyboard. For AutoCAD to position these copied objects, you must designate two points: a base point, which serves as a point of reference for where the copy move starts; and then a second point, which serves as the ending point for the Copy command. The copy is moved the same distance and direction from its original that the second point is moved from the first point. When you know the actual distance and direction to move the copy, the base point isn't critical because you will specify the second point with relative polar or Cartesian coordinates. But in this situation, you don't know the exact distance or angle to move a copy of the front door to the back door opening, so you need to choose a base point for the copy carefully.

In copying this new door and its swing to the back door opening of the cabin, you need to find a point somewhere on the existing door or swing that can be located precisely on a point at the back door opening. There are two points like this to choose from: the hinge point, or the start point of the door swing. Let's use the hinge point. You usually know where the hinge point of the new door belongs, so this is easier to locate than the start point of the arc.

> **The Copy command can also be started from the drop-down menus, by picking Modify ➤ Copy; or from the keyboard, by typing cp ↵.**

1. Click the Copy button on the Modify toolbar. The prompt asks you to select objects to copy. Pick the door and swing, then press ↵. The prompt reads Specify base point or displacement, or [Multiple]:. Activate the Endpoint Osnap and pick the hinge point. A copy of the door and swing is attached to the crosshair cursor at the hinge point (Figure 4.33). The prompt changes to Specify second point of displacement or <use first point of displacement>:. You need to pick where the hinge point of the copied door will be located at the back door opening. To do this, you need to change the view back to what it was before you zoomed into the doorway opening.

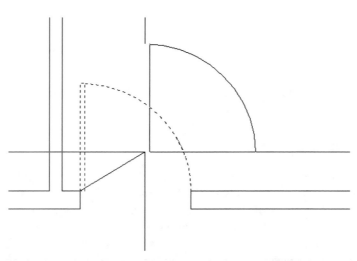

FIGURE 4.33: The copy of the door and swing attached to the crosshair cursor

2. From the Standard toolbar, click the Zoom Previous button. The full view of the cabin is restored. Move the crosshair cursor with the door in tow up to the vicinity of the back door opening. The back door should swing to the inside and be against the wall when open, so the hinge point for this opening will be at the lower end of the left jamb line.

3. Activate the Endpoint Osnap and pick the lower end of the left jamb line on the back door opening. The copy of the door and swing is placed in the opening (Figure 4.34) and, by looking at the Command window, you can see that the Copy command has ended.

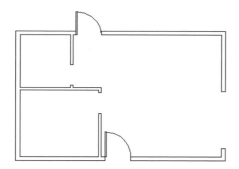

FIGURE 4.34: The door is copied to the back door opening.

◄

The Copy command ends when you pick or specify the second point of the move, unless you're copying the same object to multiple places. You'll do that in Chapter 5 when you draw the stovetop.

The door is oriented the wrong way, but you'll fix that next.

When you copy doors from one opening to another, often the orientation may not match. The best strategy is to use the hinge point as a point of reference and place it where it needs to go, as you have just done. Then flip and/or rotate the door so that it sits and swings the right way. The flipping of an object is known as *mirroring*.

Mirroring Objects

You have located the door in the opening, but it needs to be flipped so that it swings to the inside of the cabin. To do this, we'll use the *Mirror command*.

The Mirror command allows you to flip objects around an axis called the *mirror line*. You define this imaginary line by designating two points as the endpoints of the line. Strategic selection of the mirror line ensures the accuracy of the

◄

You were able to use the Zoom command while you were in the middle of using the Copy command. Most of the display commands (Zoom, Pan, etc.) can be used in this way. This is called using a command *transparently*.

mirroring action, so it's critical to visualize where the proper line lies. Sometimes you will have to draw a guideline in order to designate one or both of the endpoints.

1. Choose the Zoom Window icon from the Standard toolbar and create a window around the back door and its opening.

2. Click the Mirror button on the Modify toolbar. Select the back door and swing, and press ↵. The prompt line changes to read Specify first point of mirror line:.

3. Activate the Endpoint Osnap, then pick the hinge point of the door. The prompt changes to read Specify second point of mirror line:, and you will see the mirrored image of the door and the swing moving as you move the cursor around the drawing area. You are rotating the mirror line about the hinge point as you move the cursor. As the mirror line moves, the location of the mirrored image moves (Figure 4.35).

> **The Mirror command can also be found on the Modify drop-down menu or can be started by typing mi ↵.**

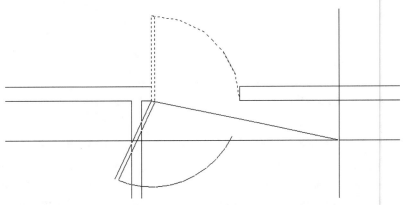

FIGURE 4.35: The mirror image moves as the mirror line moves.

4. Hold the crosshair cursor directly to the right of the first point picked, along the inside wall line. The mirror image appears where you want the door to be.

5. Activate the Endpoint Osnap again and pick the lower end of the right jamb line. The mirror image disappears and the prompt changes to read Delete source objects? [Yes/No] <N>:. You have two choices. You can keep both doors by pressing ↵ and accepting the default (No). Or you can discard the original one by typing y (for yes) in the command line and pressing ↵.

6. Type y ↵. The flipped door is displayed and the original one is deleted (Figure 4.36). The Mirror command ends. Like the Copy command, the Mirror command ends automatically after one mirroring operation.

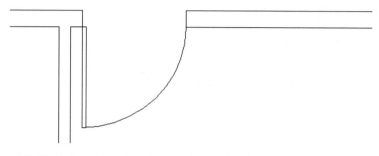

FIGURE 4.36: The mirrored door and swing

It may take some practice to become proficient at visualizing and designating the mirror line, but once you are used to it, you will have learned a very powerful tool. Because many building layouts have some symmetry to them, wise use of the Mirror command can save you a lot of drawing time.

You have two more swinging doors to place in the floor plan.

Finishing the Swinging Doors

You can't copy the existing doors and swings to the interior openings because the sizes don't conform, but you can use the same procedure to draw one door and swing, and then copy it to the other opening.

 N O T E We could have used the Stretch command to lengthen the door, but that's an advanced Modify command, and won't be introduced until Chapter 9, *Working with Hatches and Fills*. Besides, the arc would have to be modified to a larger radius. It's easier to just draw another door and swing to a different size.

1. Click the Zoom Previous button on the Standard toolbar. Then click the Zoom Window button right next to the Zoom Previous button, and make a zoom window to magnify the view of the interior door openings. Be sure to make the zoom window large enough to leave some room for the new doors to be drawn (Figure 4.37).

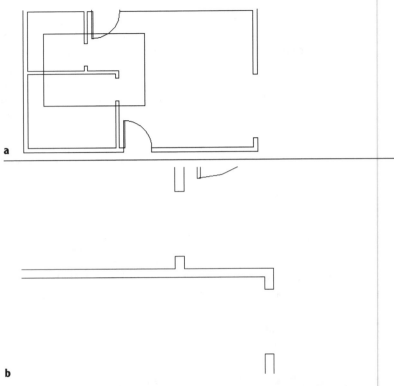

a

b

FIGURE 4.37: A zoom window in the interior door opening area (a), and the results of the zoom (b)

2. Follow the same procedure to draw the door and swing in the lower opening. Here is a summary of the steps:

A. Use the Rectangle command and Endpoint Osnap to draw the door from the hinge point to a point @1.5,-2'6.

B. Rotate the door around the hinge point to an open position. You will have to use a rotation angle of –90°.

C. Use the Start, Center, Angle option of the Arc command to draw the door swing, starting at the upper-left corner of the door, and using Endpoint Osnap for the two picks.

3. Use the Copy command to copy this door and swing to the other interior opening. The base point will be the hinge point, and the second point will be the left end of the lower jamb line in the upper opening. Use the Endpoint Osnap for both picks.

> ▶
>
> **The Start, Center, Angle options, as well as a few others, of the Arc command require that you choose the start point for the arc in such a way that the arc is drawn in a counter-clockwise direction. If you progress in a clockwise direction, use a negative number for the angle.**

4. Use the Mirror command to flip up this copy of the door and swing. The mirror line will be different from the one used for the back door. The geometrical arrangement at the back opening required that the door and its swing be flipped across the opening. For this one, the door and its swing must flip in a direction parallel to the opening. For this opening, the mirror line is the lower jamb line itself, so pick each end of this line (using Endpoint Osnap) to establish the mirror line.

5. Use the Zoom Previous button to see the four swinging doors in place (Figure 4.38).

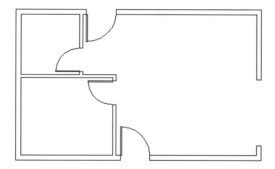

F I G U R E   4 . 3 8 :   The four swinging doors in place

The last door to draw is the sliding glass door. This kind of door requires an entirely different strategy, but you'll use commands familiar to you by now.

N O T E   The buttons you have been clicking in this chapter are also referred to as "icons" and "tools." When they are in dialog boxes or on the Status Bar, they actually look like buttons to push that have icons on them. When they are on the toolbars, they look like icons, i.e., little pictures. But when you move the Pointer Arrow cursor onto one, it takes on the appearance of a button with an icon on it. All three terms—"button," "icon," and "tool"—will be used interchangeably in this book.

Drawing a Sliding Glass Door

Sliding glass doors are usually drawn to show their glass panels within the door frames.

To draw the sliding door, you will apply the Line, Offset, and Trim commands to the 7' opening you made earlier.

1. Click the Zoom Window button on the Standard toolbar and make a zoom window closely around the 7' opening. In making the zoom window, pick one point just above and to the left of the upper door-jamb and below and to the right of the lower jamb. This will make the opening as large as possible while including everything you will need in the view (Figure 4.39).

FIGURE 4.39: The view when zoomed in as closely as possible to the 7' opening

2. You will be using several Osnaps for this procedure, so it will be convenient to have the Osnap Flyout toolbar more immediately available. Here's how:

A. Right-click on any button on any of the toolbars on your screen. The toolbar menu appears.

B. Click Object Snap on the menu. The menu closes and the Object Snap toolbar will be displayed in the drawing area. It is in floating mode.

C. Put the cursor on the colored title bar of the Object Snap toolbar, and, holding down the left mouse button, drag the toolbar to the right side of the drawing area. Dock it there by releasing the mouse button (Figure 4.40). Now all Object Snaps can easily be selected as needed.

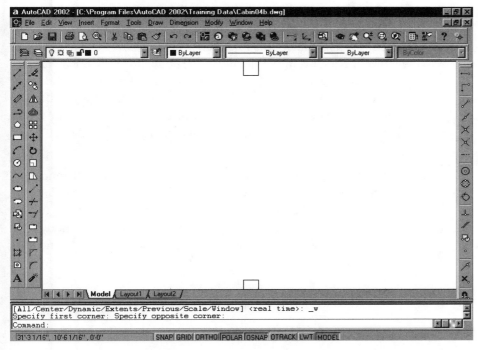

FIGURE 4.40: The Object Snap toolbar docked to the right of the drawing area

3. Offset each jamb line 2" into the doorway opening (Figure 4.41).

FIGURE 4.41: Jamb lines offset 2" into the doorway opening

4. Type l ↵ to start the Line command. Click the Midpoint Osnap button on the Object Snap toolbar, then place the cursor near the midpoint of the upper doorjamb line. Notice how a colored triangle appears when your cursor is in the vicinity of the midpoint. Each Osnap has a symbol with a distinctive shape. When the triangle appears at the midpoint of the jamb line, left-click. Click the Midpoint Osnap button again, move the cursor to the bottom jamb line, and, when the triangle appears at that midpoint, click again. Press ↵ to end the Line command.

5. Start the Offset command and type 1.5 ↵ to set the offset distance. Pick the newly drawn line, then pick a point anywhere to the right side. Then, while the Offset command is still running, pick the original line again and pick another point in a blank area somewhere to the left side of the doorway opening (Figure 4.42). Press ↵ to end the Offset command.

> A line *offset* from itself, that is, a copy of the selected line, is automatically made at a specified perpendicular distance from the selected line.

FIGURE 4.42: Offset vertical line between jambs

6. Check the Status bar to see if Ortho is on. If it's not, click it to activate it. Type l ↵ to start the Line command. Click the Midpoint Osnap button and then move the cursor near the midpoint of the left vertical line. When the colored triangle appears at the midpoint of this leftmost line, click. Hold the cursor out directly to the right of the point you just selected to draw a horizontal line through the three vertical lines. When the cursor is about two feet to the right of the three vertical lines, pick a point to set the endpoint of this guideline. Press ↵ to end the Line command (Figure 4.43).

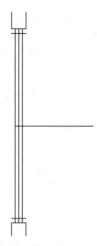

FIGURE 4.43: Horizontal guideline drawn through vertical lines

7. Type o ↵ to start the Offset command. Type 1 ↵ to set the offset distance. Select this new line, and then pick a point in a blank area anywhere above the line. Pick the new horizontal line again and then
pick anywhere below it. The new line has been offset 1" above and
below itself (Figure 4.44). Now you have placed all the lines necessary
to create the sliding glass door frames in the opening. You still need
to trim back some of these lines and erase others. Press ↵ to end the
Offset command.

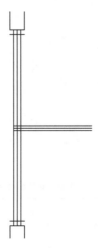

FIGURE 4.44: Offset horizontal guideline

8. Start the Trim command by typing **tr** ↵. When you are prompted to select cutting edges, pick the two horizontal lines that were just created with the Offset command. Then press ↵.

9. Now trim the two outside vertical lines by selecting them as shown in Figure 4.45a. The result is shown in Figure 4.45b.

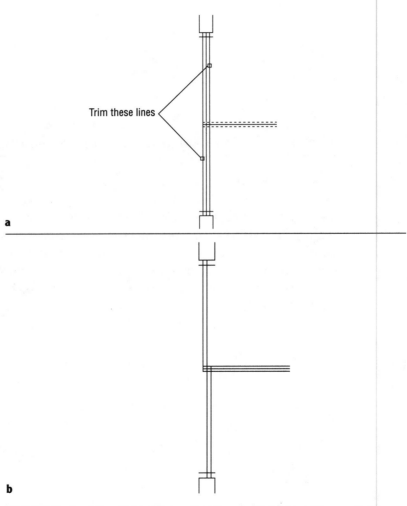

a

b

FIGURE 4.45: Picking the vertical lines to trim (a), and the result (b)

10. Press ⏎ twice to stop and restart the Trim command. When you are prompted to select cutting edges, use a special window called a *crossing window* to select all the lines visible in the drawing. A crossing window will select everything within the window or crossing it. Here's how to do it:

    A. Pick a point above and to the right of the opening.

    B. Move the cursor to a point below and to the left of the opening, forming a window with dashed lines (Figure 4.46).

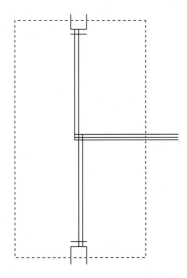

FIGURE 4.46: The crossing window for selecting cutting edges

    C. Pick that point. Everything inside the rectangle or crossing an edge of it is selected.

    D. Press ⏎.

11. To trim the lines, pick them at the points noted in Figure 4.47a. When you finish trimming, the opening should look like Figure 4.47b. Be sure to press ⏎ to end the Trim command.

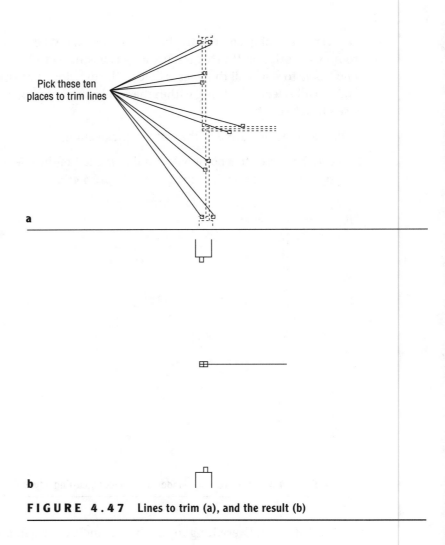

Pick these ten
places to trim lines

a

b

FIGURE 4.47   Lines to trim (a), and the result (b)

N O T E   If all lines don't trim the way you expect them to, you may have to change the setting for the Edgemode variable. It's easy. Cancel the trim operation and undo any trims you've made to the sliding glass door. Type **edgemode** ↵, then type **0** ↵. Now start the Trim command and continue trimming.

12. Start the Erase command and erase the remaining horizontal guideline.

    To finish the sliding glass doors, you need to draw in two lines to represent the glass panes for each door panel. Each pane of glass is centered inside its frame, so the line representing the pane will run between the midpoints of the inside edge of each frame section.

13. Type l ↵ to start the Line command and pick the Midpoint button on the Object Snap toolbar.

14. For each of the two sliding door frames, put the cursor near the midpoint of the inside line of the frame section nearest the jamb. When the colored triangle appears there, click. Then select the Perpendicular Osnap button from the Object Snap toolbar and move the cursor to the other frame section of that door panel. When you get near the horizontal line that represents both the inside edge of one frame section and the back edge of the frame section next to it, the colored Perpendicular Osnap symbol will appear on that line. When it does, select that point.

15. Press ↵ to end the Line command.

16. Press ↵ to restart the Line command and repeat the procedure described in step 14 for the other door panel, being sure to start the line at the frame section nearest the other jamb. The finished opening should look like Figure 4.48a.

17. Use the Zoom Previous button to see the full floor plan with all doors (Figure 4.48b).

18. Save this drawing as Cabin04c.

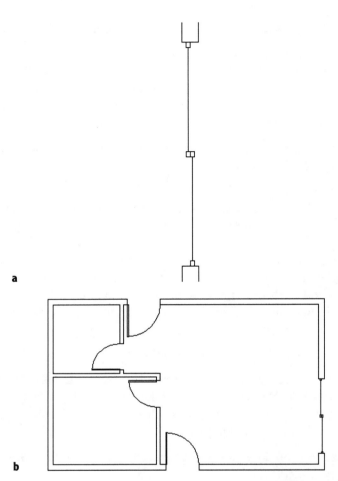

FIGURE 4.48: The finished sliding glass doors (a), and the floor plan with all doors finished (b)

This completes the doors for the floor plan. The focus here has been on walls and doors, and the strategies for drawing them. As a result, you now have a basic floor plan for the cabin, and you will continue to develop this plan in the next chapter.

The overall drawing strategy that has been emphasized in this chapter is using objects already in the drawing to create new ones. We started out with four lines that comprised the outside wall lines. By offsetting, filleting, extending, and trimming, we drew all the walls and openings without drawing any new lines. For the swinging doors, we made two rectangles and two arcs. Then by copying, rotating, and mirroring, we formed the other two swinging doors. For the sliding glass door, we drew two new lines, then used offset, trim, and erase to finish the door. So we used four lines and created six new objects to complete the walls and doors. This is a pretty good start in learning to use AutoCAD wisely.

By working with the tools and strategies in this chapter, you now should have an idea of an approach to drawing many objects. In the next one, you will continue in the same vein, learning a few new commands and strategies as you add steps, a balcony, a kitchen, and a bathroom to the floor plan.

If You Would Like More Practice...

If you would like to practice the skills you have learned so far, here are a couple of extra exercises.

An Alternate Sliding Glass Door

Here is a simplified version of the sliding glass door of the cabin. It doesn't include any representation of the panes of glass and their frames.

To draw it, use a technique similar to the one described in the previous section. Copy the jambs for the 7' opening to the right and draw this door between them.

An Addition to the Cabin

This addition is connected to the cabin by a sidewalk, and consists of a remodeled two-car garage in which one car slot has been converted into a storage area and an office (Figure 4.49). Use the same commands and strategies you have been using up to now to draw this layout adjacent to the cabin. Save this exercise as Cabin04c-addon.dwg.

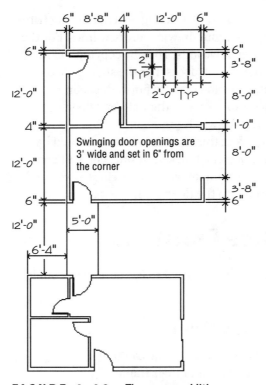

FIGURE 4.49: The garage addition

Refer back to this chapter and the previous one for specific commands. Here is the general procedure:

- ▶ Draw the two lines that represent the walkway between the two buildings.

- ▶ Draw the outside exterior wall line.

- ▶ Use Offset, Fillet, and Trim to create the rest of the walls and wall lines.

- ▶ Use Offset, Extend, and Trim to create the openings.

- ▶ Use Rectangle and Arc to create a swinging door.

- ▶ Use Copy, Rotate, and Mirror to put in the rest of the doors.

- ▶ Use Offset, Line, and Copy to draw the storage partitions.

Are You Experienced?

Now you can...

- ☑ offset exterior walls to make interior walls

- ☑ zoom in on an area with a zoom window and zoom back out with the Zoom Previous command

- ☑ use the Rectangle and Arc commands to make a door

- ☑ use the Endpoint, Midpoint, and Perpendicular Object Snap modes

- ☑ use the crossing window selection tool

- ☑ use the Copy and Mirror commands to place an existing door and swing in another opening

- ☑ use the Offset and Trim commands to make a sliding glass door

CHAPTER 5

Gaining Drawing Strategies: Part 2

- ▶ Using Object Snaps
- ▶ Using Polar Tracking
- ▶ Zooming with Realtime and Pan
- ▶ Copying and moving objects
- ▶ Using Direct Entry of Distances
- ▶ Creating circles and ellipses

n the last chapter, we emphasized using existing geometry (or objects) in the drawing to create new geometry. In this one, we'll look at new tools for forming an efficient drawing strategy. Before we get back to the cabin, I want to give you a brief overview of the tools available for starting and running commands.

Developing a drawing strategy begins with determining the best way to start, or when to start, a command. AutoCAD provides several ways to start most of the commands you will be using. You have seen how the Offset, Fillet, Trim, and Extend commands can be found on either the Modify toolbar or Modify drop-down menu. They can also be started by typing the first letter or two of the command, then pressing Enter.

> **T I P**   Here's a quick recap. To start the Offset and Fillet commands, enter o or f, respectively. To execute the Trim command, enter tr, and to execute the Extend command, enter ex. Remember also that the drop-down menus may be activated by holding down the Alt key while pressing the hotkey—the letter that is underlined in the menu name. For example, to open the Modify drop-down menu, enter Alt+m.

The choice of which method to use will be determined, to an extent, by what you are doing at the time as well as by your command of the keyboard. When using the abbreviations, keyboard entry is generally the fastest method; but if your hand is already on the mouse and the Modify toolbar is docked on the screen, selecting commands from the toolbar may be faster. The drop-down menus are slower to use because they require more selections to get to a command, but they also contain more commands and command options than the toolbars.

Remember that if you have just ended a command, that command can be restarted by pressing ↵, or by right-clicking the mouse. When you right-click, a *shortcut* menu appears near where you are holding the cursor.

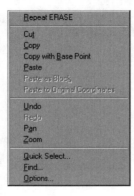

The top item on this menu says Repeat *command* with the command being the last command used. So if you just finished using the Erase command and you right-click your mouse, the top item of the shortcut menu will say Repeat Erase. Other items on this shortcut menu will be introduced in the rest of the book. It is also called a *context* menu because the particular items on it will vary depending on:

▶ Whether or not a command is running

▶ What command you are using

▶ Where you are in a command

In this chapter, you will be introduced to several new commands and, through the step-by-step instructions, be shown some alternate methods for accomplishing tasks similar to those you have previously completed. You will add front and back steps, thresholds, a balcony, and kitchen and bath fixtures to the cabin floor plan (Figure 5.1). For each of these tasks, the focus will be on noticing what objects and geometry are already in the drawing that can make your job easier, and on tools to help you accomplish the tasks more quickly and efficiently.

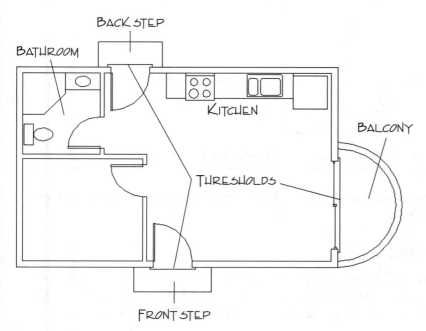

FIGURE 5.1: The cabin with front and back steps, thresholds, balcony, kitchen, and bathroom

Drawing the Steps and Thresholds

The steps and thresholds are each drawn with three simple lines. The trick is to see what part of the drawing can be effectively used to generate and position those lines. Use a width of 2' for the front and back step, and lengths of 6' and 5', respectively. The three thresholds extend 2" beyond the outside wall line and run 3" past either jamb line (Figure 5.2).

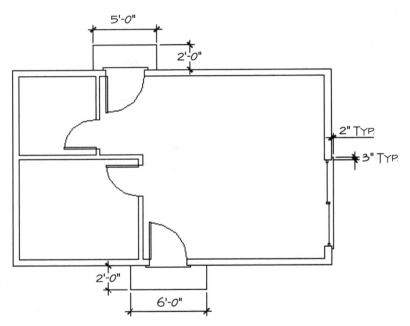

FIGURE 5.2: The steps and thresholds with their dimensions

These are simple shapes to draw, but you will learn a few new techniques as you create them.

The Front Step

As you can see in Figure 5.2, the front step is 2' wide and 6' long. Because you know the width of the doorway opening, you can determine how far past the opening the step extends, assuming it to be symmetrical. A line can then be drawn from the endpoint of one of the jamb lines, down 2', then offset the proper distance left and right to create the sides of the step. Here's how it's done:

1. With AutoCAD running, bring up your cabin drawing (last saved as Cabin04c) and use the Zoom command options to achieve a view similar to Figure 5.3.

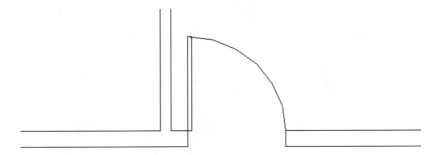

F I G U R E 5 . 3 : Zoomed into the front opening

2. Check to be sure all buttons on the Status bar except Model are in the Off position. Start the Line command, activate the Endpoint Osnap, and pick a point at the lower end of the left jamb line.

WAYS TO USE THE OBJECT SNAP TOOLS

There are several ways to access the Object Snap tools:

▶ The Object Snap toolbar may be docked on the right side of the drawing area. If not, you can bring it up and dock it.

▶ Use the Object Snap flyout. The flyout toolbar is opened by holding down the left mouse button when the cursor is on the Tracking button on the Standard toolbar.

▶ The Object Snap menu also has the Object Snaps on it. You can open this menu by holding down the Shift key and clicking the right mouse button.

▶ If you're using an Intellimouse or have a mouse with three buttons, you may be able to open the Object Snap menu by clicking the Intellimouse wheel or clicking the third mouse button.

3. Right-click the Polar button on the Status bar at the bottom of the screen, then click Settings. The Drafting Settings dialog box comes up and the Polar Tracking tab is active.

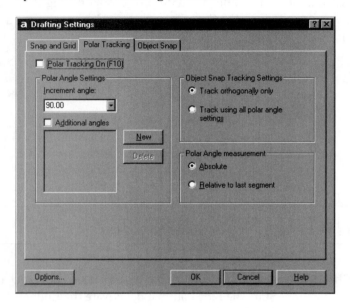

4. In the Polar Angle Settings area, check to see whether the Increment angle is set to 90.00. If it's not, open the drop-down list and select 90.00. On the right side, be sure that Absolute is selected in the Polar Angle Measurement area. Finally, in the upper-left corner, click the Polar Tracking On check box. Click OK.

5. Hold the crosshair cursor so that it is below the first point picked. Do not pick a point yet (Figure 5.4). A dashed line called a *temporary alignment path* is displayed along with a tooltip that identifies the alignment path as a Polar one, and a relative polar coordinate that confirms the angle to be 270°. As you move the cursor from left to right, notice that the alignment path and tooltip disappear when you get too far away from a point directly below the first point of the line, and reappear as you get back close to vertical.

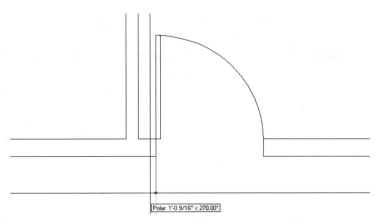

FIGURE 5.4: Line command running with Polar tracking on

6. While the alignment path and tool tip are visible, type 2' ↵. A vertical line is drawn that is two feet long. When the line command is running and the crosshair cursor is held away from the last point picked in a particular direction, you can enter a distance, and the line will be drawn to the desired length in the direction of the crosshair cursor. This is called the *Direct Entry* method of entering distances. Because you want the line to be vertical, Polar Tracking assisted you by producing an alignment path in the vertical direction.

7. Press ↵ to end the Line command. Type **o** ↵ to start the Offset command. Type **1'6** ↵ for an offset distance, and offset this line to the left.

8. Press ↵ twice to stop and restart Offset. Type **6'** ↵ and offset this new line to the right (Figure 5.5). Press ↵ to end the Offset command.

When Polar Tracking mode is on, temporary alignment paths assist you in drawing lines at angles that are multiples of the increment angle, in this case, 90°.

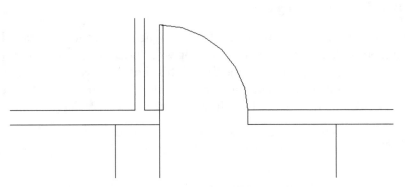

FIGURE 5.5: The sides of the front step after offsetting

9. Erase the original line and draw a line from the lower endpoints of these two new lines to represent the front edge of the step. Use the Endpoint Osnap for each point picked. Press ↵ to end the Line command. Your drawing should look like Figure 5.6.

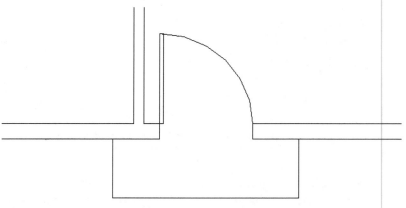

FIGURE 5.6: The completed front step

10. Zoom previous to view the entire floor plan.

The strategy here was to recognize that a line drawn from the jamb line could be used to determine the location of the sides of the step. The new technique of using Polar Tracking to draw showed you a quick method for entering distances when the lines are at angles that are multiples of the Polar tracking increment angle that you have set. For the back step, you'll build on this by adding the Temporary Tracking Point aid to your bag of tools.

The Back Step

The method used on the front step can be applied to the back step as well. The situation is identical: You will be working with the same geometry in the drawing and will accomplish the same thing. This time, however, you'll use a Temporary Tracking Point to locate the side of the step. This will cut out the need to use a guideline. Remember that the step in the back is 5' wide.

 1. Zoom into the back step area. Start the Line command and pick the Temporary Tracking Point button on the Object Snap toolbar.

The prompt line in the Command window will read: _line Specify first point: _tt Specify temporary OTRACK point:. This is actually three prompts grouped together:

▶ _line signifies the start of the Line command.

▶ Specify first point: is the first prompt for the Line command.

▶ _tt Specify temporary OTRACK point: signifies that the Temporary Tracking Point option has been selected.

In this case, because the step is 5' long, we want to begin the side of the step 1' to the left of the doorway opening. So the temporary tracking point that you need is the starting point from which you will measure the 1-foot distance—in this case, it is the upper end of the left jamb line.

2. Pick the Endpoint Osnap and pick the upper end of the left jamb line. A small cross appears at the point you just picked, and the prompt line now has _endp of Specify first point: added to it. This is actually two more prompts:

▶ _endp signifies that the Endpoint Osnap was selected.

▶ Specify first point: is the second prompt for the Temporary Tracking Point option. AutoCAD has recorded the temporary tracking point and waits for you to specify the first point of the line that is to be the left side of the back step. You will do this by using Polar Tracking and Direct Entry, telling AutoCAD how far away and in what direction from the temporary tracking point you want to begin the line—in this case, it's 1' to the left.

3. Hold the cursor to the left of the temporary tracking point. When the temporary alignment path appears with the tooltip, as shown in Figure 5.7, type 12 ↵. A line begins 1' to the left of the opening on the outside wall line. Hold the crosshair cursor directly above the beginning of the line and, when you see the vertical alignment path with the tooltip, type 2' ↵. The side of the step is drawn using the Direct Entry technique with Polar Tracking. The Line command is still running.

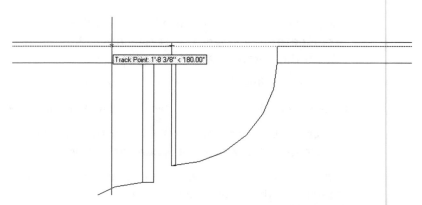

FIGURE 5.7: Using a temporary tracking point with Polar Tracking and Direct Entry

4. Hold the crosshair cursor directly to the right from the last point; then, when you see the alignment path and tooltip, type 5' ↵. The front edge of the step is drawn. You used Direct Entry with Polar Tracking again, and didn't have to enter either the relative polar or Cartesian coordinates.

5. Select Perpendicular Osnap from the Object Snap toolbar and move the cursor to the outside wall line (Figure 5.8). When the perpendicular icon appears on the wall line, click the mouse button. The right edge of the step is drawn and the back step is complete. Press ↵ to end the Line command.

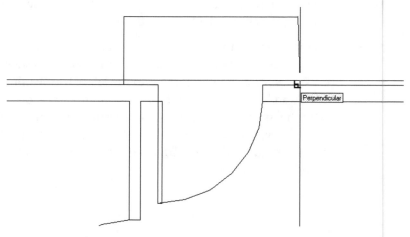

FIGURE 5.8: Completing the back step with the Perpendicular Osnap

6. Zoom Previous to view the completed back step with the whole floor plan.

Temporary Tracking is a welcome new tool for AutoCAD users. It will be used a few more times in this book. When you combine it with the technique of using Polar Tracking to help enter distances, as you have for the back step, you will be surprised at how quickly you can lay out orthogonal walls in a floor plan. The Polar Tracking technique, used by itself, powerfully facilitates drawing the footprint of a building. When you work through the next section, you'll get to practice using the Temporary Tracking tool once more.

I'm sure this seems complicated, but you'll get a chance to try the technique three more times, because you now have to do the thresholds for the three external openings.

The Thresholds

Thresholds generally are used on doorway openings where the level changes from one side of the opening to the other. This usually occurs at entrances that open from or to the outside. Though quite different in shape, each threshold for the cabin has the same geometry as the steps. The lip of each threshold is offset 2" from the outside wall, and each edge runs 3" past the doorjamb (refer to Figure 5.2). You'll use the Temporary Tracking Point tool with Polar Tracking and Direct Entry to draw the three thresholds for the cabin. Here is a summary of the steps to draw a threshold for one of the openings. We'll use the front door entry for our illustrations.

1. Zoom into the opening and its immediate surroundings.

2. Start the Line command, then click the Temporary Tracking Point button and the Endpoint Osnap button from the Osnap toolbar.

3. Click the outside endpoint of one of the jamb lines, then move the cursor along the wall line away from the opening until the Polar alignment path and tooltip appear (Figure 5.9a).

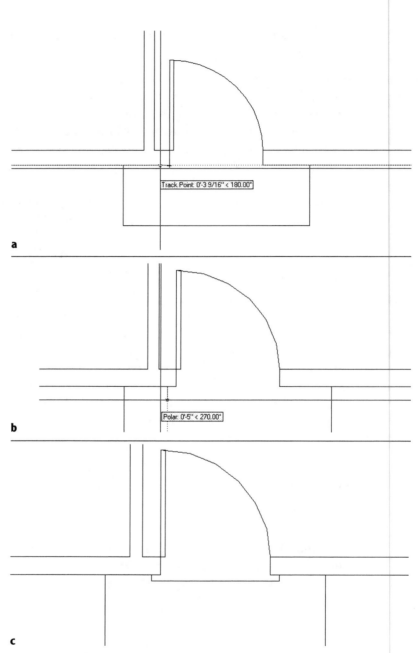

FIGURE 5.9: The tracking path and Track Point tooltip (a), the first threshold line is started (b), and the completed threshold (c)

4. Enter the distance that the threshold extends past the jamb (it's 3"). This begins the first line.

5. Move the crosshair away from the wall line in a horizontal or vertical direction (depending on which opening you are drawing) until the Polar alignment path and tooltip appear (Figure 5.9b).

6. Enter the overhang distance of the threshold (it's 2").

7. Move the crosshair in a direction perpendicular to the last point of the last segment drawn, until the Polar alignment and tooltip appear.

8. Enter the length of the threshold (it's the length of the opening + 6").

9. Invoke the Perpendicular Osnap and hold the crosshair back on the wall line, then click. Press ↵ to end the Line command (Figure 5.9c).

10. When finished, Zoom Previous to view the finished thresholds with the rest of the drawing.

USING DIRECT ENTRY OF DISTANCES

Direct Entry is a method used to specify distances for line segments. In this method, you position the crosshair in such a way that the direction from the last point picked indicates the direction for the next line segment. Then you just type in the distance. There's no need to use either the relative polar or relative Cartesian coordinates. This technique is primarily used with Polar tracking to draw line segments that are oriented at a preset angle, in this case, 90°, 180°, 270°, and 0°. It saves time because there is less data to type in. Direct Entry can also be used with the Copy and Move commands to specify displacement of selected objects being moved or copied.

The tracking features in AutoCAD are powerful tools for drawing that can be used in several ways. So far we have used Polar Tracking and the Temporary Tracking Point Osnap, and will use them again and other tracking features later in this chapter.

The Balcony: Drawing Circles

A glance back at Figure 5.1 will tell you that the balcony is made up of two semi-circles. There are several ways that these could be drawn, but you will form them from a circle. Often the easiest way to draw an arc is to draw a circle that contains the arc segment, then trim the circle back.

1. Select Draw ➢ Circle and look at the Circle menu for a moment.

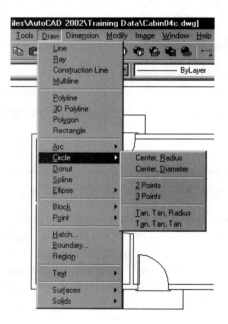

There are six options for constructing a circle. Two of them require you to specify a point as the center of the circle and to enter a radius or a diameter. The next two options are used when you know two or three points that the circle must intersect. And, finally, the last two options use tangents and a radius, or just tangents, to form a circle.

2. The balcony has a radius of 5', so select the Center, Radius option. The Command window will prompt you to specify a point as the center of the circle. The actual center for the balcony will be 5' above

the lower-right corner of the outside wall line; but, for this exercise, we will draw the circle in the living room and then move it into position later.

3. Pick a point in the middle of the largest room of the cabin. The center is now established, and, as you move the cursor, the circle changes size and becomes attached to the crosshair cursor (Figure 5.10). You could pick a point to establish the radius; but, in this case, you know exactly what you want the radius to be.

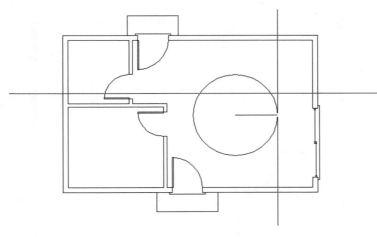

FIGURE 5.10:   The circle attached to the crosshair cursor

4. Type 5' ↵. The circle is drawn, and the command ends.

 5. Click the Move button on the Modify toolbar. The cursor changes to a pickbox. Select the circle and press ↵.

 6. On the Object Snap toolbar or flyout, pick the Quadrant button. Select the circle somewhere near its bottom extremity (Figure 5.11a). An image of the circle is attached to the crosshair cursor. Turn Polar Tracking off by clicking the Polar button on the status bar.

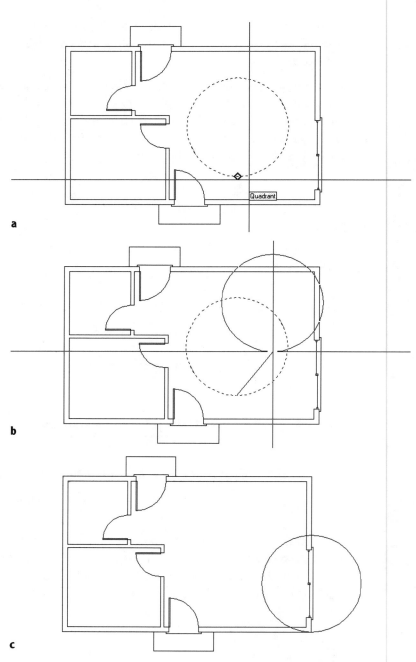

a

b

c

FIGURE 5.11: Selecting the base point with Quadrant Osnap (a), the circle attached to the crosshair cursor at its lowest point (b), and the circle positioned for the balcony (c)

7. Move the crosshair cursor around to see that the lowest point on the circle is attached at the crosshair (Figure 5.11b). This point on the circle needs to be placed at the lower-right corner of the outside wall line.

8. Select the Endpoint Osnap, then pick the lower-right corner of the cabin. The circle is positioned correctly for the balcony (Figure 5.11c). Now you can use the existing wall lines to trim the circle into a semicircle.

9. Zoom into the area of the balcony and start the Trim command.

10. Select the two outside wall lines on the far right, as shown in Figure 5.12, then press ↵.

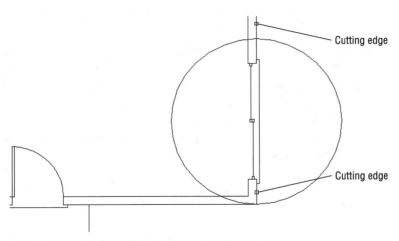

Cutting edge

Cutting edge

FIGURE 5.12: Selecting wall lines to be cutting edges

11. Select the portion of the circle that is inside the cabin. The circle is trimmed into a semicircle. Press ↵ to end the Trim command.

12. Start the Offset command, set the distance for 6", and offset the semicircle to the inside. Press ↵ to end the Offset command. The balcony is complete. Zoom previous to view the floor plan with the completed balcony. Save the drawing as Cabin05a.dwg (Figure 5.13).

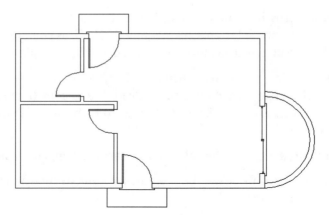

F I G U R E 5 . 1 3 : The floor plan with the balcony completed

As mentioned at the beginning of this section, there are several techniques for drawing the balcony. The one you used gave you the opportunity to use the Move command and the Quadrant Osnap, and let you see how using the lowest quadrant snap point on the circle is an easy way to locate the balcony on the building. No entry of relative coordinates was required.

In the next section, you will continue to develop drawing strategies as you focus on laying out a counter and fixtures to complete the kitchen.

Laying Out the Kitchen

The kitchen for the cabin will have a stove, a refrigerator, and a counter with a sink (Figure 5.14). The refrigerator is set 2" away from the back wall. Approaching this drawing task, your goal is to think about the easiest and fastest way to complete it. The first step in deciding on an efficient approach is to ascertain what information you have about the various parts, and what geometry in the drawing will be able to assist you. The basic dimensions are given here, and you will get more detailed information about the sink and stove as we progress through the exercise.

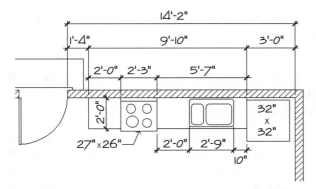

FIGURE 5.14: The general layout of the kitchen

The Counter

Although the counter is in two pieces, you will draw it as one piece and then cut out a section for the stove. Try two ways to draw the counter to see which method is more efficient.

Using Polar Tracking and Direct Entry with a Temporary Tracking Point

1. Use a zoom window to zoom your view so it is about the same magnification as Figure 5.15. On the Status bar, Model and Polar should be in the On position. The rest of the buttons should be off.

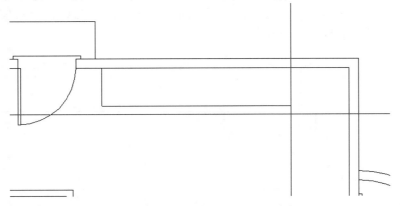

FIGURE 5.15: Drawing the counter using the Direct Entry technique

2. Start the Line command. Activate the Temporary Tracking Point Osnap and click Endpoint Osnap. Then pick the lower end of the right back doorjamb line. A small cross is placed on the point you choose.

3. Hold the crosshair cursor directly to the right of that point. When the Track Point tooltip and the dotted-line tracking path appear, type 1'4 ⏎. The line for the left side of the counter is begun.

4. Hold the crosshair cursor directly below the first point of the line and type 2' ⏎. Hold the crosshair cursor to the right and type 9'10 ⏎ (Figure 5.15). Select the Perpendicular Osnap and pick the inside wall line again. Press ⏎ to end the Line command. The counter is drawn.

Using Offset and Fillet

To do the same thing using the Offset command, you'll need to undo the effects of the previous command. Since all lines were drawn in one cycle of the Line command, one use of the U command will undo the entire counter.

1. Click the Undo button on the Standard toolbar. The counter you just drew should disappear. If you ended the Line command while drawing the counter and had to restart it before you finished, you may have to click the Undo button more than once. If you undo too much, click the Redo button, just to the right of the Undo button.

   Now draw the counter again, this time using the Offset and Fillet commands.

2. Offset the right inside wall line 3' to the left. Then offset this new line 9'-10" to the left. Finally, offset the upper inside wall line 2' down (Figure 5.16).

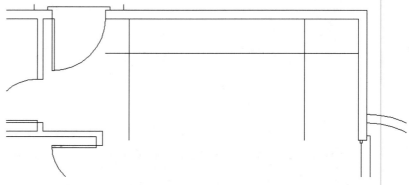

FIGURE 5.16: Offsetting wall lines to create the counter

3. Use the Fillet command with a radius of zero to clean up the two corners.

You can decide which of the two methods is more practical for you. Both are powerful techniques for laying out orthogonal patterns of lines for walls, counters, and other objects.

UNDOING AND REDOING IN AUTOCAD

AutoCAD has two Undo commands, and they operate quite differently.

▶ When you click the Undo button on the Standard toolbar, you are using AutoCAD's U command. It can also be started by typing **u** ↵. The U command works like the undo command for Windows-compatible applications by undoing the results of commands one step at a time.

▶ The Undo command in AutoCAD has many options and is started by typing **undo** ↵. This is used when you want to undo everything you've done since you last saved your drawing, or back to a point in your drawing session that you marked earlier. Be careful when you use the Undo command, as you could easily lose a lot of your work.

The Redo command will only undo the effect of one undo. So, if you undo one step too many, you can still get the last undone step back. But, undoing more than one step has the effect of deleting work permanently; your work will then have to be redrawn.

The Stove and Refrigerator

The stove and refrigerator are simple rectangles. Use the Temporary Tracking Point Osnap to locate the first corner of each shape.

1. For the refrigerator, select the Rectangle button on the Draw toolbar, then click the Temporary Tracking Point Osnap option. Use Endpoint Osnap to select a base point at the upper end of the right side of the counter. Then hold the cursor directly below that point. When the dotted tracking path and the Track Point tooltip appear, type 2 ↵. This starts the rectangle 2" away from the back wall, along the side of the counter. To specify the opposite corner of the rectangle, type @32,-32 ↵.

2. For the stove, right-click the mouse. A shortcut menu pops up next to the crosshair cursor. Click Repeat Rectangle. Use the same technique that was used in step 1, but pick the upper end of the left side of the counter as the tracking point. Hold the cursor directly to the right of that point and type 2' ⏎. Then type @27,-26 to complete the rectangle.

3. Use the Trim command to trim away the front edge of the counter at the stove (Figure 5.17).

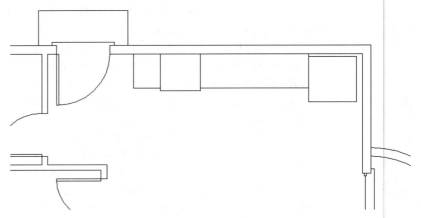

F I G U R E 5 . 1 7 : The stove and refrigerator made with rectangles

N O T E   Because the stove rectangle is drawn as a *polyline*—a special line where all segments compose one unique entity—you need to select only one segment of it for all sides of the rectangle to be selected and, in this case, become cutting edges.

Completing the Stove

The stove needs a little more detail. You will need to add circles to represent the burners and to add a line off the back to indicate the control panel (Figure 5.18). The burners are located by their centers.

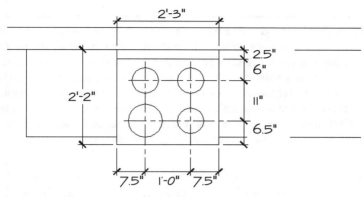

FIGURE 5.18: The details of the stove

1. Zoom into a closer view of the stove using the zoom window. You need to draw a line along the back of the stove that is 2.5" in from the wall line. Offsetting seems like the right command to use.

2. Offset the wall line down 2.5". When you pick the line, pick it somewhere to the right or left of the stove. Then, after it's offset, trim it back to the sides of the stove (Figure 5.19).

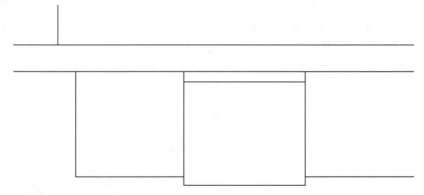

FIGURE 5.19: The stove with the control panel drawn

W A R N I N G   The back segment of the stove coincides with the wall. If you try to pick the wall line where the two lines coincide, you may pick the rectangle of the stove instead. You don't want to offset a line of the stove because it is a polyline. When any segment of a polyline is offset, all segments are offset and all corners are filleted automatically. This would be an inconvenience in this situation because only one line segment needs to be offset. When you draw the sink, you'll learn a technique for selecting the line you want when two or more lines overlap or coincide.

3. The next step is to lay out guidelines to locate the centers of the burners. Offset the line you created for the control panel in step 2 down 6". Then offset this new line down 11". Next you need vertical guidelines. Use tracking to draw the first guideline.

4. Start the Line command and select Temporary Tracking Point Osnap and then Endpoint Osnap. Then pick the upper-left corner of the stove.

5. Hold the cursor directly to the right of this point. When the dotted tracking path and the Track Point tooltip appear, type **7.5** ↵. The first guideline is started.

6. Hold the crosshair cursor below the first point of the guideline and pick a point just below the stove. Press ↵ to end the Line command.

7. Offset this line 12" to the right (Figure 5.20). The guidelines are set in place.

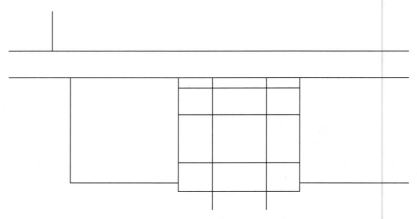

F I G U R E   5 . 2 0 : The guidelines for the centers of the burner circles

The next step is to draw a circle for one burner, copy it to the other three burner locations, and then change the radius of the left front burner.

1. Using the Intersection Osnap and the Circle command, draw a circle with its center at the lower-left intersection of the guidelines, and a radius of 3.5".

2. Start the Copy command. Select the circle and then press ↵.

3. Type **m** ↵. This starts the Multiple option. Choose Intersection Osnap. Select the intersection of the guidelines at the center of the circle as a base point. Press ↵.

4. Select the Intersection Osnap again and pick the intersection of guidelines above the first circle (Figure 5.21). Select the Intersection Osnap again and pick one of the intersections on the right side. Then select the Intersection Osnap one more time and pick the fourth intersection of guidelines. Press ↵ to end the Multiple Copy command. The burners are in place. Now you need to change the size of the lower-left burner.

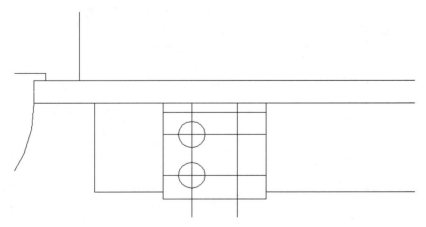

FIGURE 5.21: The first burner is copied.

5. Pick the lower-left burner. Five colored boxes will appear on the circle and at its center. These are called *grips*.

6. Click the Properties button near the right end of the Standard Toolbar. The Properties dialog box comes up on the left part of the screen (Figure 5.22). Notice the drop-down list at the top of the Properties dialog box. This tells you the currently selected object is a circle.

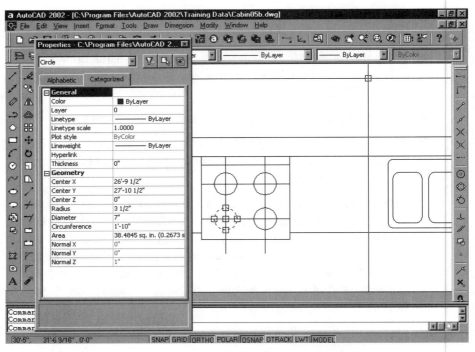

FIGURE 5.22: The Properties dialog box and the selected burner

7. Be sure that the Categorized tab below the drop-down list is selected (i.e., in front). If it isn't, click the tab to bring it forward. Now move down the categorized list of properties and click Radius.

8. Highlight the 3.5" radius setting. Change it to 4.5" and press ↵. The burner in the drawing is enlarged.

9. Click the X in the upper-right corner of the Properties dialog box to close it. Then press the Esc key to turn off the five Grips that were on the circle.

10. Erase the guidelines, and the stove is completed (Figure 5.23). Zoom Previous to see the whole kitchen with the completed stove.

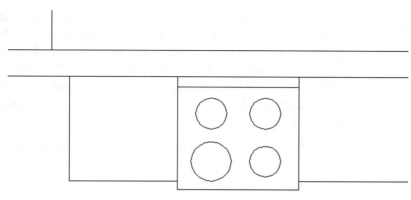

FIGURE 5.23: The completed stove

With the stove finished, the final task in the kitchen is to draw the sink.

 N O T E The Properties dialog box is an important tool for working with objects in the drawing. You will learn more about it in Chapter 6, *Using Layers to Organize Your Drawing*, and you will use it throughout the rest of the book.

The Kitchen Sink

The sink you will draw is a double sink, with one basin larger than the other (Figure 5.24). You will use Offset, Fillet, and Trim to create it from the counter and wall lines.

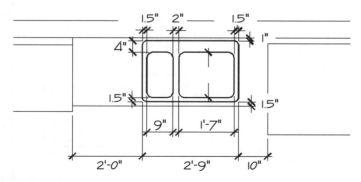

FIGURE 5.24: The sink with dimensions

1. Zoom into the sink area, keeping the edges of the refrigerator and stove in view. Offset the wall line 1" down and the front edge of the counter 1.5" up.

We could have used cycling when we drew the detail onto the stove, to select the wall line where it coincided with the stove outline. We didn't need to because we could select the wall line at a point where the stove wasn't interfering.

2. Offset the right side of the counter 10" to the left. Hold down the Ctrl key as you pick the line. Then release the Ctrl key. If the refrigerator ghosts, pick the line again. The selected line will switch to the one representing the edge of the counter. When the counter edge is selected, press ↵, then complete the offset. This selection technique is called *cycling*. It allows you to select a line that may coincide with another line.

3. Offset this new line 2'-9" to the left. This forms the outside edge of the sink (Figure 5.25a).

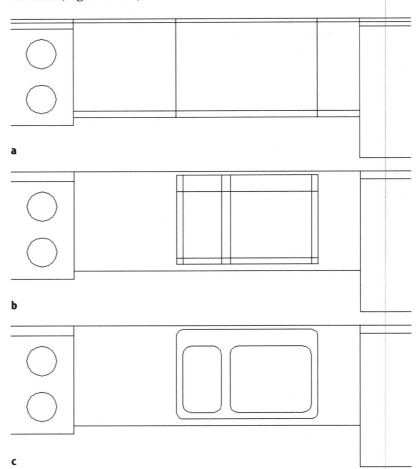

a

b

c

FIGURE 5.25: The offset lines to form the outside edge of the sink (a), the offset lines to form the inside edges of the sink (b), and the finished sink (c)

4. Fillet the corners of this rectangle to clean them up, using a radius of zero.

5. Offset the left side, bottom, and right side of the sink 1.5" to the inside. Offset the top side 4" to the inside. Then offset the new line on the left 9" to the right, and then again, 2" further to the right. This forms the basis of the inside sink lines (Figure 5.25b).

6. Trim away the horizontal top and bottom inside sink lines between the two middle vertical sink lines. Then fillet the four corners of each sink with a 2" radius to clean them up.

7. Fillet all outside sink corners with a 1.5" radius. This will finish the sink (Figure 5.25c). Zoom Previous to view the whole kitchen with the completed sink.

This completes the kitchen area. Very few new lines were drawn to accomplish this task because most of them were created by offsetting existing lines, then trimming or filleting them. Keep this in mind as you move on to the bathroom.

Constructing the Bathroom

The bathroom has three fixtures: sink, shower, and toilet (Figure 5.26). In drawing these fixtures, you will be using a few Object Snaps over and over again. You can set one or more of the Osnap choices to be continually running until you turn them off. That way, you won't have to select them each time.

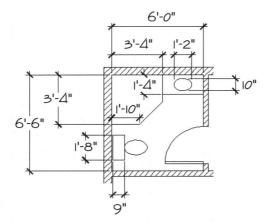

F I G U R E 5 . 2 6 : The bathroom fixtures with dimensions

Setting Running Object Snaps

You will set only two Osnaps to run continually for now, until you get used to how they work.

1. Right-click the Osnap button on the Status bar and choose Settings on the shortcut menu. The Drafting Settings dialog box comes up with the Object Snap tab on top.

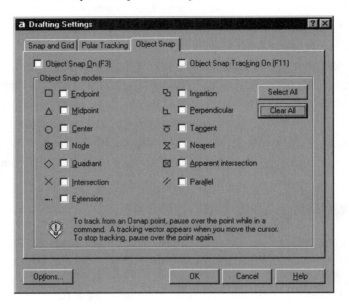

Each of the 13 Osnap options has a check box and a symbol next to it. The symbol appears in the drawing when a particular Osnap is selected and the cursor is near a point where that Osnap can be used. You can check any number of Osnaps to be running at a time.

 N O T E   The symbols or icons that appear on an object when an Osnap is active and when you move the cursor near the object are called *Autosnaps.* They're quite helpful, and you can choose a different color for them if you wish. If you're using a dark background in the drawing area, use a bright color, like yellow. For a white background, try blue.

2. In the lower-left corner of the Drafting Settings dialog box, click Options. In the Options dialog box, the Drafting tab should be on top.

Then, on the left side in the AutoSnap Settings area, open the AutoSnap Marker Color drop-down list and select a color. While you're in this area, make sure the Marker, Magnet, and Display AutoSnap Tooltip check boxes are selected. Also make sure that the Display AutoSnap Aperture Box is unchecked. Then click OK.

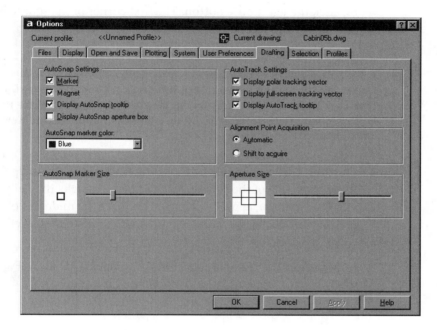

3. Back in the Object Snap tab of the Drafting Settings dialog box, click the check boxes next to Endpoint and Midpoint. Then, above the list and to the left, be sure there's a check mark in the box next to Object Snap On. Click OK to close the dialog box. These Osnaps will now be active any time you are prompted to select a point on the drawing.

Now you are ready to begin drawing the three fixtures for the bathroom. The shower determines the placement of the other two, so let's start there.

Drawing a Shower Unit

You will start the shower unit with a square, then trim away one corner. As you start this exercise, check the Status bar. The Polar, Osnap, and Model buttons should be in the On position. The rest of the buttons should be off.

1. Zoom to Extents. Then use the Zoom window to view the bathroom close-up. Start the Rectangle command. For the first point, move the cursor to the upper-left inside corner of the room. Notice the square that appears at the corner. This is the Autosnap symbol for the Endpoint Osnap. As soon as it appears on the endpoint you want to snap to, click the left mouse button. The first corner of the square is placed. For the second point, type @40,-40 ↵.

T I P   If you don't get the square you want after entering the relative coordinates for the second corner, check this setting. Choose Tools ➤ Options. Then click the User Preferences tab. In the upper-right corner of the Priority for Coordinate Data Entry area, be sure that the button next to Keyboard Entry Except Scripts is active. Then click OK. Try the square again.

2. Start the Line command and move the cursor near the midpoint of the bottom line of the square. Notice how a triangle, the Midpoint Autosnap symbol, appears when you get near the midpoint of the line. When you see the triangle on the midpoint you want, click.

3. Move the cursor near the midpoint of the right side of the rectangle until you see the triangle appear at the midpoint location (Figure 5.27). Click again. Press ↵ to end the Line command.

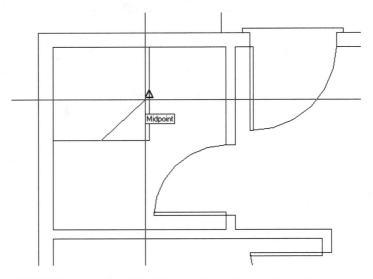

F I G U R E 5 . 2 7 : Using Midpoint Osnap to complete a line across the corner of the shower

4. Use this line as a cutting edge and trim away the lower-right corner of the shower rectangle. The trimming will require only one pick because you are trimming a polyline. Press ↵ to stop the Trim command. This completes the shower.

Next, draw the sink to the right of the shower.

The Bathroom Sink

You will offset a line and draw an ellipse for this fixture, while practicing the Temporary Tracking Point Osnap option in the process. The Endpoint and Midpoint Osnaps are still running.

1. Zoom into the sink area with a zoom window. Offset the top inside wall line down 16". Then use the shower wall as a cutting edge and trim back the line.

2. Click the Ellipse button on the Draw toolbar. Type c ↵ to select the Center option.

3. Click the Temporary Tracking Point Osnap button and then move the cursor near the midpoint of the newly offset line. When the Autosnap symbol appears at the midpoint of this line, click. This establishes a tracking point (small cross).

4. Move the crosshair cursor directly above the tracking point. When the dotted tracking path and the Track Point tooltip appear, type 8 ↵ to locate the center of the counter. The Command window will prompt you for the location of the ends of two perpendicular axes. You will start with the left/right axis and enter the distance using Direct Entry and Polar Tracking, as you did for the steps earlier in the chapter.

5. Hold the crosshair cursor directly to the right of the center point. Type 7 ↵. Hold the crosshair cursor directly above the center and type 5 ↵. The ellipse is constructed, and the sink fixture is complete (Figure 5.28). Leave the view on your screen as it is for a moment.

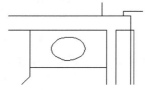

FIGURE 5.28: The completed sink fixture

Drawing the toilet will be the final task in this chapter. You will use the Ellipse command again, along with the Rectangle command. You will also be introduced to a couple of new display options.

Positioning a Toilet

The toilet consists of a rectangle and an ellipse centered between the shower and the wall. The tank is offset 1" from the back wall, and is 9" × 20". The ellipse representing the seat measures 18" in one direction and 12" in the other.

1. On the Standard toolbar, click the Pan Realtime button. The cursor changes to a small hand when you return it to the drawing area. Position it in the lower-left corner of the drawing area with the view still zoomed in on the sink.

2. Hold down the left mouse button and drag the hand up and to the right. When the toilet area comes into view, release the mouse button. The drawing slides along with the movement of the cursor. If necessary, do this again until you have the toilet area centered in the drawing area.

3. Right-click the mouse. On the shortcut menu, select Zoom. Back on the drawing, the cursor changes to a magnifying glass with a plus and minus sign.

> With Zoom Realtime, moving the cursor to the left or right has no effect on the view. The magnification is controlled solely by the up-and-down motion.

4. Position the Zoom Realtime cursor near the top of the drawing and hold down the left mouse button. Drag the cursor down and watch the view being zoomed out in real time. Move the cursor up, still holding the mouse button down. Position the cursor in such a way that you have a good view of the toilet area, then release the mouse button. Right-click again and select Exit from the shortcut menu. This will end the Zoom Realtime command.

These zooming options are convenient tools for adjusting the view of your drawing. Let's move on to the toilet. You need to find a way to position the toilet accurately, centering it between the wall and shower. The midpoint of the left wall line won't be useful because the wall line runs behind the shower. You will have to construct a guideline.

1. With the Rectangle command, draw the toilet tank a few inches to the right of the wall, not touching any lines. (See Figure 5.26 for the dimensions.) Then offset the left wall line 1" to the right to make a guideline. Use the shower as a cutting edge and trim this guideline down to the shower (Figure 5.29a).

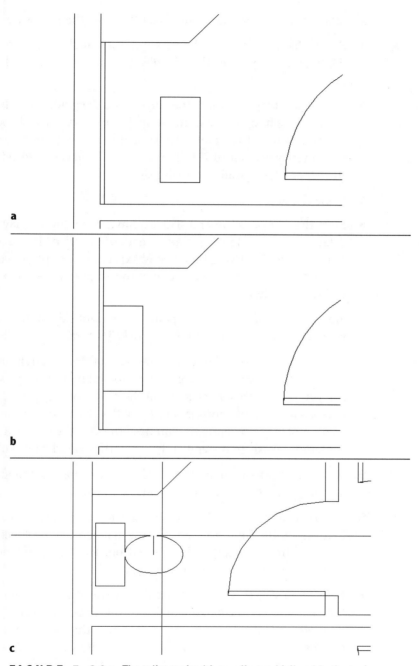

FIGURE 5.29: The toilet tank with an offset guideline (a), the tank correctly positioned (b), and the cursor controlling the size of the second axis for the toilet seat (c)

2. Start the Move command and select the tank, then press ↵.

3. For the base point, move the cursor to the middle of the left side of the tank. When you see the triangle at the midpoint, click the left mouse button.

4. For the second point, move the cursor onto the guideline. When it gets closer to the midpoint than the endpoint, the triangle will appear at the midpoint. At this point, click the left mouse button. The rectangle is accurately positioned 1" from the left wall and centered between the shower and lower wall (Figure 5.29b).

5. Erase the guideline.

6. Start the Ellipse command. The Command window displays a default prompt of `Specify axis endpoint of ellipse or [Arc/Center]:`. Using the Specify Axis endpoint option, you can define the first axis from one end of the ellipse to the other. This will help you here.

7. Move the cursor near the midpoint of the right side of the tank and, when the triangle shows up there, click. This starts the ellipse.

8. Hold the crosshair cursor out to the right of the rectangle and type 1'6 ↵. The first axis is positioned. Now as you move the crosshair cursor, you will see that a line starts at the center of the ellipse, and the cursor's movement controls the size of the other axis (Figure 5.29c). To designate the second axis, you need to enter the distance from the center of the axis to the end of it, or half the overall length of the axis.

9. Hold the crosshair cursor directly above the center point and type 6 ↵. The ellipse is complete, and the toilet is finished.

10. Go to the Status bar and right-click on the Osnap button, then choose Settings on the shortcut menu. In the dialog box, the Object Snap tab will be in front. Click the Clear All button. This turns off all running Osnaps. Click OK to close the dialog box.

11. Before you save this drawing, use the Pan Realtime and Zoom Realtime commands to zoom out and pan your drawing until the whole floor plan fills the drawing area, except for a thin border around the outside of the plan (Figure 5.30). Save this drawing as Cabin05b.

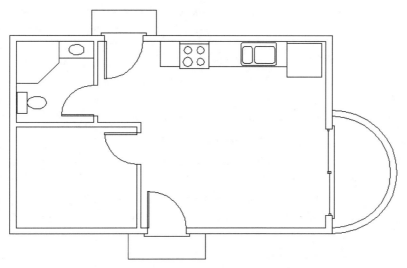

FIGURE 5.30: The completed floor plan zoomed and panned to fill the screen

USING REALTIME PAN AND REALTIME ZOOM

The Realtime Pan and Zoom buttons are next to each other on the Standard toolbar. Realtime Pan can be started by typing **p** ↵. Realtime Zoom can be started by typing **z** ↵ ↵. You can also start Realtime Pan or Zoom by right-clicking at the Command: prompt, then choosing Pan or Zoom on the shortcut menu that appears. If you try this, you will find that it is easier than clicking the Realtime Pan or Zoom buttons.

Once one of these Realtime commands is running, you can switch to the other one by clicking on the other Realtime button, or by right-clicking and choosing the other one on the shortcut menu that appears. The shortcut menu also has other options that help make Realtime Pan and Zoom quite useful commands.

▶ Exit: Ends the Realtime Zoom or Pan commands.

▶ Pan: Switches to Realtime Pan from Realtime Zoom.

▶ Zoom: Switches to Realtime Pan from Realtime Zoom.

▶ 3D Orbit: This is a special viewing tool for 3D and will be covered in Appendix A, *A Look at Drawing in 3D*.

Continued on next page

▶ Zoom Window: Allows you to make a Zoom window without first ending Realtime Pan or Zoom. You pick a point and hold down the left mouse button, then drag open a window in your drawing. When you release the button, you are zoomed into the window you made, and Realtime Pan or Zoom resumes.

▶ Zoom Original: Restores the view of your drawing that you had when you began Realtime Pan or Zoom.

▶ Zoom Extents: Zooms to the drawing Extents.

To end Realtime Pan or Zoom, press the Esc key, then ↵, or right-click and choose Exit on the shortcut menu.

When Realtime Pan or Zoom is running, AutoCAD is in a special mode that makes the Status Bar and the Grid (if it is on) invisible and, therefore, unusable.

The bathroom is complete, and you now have a fairly complete floor plan for the cabin. In accomplishing the drawing tasks for this chapter, you have been exposed to several new commands and techniques to add to those introduced in Chapter 4, *Gaining Drawing Strategies: Part 1*. Combined, you now have a set of tools for drawing that will take you a long way toward being able to lay out a floor plan of any size.

Chapters 1 through 5 fill out the basic level of skills in AutoCAD that allow you to draw on the computer approximately as you would with pencil and vellum, though you may already see some of the advantages CAD offers over traditional board drafting. Beginning with the next chapter, you will be introduced to concepts of AutoCAD that do not have a counterpart in board drafting. These features will take you to a new level of knowledge and skill, and you will start to get an idea of what sets computer drafting apart.

If You Would Like More Practice...

Draw the Cabin Again

As is true for almost any skill, the key to mastery is practice. Redrawing the entire cabin may seem daunting at this point when you think of how long it took you to get here. But if you try it all again, starting with Chapter 3, *Setting Up a Drawing*, you will find that it will take about half the time that it did the first time, and if you do it a third time, half that time again. Once you understand the techniques used and how the commands work, feel free to experiment with alternative techniques to accomplish tasks and with other options on the commands.

Draw Something Else

If you have a specific project in mind you would like to draw in AutoCAD, so much the better—try it out.

Draw Some Furniture for the Cabin

Once you put some furniture in the cabin, you will quickly see how small it is! But it can still accept some basic furniture without seeming too cramped. You should be able to add the following:

- ► Kitchen—a table and chairs

- ► Living room—a short couch, coffee table, and easy chair

- ► Bedroom—a double bed, dresser, and side table

Use a tape measure and go around your office or home to determine the approximate dimensions of each piece. The goal here is not so much accuracy of scale but to practice drawing in AutoCAD. Figure 5.31 shows the floor plan with these items of furniture.

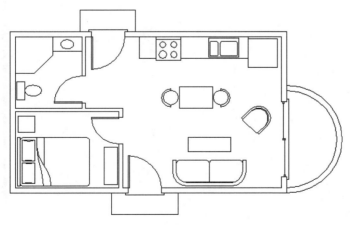

FIGURE 5.31: The floor plan with furniture

Are You Experienced?

Now you can...

- ☑ use the Temporary Tracking Point tool to create and use tracking points

- ☑ use the Quadrant and Intersection Osnaps

- ☑ set up and use running Osnaps

- ☑ move around the drawing area with Realtime Zoom and Pan

- ☑ use the Circle and Ellipse commands

- ☑ move and duplicate objects with the Move and Copy Multiple commands

- ☑ use a circle and the Trim command to make a semicircle arc

- ☑ use guidelines to locate the center of circles for a stove top

CHAPTER 6

Using Layers to Organize Your Drawing

- ▶ Creating new layers
- ▶ Assigning a color and linetype to layers
- ▶ Moving existing objects onto a new layer
- ▶ Controlling the visibility of layers
- ▶ Working with linetypes

I n pre-computer days, drafters used sets of transparent overlays on their drafting tables. These were sheets that stacked on top of one another, and the drafters could see through several at a time. Specific kinds of information were drawn on each overlay, all related spatially so that several overlays might all be drawn to the same floor plan. Each overlay had small holes punched near the corners so the drafter could position it onto buttons, called registration points, which were taped to the drawing board. Because all overlays had holes punched at the same locations with respect to the drawing, information on the set of overlays was kept in alignment.

To help you organize your drawing, AutoCAD provides you with an amazing tool, called *layers,* which is a computerized metaphor for the transparent overlays, only much more powerful and flexible. In manual drafting, you could use only four or five overlays at a time before the information on the bottom overlay became unreadable. In AutoCAD, you are not limited in the number of layers that you can use. You can have hundreds of layers, and complex CAD drawings often do.

Layers as an Organization Tool

To understand what layers are and why they are so useful, think again about the transparent overlay sheets used in hand drafting. Each overlay is designed to be printed. The bottom sheet may be a basic floor plan. To create an overlay sheet for a structural drawing, the drafter traces over the lines of the floor plan that they need in the overlay, then adds new information pertinent to that sheet. For the next overlay, the same thing is done again. Each sheet, then, contains some information in common, in addition to data unique to that sheet.

In AutoCAD, using layers will allow you to generate all the sheets for a set of overlays from a single file (Figure 6.1). Nothing needs to be drawn twice or traced. The wall layout will be on one layer and the roof lines on another. Doors will be on a third. The visibility of layers can be controlled so that all objects residing on a layer can be made temporarily invisible. This feature lets you put all information keyed to a particular floor plan in one .dwg file and, from that drawing, to produce a series of derived drawings, such as the foundation plan, the second floor plan, the reflected ceiling plan, and the roof plan, by making different combinations of layers visible for each drawing. When you make a print, you decide which of the layers will be visible in the print. Consequently, in a set of drawings, each sheet based on the floor plan will display a unique combination of layers, all of which are in one file.

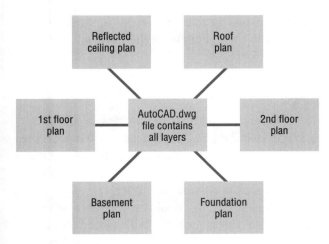

FIGURE 6.1: Diagram of several drawings coming from one file

Layers, as an organization tool, allow you to classify the various objects in a computerized drawing—lines, arcs, circles, etc.—according to the component of the building they represent, such as doors, walls, and windows. Each layer is assigned a color, and all objects placed on the layer take on that assigned color. This lets you easily distinguish between objects that represent separate components of the building (Figure 6.2). And you can quickly tell what layer a given object or group of objects is on.

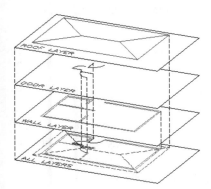

FIGURE 6.2: Separate layers combined to make a drawing

The procedure for achieving this level of organization is to set up the new layers, and then move existing objects onto them. Following that, you will learn how to create new objects on a specific layer.

Setting Up Layers

All AutoCAD drawings have one layer in common—the 0 layer. The 0 layer is the default layer in all new drawings. If you don't add any new layers on a drawing, everything you create in that drawing will be on the 0 layer. Everything you have drawn so far in the cabin drawing has been drawn on the 0 layer.

All objects in AutoCAD are assigned a layer. In this book, I will refer to objects assigned to a particular layer as "being on" that layer. Objects get placed on a layer in two ways: Either they are moved to the layer, or they are created on the layer in the first place. You will learn to do both in this chapter. But first you need to learn how to set up layers. To see how this is done, you will create seven new layers for your cabin drawing—Walls, Doors, Steps, Balcony, Fixtures, Headers, and Roof— then move the existing objects in your drawing onto the first five of these layers. After that, you will create new objects on the Header and Roof layers. Let's begin by creating a few new layers.

> A good way to think about objects and layers is the analogy of people and countries: Just as all people must reside in some country, so must all objects be on some layer.

1. Bring up AutoCAD and open Cabin05b.dwg. The Object Properties toolbar, just above the drawing area on your screen, contains three buttons and five drop-down lists for controlling layers, linetypes, colors, and other layer properties. The layer controls are on the left end of the toolbar.

> A *linetype* is the style of appearance of a line, such as continuous, dashed, dash-dot, etc.

Layer controls

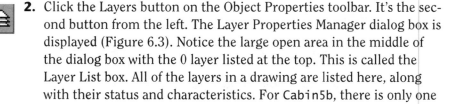

2. Click the Layers button on the Object Properties toolbar. It's the second button from the left. The Layer Properties Manager dialog box is displayed (Figure 6.3). Notice the large open area in the middle of the dialog box with the 0 layer listed at the top. This is called the Layer List box. All of the layers in a drawing are listed here, along with their status and characteristics. For Cabin5b, there is only one layer so far.

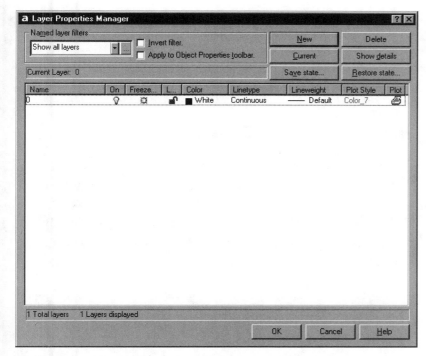

FIGURE 6.3: The Layer Properties Manager dialog box

The Layer Properties Manager Dialog Box

Besides the Layer List box, there is also a drop-down list, titled Named Layer Filters, a couple of check boxes, and several command buttons in the dialog box. Before setting up new layers, look for a moment at the Layer List box.

The Layer List Box

The Layer List box lists all the layers in the drawing along with each layer's properties and modes.

Each layer has four properties: Color, Linetype, Lineweight, and Plot Style. Look at the 0 layer row in the list and notice the square and the word "White" in the color column. The square is black (or white if you have a black background for your drawing area), but the name of the color is called White whether the square is black or white. Continuous is in the Linetype column. This tells us that the 0 layer has been assigned the color White (black or white) and the Continuous linetype by default.

The three columns to the left of the Color column are titled On, Freeze, and Lock. They have picture icons in the 0 layer row. These columns represent some of the status modes of the layer and control whether objects on a layer are visible or can be changed. The visibility status of a layer will be discussed later in this chapter. The columns to the right of the Linetype column—Lineweight, Plot Style, and Plot—will be discussed in Chapter 14, *Printing an AutoCAD Drawing*.

Creating New Layers and Assigning Colors

Let's create a few new layers, name them, and assign them colors.

1. In the upper-right corner of the dialog box, click New. A new layer called Layer1 appears in the list. The layer's name is highlighted, which means that it can be renamed by entering another name now.

2. Type Walls ↵. Layer1 changes to Walls. Walls should still be highlighted (Figure 6.4).

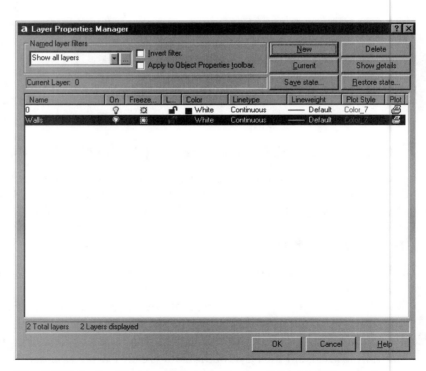

FIGURE 6.4: The Layer Properties Manager dialog box with a new layer named Walls

3. Click the word White in the Color column for the Walls row. The Select Color dialog box comes up (Figure 6.5). There are four areas of color choices. In the Standard Colors area, click the cyan (turquoise) square. In the Color text box, under the Full Color Palette, white has changed to cyan, and the square just to the right has taken on the color cyan.

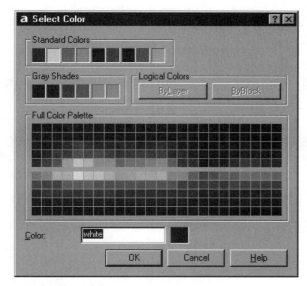

FIGURE 6.5: The Select Color dialog box

4. Click OK. The Select Color dialog box disappears. In the Layer List box of the Layer Properties Manager dialog box, you can see that the color square for the Walls layer has changed to cyan.

As you create your new list of layers and assign them colors, notice how each color looks in your drawing. Some are easier to see on a screen with a light background, and others do better against a dark background. In this book, I will be assigning colors that work well with a black background. If your system has a white background, you may want to use darker colors, which can be found on the Full Color Palette in the middle of the Select Color dialog box.

Let's continue creating new layers and assigning them colors. You'll master this procedure as you add a new layer or two in each chapter throughout the rest of the book.

1. In the Layer Properties Manager dialog box, click New.

2. Type **Doors** ↵ to change the name of the layer.

3. Pick the color square in the Doors row. When the Select Color dialog box comes up, click the red square in the Standard Colors area. Then click OK.

4. Repeat these steps, creating each of the following layers with their assigned colors. Pick the colors from the Standard Colors area of the Select Color dialog box.

Layer Name	Color
Steps	9 (Light Gray)
Balcony	Green
Fixtures	Magenta
Headers	Yellow
Roof	Blue

T I P   The color blue may or may not read well on a black background. If you don't like the way it looks, try picking a lighter shade of blue from the Full Color Palette in the Select Color dialog box.

When finished, the layer list should have eight layers listed with their assigned colors in the color squares of each row (Figure 6.6). All layers are assigned the Continuous linetype by default. This is convenient since most building components are represented in the floor plan by continuous lines, but the roof— because of its position above the walls—needs to be represented by a dashed line. Later, you will assign a Dashed linetype to the Roof layer.

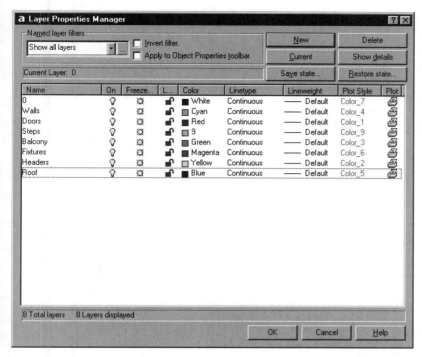

FIGURE 6.6: The Layer List box, in the Layer Properties Manager dialog box, with the seven new layers and the 0 layer

NAMING LAYERS

There are a variety of methods for naming layers. With their different color assignments, layers make it possible for you to easily distinguish which objects in your drawing represent walls or other parts of your building. Most offices have a standard they follow for organizing layers by name, color, and linetype. The American Institute of Architects publishes its Layering Standards, which are often adapted by architecture firms and customized to fit their specific needs. Before version 2000, lineweights in AutoCAD drawings were controlled by color, so the layer standards were developed around this determining factor. Since version 2000, this is no longer the case. As a result, you can expect that layering standards used for years will be changing. With the cabin drawing, you will start out developing a basic set of layers. Once you learn how to manage this set, tackling more complex layering systems will come naturally.

In more complex drawings, you may need to have several layers for variations of the same building components, such as Existing Walls to Remain, Walls to Be Demolished, and New Walls. Once you acquire the skills presented here, you will have no difficulty progressing to a more complex layering system.

N O T E   When you name layers, you can use upper- and lowercase letters, and AutoCAD will preserve them. But it does not distinguish between them, and treats "Walls", "WALLS", and "walls" as the same layer.

USING AUTOCAD'S COLORS

As you saw in the Select Color dialog box, there are four groupings of colors:

Standard Colors: This group includes colors 1–9. The first 7 colors in this group also have names: Red (1), Yellow (2), Green (3), Blue (4), Cyan (5), Magenta (6), and White/Black (7). Colors 8 and 9 have numbers only. Color 7 is named White, but will actually be black if you are using a white background color.

Full Color Palette: In the middle of the dialog box are colors 10–249, and they represent the full color palette that AutoCAD uses. They are variations of the first 6 colors in the Standard group, with 40 shades between Red and Yellow, 40 shades between Yellow and Green, etc.

Gray Shades: Between the Standard colors and the Full Color Palette are 6 gray shades, numbering 250–255, and ranging from almost black to almost white.

These 255 colors, plus the background color, make up AutoCAD's 256-color palette. There are two additional colors that are in a group by themselves:

Logical Colors: The two buttons in this grouping—ByLayer and ByBlock—represent two ways that a color can be assigned to a layer or a *block*, rather than to objects in the drawing such as lines, circles, text, etc. (Blocks will be covered in the next chapter, *Grouping Objects into Blocks*.) When you assign the color cyan to the Walls layer and place all objects representing walls on that layer, all wall objects will be assigned the color ByLayer, and take on the color of the assigned layer, in this case, cyan.

Assigning Linetypes to Layers

When you assigned a color to a layer, you could choose any color supported by your system. Not so with linetypes. Each new drawing has only one linetype loaded into it by default (the Continuous linetype). You must load in any other linetypes you need from an outside file.

1. In the Layer Properties Manager dialog box, click Continuous in the row for the Roof layer. The Select Linetype dialog box comes up

(Figure 6.7). In the Loaded Linetypes list, only Continuous is displayed. No other linetypes have been loaded into this drawing.

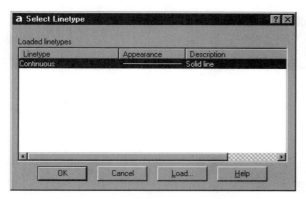

F I G U R E   6 . 7 : The Select Linetype dialog box

2. Click Load. The Load or Reload Linetypes dialog box comes up. Scroll
down the list to where the Dashed, Dashed2, and DashedX2 linetypes
are located (Figure 6.8). Notice how, in this family, the dashed lines are
different sizes.

F I G U R E   6 . 8 : The list scrolled to the three Dashed linetypes

3. Click the word Dashed in the left-hand column, then click OK. You
are returned to the Select Linetype dialog box. In the Select Linetype
dialog box, the Dashed linetype has been added to the Linetypes list
under Continuous (Figure 6.9). Click Dashed to highlight it and click

OK. In the Layer Properties Manager dialog box, the Roof layer has been assigned the Dashed linetype (Figure 6.10).

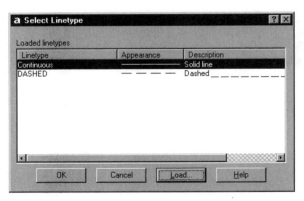

FIGURE 6.9: The Select Linetype dialog box with the Dashed linetype loaded

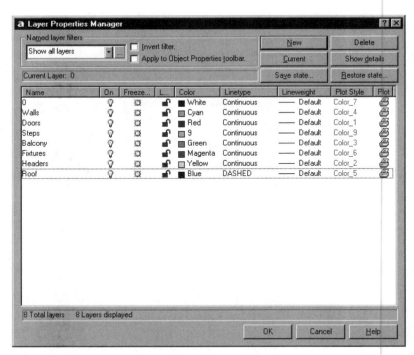

FIGURE 6.10: The Layer Properties Manager dialog box with the Roof layer assigned the Dashed linetype

AUTOCAD'S LINETYPES

In the Available Linetypes list in the Load or Reload Linetypes dialog box, there are 45 linetypes listed. They fall into three groups:

ACAD_ISO family: The first 14 linetypes are in the Acad_ISO family (International Standards Organization). They have been set up to be used in metric drawings, and have *lineweight,* or pen-width, settings.

Standard AutoCAD Linetypes: Below the ISO linetypes are eight families of 3 linetypes each, mixed with 7 special linetypes that contain graphic symbols. Each family has one basic linetype and two that are multiples of it: one has dashes twice the size (called, for example, Dashed×2), and one has dashes half the size (called Dashed2). (See Figure 6.8.) Having an assortment of different sizes of one style of linetype will be helpful for distinguishing between building components, such as foundation walls and beams, which, in addition to roof lines, may also need dashed lines.

Complex Linetypes: Mixed in with the Standard linetypes are 7 linetypes that contain symbols, letters, or words. These are used to indicate specific elements in the drawing, like fences, hot-water lines, railroad tracks, and others.

It is not difficult to create your own Custom linetypes. AutoCAD provides two methods:

▶ Using Notepad: Start the Notepad program and navigate to the Support folder for AutoCAD 2002. Open the acad.lin file. It has the definition codes for all the linetypes and is pretty easy to figure out. Use the existing pattern and create your own.

▶ Using the Linetype command: Type **linetype** ↵, then type **c** ↵ for the Create option. You will be guided through the steps to create your own .lin file or add to one of the existing ones. To use this method, you will need to know the definition codes. Use the first method until you get the feel for the codes.

A Word About Lineweight

In the Layer Properties Manager dialog box, there is a column for the Lineweight property. When a layer is first created, it is assigned the Default lineweight. Just as you assigned a color and a linetype for each of the new layers in the cabin drawing, you can also assign a lineweight. Once assigned, lineweights can be displayed so you can see how your drawing will look when printed. In Chapter 14 you will learn more about lineweights, how to assign them to layers, and how to view your drawing as it will look when printed, or in *wysiwyg* mode.

The Current Layer as a Drawing Tool

Now is a good time to look at what it means for a layer to be current.

Notice the Current button in the top-right corner of the Layer Properties Manager dialog box. On the left side, just above the Layer List box, is the name of the current layer, in this case, 0.

At any one time, there is always one, and only one, layer that is set as the current layer. When a layer is current, all objects you draw will be on that layer and take on the properties assigned to it. Because the 0 layer is current—and has been current so far in this book—all objects that you have drawn so far are on the 0 layer and have the linetype and color that are specified by default for the 0 layer: Continuous and White (or Black), respectively. If you make the Walls layer current, any new lines you draw will be Cyan and Continuous. If the Roof layer is current, any new lines will be Blue and Dashed.

1. Click the Walls layer in the Layer List box to highlight it. Then click Current. The Walls layer replaces 0 layer as the current layer.

2. Click OK at the bottom of the Layer Properties Manager dialog box. The dialog box closes, and you are returned to your drawing.

3. Look at the Layer Control drop-down list on the Object Properties toolbar. Most of the symbols you saw in the Layer List box, in the Layer Properties Manager dialog box, are on this drop-down list. The Walls layer is the visible entry on the list and has a cyan square (the color you assigned to the Walls layer earlier). The layer visible in this list when it is closed is the current layer.

4. Now look at your drawing. Nothing has changed because the objects in the drawing are still on the 0 layer.

You need to move the objects in the drawing onto their proper layers. To do this, you'll use the Layer Control drop-down list on the Object Properties toolbar to assign each object to one of the new layers.

Assigning Objects to Layers

When assigning existing objects in the drawing to new layers, our strategy will be to begin by selecting all the objects that belong on the same layer and that are easiest to select. We'll reassign them to their new layer, using the Layer Control drop-down list. Then we'll move to a set of objects that belong on a different layer and are slightly more difficult to select, and so on.

1. In the drawing, pick the two arcs of the balcony. Small squares, called *grips*, appear on the arcs to signal that they have been selected (Figure 6.11). Notice also that in the Layer Control drop-down list, the layer being displayed now is the 0 layer rather than Walls, the current layer. When objects are selected with no command running, the Layer Control drop-down list displays the layer that the selected objects are currently assigned to. If selected objects are on more than one layer, the Layer Control drop-down list goes blank.

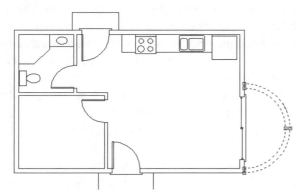

FIGURE 6.11: The balcony arcs, selected and displaying their grips

2. Click the Layer Control drop-down list to open it (Figure 6.12).

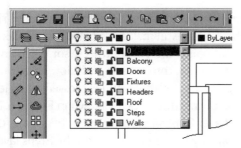

FIGURE 6.12: The opened Layer Control drop-down list

3. Click the Balcony layer. The list closes. The Balcony layer is displayed in the Layer Control drop-down list. The balcony arcs have been moved to the Balcony layer and are now green.

4. Press Esc to remove the grips. The current layer, Walls, returns to the Layer Control drop-down list.

This is the process you need to go through for each layer, so that the new layers can receive objects that are currently on the 0 layer. This time, move the threshold and steps to the Steps layer. You will select the threshold and steps by using a selection window.

Selecting Objects with Windows

AutoCAD provides many tools for selecting objects in your drawing. Two of the most powerful are the crossing and regular selection windows. The size and location of these selection windows are determined by picking points on your drawing to be opposite corners of a rectangle that will serve as the window. The *regular window* selects any objects completely enclosed by the window. The *crossing window* selects objects that are completely enclosed by, or cross through an edge of, the window. The crossing window is represented by dashed lines, and the regular window is represented by solid ones.

By default, AutoCAD is set up so that whenever there is no command running and the prompt in the Command window is Command:, you can pick objects one at a time or start a regular or crossing window. If you pick an object, it is selected and its grips are displayed. If you select a blank area of the drawing, a selection window is started. If you then move the cursor to the right of the point just picked, a regular window is started. If you move the cursor to the left, a crossing window is started. You'll use three crossing windows to select the thresholds and the front and back steps.

1. Zoom into the sliding glass door area. Click the Osnap button on the Status bar to put it in the off position, if it isn't already off.

2. Hold the crosshair cursor above and to the right of the upper-right corner of the balcony threshold—still inside the balcony wall—as shown in Figure 6.13a. Click that point, then move the cursor down and to the left until you have made a tall, thin crossing window that completely encloses the right edge of the threshold, and is crossed on its left edge by the short horizontal connecting lines, as shown in Figure 6.13b. Then click again. Click the Layer Control drop-down list to open it, then click the Steps layer. The balcony threshold is now on the Steps layer.

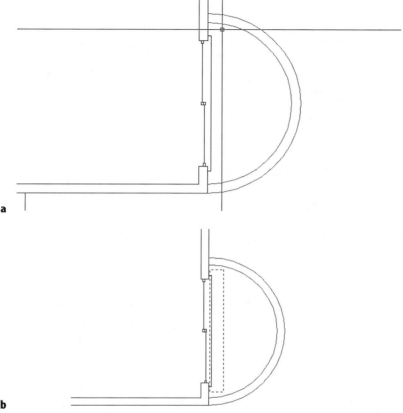

FIGURE 6.13: Starting the crossing selection window (a), and completing it (b)

3. Zoom previous to return to a view of the entire drawing. Make two regular windows to select the front and back steps and their thresholds. Be sure your first pick starts a window at the left and finishes to the right of each step, so the window completely encloses the horizontal and vertical lines that make up each step and threshold. Figure 6.14 illustrates the two regular selection windows and the points to pick to create them. Once selected, the objects display their grips. For lines, grips appear at each endpoint and at the midpoint of each segment. When endpoints of lines coincide, some of the grips overlap.

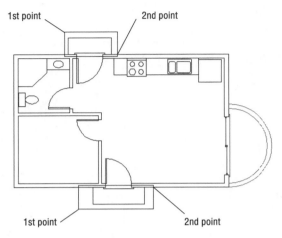

FIGURE 6.14: The two regular selection windows used to select the front and back steps and thresholds

4. Click the Layer Control drop-down list, then click the Steps layer. The front and back steps and their thresholds are now on the Steps layer.

5. Press the Esc key to remove the grips.

Selecting the Doors and Swings

To select the door and swings, you can use crossing windows. Let's examine this task closely to learn more valuable skills about how to select objects.

1. Place the crosshair cursor in a clear space below and to the right of the back door, then pick that point. This starts the selection window. Move the cursor up and to the left until the crossing window crosses the back door and swing, but does not cross the wall line, as in Figure 6.15a.

2. When you have the crossing window positioned correctly, click again. This selects the back door and its swing.

3. Move to the bathroom and position the crosshair cursor in the clear space directly above the swing. When the crosshair is positioned, click. Then move the cursor down and to the left until the window you are creating crosses the bathroom door and swing, without crossing any wall lines (Figure 6.15b). Then click in a clear space again. The bathroom door and swing are selected.

4. Continue this procedure to select the other two doors and their swings. For the bedroom door, start the crossing window directly below the door swing. For the front door, start a crossing window

Grips have other uses besides signaling that an object has been selected. You'll learn about some of these other uses as we progress through the chapters.

above and to the right of the door. Figure 6.15c shows the two cross-ing windows that will select the bedroom and front doors.

5. Open the Layer Control drop-down list and select the Doors layer. Then press Esc to remove the grips. The swinging doors are now red and on the Doors layer.

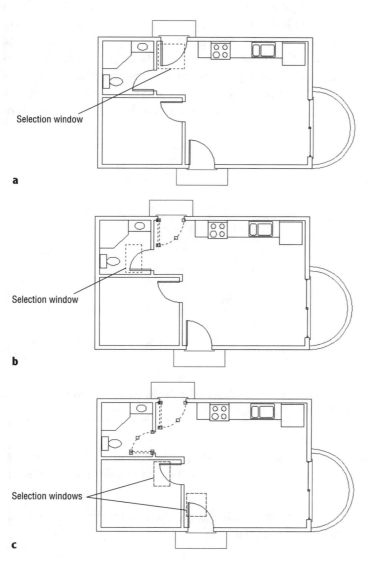

FIGURE 6.15: Using a crossing window to select the doors and swings: the back door (a), the bathroom door (b), and the bedroom and front doors (c)

For the sliding glass door, it is awkward to create a crossing window from left to right because it may be difficult to position the pickbox between the threshold lines and the sliding door. In this situation, use a regular window to select the objects.

1. Zoom into the sliding glass door area. Pick a point to the left of the balcony opening, just above the upper jamb line. Move the crosshair down and to the right until the right edge of the window sits inside the wall but to the right of the sliding glass window frames. When your window is positioned as in Figure 6.16, click. The entire sliding glass door assembly will be selected, but not the jambs, walls, threshold, or balcony. Many grips appear: There are 13 lines making up the sliding glass door and each one has three grips. Many of the grips overlap.

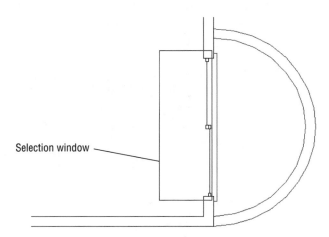

Selection window

FIGURE 6.16: Using a Regular Selection Window to select the sliding glass door

2. Open the Layer Control drop-down list and select the Doors layer. Back in your drawing, all doors are the color red and are on the Doors layer.

3. Press Esc to remove the grips, then Zoom Previous. You will have a full view of the floor plan.

The next task is to move the kitchen and bathroom counters and fixtures onto the Fixtures layer. In doing this, you'll learn how to de-select some objects from a group of selected objects.

Selecting the Kitchen and Bathroom Fixtures

Sometimes it is more efficient to select more objects than you want, and then de-select those you don't want. You'll see how this is done when you select the kitchen and bathroom fixtures.

1. Pick a point in the kitchen area just below the refrigerator to start a crossing window.

2. Move the cursor to the left and up until the upper-left corner of the crossing window is to the left of the left edge of the counter, and inside the back wall, as in Figure 6.17a. When you have it right, click that point. The entire kitchen counter area and the back wall line are selected.

3. Now move over to the bathroom and pick a point in the middle of the bathroom sink, being careful to not touch any lines with the cross-hair cursor.

4. Move the crosshair cursor down and to the left until the lower-left corner of the crossing window is in the middle of the toilet tank (Figure 6.17b). When you have it positioned this way, click that point. All the bathroom fixtures and the door swing are selected.

5. Hold down the Shift key, then pick the selected door swing in the bathroom and the back wall line in the kitchen. As you pick them, their lines become solid again, letting you know that they have been de-selected or removed from the selection set, but their grips remain (Figure 6.17c). Be sure to pick the back wall line in the kitchen where it doesn't coincide with the stove.

6. Release the Shift key. Open the Layer Control drop-down list and select the Fixtures layer. The fixtures are now on the Fixtures layer and are magenta in color.

7. Press the Esc key to remove the grips.

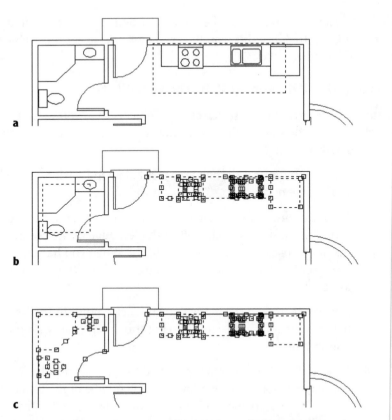

FIGURE 6.17: A crossing window to select the kitchen objects (a), another crossing window to select the bathroom objects (b), and the completed selection set after removing the door swing and back wall line (c)

The last objects to move onto a new layer are the wall lines. As the drawing is now, it will not be easy to select the wall lines because there are so many other objects in the drawing that are in the way. However, these other objects are now on their own layers, while the wall lines are still on the 0 layer. If you make all of your layers temporarily invisible except for the 0 and Walls layers, selecting the wall lines will be easy.

SELECTING OBJECTS IN YOUR DRAWING

As you have been selecting objects in the cabin drawing to move them onto their prescribed layers, you are using various selection tools. These tools are important, and mastering them will greatly enhance your performance as an AutoCAD user. As objects are selected by picking them and windowing them, you are building a *selection set*. You may later want to remove objects from that selection set. Here is a summary of the basic selection tools that you have used so far, with a couple of additions.

Picking: This is the basic, bottom-line selection tool. Click on the line, circle, or other object, and it is selected. If no command is running, grips appear on the selected object and the object ghosts. If a command is running and you are being prompted to Select objects:, grips do not appear but the object is selected and ghosts.

Automatic Window Selection: Click a location that is in an empty portion of the screen, where there are no objects. A window will be started. As you move your cursor to the right, a regular window will be formed. If you move your cursor to the left, a crossing window will be formed. This feature is called *implied windowing* and it works this way if no command is running or if one is running and the prompt line says Select objects:. If the geometry of your drawing makes forming a crossing or regular selection window difficult because of the need to move from right to left (crossing) or from left to right (regular), you can force one or the other by typing **c** ↵ or **w** ↵, respectively.

Removing Objects from a Selection Set: At some point, you will find it more efficient to select more objects than you want, then remove the unwanted ones. There are two ways to do this:

> ▶ To remove a couple of objects, hold down the Shift key and pick the objects.

> ▶ To remove many objects, type **r** ↵, then use the same selection tools (picking, windows, etc.) to remove them from the selection set.

If you need to add objects back to the selection set after removing some, type **a** ↵. This will put you back into selection mode, and you can continue adding objects to the set.

Turning Off and Freezing Layers

Layers can be made invisible either by turning them off or by *freezing* them. When a layer is turned off or frozen, the objects on that layer are invisible. These two procedures operate the same way and do about the same thing. The difference between freezing and turning a layer off is technical and beyond the scope of this book. However, here is a good rule to follow: If you want a layer to be invisible for only a short time, turn it off; if you prefer that it be invisible semi-permanently, freeze it. For the task at hand we will turn off all the layers except the 0 layer and the Walls layer. Then we will move the wall lines onto the Walls layer.

Layers beginning with numbers are listed first in numerical order. Following them, the rest of the layers are listed alphabetically.

1. Click the Layers button on the Object Properties toolbar. The Layer Properties Manager dialog box comes up. Notice that the 0 layer is still first in the list, and the other layers have been reorganized alphabetically (Figure 6.18a).

2. Click the Balcony layer to highlight it. Then hold down the Shift key and click the Steps layer. All layers have been selected except the 0 layer and the Walls layer.

3. Move the arrow cursor over to the On column, which has a lit light bulb as a symbol for each layer row.

4. Click one of the light bulbs of the selected layers. The lit light-bulb symbols have all changed to unlit bulbs except the ones for the 0 layer and the Walls layer (Figure 6.18b).

5. Click OK. All objects in your drawing are invisible except the wall lines (Figure 6.19). The wall lines are still on the 0 layer.

6. Start a regular selection window around the cabin by clicking the upper-left corner of the drawing area, above and to the left of any lines. Then click the lower-right corner in the same way. All the wall lines are selected, and grips appear on all of them.

7. Open the Layer Control drop-down list, then click the Walls layer. The walls move to the Walls layer and are now cyan. Press Esc to remove the grips.

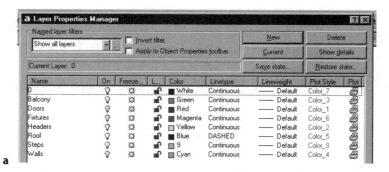

a

b

FIGURE 6.18: The layers, now listed alphabetically (a), and newly turned-off layers (b)

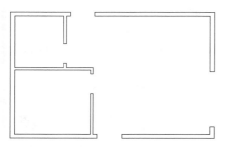

FIGURE 6.19: The floor plan with all layers frozen except the Walls layer and the 0 layer

8. Click the Layers button on the Object Properties toolbar. In the Layer Properties Manager dialog box, right-click on any layer. Pick Select All from the shortcut menu that appears. All layers are highlighted.

9. Click one of the unlit bulbs in the On column. All unlit bulbs become lit. Click OK. Back in your drawing, all objects are now visible and on their correct layers (Figure 6.20).

10. Save this drawing in your training folder as Cabin06a.

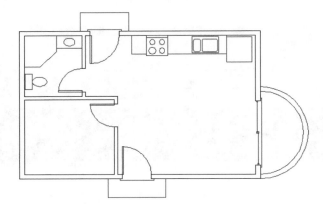

FIGURE 6.20: The floor plan with all layers visible and all objects on their correct layers

Two of your layers, Roof and Header, still have no objects on them because these components haven't been drawn yet. We'll draw the headers now.

Drawing the Headers

Most door and window openings do not extend to the ceiling. The portion of the wall above the opening and below the ceiling is the *header*. The term comes from the name of the beam inside the wall that spans the opening. In a floor plan, wall lines usually stop at the door and window openings, but you need lines across the gap between jamb lines to show that an opening does not extend to the ceiling, hence, the header.

To draw headers you need to make the Header layer current. As you've seen above, you can use the Layer Properties Manager dialog box. But there is a short-cut, the Layer Control drop-down list, which you have just been using to move objects from one layer to another.

1. Click anywhere on the drop-down list or the down-arrow button on the right end. The drop-down list opens, displaying a list of the layers in your drawing. If you have more than 10 layers, a scroll bar becomes operational, giving you access to all of the layers.

2. Click the Headers layer. The drop-down list closes. Header is now in the box; this tells you that the Header layer has replaced Walls as the current layer.

3. Right-click the Osnap button on the Status bar, then select Settings from the shortcut menu that appears. The Drafting Settings dialog box comes up and the Object Snap tab is on top. Be sure Endpoint is the only Object Snap mode with a check mark, and be sure that Object Snap On is checked, then click OK.

4. The doors and steps may be in your way. Click the Layer drop-down list. When the list of layers appears, click the light-bulb icons for the Doors and Steps layers to turn them off. Then click Header at the top of the list. The drop-down list closes; the Header layer is still current. The doors, steps, and thresholds have temporarily disappeared.

You need to draw two parallel lines across each of the five openings, from the endpoint of one jamb line to the corresponding endpoint of the jamb on the opposite side of the opening.

5. To start the Line command, type l ↵. Move the cursor, with its target box, near the upper end of the left jamb for the back door until the colored square appears at the upper endpoint of the jamb line, then click.

6. Move the cursor to the upper end of the right jamb and do the same thing as you did in the previous step.

7. Right-click once. A menu appears near your cursor.

8. Choose Enter on the menu, then right-click again. Another menu appears at the cursor.

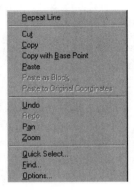

9. Click Repeat Line on the menu.

10. Move to the lower endpoint of the right jamb line for the back door and—with the same technique used in steps 5 through 9—draw the lower header line across the opening. The results are shown in Figure 6.21a.

Keep using the same procedure to draw the rest of the header lines for the remaining four doorway openings. Use a *click, click, right-click, click, right-click, click* pattern on your mouse that repeats for each header line. Here's the pattern:

A. Click one of the jamb corners.

B. Click the opposite jamb corner.

C. Right-click. A small menu comes up.

D. Click Enter to end the line command.

E. Right-click again. Another small menu comes up.

F. Click Repeat Line.

G. Click one of the Jamb corners.

H. And so on.

When you're finished, turn on the Doors and Steps layers. The floor plan will look like Figure 6.21b.

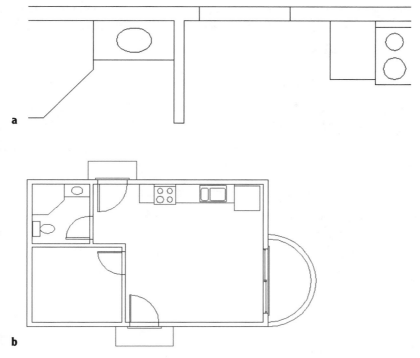

a

b

F I G U R E 6 . 2 1 : The header lines drawn for the back door opening (a), and for the rest of the doorway openings (b)

N O T E   These menus that appear are called right-click menus, shortcut menus, or context menus. They contain frequently used tools. The specific tools on a menu will vary depending on what you're doing when you right-click. It was not terribly efficient to use them to draw in the header lines, but it was a good way to introduce them to you. It's also a method of drawing without using the keyboard.

The Layer drop-down list box is a shortcut that allows you to quickly pick a different layer as the current layer and to turn off or turn on individual layers. To create new layers, or to turn off many layers at a time, use the Layer Properties

Manager dialog box, accessed by clicking the Layers button on the Object Prop-erties toolbar. You'll learn another tool for changing the current layer as you draw the roof lines.

Drawing the Roof

Before starting to draw the roof lines, refer to Figure 6.22 and note the lines rep-resenting different parts of the roof:

▶ Four *eaves lines* around the perimeter of the building, representing the lowest edge of the roof

▶ One *ridgeline*, representing the peak of the roof

▶ Four *hip lines*, connecting the endpoints of the eaves line to an end-point of the ridgeline

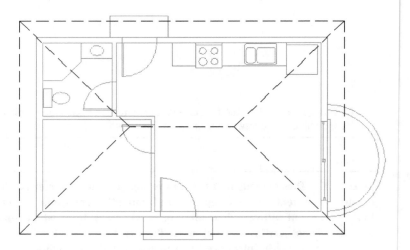

FIGURE 6.22: **The floor plan with the roof lines**

The roof for the cabin is called a *hip roof* because the end panels slope down to the eaves just as the middle panels do. The intersections of the sloping roof planes form the hip lines. We'll start with the eaves.

Creating the Eaves

Because the roof is cantilevered out beyond the exterior walls the same distance on all sides of the building, we can generate the eaves lines by offsetting the outside wall lines.

1. Start the Offset command. Then type 1'-6"⤶ to set the offset distance. Pick the left outside wall line and then pick a point to the left of that line to offset it to the outside.

2. Move to another side of the building and pick one of the outside wall lines on that side and offset it to the outside.

3. Repeat this for the other two sides of the building until you have offset one outside wall line to the outside of the building on each side of the cabin (Figure 6.23). Press ⤶ to end the Offset command. Be sure you have only one line offset on each side of the building. If you offset two lines on one side, erase one.

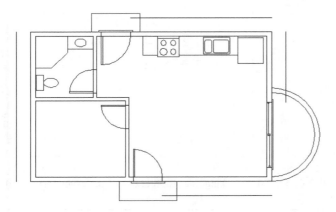

FIGURE 6.23: One outside wall line is offset to each side of the building.

4. Type f ⤶ to start the Fillet command. Make sure that the radius is set to zero. If it is, go on to step 5. If not, type r ⤶. Then type 0 ⤶ to reset the radius.

5. Click any two of these newly offset lines that are on adjacent sides of the building. Click the half of the line nearest the corner that the two

selected lines will meet (Figure 6.24a). The lines extend to meet each other and form a corner (Figure 6.24b). The Fillet command ends.

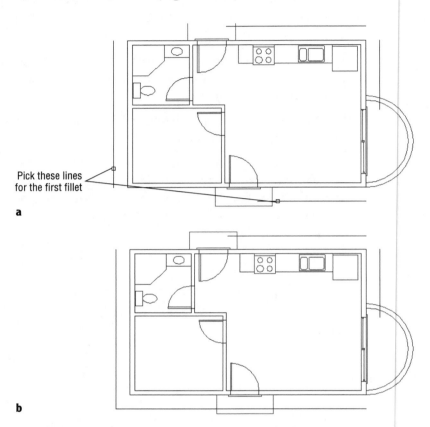

Pick these lines
for the first fillet

a

b

FIGURE 6.24: Picking lines to fillet one of the eaves corners (a), and the result (b)

6. Press ↵ to restart the Fillet command. Pick two more adjacent lines that will meet at another corner.

7. Start the Fillet command again and keep picking pairs of lines until all the corners are filleted and the result is a rectangle that represents the eaves of the roof surrounding the building, offset 1'-6" from the outside exterior walls (Figure 6.25).

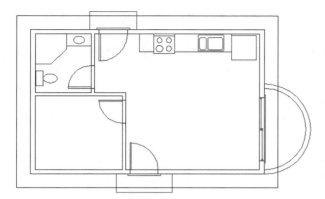

FIGURE 6.25: The eaves lines after filleting

Because the eaves lines were offset from wall lines, they are on the Walls layer. You need to move them onto the Roof layer. Then you'll make the Roof layer current so when you draw the hip lines and the ridgeline, they will be on the Roof layer.

1. Select the four eaves lines, then click the Layer Control drop-down list on the Object Properties toolbar.

2. Click Roof. The eaves lines are now on the Roof layer.

3. Press Esc to remove the grips.

The eaves lines are still solid lines, even though the Roof layer has been assigned a dashed linetype. Actually, the lines are dashed, but the dashes are so small the monitor can't display them.

Setting a Linetype Scale Factor

By default, the dashes are set up to be ½" long with ¼" spaces. This is the right size for a drawing that is close to actual size on your screen, like the box you drew in Chapter 2, *Basic Commands to Get Started*. But for something the size of your cabin, you must increase the linetype scale to make the dashes large enough to see. If the dashes were 12" long with 6" spaces, they would at least be visible, though possibly not exactly the right size. To make such a change in the dash size, ask what you must multiply ½" by to get 12". The answer is 24—so that's your scale factor. AutoCAD stores a Linetype Scale Factor setting that controls the size of the dashes and spaces of non-continuous linetypes. The default is 1.00, which gives you the ½" dash, so we need to change it to 24.00.

1. Type ltscale ↵. The prompt in the Command window reads New scale factor <1.0000>:.

2. Type 24 ↵ to set the linetype scale factor to 24. Your drawing changes, and you can see the dashes (Figure 6.26). If you are not satisfied with the dash size, restart the Ltscale command and increase the scale factor for a longer dash or decrease it for a shorter one. This linetype scale factor is a global one, meaning it affects every non-continuous line in the drawing. There is also an individual scale factor for linetypes. You'll see that after you finish the roof.

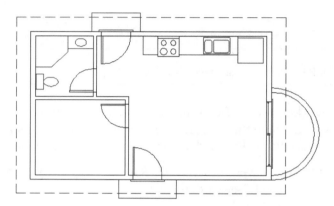

FIGURE 6.26: The eaves lines on the roof layer with visible dashes

Assigning an Individual Linetype Scale Factor

Although the Ltscale command sets a linetype scale factor for all non-continuous lines in the drawing, you can adjust the dash and space sizes for individual lines by using the Properties button to change the current linetype scale. If you want to change the dash and space size for one of the eaves lines of the roof to make them larger, follow these steps:

1. Select an eaves line. Grips will appear.

2. Click the Properties button on the Standard toolbar.

3. In the Properties dialog box, click Linetype Scale. Highlight the current scale of 1.0000 and type 3 ↵.

4. Close the Properties dialog box and press Esc to remove the grips. The dashes and spaces of the ridgeline are three times larger than those for the rest of the roof lines.

5. Click the Properties button and use the same procedure to change the current linetype scale factor for the ridgeline back to 1.

N O T E   If no objects are selected, and you set the Linetype Scale in the Properties window to a number other than 1.000, any non-continuous lines that are subsequently drawn will be controlled by this new Linetype Scale.

This tool allows you to get subtle variations in the size of dashes and spaces for individual, non-continuous lines. But remember that all lines are controlled by an individual linetype scale factor and by the global linetype scale factor. The actual size of the dashes and spaces for a particular line is a result of the two linetype scale factors working together. This additional flexibility requires you to keep careful track of the variations you are making. To find out the current values for the individual (called *object*) and global linetype scale factors:

1. With Cabin06a as the current drawing, type **linetype** ↵.

2. In the Linetype Manager dialog box, make sure the Details area is visible at the bottom of the dialog box. If it isn't, click Show Details in the upper-right corner.

3. Note the bottom-right corner. The current Global and Object linetype scales are displayed here. They can also be modified here.

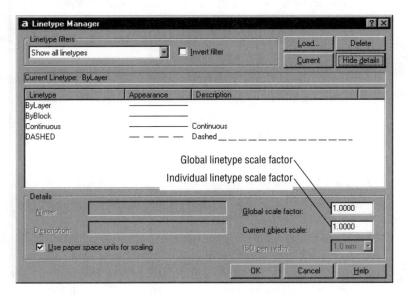

4. For now, click Cancel.

Drawing the Hip and Ridge Lines

Next, you'll draw two of the diagonal hip roof lines, then use the Mirror command to create the other two. To do this, you need to assign the Roof layer as the current layer. Because you have moved the lines you just offset to the Roof layer, you can use the Make Object's Layer Current button to make the Roof layer current.

1. Click the Make Object's Layer Current button on the left end of the Object Properties toolbar. You will get the `Select object whose layer will become current:` prompt.

2. Pick one of the dashed eaves lines. The Roof layer replaces Header in the Layer drop-down list, telling you the Roof layer is now the current layer. Look at the Linetypes drop-down list on the Object Properties toolbar. A dashed line with the name ByLayer appears there. ByLayer tells you that the current linetype is going to be whatever linetype has been assigned to the current layer. In the case of the Roof layer, the assigned linetype is dashed. You will read more about ByLayer at the end of this chapter.

3. The Endpoint Osnap should still be running. How can you tell? Type os ↵. The Osnap tab on the Drafting Settings dialog box comes up and you can easily see which Osnaps are checked. First, be sure Object Snap On is checked. Then, if Endpoint is checked, click the Polar Tracking tab. Otherwise, click in the check box next to Endpoint and then click the Polar Tracking tab (Figure 6.27).

4. At the top, click the Polar Tracking On (F10) check box to turn Polar Tracking on.

5. In the Polar Angle Settings area, open the Increment Angle drop-down list and select 45.

6. Click OK to close the Drafting Settings dialog box.

7. Start the Line command. Move the crosshair cursor to the lower-left corner of the rectangle representing the roof until the square appears on the corner, then click. A line is started.

8. Move the crosshair cursor up and to the right at a 45° angle from the lower-left corner of the roof. When the angle of the line being drawn approaches 45°, a tracking path and a Polar tooltip will appear, along with a small *x* near the crosshair cursor (Figure 6.28a).

9. While the tracking path is visible, type 15' ↵↵. The first hip line is drawn and the Line command ends (Figure 6.28b).

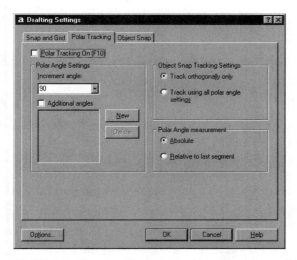

FIGURE 6.27: The Polar Tracking tab on the Drafting Settings dialog box

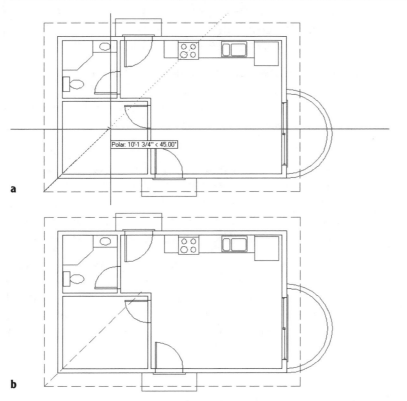

FIGURE 6.28: The 45° tracking path for the first hip line of the roof (a), and the completed first hip line (b)

Use the same procedure to draw another hip line from the upper-left corner of the roof. Here's a summary of the steps:

1. Restart the line command and start a line at the upper-left corner of the roof.

2. Hold the crosshair cursor down and to the right at an angle of approximately 45° until the Polar tracking path with its tooltip appears. (The tooltip will confirm that the actual angle is 315°.)

3. Type 15' ↵ ↵. The second hip line is completed.

The two hip lines need to be filleted together at their intersection, but the bedroom door is in the way.

1. Open the Layer Control drop-down list and turn off the Door layer. Then click the Roof layer in the list to close the list.

2. Start the Fillet command. The radius should still be set to zero. Click the two diagonal lines at a place that is close to their intersection. The lines are filleted together (Figure 6.29a). Now you need to mirror these two diagonal lines to the right side of the roof.

3. Start the Mirror command. At the prompt to select objects, select the two diagonal lines, then press ↵. Click the Midpoint Osnap button and place the cursor on the horizontal eaves line above the cabin. When the triangle appears at the midpoint of the eaves line, click.

4. Then move the crosshair cursor down into the living room, keeping it directly below the point just picked, and, when the tracking line and Polar tooltip appears, click a clear space. Press ↵ when asked whether to delete old objects. The diagonal lines from the left are mirrored to the right (Figure 6.29b). The Mirror command automatically ends. To finish the roof, we'll draw in the ridgeline.

5. Start the Line command. Endpoint Osnap is still running. Pick the two intersections of the diagonal lines, then press ↵. Open the Layer Control drop-down list and turn on the Doors layer. Then click the roof layer to close the drop-down list. This completes the ridgeline and finishes the roof (Figure 6.30). Save this drawing as Cabin06b.

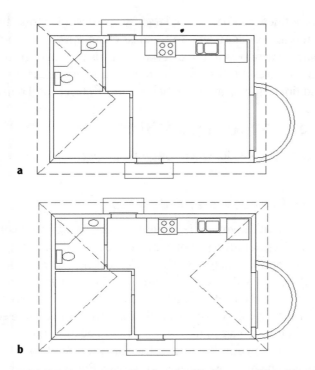

a

b

FIGURE 6.29: The first two hip lines are filleted together (a), and then mirrored to the right (b).

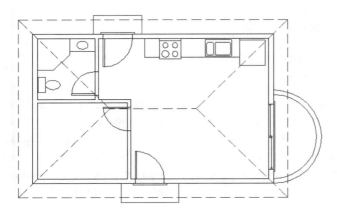

FIGURE 6.30: The completed roof

By drawing the roof lines, you have completed the exercises for this chapter. The cabin floor plan is almost complete. In the next chapter, you will complete the floor plan by placing windows in the external walls using a new grouping tool called the *block*. The rest of this chapter contains a short discussion on color, linetypes, and lineweights, and how they work with layers and objects.

Properties of Layers and Objects

Here are a few concepts to consider when assigning properties to Layers and Objects.

Selecting Colors for Layers and Objects

First, you must decide whether you prefer a light or dark background color for the drawing area. This is generally a personal preference, but the lighting in your work area can be a contributing factor. Bright work areas usually make it difficult to read monitors easily; and, with a dark background color on your screen in a brightly lit room, you will often get distracting reflections on the screen. Eyestrain can result. Darkening your work area will usually minimize these effects. If that's not possible, you might have to live with a lighter background.

Next, look at the colors in your drawing. If the background of your drawing area is white, notice which colors are the easiest to read. For most monitors, yellow, light gray, and cyan are somewhat faded out, while blue, green, red, and magenta are read very easily. If your drawing area background is black, the blue is sometimes too dark to read easily, but the rest of the colors that we have used so far usually read very well. This is one reason why most users prefer the black, or at least a dark background color.

Assigning a Color or Linetype to an Object Instead of a Layer

Properties of layers, such as color, linetype, and lineweights, can also be assigned to objects. So, for example, think about the Roof layer. It is assigned the Dashed linetype. A line on the Roof layer can be assigned the Continuous linetype, even though all other lines on the Roof layer may be dashed. The same is true for color and lineweights. There may be an occasion where it makes sense to do this, especially for linetypes, but that would be the exception, rather than the rule. To make such a change, you would select the line, open the Properties window, and change the linetype from By Layer to the Linetype of your choice.

In this chapter you have been taught to assign colors and linetypes to layers, in order to control the way objects on those layers appear. That is the rule to follow. When objects are assigned properties that vary from those of their layer, the resulting situation can be confusing to someone working with your drawing file because the objects don't appear to be on their assigned layer. If the object's properties match those of another layer, you may mistakenly think the object is on that layer.

Making a Color or Linetype Current

If you look at the Object Properties toolbar for a moment, you will see, to the right of the Layer Control drop-down lists, more such lists. The first three are the Color, the Linetype, and the Lineweight controls. These tools allow you to set a color, linetype, or lineweight to be current. When this is done, each object subsequently created will be assigned the current linetype, lineweight, and/or color, regardless of which linetype, lineweight, and color have been assigned to the current layer. If, for example, the Doors layer was set as the current layer, and the dashed linetype and green color were also assigned as current, any lines drawn would be dashed and green, but still on the Doors layer. This is not a good way to set up the system of layers, linetypes, and colors because of the obvious confusion it would create in your drawing, but beginners often accidentally do this.

The best way to keep all this straight is to keep the current linetype, lineweight, and color set to ByLayer, as they are by default. When you do this, colors and linetypes are controlled by the layers, and objects take on the color and linetype of the layers they are on. If this configuration is accidentally disturbed and objects are created with the wrong color or linetype, you can correct the situation without too much trouble. First, reset the current color, lineweight, and linetype to ByLayer by using the Property Control drop-down lists on the Object Properties toolbar. Then use the Properties button to change the linetype, lineweight, or color of the problem objects to ByLayer. They will then take on the color, lineweight, and linetype of the layer to which they have been assigned.

If You Want More Practice...

Use Save As to save Cabin06b to a new file called Cabin06b_Linetype. Then experiment with the linetypes and linetype scales (Global and Object) to get a feel for how the linetypes look and how the scales work. You won't be using this practice file again, so feel free to draw new objects that will make it convenient for you to work with linetypes. Here are some suggestions for linetypes to experiment with:

- ► Dashed (.5×)
- ► Dashed (2×)
- ► Hidden (as compared to Dashed)
- ► Phantom
- ► DashDot
- ► Fenceline2
- ► HotWaterLine

Here is a summary of the steps to get a new linetype into your drawing:

- ► Create a new layer or highlight an existing layer.
- ► Click Continuous in the Linetype column for the chosen layer.
- ► Click the Load button.
- ► Highlight a linetype in the list and click OK.
- ► Highlight the new linetype in the Linetype Manager dialog box and click OK.
- ► Make the layer with the new linetype the Current layer, then click OK to close the Layer Properties Manager dialog box.
- ► Draw objects.

Once you have a few linetypes represented in the drawing, open the Linetype Manager dialog box and experiment with the Global and Object linetype scale factors.

Are You Experienced?

Now you can...

- ☑ create new layers and assign them a color and linetype

- ☑ load a new linetype into your current drawing file

- ☑ move existing objects onto a new layer

- ☑ turn layers off and on

- ☑ make a layer current and create objects on the current layer

- ☑ reset the linetype scale factor to make non-continuous lines visible

- ☑ use Polar Tracking to draw a diagonal line

- ☑ use the individual linetype scale factor to adjust the size of one dashed line

CHAPTER 7

Grouping Objects into Blocks

▶ Creating and inserting blocks

▶ Using the Wblock command

▶ Detecting blocks in a drawing

▶ Using point filters and blips

▶ Working with AutoCAD's Design Center

C omputer drafting gains much of its efficiency from a feature that makes it possible to group a collection of objects into an entity that behaves as one object. AutoCAD calls these grouped objects a *block*. The AutoCAD tools that work specifically with blocks make it possible to:

▶ Create a block in your current drawing.

▶ Repeatedly place copies of a block in precise locations in your drawing.

▶ Share blocks between drawings.

▶ Create .dwg files either from blocks or from portions of your current drawing.

In general, objects best suited to becoming part of a block are the components of your building that are repeatedly used in the drawing, such as doors, windows, and fixtures, or drawing symbols, like a North arrow or labels for a section cut line (Figure 7.1). In your cabin drawing, you will convert the doors with swings into blocks. Then you will create a new block that you will use to place the windows in the Cabin drawing. To accomplish these tasks, you will need to learn two new commands.

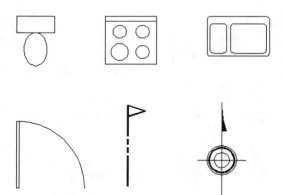

FIGURE 7.1: Examples of blocks often used in drawings

Making a Block for a Door

When making a block, you will create a *block definition*. This is an invisible entity that is stored in the drawing file and consists of:

▶ The block name

▶ An insertion point to help you place the block in the drawing

▶ The objects to be grouped into the block

You will specify each of these in the course of using the Make Block command. When the command is completed, the block definition is stored with the drawing file. Then you will insert the object (as a block) back into the drawing using the Insert Block command.

Before you create a block, you must consider the layers on which the objects to be blocked reside. When objects on the 0 layer are grouped into a block, they will take on the color and linetype of the layer that is current when the block is inserted. Objects on other layers retain the properties of their original layers, regardless of which color or linetype has been assigned to the current layer. This characteristic distinguishes the 0 layer from all other layers.

As you define a block, you must decide which—if any—of the objects to be included in the block will need to be on the 0 layer before they are blocked. If a block is always going to be on the same layer, the objects making up the block can remain on that layer. On the other hand, if a block may be inserted on several layers, the objects in the block will need to be moved to the 0 layer before the block definition is created, so as to avoid confusion of colors and linetypes.

As you learn to make blocks for the doors, you will also see how layers work in the process of creating block definitions. We'll create a block for the exterior doors first, using the front door, and call it door3_0 to distinguish it from the smaller interior door. For the insertion point, you will need to assign a point on or near the door that will facilitate its placement as a block in your drawing. The hinge point will make the best insertion point.

For this chapter, the Endpoint Osnap should be running most of the time, and Polar tracking should be off. Follow the first five steps below to get your drawing set up:

1. If you are continuing on from the last chapter, go on to step 2. If you are starting up a new session, start AutoCAD. In the Startup dialog box, click Open a Drawing. In the Select a File list, highlight Cabin06b and click OK. If this .dwg file is not in the list, use the Browse button to navigate to your training folder and select the file.

In complex blocks, the objects that comprise them may reside on more than one layer.

We are using the Freeze option for layers this time because we won't need to see the lines on the Roof and Headers layers for a while.

2. The Roof layer should be visible in the Layers drop-down list on the Object Properties toolbar. Click the list to open it, then click Doors to make the Doors layer current. The list will close. Click the drop-down list again and this time click the sun icons for the Roof and Header layers to freeze them. The suns turn into snowflakes. Then click the Doors layer to close the list. The Doors layer is now current, and the Headers and Roof are no longer visible in the drawing (Figure 7.2).

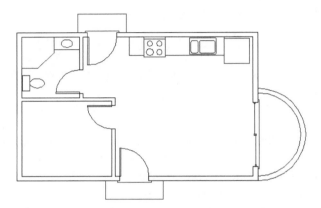

F I G U R E   7 . 2 :   The floor plan with the Headers and Roof layers frozen

3. Check the Status bar and note whether the Osnap button is in the On position, then right-click that button and pick Settings from the shortcut menu that appears.

4. In the Object Snap tab of the Drafting Settings dialog box, be sure the check box next to Endpoint is marked. Also, be sure Object Snap On is checked.

5. Then click OK. In the Status bar, click Polar off if it is on, and be sure only the Model and Osnap buttons are in the On position.

Now you're ready to make blocks.

The Block command can also be started by choosing Draw ➢ Block ➢ Make, or by typing b ↵.

1. Click the Make Block button on the Draw toolbar. The Block Definition dialog box comes up (Figure 7.3). Notice the flashing cursor in the text box next to Name. Type **door3_0** but do not press ↵.

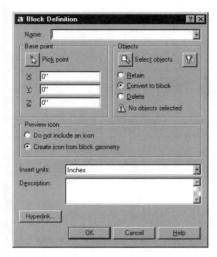

FIGURE 7.3: The Block Definition dialog box

2. Click the Pick Point button in the Base Point area. The dialog box momentarily disappears, and you are returned to your drawing.

3. You need to zoom into the front door area. In your drawing, click the Zoom Window button on the Standard toolbar and make a window around the front door area. The area in the zoom window will fill the screen.

4. Move the cursor to the front door area and position it near the hinge point of the door. When the square appears on the hinge point (Figure 7.4a), click. This selects the insertion point for the door, and the Block Definition dialog box returns.

5. Click the Select Objects button in the Objects area. You are returned to the drawing again. The cursor changes to a pickbox, and the Command window displays the `Select objects:` prompt.

6. Select the door and swing, then press ↵. You are returned to the Block Definition dialog box. At the bottom of the Objects area, the count of selected objects is displayed. Just above that, there are three radio buttons. Click the Delete radio button if it's not already selected.

7. Finally, in the middle of the dialog box, be sure Create Icon From Block Geometry is selected, then click OK, and the dialog box disappears. The door and swing disappear (Figure 7.4b).

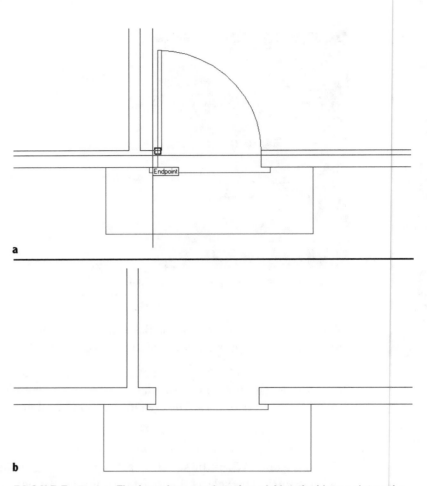

FIGURE 7.4: The front door opening when picking the hinge point as the insertion point (a), and after creating the door3_0 block and deleting the door and swing (b)

You have now created a block definition, called door3_0. Block definitions are stored electronically with the drawing file. You need to insert the door3__0 block (known formally as a *block reference*) into the front door opening to replace the door and swing that were just deleted when the block was created.

Inserting the Door Block

You will use the Insert command to place the door3_0 block back into the drawing.

1. On the Draw toolbar, click the Insert Block button. The Insert dialog box comes up (Figure 7.5). At the top, the Name drop-down list contains the names of the blocks in the drawing. In this case, there is only one so far, door3_0, so it is on top. Below the Name list, there are three areas with the Specify On-screen option. These are used for the insertion procedure.

The Insert command can also be started by selecting Insert ➢ Block, or by typing i ↵.

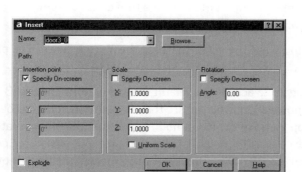

FIGURE 7.5:   The Insert dialog box

2. Be sure the Specify On-screen option is checked for all three areas.

3. Click OK. You are returned to your drawing and the door3_0 block is now attached to the cursor, with the hinge point coinciding with the intersection of the crosshairs (Figure 7.6). The Command window reads `Specify insertion point or [Scale/X/Y/Z/Rotate/ PScale/PX/PY/PZ/PRotate]:`.

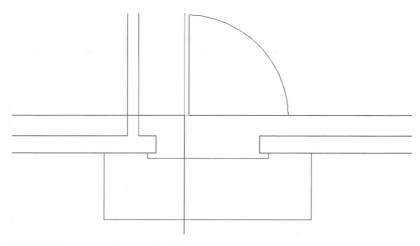

FIGURE 7.6:   The door3_0 block attached to the cursor

4. With Endpoint Osnap running, move the cursor toward the upper end of the left jamb line in the front door opening. When a colored square appears at the jambline's upper endpoint, click. The insertion point has been positioned, and the Command window now displays an additional prompt: Enter X scale factor, specify opposite corner, or [corner/XYZ]<1>:.

5. Press ↵ to accept the default of 1 for the *X* scale factor. The prompt changes to Y scale factor <use X scale factor> :.

6. Press ↵ again to accept the default for this option. The door3_0 block comes into view, and you can see that its insertion point has been placed at the upper end of the left jamb line, and that the block rotates as you move the cursor (Figure 7.7a). Another prompt comes up: Specify rotation angle <0>:. Press ↵ again to accept the default of 0. The door3_0 block is placed in the drawing (Figure 7.7b).

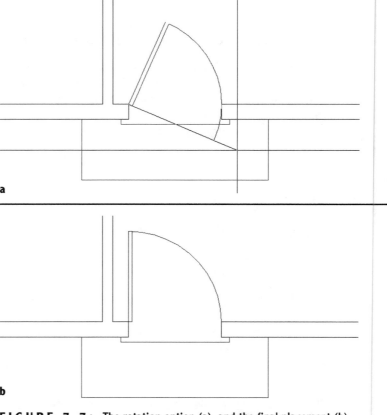

a

b

FIGURE 7.7: The rotation option (a), and the final placement (b)

Each time a block is inserted, you have the option of specifying the following on-screen or in the Insert dialog box:

▶ The location of the insertion point of the block

▶ The X and Y scale factors

▶ The Z factor in the dialog box (used in 3D drawings only)

▶ A rotation angle

When blocks are inserted, they can be stretched or flipped horizontally (the X scale factor) or vertically (the Y scale factor), or they can be rotated from their original orientation. Because the door3_0 block was created from the door and swing that occupied the front door opening, and the size was the same, inserting this block back into the front door opening required no rotation, so we followed the defaults. When you insert the same block into the back door opening, you will have to change the Y scale factor, because the door will be flipped vertically.

Flipping a Block While Inserting It

The X scale factor controls the horizontal size and orientation. The Y scale factor mimics the X scale factor unless you change it. For the next insertion, you will make such a change.

1. Click the Zoom Previous button on the Standard toolbar to zoom back out to a full view of the floor plan.

2. Click the Zoom Window button and make a window around the back door area, including plenty of room inside and outside the opening so that you can see the door3_0 block as it is being inserted. You will be zoomed into a close view of the back door (Figure 7.8).

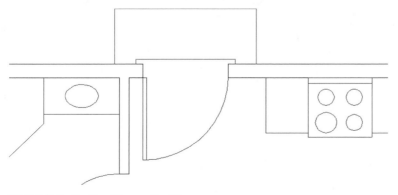

FIGURE 7.8: The result of the zoom

3. Use the Erase command to erase the door and swing from the back door opening.

4. Choose Insert ➤ Block. In the Insert dialog box, door3_0 should still be in the Name drop-down list.

5. Click OK. You are returned to your drawing, and the door3_0 block is attached to the cursor.

6. Move the cursor to the lower end of the left jamb line. When the colored square appears at that endpoint (Figure 7.9a), click. The insertion point has been placed and the prompt reads Enter X scale factor, specify opposite corner, or [corner/XYZ]<1>:.

7. Press ⏎ to accept the default *X* scale factor of 1. The prompt changes to read Specify Y scale factor <use X scale factor:. In order to flip the door down to the inside of the cabin, you need to give the *Y* scale factor a value of -1.

8. Type -1 ⏎. Then press ⏎ again to accept the default rotation angle of 0°. The Insert command ends, and the door3_0 block is placed in the back door opening (Figure 7.9b). Figure 7.9b will look exactly like Figure 7.8.

9. Click the Zoom Previous button on the Object Properties toolbar to zoom back out to a full view of the floor plan.

N O T E   When inserting a block, giving a value of -1 to the *X* or *Y* scale factor has the effect of flipping the block, much like the Mirror command did in Chapter 4, *Gaining Drawing Strategies: Part 1*, when you first drew the doors. Because you can flip or rotate the door3_0 block as it is inserted, it can be used to place a door and swing in any 3'-0" opening, regardless of its orientation.

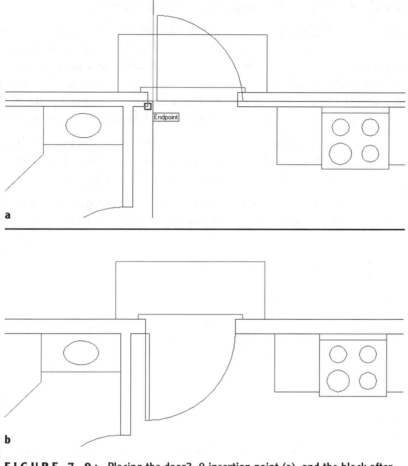

FIGURE 7.9: Placing the door3_0 insertion point (a), and the block after insertion (b)

Doors are traditionally sorted into four categories, depending on which side the hinges and doorknob are on and which way the door swings open. To be able to use one door block for all openings of the same size, you need to know:

► How the door and swing in the block is oriented

► Where the hinge point is to be in the next opening

► How the block has to be flipped and/or rotated during the insertion process to properly fit in the next doorway opening

◄

Nothing has changed about the geometry of the door, but it is now a different kind of object. Before it was a rectangle and an arc, now it's a block reference made up of a rectangle and an arc.

Blocking and Inserting the Interior Doors

Because the interior doors are smaller, you will need to make a new block for them. We could insert the door3_0 block with a 5⁄6 scale factor, but the door thickness would also be reduced by the same factor, and we don't want that.

On the other hand, it's a good idea to have all door blocks oriented the same way, and the bath and bedroom doors are turned relative to the door3_0 block. We'll move and rotate the bathroom door and its swing like the front door.

1. Use Zoom Window to define a window that encloses both the bathroom and bedroom doors. The view will change to a close-up view of the area enclosed in your window (Figure 7.10a).

2. Use the Move command to move the bathroom door to the right, then use the Rotate command to rotate it -90° (Figure 7.10b).

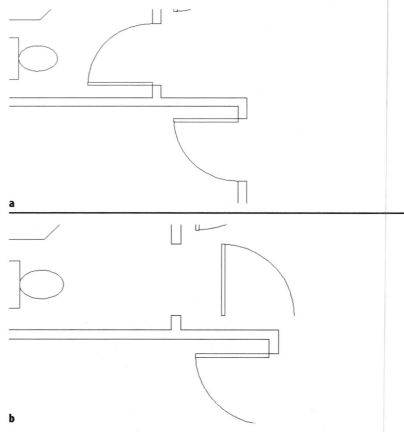

a

b

F I G U R E   7 . 1 0 :   The result of a zoom window (a), the bathroom door moved and rotated (b)

3. Repeat a procedure similar to the one you used to make a block out of the front door and swing to make a block out of the bathroom door and swing. Here is a summary of the steps:

A. Start the Block command (click the Make Block button on the Draw toolbar).

B. In the dialog box, type **door2_6** to name the new block. Don't press ↵.

C. Click the Pick Point button and pick the hinge point of the bathroom door.

D. Click the Select Objects button and pick the door and swing. Then press ↵.

E. In the Objects area, select the radio button for Delete.

F. Click OK. The door and swing disappear.

4. Start the Insert command and insert the door2_6 block into the bathroom doorway opening. Follow the steps carefully. Here's a summary of the steps:

A. Start the Insert command.

B. Open the Name drop-down list and select door2_6, then click OK.

C. Pick the left end of the lower jamb line.

D. Accept the default of 1 for the *X* scale factor.

E. Accept the default of <use X> for the *Y* scale factor.

F. Enter **90** ↵ for the rotation.

5. Erase the bedroom door, then restart the Insert command and insert the door2_6 block into the bedroom door opening. Here are the parameters:

▶ Specify On-screen checked for Insertion Point, Scale, and Rotation.

▶ Insertion point: left endpoint of upper jamb line.

▶ *X* scale factor will be -1.

▶ *Y* scale factor will be 1.

▶ Rotation will be 90.

6. Zoom Previous (Figure 7.11).

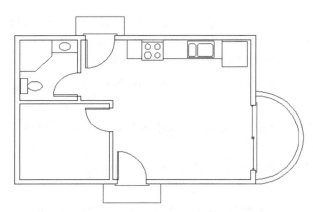

F I G U R E   7 . 1 1 :   The floor plan with all swinging doors converted into blocks

This view looks the same as the view you started with at the beginning of this chapter; see Figure 7.2. Blocks look the same as other objects and can't be detected by viewing only. Their usefulness comes from our being able to use them over and over again in a drawing or many drawings, and the fact that the block is a grouping of two or more (and sometimes many more) objects together into a single object. The next section will go into how you can detect a block.

THE FATE OF OBJECTS USED TO MAKE A BLOCK

The three radio buttons in the Objects area of the Block Definition dialog box represent the options you have for objects transformed into a block:

- ▶ ***Retain***: The objects remain unblocked. Use this if you want to make several similar blocks from the same set of objects.

- ▶ ***Convert to Block***: The objects become a block reference. Use this if the first use of the block has geometry identical to that of the set of objects it is replacing.

- ▶ ***Delete***: The objects are automatically erased after the block has been defined. Use this if the first use of the block will be at a different scale, orientation, or location from the set of objects it is replacing.

NOTE: When we made the first door block, we could have used the Convert to Block option because the door3_0 block replaced the front door and its swing. I decided not to use this option so I could show you the insertion process with default *X* and *Y* scale factors and Rotation.

Finding Blocks in a Drawing

There are three ways of detecting blocks in a drawing: with grips, with the List command, or with the Properties button. Each method is detailed below.

Using Grips to Detect a Block

Grips appear on objects that are selected when no command is started. When an object that is not a block is selected in the above manner, grips appear at strategic places. But if you select a block, by default, only one grip appears and it's always located at the block's insertion point. Because of this, clicking an object when no command started is a quick way to see if it is a block.

1. At the Command: prompt, click one of the door swings. The door and swing ghost and a colored square appears at the hinge point.

2. Press Esc to clear the grip.

3. Choose Tools ➢ Options, then click the Selection tab. The Grips area is in the upper-right corner. Enable Grips within Blocks is unchecked by default. If this is checked, when you click on a block with no command running, grips appear on all objects in the block as if they weren't blocked. Leave this setting unchecked.

4. Click OK to close the Options dialog box.

We'll look at grips in more detail in Chapter 11, *Dimensioning a Drawing*. You may need to know more about a block than just whether or not something is one. If that is the case, you will need to use the List command.

Using the List Command to Detect a Block

1. Choose Tools ➢ Inquiry ➢ List.

2. Click the bedroom door block, then press ↵. The AutoCAD Text Window temporarily covers the drawing (Figure 7.12). In the text window, you can see the words BLOCK REFERENCE Layer: DOORS, followed by eight lines of text. These nine lines describe the block you selected.

Each time you use the List command and select an object, the text screen will display information that is tailored to the kind of object selected.

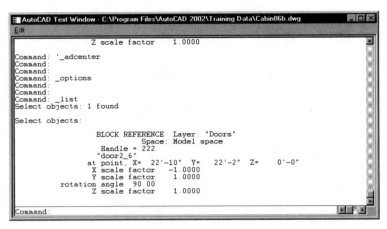

FIGURE 7.12: The AutoCAD Text Window

Some of the information stored here about the selected object is:

▶ What the object is (Block Reference)

▶ The layer the object is on (Doors layer)

▶ The name of the block (door2_6)

▶ The coordinates of the insertion point in the drawing

▶ The *X* and *Y* scale factors

▶ The rotation angle

3. Press F2. The drawing area returns.

4. Right-click and select Restart List from the top of the shortcut menu that appears.

5. At the Select objects: prompt, click one of the arcs that represent the balcony, then click one of the wall lines and press ↲.

6. The text screen comes up again, and you see information about the arc that you selected, followed by information about the selected wall line.

7. Press F2, then slowly press it a few more times. As you switch back and forth between the text screen and the drawing, notice that the last three lines on the text screen are the three lines of text in the Command window of the drawing (Figure 7.13). The Command window is displaying a strip of text from the text screen, usually the last three lines.

8. Press F2 to display the drawing.

> The F2 key toggles the text screen on and off.

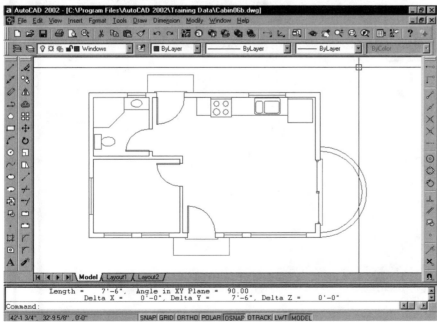

FIGURE 7.13: Toggling between the text window (a), and the drawing with its Command window (b)

Using the Properties Dialog Box to Detect a Block

In Chapter 6, *Using Layers to Organize Your Drawing*, we used the Properties button on the Standard Properties toolbar to change the individual linetype scale for the ridgeline of the roof. It can also be a tool for investigating objects in your drawing. When the Properties command is started, and only one object is selected, the Properties dialog box will display data specific to the selected object.

1. Click one of the door blocks.

2. Click the Properties button on the Object Properties toolbar. The Properties dialog box appears. If the Categorized tab is not on top, click it.

   The data displayed in the dialog box is similar to that displayed when you used the List Command, but in slightly different form (Figure 7.14). At the top of the dialog box, a drop-down list displays the type of object selected—in this case, a Block Reference.

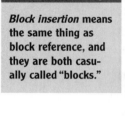

Block insertion means the same thing as block reference, and they are both casually called "blocks."

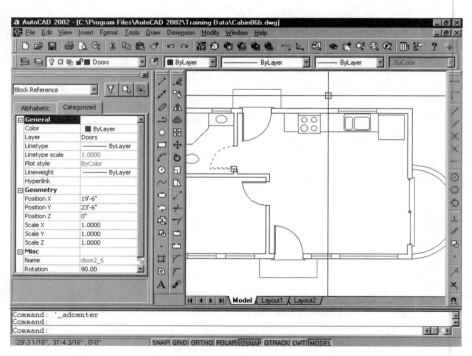

FIGURE 7.14: The Properties dialog box

3. Close the Properties dialog box by clicking the *X* in the upper-right corner, then press Esc to remove the grip on the door block.

If you are ever working on a drawing that you did not draw, these tools for finding out about objects will be invaluable. The next exercise on working with blocks will involve the placement of windows in the walls of the cabin.

The Properties window may be docked or floating. The one illustrated in Figure 7.14 is in docked mode.

Creating a Window Block

The windows in the cabin floor plan can all be created from one block, even though they are four different sizes (Figure 7.15). You'll create a window block, then go from room to room to insert the block into the walls.

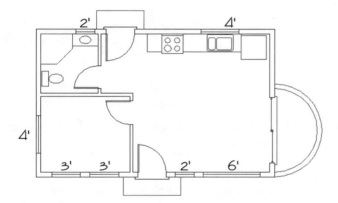

FIGURE 7.15: The cabin windows in the floor plan

1. Click the Layers list on the Object Properties toolbar to open the drop-down list and click the 0 layer in the list to make it current.

2. Right-click the Osnap button on the Status bar and pick Settings from the shortcut menu. Add check marks to Midpoint and Perpendicular Osnaps. Then click OK.

3. Zoom into a horizontal section of wall where there are no jamb lines or intersections with other walls, by clicking the Zoom Window button on the Standard toolbar and picking two points to be opposite corners of the zoom window (Figure 7.16). Because the widths of the windows in the cabin are multiples of 12", a block made from a

12"–wide window can be inserted for each window, and an *X* scale
factor can be applied to the block to make it the right width. The first
step is to draw a 12"–wide window inside the wall lines.

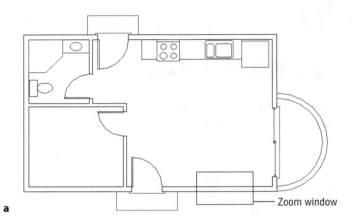

a

b

FIGURE 7.16: Making a zoom window (a), to zoom into a section of
straight length of wall (b)

4. Start the Line command, then click the Nearest Osnap button from
the Object Snap toolbar or the Osnap flyout on the Standard toolbar.
The Nearest Osnap will allow you to start a line on one of the wall
lines. It finds the point on the wall line nearest to the point you pick.

5. Move the cursor to the upper wall line, a little to the left of the center
of the screen and, with the hourglass symbol still displayed, click. A
line begins.

6. Move the cursor to the lower wall line. A colored perpendicular icon
will appear directly below the point you previously picked. When it is
displayed, click. The line is drawn between the wall lines. Press ↵ to
end the Line command.

7. Start the Offset command. Type **12** ↵ to set the offset distance to 12".
Pick the line you just drew, then pick a point to the right of that line.
The line is offset 12" to the right. Press ↵ to end the Offset command.

8. Start the Line command again. Move the cursor near the midpoint of the line you first drew. When the midpoint symbol appears, click. Move the cursor near the midpoint of the line that was just offset. When the Perpendicular or Midpoint symbol appears, click. Press ↵ to end the Line command. Your drawing should look like Figure 7.17.

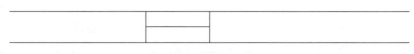

F I G U R E 7 . 1 7 : Completed lines for the window block

The three lines you've drawn will make up a window block. They represent the two jamb lines and the glass (usually called *glazing*). When inserted, by varying the X scale factor from 2 to 6, you will be able to create windows 2', 3', 4', and 6' wide.

Before you create the block, you need to decide the best place for the insertion point. For the doors, you chose the hinge point because you always know where it will be in the drawing. Locating a similar strategic point for the window is a little more difficult, but certainly possible. We know the insertion point can't be on the horizontal line representing the glazing, because it will always rest in the middle of the wall, and there is no guideline in the drawing for the middle of the wall. Windows are usually dimensioned to the midpoint of the glazing line rather than to either jamb line, so we don't want the insertion point to be at the endpoint of a jamb line. The insertion point will need to be positioned on a wall line but also lined up with the midpoint of the glazing line.

To locate this point, draw a guideline from the midpoint of the glazing line straight to one of the wall lines.

1. Press ↵ to restart the Line command. Move to a point near the midpoint of the glazing line. When the midpoint symbol appears, click.

2. Move to the bottom wall line. When the Perpendicular symbol appears, click. A guideline is drawn from the midpoint of the glazing line that is perpendicular to the lower wall line (Figure 7.18). The lower endpoint of this line is the location of the window block insertion point. Press ↵ to end the Line command. Now you are ready to define the window block.

Guideline

F I G U R E 7 . 1 8 : The guideline is completed.

3. Type b ↵ to start the Block command. In the dialog box, type **win-1** for the block name. Then click the Pick Point button.

4. Back in the drawing, with Endpoint, Midpoint, and Perpendicular Osnaps running, move the cursor to the lower end of the guideline you just drew. When the Endpoint symbol appears at that location, click.

If only the Perpendicular Osnap symbol appears, click Endpoint of the Object Snap toolbar, then try again.

5. In the dialog box, click the Select Objects button.

6. Back in the drawing, select the two jamb lines and the glazing line, but don't select the guideline whose endpoint locates the insertion point. Press ↵.

7. Back in the dialog box, click the radio button next to Delete. Then click OK. The win-1 block has been defined, and the 12" window has been erased.

8. Erase the guideline with the Erase command.

9. Zoom Previous to zoom out to a view of the whole floor plan.

This completes the definition of the block that will represent the windows. The next task is to insert the win-1 block where the windows will be located.

Inserting the Window Block

Several factors come into play when deciding where to locate windows in a floor plan:

▶ The structure of the building

▶ The appearance of windows from outside the building

▶ The appearance of windows from inside a room

▶ The location of fixtures that may interfere with placement

▶ The sun angle and climate considerations

For this exercise, we will work on the windows for each room, starting with the bedroom.

Rotating a Block during Insertion

The bedroom has windows on two walls: two 3' windows centered in the front wall 12" apart, and one 4' window centered in the left wall (Figure 7.19). You'll make the 4' window first.

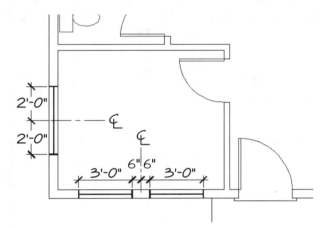

FIGURE 7.19: The bedroom windows

1. Use a zoom window to zoom into a view of the bedroom similar to that of Figure 7.19. Click the Polar button on the Status bar to turn on Polar tracking. Polar, Osnap, and Model should now be in the On position.

2. Create a new layer by clicking the Layer button and then clicking the New button in the Layer Properties Manager dialog box. Layer1 will appear and be highlighted. Type **Windows** ↵ to rename Layer1.

3. Click the color square in the Windows row. When the Select Color dialog box comes up, White will be highlighted in the Color text box. Type **30** ↵ to change the color to a bright orange. (If you don't have 256 colors available, choose any color.) The Select Color dialog box will close.

4. With Windows still highlighted in the Layers Properties Manager dialog box, click the Current button to make the Windows layer current. Then click OK. You are returned to your drawing, and Windows is the current layer.

5. Start the Insert command (it's on the Draw toolbar). Open the Name drop-down list in the Insert dialog box. In the list of blocks, click win-1.

Be sure all three of the Specify On-screen check boxes are selected, then click OK.

6. In your drawing, the 12" window block is attached to the cursor at the insertion point (Figure 7.20). Note that it is still in the same horizontal orientation that it was in when you defined the block. To fit into the left wall, you will need to rotate it as you insert it.

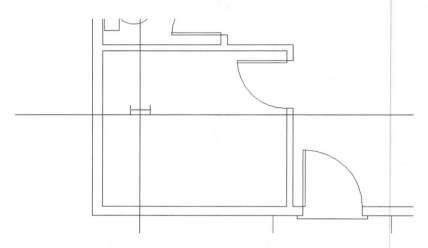

FIGURE 7.20: The win-1 block attached to the cursor

7. Move the cursor near the midpoint of the left inside wall line. When a colored triangle appears at the midpoint of that wall line, click.

8. You will be prompted for an *X* scale factor. This is a 4' window, so type 4 ↵. For the *Y* scale factor, type 1 ↵.

> The *Y* scale factor will be 1 for all the win-1 blocks because all walls that have windows are 6" wide— the same width as the win-1 block.

9. You are prompted for the rotation angle. The window block is now 4' wide and rotates with movement of the cursor. Move the cursor so that it's directly to the right of the insertion point. The Polar tracking lines and tooltip appear (Figure 7.21a). This will show you how the window will be positioned if the rotation stays at 0°. Obviously, you don't want this.

10. Move the cursor so that it is directly above the insertion point. Another tracking line and tooltip appear. This shows what position a 90° rotation will result in (Figure 7.21b). The window fits nicely into the wall here.

11. With the tracking line and tooltip visible, click. The win-1 block is placed in the left wall. The Insert command ends (Figure 7.21c).

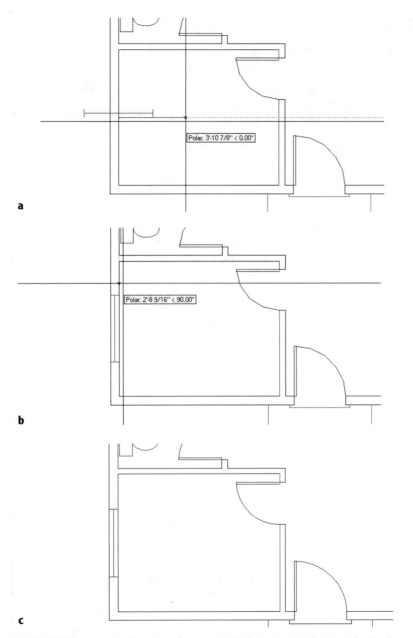

Polar: 3'-10 7/8" < 0.00°

a

Polar: 2'-8 9/16" < 90.00°

b

c

FIGURE 7.21: Rotating the win-1 block 0° (a), 90° (b), and the final position (c)

Using Guidelines When Inserting a Block

The pair of windows in the front wall of the bedroom are 3' wide, 12" apart, and centered horizontally in the bedroom wall (refer to Figure 7.19). You can use a guideline to locate the insertion points for these two windows.

1. Start the Line command and locate the cursor on the inside, horizontal exterior wall line near its midpoint. When the colored triangle appears at the midpoint of this line, click. A line starts.

2. Hold the cursor at a point a few feet below the first point of the line. When the Polar tracking line and tooltip appear, click. Press ↵ to end the Line command. This establishes a guideline at the center of the wall. The insertion points for each window will be at its center. The distance between the center of the wall and the insertion point will be half the width of the window, plus half the distance between the windows, in other words, 2 feet.

3. Offset the line that you just drew 2' to the right and left (Figure 7.22). Now you have established the locations for the insertion points of the win-1 blocks, and you are ready to insert them.

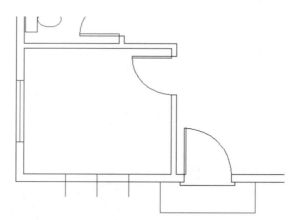

FIGURE 7.22: Guidelines for the pair of window blocks

4. Click the Insert button on the Draw toolbar to start the Insert command. In the Insert dialog box, the win-1 block will still be displayed in the Name drop-down list because it was the last block inserted. Click OK.

5. Back in the drawing, the win-1 block is again attached to the cursor. To locate the insertion point, you can choose the upper endpoint of one of the outer guidelines, or the intersection of this guideline with

the exterior outside wall line. Which one would be better? The second choice requires no rotation of the block, so it's easier and faster to use that intersection.

6. Click the Intersection Osnap button on the Object Snap toolbar and position the cursor on the outside wall (Figure 7.23a). A colored × appears with three dots to its right, along with a tooltip that says "Extended Intersection." Click. Now hold the crosshair cursor on the lower portion of the leftmost offset guideline, again without touching any other lines. The × will appear, this time at the intersection of this guideline with the outside wall line, and without the three dots. The tooltip now says "Intersection" (Figure 7.23b). Click again. The insertion point is set at the intersection of the guideline and the outside wall line.

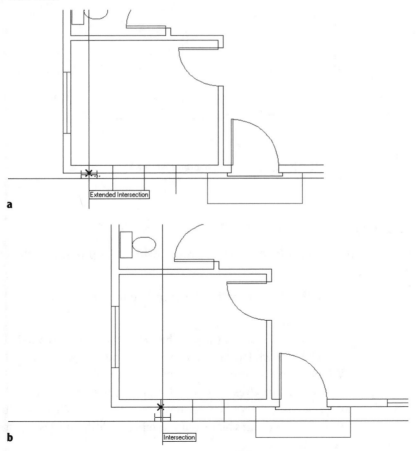

FIGURE 7.23: Selecting the first line (a), and the second (b)

7. Type 3 ↵ for the *X* scale factor, then type 1 ↵ for the *Y* scale factor. At the rotation angle prompt, press ↵ to accept the default of 0°. The 3' window on the left is inserted in the front wall.

8. Repeat this procedure for the other 3' window.

9. Erase the three guidelines.

Because you chose to locate the insertion point on the lower of the two wall lines, the block needed no rotation. When finished, the bedroom will look like Figure 7.24.

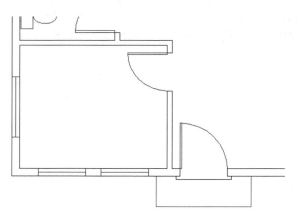

FIGURE 7.24: The bedroom with all windows inserted

Using Tracking to Insert a Block

The next room to work on is the bathroom, which has one small window over the sink.

1. Click the Pan button on the Standard toolbar. The cursor changes to a hand.

2. Position the hand on the wall between the bedroom and bathroom, then hold down the left mouse button and drag the drawing down. When the bathroom is in the middle of the drawing area, release the mouse button. Press Esc or ↵ to cancel the Pan command. You want to create one 2' window, centered over the sink. This time you'll insert the block without the use of guidelines. Endpoint Osnap should be running.

3. Start the Insert command, be sure win-1 is in the Name drop-down list, and check that all Specify On-screen check boxes are marked. Then click OK and, at the `Specify insertion point:` prompt, click the Temporary Tracking Point button on the Object Snap toolbar.

4. Position the crosshair cursor on the line representing the front edge of the sink counter. A colored triangle will appear at the midpoint of that line (Figure 7.25a). When it does, click. You have set a temporary tracking point, and a cross appears at that point.

5. Move the cursor to the lower outside wall line, just in back of the sink. When the colored perpendicular symbol appears on the line (Figure 7.25b), click. The insertion point has been placed on the inside wall line, centered over the sink.

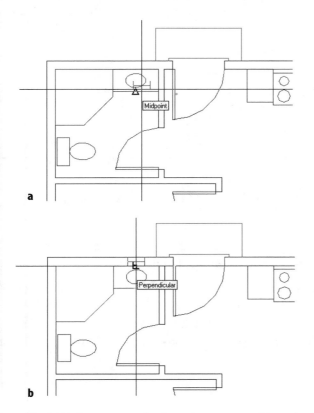

FIGURE 7.25: Setting a temporary tracking point (a), and using Perpendicular Osnap to locate the insertion point (b)

6. At the X scale factor prompt, Type 2 ↵. Then, at the Y scale factor prompt, type 1 ↵. Press ↵ again to accept the default rotation angle of 0°. The 2' window is inserted into the wall behind the sink (Figure 7.26).

Note that no mark is left at the insertion point location on the wall. You have to wait until the insertion process is over to see if everything has been done correctly. When I walk you through the next insertion, you'll learn how to change a setting so that AutoCAD will leave a mark.

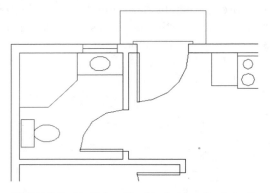

FIGURE 7.26: The 2' window after insertion

Using Blips with Point Filters to Insert Blocks

You're more than halfway done with the windows. Just three remain to be inserted: one in the kitchen and two in the living room.

1. Click the Pan button on the Standard toolbar. Then position the hand cursor on the back door swing. Hold down the left mouse button and drag the drawing over to the left until the kitchen is in the middle of the drawing area. Release the mouse button. Then press the Esc key or ↵ to cancel the Real Time Pan.

2. Zoom into the sink area. Type **blipmode** ↵, then type **on** ↵. Blipmode feature is activated.

3. You need to insert a 4' window in the back wall, centered behind the sink (see Figure 7.15). Start the Insert command. Click OK when the Insert dialog box comes up. The win-1 block appears on the cursor.

4. At the Specify insertion point: prompt, type .x ↵ to activate the point filters. You need to pick the midpoint of the back or front edge of the sink. Since the front edge is more accessible, select that one.

5. Put the target box on the front edge of the sink. When the colored triangle appears on the front edge, click. A small + is placed at the midpoint of the front edge of the sink (Figure 7.27a). This is called a *blip* or a *blipmark*.

6. Click the Nearest Osnap, then position the target box on the inside wall line of the back wall where it's not touching any other lines. When an hourglass symbol appears on the wall line, click. The + is placed where you clicked the wall line and at a position on the wall line directly behind the midpoint of the sink's back edge (Figure 7.27b). This assures you that the point filters successfully set the insertion point exactly where you need it.

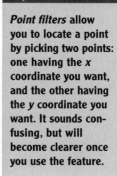

Point filters allow you to locate a point by picking two points: one having the *x* coordinate you want, and the other having the *y* coordinate you want. It sounds confusing, but will become clearer once you use the feature.

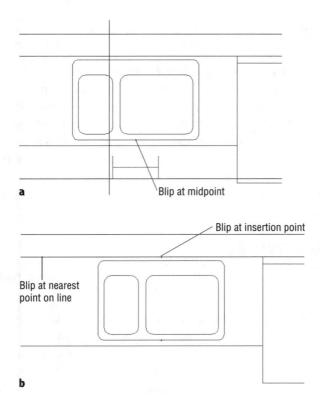

FIGURE 7.27: A blip marks the midpoint of the front edge of the sink (a), and the resulting insertion point location (b)

7. Type 4 ↵ for the *X* scale factor. Then type **1** ↵ for the *Y* scale factor. For the rotation angle, press ↵ again to accept the default angle of 0°. The window is placed in the back wall, centered behind the sink.

8. Zoom Previous (Figure 7.28).

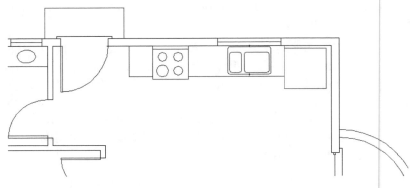

FIGURE 7.28: The inserted window behind the sink

You can also redraw the screen and get rid of blips by choosing View ≻ Redraw.

When Blipmode is on, a + is placed wherever you pick a point in the drawing area, whether you are drawing or selecting objects. These are temporary markers and are not saved with the drawing file, nor do they show up in printouts. As they accumulate, you can delete them by typing **r** ↵ at the Command: prompt, or by any use of the Zoom or Pan commands. Using blips is up to you. Some people find them irritating and would rather not see them. Others find them useful because they are a record of what you've done, as you just saw when placing an insertion point. Let's leave them visible through the next two sections so you can see how you feel about them.

Finishing the Windows

The last two windows to insert are both in the front wall of the living room. You will use skills you've already worked with to place them.

1. Use the Pan command to move the drawing down to the front wall of the living room. One window is 6' wide. Its right jamb is 12" to the left of the inside corner of the wall. The other one is a circular window, 2' in diameter, positioned halfway between the 6' window jamb and the front doorjamb (Figure 7.29). We don't know that distance yet.

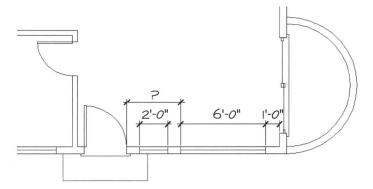

FIGURE 7.29: The windows in the front wall of the living room

2. Turn off Perpendicular and Midpoint running osnaps. (To review how to do this, go back to the section in which you created the win-1 block.) Start the Insert command and click OK in the Insert dialog box to select the win-1 block.

3. Select the Temporary Tracking Point Osnap button. Then, with Endpoint Osnap running, pick the lower right inside corner of the cabin. The insertion point will be positioned to the left of this corner at a distance of 12" in plus half the width of the 6' window, in other words, 4' from the corner.

4. Hold the crosshair cursor directly to the left of the point just picked. When the tracking path and tooltip appear, type 4' ↵. This sets the insertion point 4' to the left of the corner, on the inside wall line. A blip appears there.

5. For the scale factors, type 6 ↵, then type 1 ↵.

6. For the rotation angle, hold the cursor directly to the right of the insertion point to see the position of the window at 0° rotation. Then hold the cursor directly above the insertion point to see how a 90° rotation would look. Finally, hold the cursor directly to the left for a view of the effect of a 180° rotation. The 180-degree view is the one you want.

7. Type 180 ↵. The 6' window is placed in the front wall.

Finally, you need to locate the 2' circular window halfway between the left jamb of the 6' window and the right jamb of the front door opening. Use the Distance command to find out the distance between the two jambs. Then offset

> To turn Osnaps off, right-click Osnap in the Status bar, choose Settings from the menu, then uncheck any osnaps that are checked. Then click OK.

one of the jambs half that distance to establish the location of the insertion point on the wall lines. Of the two jamb lines, you must offset the doorjamb because the window jamb is part of the window block and can't be offset.

1. Type **di** ↵ to start the Distance command. With Endpoint Osnap running, pick the upper end of the front doorjamb, then pick the upper end of the left window jamb. In the Command window, the distance is displayed as 3'-10". You need to offset the doorjamb half that distance to locate the insertion point for the 2' window.

2. Start the Offset command, then type **1'-11** ↵ to set the offset distance.

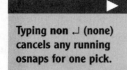

Typing **non** ↵ (none) cancels any running osnaps for one pick.

3. Pick the doorjamb and type **non** ↵. Then pick a point to the right of the doorjamb. Press ↵ to end the Offset command.

4. Start the Insert command. Click OK to accept the win-1 block. Pick the bottom endpoint of the offset jamb line to establish the insertion point.

5. Type **2** ↵ for the *X* scale factor. Type **1** ↵ for the *Y* scale factor.

6. For the rotation angle, press ↵ to accept the default of 0°. The last window is inserted in the front wall, and the Insert command ends. Erase the offset jamb line (Figure 7.30).

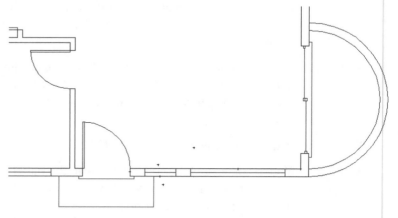

FIGURE 7.30: The two windows inserted in the front wall of the living room

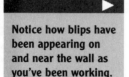

Notice how blips have been appearing on and near the wall as you've been working.

7. Type **r** ↵ to use the Redraw command to refresh the screen. The blips disappear.

8. Type z ↵ e ↵ to zoom out to the Extents view of the drawing. This changes the view to include all the visible lines. The view fills the drawing area.

9. Type z ↵ .85x ↵ to zoom out a little from the Extents view, so all objects are set in slightly from the edge of the drawing area (Figure 7.31).

Zooming to *Extents* is one of the zoom options, and is the bottom button of the Zoom flyout on the Standard toolbar.

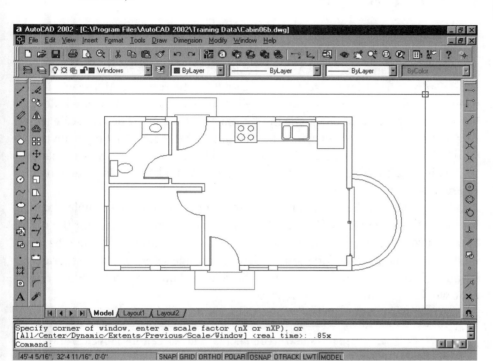

FIGURE 7.31: Zooming to .85× after zooming to Extents

10. Save this drawing as Cabin07a.

You have inserted seven windows into the floor plan, each of them generated from the win-1 block. You created the win-1 block on the 0 layer and then made the Windows layer current, so each window block reference took on the characteristics of the Windows layer when it was inserted.

Blocks can be ungrouped by using the *Explode* command. Exploding a block has the effect of reducing the block to the objects that make it up. For the win-1 block, exploding it would reduce it to three lines, all on the 0 layer. If you exploded one of the door blocks, it would be reduced to a rectangle and an arc, with both objects on the Doors layer because these components of the door block were on the Doors layer when the block was defined.

Revising a Block

If you need to revise a block that has already been inserted in the drawing several times, explode one of these blocks and then modify it. You will need to choose a block whose parameters—the X and Y scale factors, and the rotation—were all at the default values: 1 for the scale factors and 0 for the rotation. All the windows were inserted using different X and Y scale factors, so to revise the win-1 block, we'll need to insert that block one more time, this time using default scale factors and rotation. Then you can make changes to the objects that make up the win-1 block reference. When finished with the changes, you can save the changes to the block definition. This redefines the block and updates all associated block references.

Let's say that the client who's building the cabin finds out that double glazing is required in all windows. You want the windows to show two lines for the glass. You can't make such a change in each window block because blocks can't be modified in this way, and you don't want to have to change seven windows separately. If you revise the win-1 block definition, the changes you make in one block reference will be made in all seven windows.

 N O T E   Using standard commands, blocks can be moved, rotated, copied, erased, scaled, and exploded. They can't be trimmed, extended, offset, or filleted, and you can't erase or move part of a block. All objects in a block are grouped together and behave as if they were one object.

1. Start the Insert command and click OK to accept the win-1 block to be inserted.

2. Pick a point in the middle of the living room. This establishes the insertion point location.

3. Press ⌡ three times to accept the defaults for X and Y scale factors and the rotation angle. The win-1 block is inserted in the living room (Figure 7.32).

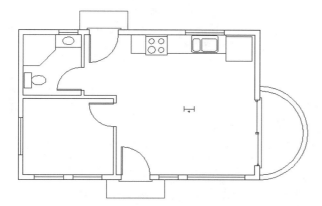

FIGURE 7.32: The win-1 block inserted into the living room

4. Zoom into a closer view of the window, then choose Modify ➢ In-place Xref and Block Edit ➢ Edit reference.

5. Select the new block reference in the middle of the living room. The Reference Edit dialog box comes up. The win-1 block is identified and a preview is displayed.

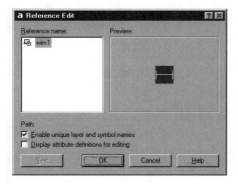

6. Click OK. You are prompted to select nested objects.

7. Select the glazing line in the win-1 block, then press ↵. The glazing line turns white (or black) and the Refedit toolbar appears.

8. Use the Offset command to offset the glazing line 0.5" up and down. Then erase the original horizontal line (Figure 7.33). This window block now has double-glazing.

FIGURE 7.33: The result of the modifications to the win-1 block

 9. On the right side of the Refedit toolbar, click the rightmost button, whose tooltip says "Save back changes to reference."

10. An AutoCAD warning window appears. Click OK. The glazing lines change back to orange and the Refedit toolbar disappears, and the blips are deleted. The block definition has been revised.

11. Erase this block reference; we don't need it any more.

12. Zoom Previous to view the entire drawing. All windows in the cabin now have double glazing.

13. Zoom into a closer look at the bedroom in order to view some of the modified window block references (Figure 7.34).

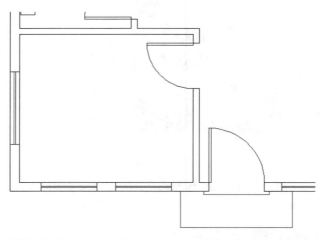

FIGURE 7.34: Zooming in to see the revised window blocks with double glazing

14. This is a good time to turn off the blips if you find them more of a nuisance than an aid. To turn them off, type **blipmode** ↵, then type **off** ↵.

15. Zoom Previous to a view of the entire floor plan. Save this drawing as Cabin07b.

Sharing Information Between Drawings

Most information in a drawing can be transferred to another drawing. There are several ways of doing this, depending on the kind of information that needs to be transferred. Blocks and lines can be dragged over from one open drawing to another when both drawings are visible on the screen. Layers, blocks, and other *named objects* can be copied out of a closed drawing into an open one using the Design Center. We'll demonstrate these two features as we end this chapter.

Dragging and Dropping between Two Open Drawings

AutoCAD is capable of supporting several drawings open at the same time, just like a word processor. You can control which one is visible, or tile two or more to be visible simultaneously. When more than one drawing is visible at once, objects can be dragged from one drawing to another.

1. With Cabin07b as the current drawing, click the New button on the Standard toolbar. In the Create New drawing dialog box, click the Start From Scratch button and click OK.

2. Choose Window ➤ Tile Vertically. The new drawing (called Drawing1) appears alongside Cabin07b (Figure 7.35).

   Each drawing has a title bar, but only one drawing can be active at a time. At this time, Drawing1 should be the active one. If it is, its title bar will be dark blue or some other color, and the Cabin07b title bar will be grayed out. If your Cabin07b drawing is active instead, click once in Drawing1.

Named objects are, quite simply, Auto-CAD objects with names, like blocks and layers. Lines, circles, and arcs don't have individual names, so they are not named objects.

Like most Windows-based programs, AutoCAD 2002 can have multiple drawing files open in a session. When you open the Window menu, the bottom of the menu contains a list of AutoCAD files currently open. Click the file you want to be the current one.

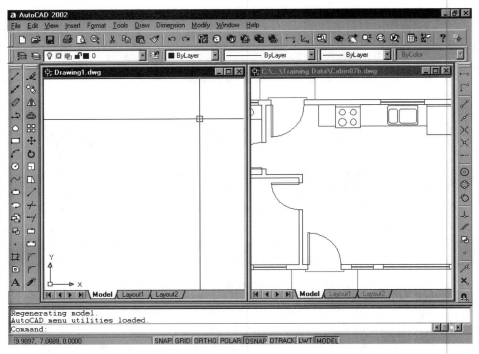

FIGURE 7.35: The user interface with two drawings tiled

3. Choose Format ➤ Units. In the Drawing Units dialog box, change the type of units in the Length area to Architectural, then click OK.

4. Click the Cabin07b drawing to make it the active drawing.

5. Zoom to Extents, then use Realtime Zoom to zoom out a little.

6. Use the Layer Control drop-down list to turn off the Doors, Fixtures, Steps, and Windows layers, and to make the Walls layer current. The walls and balcony should be the only lines visible.

7. Form a selection window to surround the cabin with its balcony. Grips will appear on all lines.

8. Place the cursor on one of the wall lines at a point where there are no grips, then click and hold down the left mouse button. Drag the cursor across the drawing to the center of Drawing1, then release the mouse button. Drawing1 is now active and contains the lines for the walls and balcony.

9. Zoom to Extents in Drawing1, then type **ucsicon** ↵ **off** ↵ (Figure 7.36).

10. Open the Layer Property Manager and note that Drawing1 now has the Walls and Balcony layers.

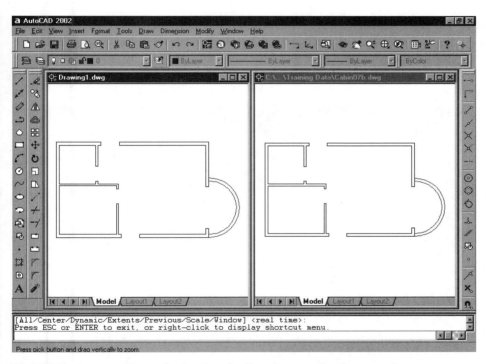

FIGURE 7.36: The result after dragging lines from one drawing to another

Any visible objects can be dragged in this fashion from one drawing into another, including blocks. If you *drag and drop* a block, its definition will be copied over to the new drawing, along with all layers used by objects in the block. If you use the right mouse button to make the drag, you get a few options as to how to place the objects in the receiving drawing.

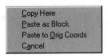

If you don't choose to have both open drawings visible at the same time, you can always use the Copy and Paste tools available on most Windows-based programs. Here's the general procedure:

1. Click the Maximize icon in the upper-right corner of the new drawing. The new drawing will fill the screen.

2. Click Window in the pull-down menu bar. When the menu opens up, notice at the bottom that the open drawings are displayed with the active one checked (Figure 7.37).

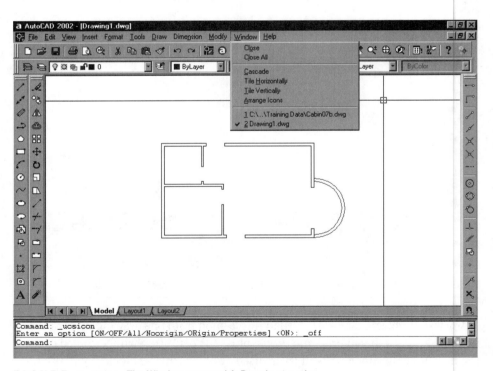

FIGURE 7.37: The Window menu with Drawing1 active

3. Click the Cabin07b drawing. It replaces Drawing1 as the active draw-
    ing and fills the screen. Turn back on the layers you turned off previ-
    ously. Leave the Headers and Roof layers frozen.

4. Select objects from this drawing, then right-click. In the menu that
    appears, select Copy or Copy with Base Point. If you choose Copy
    with Base Point, you will be prompted to specify a base point in the
    Cabin07b drawing.

5. Click Window in the pull-down menu bar. When the menu opens up,
    click Drawing1 to make it active.

6. Click the Paste button on the Standard toolbar. Pick a point in the
    drawing to locate the copied objects.

Using AutoCAD's Design Center

Design Center is a tool for copying named objects (block, layers, text styles,
etc.) to an opened drawing from an unopened one. Lines, circles, and other
unnamed objects cannot be copied unless they are part of a block. We'll demonstrate this feature by bringing some layers and a block into Drawing1 from
Cabin07b.

1. Close Cabin07b. Do not save changes. Maximize the window for
    Drawing1 if it is not already maximized.

2. Click the Design Center button on the Standard toolbar. It's just to
    the left of the Properties button. The Design Center appears on the
    drawing area. It may be docked or floating (Figure 7.38). Your screen
    may not look exactly like the samples shown here. The tree diagram
    of file folders on the left half may or may not be visible. Your Design
    Center may be wider or narrower.

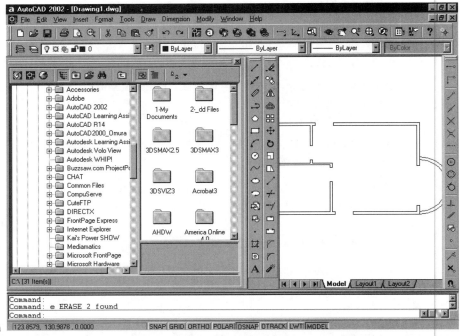

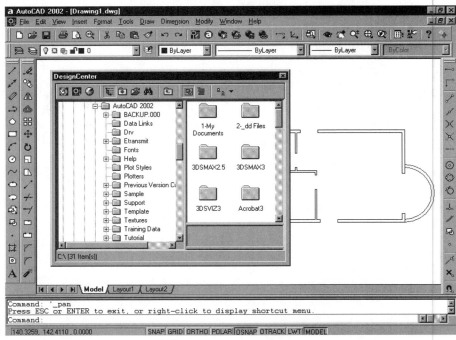

FIGURE 7.38: The Design Center docked (a) and floating (b)

3. Click the Tree View Toggle at the top of the Design Center to close and open the file folder tree diagram. Notice that when it's open, more buttons are visible at the top on the left. The Design Center can be resized horizontally (and vertically as well, if it is floating). Leave the Tree View open.

4. Use the same procedure you would in Windows Explorer to navigate to the AutoCAD 2002 folder, open it, then click your Training Data folder to open it (Figure 7.39a). If yours is stored somewhere else, navigate to its location and click it to open it. On the right side of the Design Center, the drawings in your Training Data folder are displayed, either in icon or listed form.

5. On the right side, find Cabin07b and double-click it. Now the left side displays a list of your drawings in the Training Data folder with Cabin07b highlighted, and the right side shows the types of objects in Cabin07b that are available to be copied into the current drawing—in this case, Drawing1 (Figure 7.39b).

6. Double-click the Layers symbol. Now the individual layers are displayed on the right side and a list of available types of objects is displayed on the left, under Cabin07b (Figure 7.39c).

7. Click the Views button above the right window of the Design Center. This changes the view of layers displayed below. It's a four-way toggle. Click until you get a view of the layers in a list.

8. Use the Shift+ and Ctrl+ keys to help you select all the layers except 0, Balcony, and Walls (Figure 7.40).

9. Right-click somewhere on the highlighted layers in the right window. Pick Add Layers from the shortcut menu that appears.

10. Open the Layer Control drop-down list on the Object Properties toolbar. It will now display all the layers of the Cabin07b drawing, including those you just transferred.

◄

If you prefer dragging and dropping, use the left mouse button, click and hold, drag the cursor onto the drawing, then release.

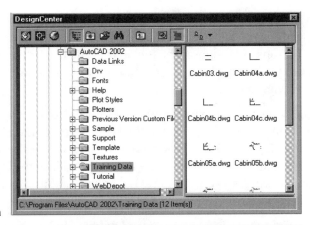

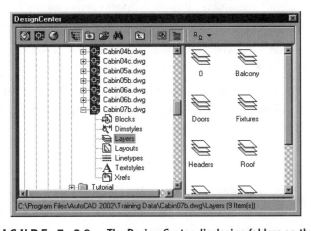

FIGURE 7.39: The Design Center displaying folders on the left and files on the right (a), files on the left and types of accessible objects on the right (b), and types of accessible objects on the left and actual accessible layers on the right (c)

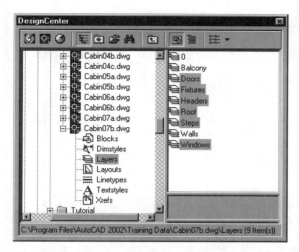

FIGURE 7.40: The Design Center with layers to grab highlighted

Now let's see how this process works when we want to get a block from another drawing.

1. On the left side of the Design Center, click Blocks in the list under the Cabin07b drawing. On the right side, the list of blocks in that drawing is displayed (Figure 7.41a).

2. Click on the Preview button at the top of the Design Center, then click on door3_0. A picture of the block is displayed in the lower-right corner of the Design Center (Figure 7.41b). The preview picture window can be resized.

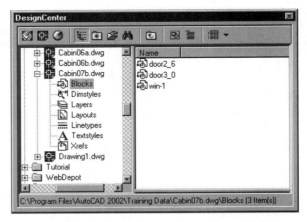

a

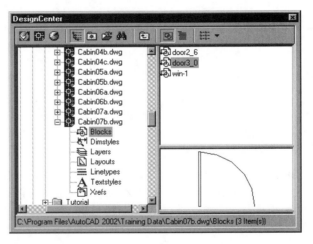

b

FIGURE 7.41: The Design Center with Blocks selected (a) and with the door3_0 block selected and Preview on (b)

3. Open the Layer Control list and make Doors the current layer.

4. Dock Design Center on the left side of the drawing area if it's not already there, then zoom into the front door area of the drawing (Figure 7.42).

5. In the Design Center, left-click and drag door3_0 from the list over to the drawing. As the cursor comes onto the drawing, the door3_0 block appears. Use Endpoint Osnap to locate the block at the opening, as you did earlier in the chapter (Figure 7.43).

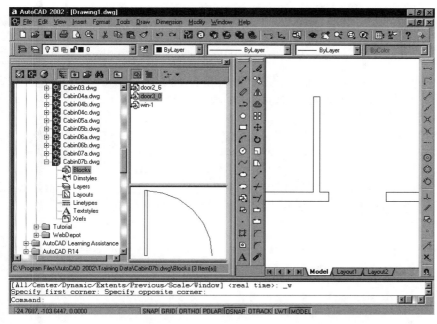

FIGURE 7.42: Zoomed into the front door area with the Design Center docked

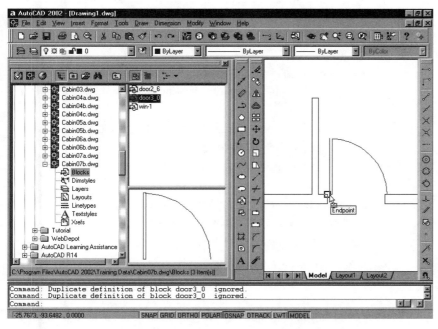

FIGURE 7.43: Dragging the door3_0 block into Drawing1 from the Design Center

6. Click the Close icon in the upper-right corner to close Design Center.

7. Keep Drawing1 open in case you want to use it in the practice exercises at the end of the chapter. Otherwise, close it without saving it.

By doing this insertion, the door3_0 block is now a part of Drawing1 and you can reinsert it in that drawing without Design Center.

The Design Center is a very simple yet powerful tool. Its function is to find named objects in unopened drawings that you have access to, and pull them into your current drawing. These drawings may be located on your hard drive, on a network, or on the Internet. At the top of the Design Center window, the buttons on the left are tools for navigating through drives and folders to find the files you need to access; the buttons on the right give you options for viewing the named objects in the window.

DESIGN CENTER OPTIONS

Here's a brief description of the functions of the Design Center buttons, from left to right:

Desktop: Makes the left window display the regular Windows Explorer–type file tree that can include drive, folder, subfolders, drawing files, and object types.

Open Drawings: Displays a list of currently open drawings, and will show object types.

History: Displays a list of the last few drawings that were opened, along with their paths. When this is open, the viewing palette window on the right is temporarily closed.

Tree View Toggle: Opens or shuts the left window, and controls the visibility of the three previous buttons.

Favorites: Displays the list of favorite files and folders that you have previously set up.

Load: Opens a file selection dialog box where you can navigate to a drawing whose contents you wish to view.

Find: Opens the Find dialog box where you can search for a particular file.

Up: In the left window, moves up one level in the tree from the highlighted item.

Preview: Enables a preview window at the bottom of the right *palette window*. When you highlight a drawing or block in the palette window, a preview is displayed. The preview window may be resized.

Continued on next page

Description: Enables a previously written description of a block or drawing to be displayed. The description window may be resized.

Views: Controls how the item in the palette window are displayed. There are four choices. Each click on this button toggles from one type of view to another. When you click the arrow to the right, the list of four options is displayed.

Other Ways to Share Information Between Drawings

There are two other ways to transfer information between drawings that deserve mention. First, you can use the Wblock command to take a portion of a drawing and create a new drawing file from the selected objects. Second, any .dwg drawing file can be inserted into any other drawing file. I'll summarize the two procedures below.

Wblocking

To perform a Wblock operation, you create a new file, then tell AutoCAD what elements of the current drawing you want in the new file. Let's say you want to create a new .dwg file for the bathroom of the cabin. Here are the steps to accomplish this:

1. With Cabin07b as the current drawing, type w ↵. The Write Block dialog box comes up (Figure 7.44).

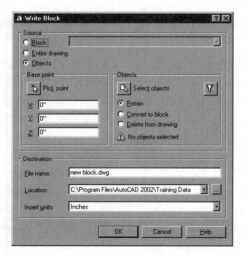

FIGURE 7.44: The Wblock dialog box

When you select with a crossing window here, you'll get more than you need, but you can clean up the new drawing later.

2. At the top, in the Source area, select the Objects radio button.

3. In the middle portion, the Base Point and Objects choices are similar to those for creating a block. For the Base Point, the default is 0,0. Click the Pick Point button and, in the drawing, pick a point just below and to the left of the area to be captured. For the Objects, click Select Objects and use a crossing window to select everything near the part of the drawing you want. For the radio button in this area, choose Retain so the selected material is not deleted from the current drawing.

4. In the Destination area, enter a filename for the new drawing and choose a folder in which to save it.

5. The units in the Insert Units drop-down list should be set to Inches, in case the new drawing is used in a drawing that has units other than Architectural.

6. Click OK. The command ends and the selected material is now a new drawing file located in the folder that you specified.

There are three ways to use the Wblock command. The other two are shown as radio buttons at the top of the Wblock dialog box. Here's a brief description of them.

▶ Block: For making a drawing file out of a block that's defined in the current drawing. You will select the name of the block from the drop-down list at the top, then follow the same procedure described in steps 4–6 above. When this procedure is followed, the objects in the new drawing are no longer in a block. Wblocking a block has the effect of unblocking it.

▶ Entire Drawing: For *purging* a drawing of unwanted objects such as layers that have no objects on them and block definitions that have no references in the drawing. You are not prompted to select anything except the information called for in steps 4–6 above. You can keep the same drawing name or type in a new one.

Inserting a Drawing into a Drawing

When you insert a drawing into another drawing, it comes in as a block. You use the same Insert command that you use to insert blocks, in a slightly different way. For example, say you have wblocked a portion of Cabin07b.dwg and made a new file called Bath.dwg (see previous section). Now you want to insert Bath into DrawingC.dwg. Use this procedure:

1. Make DrawingC current.

2. Start the Insert command.

3. In the Insert dialog box, click the Browse button, then navigate to the folder containing `Bath.dwg`.

4. Open that folder, highlight `Bath.dwg`, then click Open.

5. The Insert dialog box comes up again, this time with the drawing file that you selected now displayed in the name drop-down list. At this point Bath has been converted into a block definition in `DrawingC`.

6. Set the insertion parameters in the dialog box, then click OK.

7. Finish the insertion procedure as if you were inserting block..

Blocks are transferred between drawings by dragging and dropping or by use of the Design Center. They can also be converted into .dwg files by use of the Wblock command, and inserted back into other .dwg files as blocks by use of the Insert command. So they become unblocked when they leave the drawing and reblocked when they enter another drawing.

This chapter has outlined the procedure for setting up and using blocks, the Wblock command, and AutoCAD's Design Center. Blocks follow a set of complex rules, some of which are beyond the scope of this book. For a more in-depth discussion on blocks, refer to *Mastering AutoCAD 2002* by George Omura (Sybex, 2001).

If You Want More Practice...

Here are a couple of suggestions that will give you practice working with blocks, drag-and-drop procedures, and the Design Center:

▶ Use Design Center to bring the door2_6 and win_1 blocks into `Drawing1`. Position the win-1 blocks into new locations in the walls of this drawing. Then open `Cabin07b` and drag and drop the kitchen and bathroom fixtures into `Drawing1`.

▶ Make blocks out of any of the fixtures in the bathroom or kitchen. Try to decide on the best location to use for the insertion point of each fixture. Then insert them back into the `Cabin07b` drawing in their original locations. Create them on the 0 layer, then insert them on the Fixtures layer. Here's a list of the fixtures:

1. Shower

2. Bath sink

3. Toilet

    4. Oven/range

    5. Kitchen sink

    6. Refrigerator

▶ At the end of Chapter 5, *Gaining Drawing Strategies: Part 2*, I suggested creating pieces of furniture for the kitchen, living room, and bedroom of the cabin. If you did that, it will be good practice to make blocks out of those pieces and insert them into the cabin floor plan. If you did not do that exercise, you could do that now and then convert them into blocks.

▶ If you have access to the sample files that come with AutoCAD 2002, use Design Center to find the drawing called db_sam.dwg and view the blocks and layers inside it. Freeze the Doors layer in the Cabin drawing, then transfer some of the office furniture and door blocks into the cabin floor plan and see how the cabin might work as a small office.

Are You Experienced?

Now you can...

☑ **create blocks out of existing objects in your drawing**

☑ **insert blocks into your drawing**

☑ **vary the size and rotation of blocks as they are inserted**

☑ **detect blocks in a drawing**

☑ **use point filters to locate an insertion point**

☑ **revise a block**

☑ **drag and drop objects from one drawing to another**

☑ **use AutoCAD's Design Center**

☑ **use the Wblock command**

CHAPTER 8

Generating Elevations

- ▶ Drawing an exterior elevation from a floor plan

- ▶ Using grips to copy objects

- ▶ Setting up, naming, and saving a User Coordinate System and a new view

- ▶ Transferring height lines from one elevation to another

- ▶ Moving and rotating elevations

Now that you have created all the building components that will be in the floor plan, it's a good time to draw the exterior elevations. *Elevations* are horizontal views of the building, seen as if you were standing facing the building instead of looking down at it, as you do in the floor plan. An elevation view shows you how windows and doors fit into the walls, and gives you an idea of how the building will look from the outside. In most design projects, the drawings include at least four exterior elevations: front, back, and one from each side. We'll go over how to create the front elevation first. Then we'll discuss some of the considerations necessary to complete the other ones, and you will have the chance to draw these on your own. Finally, we will look at how interior elevations are set up. They are similar to exterior elevations, but are usually of individual walls on the inside of a building to show how objects, such as doors, windows, cabinets, shelves, and finishes will be placed on the walls.

Drawing the Front Elevation

The front elevation is drawn using techniques very similar to those used on a traditional drafting board. You will draw the front elevation view of the cabin directly below the floor plan by dropping lines down from key points on the floor plan and intersecting them with horizontal lines representing the heights of the corresponding components in the elevation. Those heights are shown in Figure 8.1.

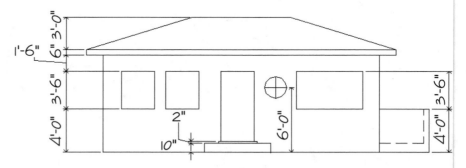

FIGURE 8.1:   The front elevation with heights of components

1. Open Cabin07b.

2. Create a new layer called F-elev. Assign it color 42 and make it current. Here's a summary of the steps to do this:

   A. Click the Layers button, then click New.

   B. Type **F-elev** and press ↵.

   C. Click the colored square for the F-elev layer. Type 42 ↵.

   D. Click Current, then click OK.

3. Thaw the Roof and Headers layers. Then offset the bottom horizontal roofline 24' down. The offset line will be off the screen.

4. Click the Zoom Extents button on the Zoom flyout toolbar.

5. Use Realtime Zoom to zoom out just enough to bring the offset roofline up off the bottom edge of the drawing area.

6. Erase this offset line. Your drawing should look like Figure 8.2.

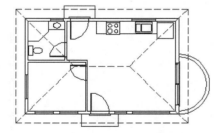

F I G U R E   8 . 2 :   The floor plan with space below it for the front elevation

Setting Up Lines for the Heights

You need to establish a base line to represent the ground. Then you can offset the other height lines from the base line or from other height lines.

1. Check the Status bar to see that Polar, Osnap, and Model are in the On position while the other buttons are off. Draw a horizontal ground line across the bottom of the screen using the Line command. Make sure the line extends on the left to a few feet beyond a point directly below the outside edge of the roof, and on the right to a few feet beyond a point directly below the right edge of the balcony (Figure 8.3).

Ground line

F I G U R E   8 . 3 :   **The floor plan with the ground line**

2. Offset the ground line 10" up to mark the height of the step. Then offset this new line 2" up to mark the top of the threshold.

3. Move back to the ground line and offset it 4' up to mark the top of the balcony wall and the bottom of the windows.

4. Offset the bottom line for the windows 3'-6" up to mark the top of the door and windows.

5. Offset the top line for the windows and door 1'-6" up to mark the soffit of the roof.

6. Offset the soffit line 6" up to mark the lower edge of the roof's top surface.

7. Offset this lower edge of the roof's top surface 3' up to mark the roof's ridge (Figure 8.4).

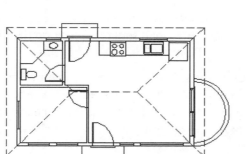

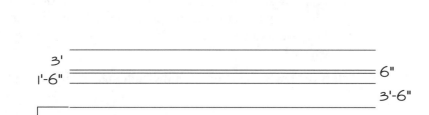

FIGURE 8.4: The horizontal height lines for the elevation in place

8. Press ↵ to end the Offset command.

Each of these lines represents the height of one or more components of the cabin. Now you will drop lines down from the points in the floor plan that coincide with components that will be visible in the front elevation. The front elevation will consist of the balcony, front step, front door, and windows, the front corners of the exterior walls, and parts of the roof.

A *soffit* is the underside of the roof overhang that extends from the outside edge of the roof back to the wall.

Using Grips to Copy Lines

In the following steps, you will learn how to use grips to copy the dropped lines.

1. Start a line from the lower-left corner of the walls of the building. Select Perpendicular Osnap and click the ground line. Press ↵ to end the Line command (Figure 8.5a).

2. At the Command: prompt, select the line you just drew. The line is selected and small squares appear on the line's midpoint and endpoints (Figure 8.5b). These are grips.

3. Click the grip on the upper endpoint. The grip changes color and the prompt changes to Specify stretch point or [Base point/ Copy/Undo/eXit]:. This is the Stretch command, which is activated by grips. Any time you activate a grip, the Stretch command automatically starts.

4. Right-click. A shortcut menu appears. Select Move. Right-click again and select Copy from the menu. This selects the Copy option. You'll use the Move command with its Copy option to copy the line that you just selected.

5. Select the lower-right corner of the building. The line is copied to this corner.

6. Select the Quadrant Osnap and click the right extremity of the outside wall line of the balcony. Another line is copied, this time to the balcony. It does not extend to the ground line because it was directly copied and therefore is the same length as the other two lines. You will extend it later.

7. Type x ↵ to end the Move command. Press Esc to remove the grips. Your drawing will resemble Figure 8.5c.

The *Stretch command* is a modifying tool that you use to lengthen or shorten lines and other objects. You'll have a chance to use it in Chapter 9, *Working with Hatches and Fills*.

Each of the commands that work with grips has a Copy option, which keeps the original object as is while you modify the copy. You can copy with grips in several ways that are not possible with the regular Copy command.

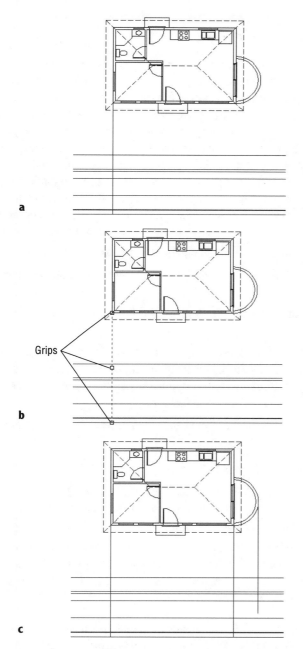

Grips

a

b

c

FIGURE 8.5: Dropping a line from the floor plan to the elevation (a), the dropped line with grips (b), and the copied lines (c)

GETTING A GRIP ON GRIPS

In Chapter 7, *Grouping Objects into Blocks,* you saw how grips could be used to detect whether an object is a block or not. They actually serve a larger function. The grips feature is a tool for editing objects quickly, using one or more of the following five commands: Stretch, Move, Rotate, Scale, or Mirror. These commands operate a little differently when using grips than when using them normally. There are a few more things the commands can do with the help of grips. Each command has a Copy option; so, for example, if you rotate an object with grips, you have the option of having the original object stay unchanged while you make multiple copies of the object in various angles of rotation. This can't be done using the Rotate command in the normal way, or by using the regular Copy command.

The steps to use grips are summarized as follows:

1. Click an object you wish to modify when no commands have been started.

2. Click the grip that will be the base point for the command's execution.

3. Right-click at this point and choose any of the five commands from the shortcut menu that comes up on the drawing area. (You can also cycle through the five commands by pressing the spacebar and watching the command prompt.)

4. When the command you need comes up, execute the necessary option.

5. Type **x** ↵ when finished.

6. Press Esc to remove the grips.

The key to being able to use grips efficiently is knowing which grip to select to start the process. This requires a good understanding of the workings of the five commands that work with grips.

This book will not cover grips in depth, but will introduce you to the basics. You will get a chance to use the Move command with grips in this chapter, and we will use grips again when we get to Chapter 11, *Dimensioning a Drawing.*

Note:

▶ Each of the five commands available for use with grips requires a base point. For Mirror, the base point is the first point of the mirror line. By default, the base point is the grip that you pick to activate the process, but you can change base points. After selecting a grip,

Continued on next page

type **b** ↵ and pick a different point to serve as a base point, then continue the command.

▶ When you use the Copy option with the Move command, you are essentially using the regular Copy command with the Multiple option.

Trimming Lines in the Elevation

The next task is to trim the appropriate lines in the elevation, but first you need to extend the line dropped from the balcony down to the ground line.

1. Click the line dropped from the balcony. Grips appear on the line. Click the bottom grip. Select Perpendicular Osnap, then place the cursor on the ground line. When the perpendicular symbol appears on the ground line, click.

2. Start the Trim command. Select the soffit line for a cutting edge for the two building lines, then press ↵. The two lines to be trimmed are the ones that were dropped from the corners of the building. Pick them anywhere between the soffit line and the floor plan. The lines are trimmed (Figure 8.6).

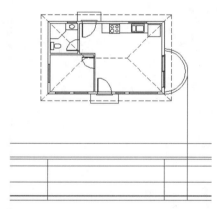

FIGURE 8.6: The building corner lines after being trimmed to the soffit line

3. Press ↵ twice to stop and restart the Trim command. You need to trim a horizontal height line and a vertical dropped line for the balcony. To select cutting edges, pick the line dropped from the balcony and the horizontal height line that represents the top of the balcony wall and the bottom of the windows (Figure 8.7a). Press ↵.

4. To trim the lines properly, click the line dropped from the balcony anywhere above the balcony in the elevation. To trim the horizontal

line representing the top of the balcony wall, pick this line anywhere to the right of the line dropped from the balcony (Figure 8.7b). The lines are trimmed (Figure 8.7c). Press ↵ to end the Trim command.

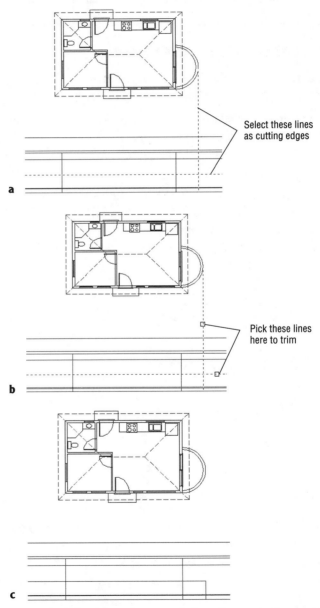

FIGURE 8.7: Trimming the balcony lines: selecting cutting edges (a), picking lines to be trimmed (b), and the result (c)

This is the basic process for generating an elevation: Drop lines down from the floor plan and trim the lines that need to be trimmed. The trick is to learn to see the picture you want somewhere in all the crossed lines and then be able to perform the Trim command accurately to cut the appropriate lines away.

TIPS FOR USING TRIM AND EXTEND COMMANDS

Basic Operation—Both commands have two steps: selecting cutting edges (trim) or boundary edges (extend), and selecting the lines to be trimmed or extended. Select the cutting or boundary edges first, then press ↵.Then pick lines to trim or extend. Press ↵ to end the commands.

Trimming and Extending in the Same Command—If you find that a cutting edge for trimming can also serve as a boundary edge, hold down the Shift key and click a line to extend it to the cutting edge.The opposite is true for the Extend command.

Correcting Errors—It's easy to make a mistake in selecting cutting or boundary edges, or in trimming and extending.They are corrected in two different ways:

▶ If you select the wrong cutting or boundary edge, type **r** ↵, then rechoose the lines that were picked in error.They will unghost. If you need to keep selecting cutting or boundary edges, type **a** ↵ and select new lines. When finished, press ↵ to move to the second part of the command.

▶ If you trim or extend a line incorrectly, click the Undo button on the Standard toolbar.This will undo the last trim. Click Undo again if you need to untrim or unextend more lines.When all corrections have been made, continue trimming or extending. Press ↵ to end the command.

If the command ended and you click the Undo button, all trimming or extending that was done in the last command will be undone.

Drawing the Roof in Elevation

To draw the roof in elevation, follow these steps:

1. Use the Line command to start a line from the right endpoint of the ridgeline of the roof. Then click the Snap to None Osnap button on

If the Osnaps that you have running get in the way of your trying to pick a point near but not on an object, click the Snap to None Osnap. This will turn off any running Osnaps for the next pick. After that pick, the running Osnaps are reactivated.

the Object Snap toolbar. Draw the line straight down past the soffit line (Figure 8.8a). End the Line command.

2. Click this line to activate grips. Select the grip at its upper endpoint. Press the spacebar once to access the Move command.

3. Type c ↵ and then click the lower-right and lower-left corners of the roof, and the left endpoint of the ridgeline. This will copy the dropped line to these three locations (Figure 8.8b).

T I P   If you have difficulty picking the left end of the ridgeline, hold the cursor on the lower-left hip line, just above the midpoint. That should produce an Endpoint symbol where you want it.

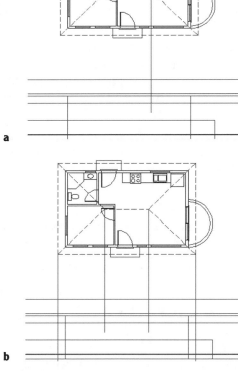

FIGURE 8.8: Dropping a line from the roof (a), and copying this line (b)

4. Type x ↵ to end the Move command, then press Esc to remove the grips.

5. Start the Trim command and select the two lines dropped from the ridgeline. Press ↵.

6. In the elevation, pick the ridgeline to the left and right of these dropped lines (Figure 8.9a). The ridgeline is trimmed back to its correct length (Figure 8.9b). Press ↵.

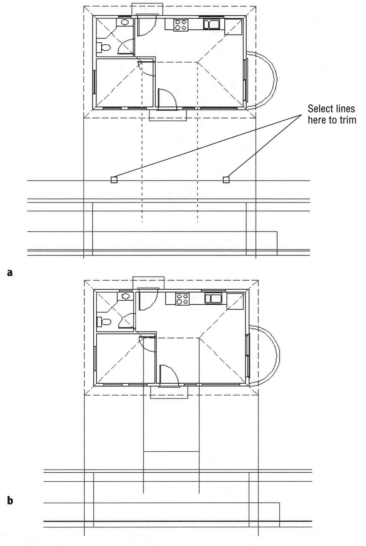

FIGURE 8.9: Selecting the lines to trim (a), and the result (b)

7. Erase the two dropped lines that were just used as cutting edges.

8. Restart the Trim command. Select the two lines dropped from the corners of the roof, the horizontal soffit line, and the line 6" above the soffit line to be cutting edges—four lines in all. Press ↵.

9. To do the trim, click the dropped lines above and below the two horizontal cutting edges, then click the two selected horizontal lines to the left and right of the dropped lines—eight picks in all (Figure 8.10a). Press ↵. The roof edge is complete (Figure 8.10b).

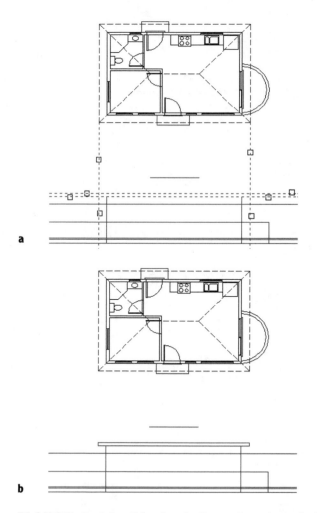

FIGURE 8.10: Trimming the lines to form the roof edge (a), and the result (b)

10. Use the Line command to draw the two hip lines from the roof edge to the ridgeline. Zoom in to do this if you need to, then Zoom Previous when you're finished to view the completed front elevation of the roof (Figure 8.11).

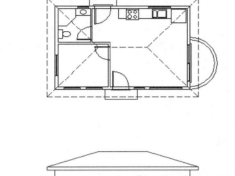

FIGURE 8.11: The completed roof in elevation

Putting in the Door, Step, and Windows

To finish the front elevation, all we need to put in are the front door, windows, front step and threshold, and a few finishing touches. We'll do the door and all of the windows, except the round one, in one cycle. We'll save the step and threshold for later.

1. Use Zoom Window to zoom into as close a view as possible that still displays as much of the drawing as you need. You will need to see the entire elevation, the front wall of the floor plan, and the lower half of the balcony, so make your zoom window large enough to enclose just those elements (Figure 8.12a). I call this process *strategic zooming*.

2. Draw a line from the left end of the leftmost window in the front wall of the floor plan to the ground line, using Perpendicular Osnap for the second point. End the Line command.

3. Click the line to display its grips, then click the upper grip on this line at the Command: prompt to activate it. Follow the same process as you did in steps 2 and 3 of the "Drawing the Roof in Elevation"

You can't Zoom or Pan while using grips. If you need to adjust your view, do so before bringing them up.

section to copy this line to (a) each endpoint of the jamb line of each window in the front wall, except the 2' circular one to the right of the front door, and (b) each edge of the front door opening. Watch your Endpoint Osnap symbol carefully.

4. Type x ↵ to end the Move command. Press Esc to remove the grips (Figure 8.12b).

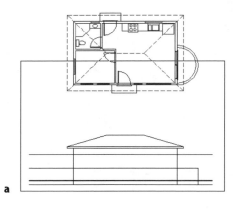

a

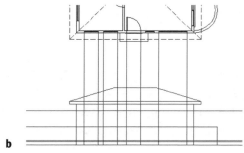

b

FIGURE 8.12: The window for zooming in closer (a), and dropping a line from a window and copying it to the edges of the windows and the front door (b)

Before we begin trimming all these lines, study the floor plan and elevation for a minute and try to visualize the three windows and the door in the middle of all the crossing lines.

We'll trim a few at a time, working from the top down.

5. Start the Trim command. For cutting edges, select the horizontal line representing the top of the windows and doors, and the eight lines you just dropped from the floor plan. Press ↵.

6. To trim, pick the horizontal line at each segment between the windows and the door and near the endpoints of the line (five places). Then pick each selected dropped line above the tops of the windows and door (eight places). This makes 13 places to pick. Then press ↵. The results of the trim are shown in Figure 8.13.

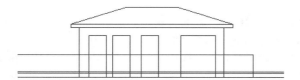

FIGURE 8.13: Trimming the top of the door and windows

Moving down, trim the lines that form the bottom of the windows.

7. Start the Trim command. Select as cutting edges (a) the horizontal line representing the bottom of the window and the top of the balcony wall, (b) the six vertical lines forming the sides of the windows, and (c) the vertical line representing the right edge of the front wall. Press ↵.

8. To trim, pick the horizontal line (a) at each segment between the windows (two picks), (b) between the right edge of the 6' window and the right edge of the building (one pick), and (c) where it extends to the left of the leftmost window (one pick). Then pick the vertical lines that extend below the bottoms of the windows (six picks). This will be a total of 10 picks. Then press ↵. The results of the trim are shown in Figure 8.14.

T I P   It will be helpful if you zoom into a closer view of the Front Elevation when you are picking lines to trim. After step 8, Zoom Previous.

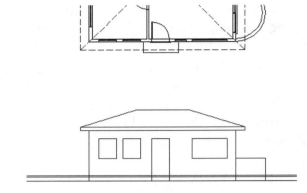

FIGURE 8.14: Trimming the bottom of the windows

Now we will draw the step and threshold, the bottom of the door, and the balcony floor.

1. Drop a line down from the left corner of the threshold to a point past the ground line. Use grips to copy this line to the other corner of the threshold and to the two corners of the step. End the grips (Figure 8.15a).

2. Zoom into a close view of the step and threshold. Use the Trim command to trim away the lines so that the result looks like Figure 8.15b. You'll probably have to stop and restart the command a couple of times in order to make all the trims you need. Here's one way to do it, in summary form:

   A. Create the step first. For cutting edges, select the two lower horizontal lines and the two outer vertical lines. To trim, pick each of these lines (except the ground line) in two places above and below, or to the left and right of, the step (6 picks).

   B. Create the threshold. For cutting edges, select the four lines that form the outside edges of the threshold. To trim, pick each of these lines (except the line that forms the top of the step) in two places above and below, or to the left and right of, the threshold (6 picks).

   C. Trim the left and right edges of the door up to the top of the threshold (Figure 8.15b).

3. When finished, Zoom Previous to a view of the front elevation and the bottom of the floor plan.

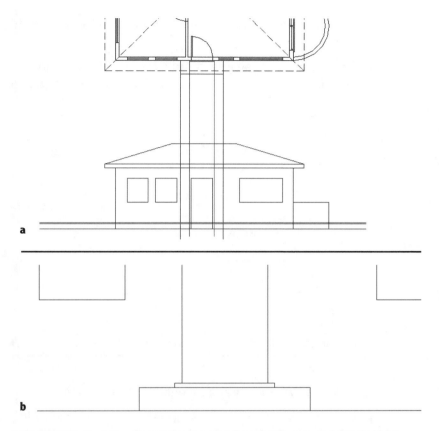

a

b

FIGURE 8.15: Dropped and copied lines for the step and threshold (a), and the finished step and threshold (b)

The results show a nearly complete front elevation. To finish it off, you need to put in the round window and finish the balcony. Then we'll add some final touches. Take another look at Figure 8.1 and note that the center of the round window is 6' above the ground line.

1. Offset the ground line 6' up.

2. Start the line command, then click the Snap to Insert button on the Object Snap toolbar. Click the 2' window in the floor plan to start a line at the insertion point of this block reference. Draw the line down through the newly offset line. Then draw a circle, using the intersection of these two lines as the center, and give it a 12" radius.

3. Start the Trim command and select the circle as a cutting edge, then press ↵.

4. Pick the intersecting lines passing through the circle in four places outside of the circle. The round window is finished (Figure 8.16).

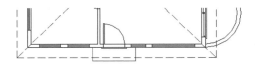

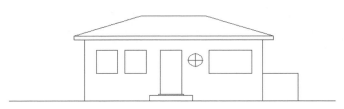

FIGURE 8.16: The completed round window

5. Make a zoom window around only the front elevation.

6. Offset the vertical line representing the balcony's right edge 6" to the left. Then offset the ground line up 10". These lines will serve to indicate the balcony's floor and inside wall.

7. Fillet these two lines at their intersection with a radius of zero. Then trim the balcony floor line back to the right wall line of the cabin.

8. Select these two new lines. Click the Properties button.

9. In the Properties dialog box, click Linetype. Then open the Linetype list and click Dashed. Close the Properties dialog box and press the Esc key. The lines are changed to dashed lines to indicate that they are hidden in the elevation (Figure 8.17).

10. Zoom Previous twice to a view of the completed front elevation with the entire floor plan. Save this drawing as Cabin08a.

This is a rare case where we are assigning a linetype to an object rather than a layer. See the discussion at the end of the previous chapter.

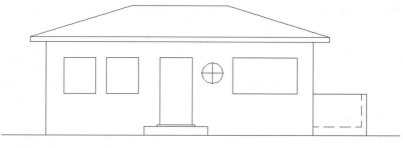

FIGURE 8.17: The completed balcony

Finishing Touches

You have gotten all the information you can from the floor plan to help you with the front elevation. You may, however, want to add some detail to enhance the appearance of the elevation.

1. Try zooming in and adding detail to the windows and door, and placing an extra step leading to the front step. Figure 8.18 shows an example. Yours can be different.

FIGURE 8.18: The front elevation with detail added

2. Zoom Previous to a full view of your drawing when finished.

3. Save this drawing as Cabin08b.

Generating the Other Elevations

In a full set of construction drawings to be used by contractors to build a building, there will be an elevation for each side of the building. In traditional drafting, the elevations are usually drawn on separate sheets. This requires transferring measurements from one drawing to another by taping drawings next to each other, turning the floor plan around to orient it to each elevation, and several other cumbersome techniques. You do about the same thing on the computer, but it is much easier to move the drawing around, and you can quickly borrow parts from one elevation to use in another.

Making the Rear Elevation

Because the rear elevation shares components and sizes with the front elevation, you can mirror the front elevation to the rear of the building and then make the necessary changes.

1. Open Cabin08a. You need to change the view to include space above the floor plan for the rear elevation.

2. Use Realtime Pan to move the floor plan to the middle of the screen. Then use Realtime Zoom to zoom the view out enough to include the front elevation.

3. Start the Mirror command. Use a window to select the front elevation and press ↵.

4. For the mirror line, select the Midpoint Osnap and pick the right edge line of the roof in the floor plan.

5. With Polar Tracking on, hold the crosshair cursor directly to the right of the point you just picked (Figure 8.19a) and pick another point. At the Delete source objects?[Yes/No]<N> prompt, press ↵ to accept the default of No. The front elevation is mirrored to the rear of the cabin (Figure 8.19b). You can now make the necessary changes to the rear elevation so that it correctly describes the rear of the cabin. But you may find it easier to work if the view is right side up.

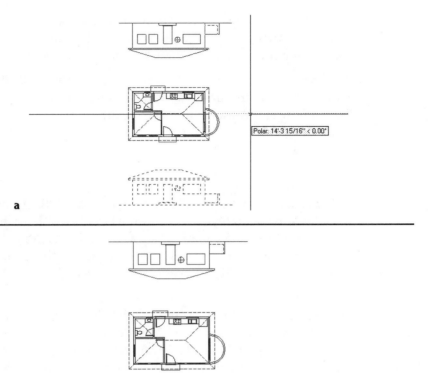

a

b

FIGURE 8.19: Specifying a mirror line (a), and the result (b)

6. Choose View ➤ Display ➤ UCS Icon ➤ On to make the User Coordinate System icon visible. (We turned it off in Chapter 5, *Gaining
   Drawing Strategies: Part 2*.) Take a look at the icon for a moment.
   The two arrows in the icon show the positive *X* and *Y* directions of
   the current user coordinate system, the *World Coordinate System*,
   which is the default system for all AutoCAD drawings. We'll change
   the orientation of the icon to the drawing, and then change the orientation of the drawing to the screen.

The *User Coordinate
System* (UCS) defines
the positive *X* and *Y*
directions relative to
your drawing. A draw-
ing may have several
UCSs but can use only
one at a time. The
*World Coordinate
System* (WCS) is the
default UCS for all
new drawings, and
remains available in
all drawings.

When there's a check mark next to Origin in the menu, the UCS icon will sit at the origin (or the 0,0 point) of the drawing. When Origin is unchecked, the icon will sit in the lower-left corner of the screen.

You used the UCS command to reorient the UCS icon relative to the drawing. Then you used the *Current* option of the Plan command to reorient the drawing on the screen so that the positive *X* and *Y* directions of the current user coordinate system are directed to the right and upwards, respectively. This process is a little bit like turning your monitor upside down to get the correct orientation, but easier.

When you access Zoom Window from the Realtime Zoom shortcut menu, it behaves differently from the regular Zoom Window. It requires a click-and-drag technique.

7. If your UCS icon is in the lower-left corner of the screen, go on to step 8. Otherwise, choose View ➤ Display ➤ UCS Icon ➤ Origin. This should move the icon to the lower-left corner of the screen.

8. Type ucs ↵ z ↵ 180 ↵. This will rotate the icon to an upside-down position. The square box disappears, meaning that we are no longer using the default World Coordinate System.

9. Choose View ➤ 3D Views ➤ Plan View ➤ Current UCS. The entire drawing is rotated 180°, and the mirrored front elevation, which will eventually be the back elevation, is now right side up. Note that the UCS icon is now oriented the way it used to be, but the square in the icon is still missing. This signals that the *current* UCS is no longer the World UCS.

10. Use Realtime Zoom to zoom out enough to bring the outermost lines of the drawing slightly in from the edge of the drawing area. Then right-click and pick Zoom Window from the menu that appears. Move the cursor above and to the left of the floor plan, then click and hold down the mouse button. Drag open a window that encloses the floor plan and mirrored elevation. Release the mouse button. Press Esc to end Realtime Zoom (Figure 8.20). Now you can work on the rear elevation.

FIGURE 8.20: The cabin drawing rotated 180° and zoomed in

Revising the Rear Elevation

A brief inspection will tell us that the roof, balcony, and building wall lines need no changes. The windows and door need revisions, as do the step and threshold:

▶ The round window and one of the 3' windows need to be deleted.

▶ The two remaining windows need resizing and repositioning.

▶ The door, threshold, and step need repositioning.

▶ The step needs resizing.

These tasks can be accomplished quickly by using commands with which you are now familiar:

1. Erase the round window and one of the 3' windows.

2. Erase the sides of the remaining windows (Figure 8.21a).

3. Drop lines down from the jambs of the two windows in the back wall of the floor plan, past the bottoms of the windows in elevation (Figure 8.21b).

4. Extend the horizontal window lines that need to meet the dropped lines, and trim all lines that need to be trimmed. (The Fillet command can be used here instead of the Trim and Extend commands, but pick lines carefully.)

5. Use a similar strategy to relocate and resize the step. The door and threshold can be moved into position by using point filters, by dropping a guideline, or by using the Temporary Tracking Point Osnap with Polar tracking. Use Zoom Window and Zoom Previous as needed. The finished rear elevation looks like Figure 8.21c.

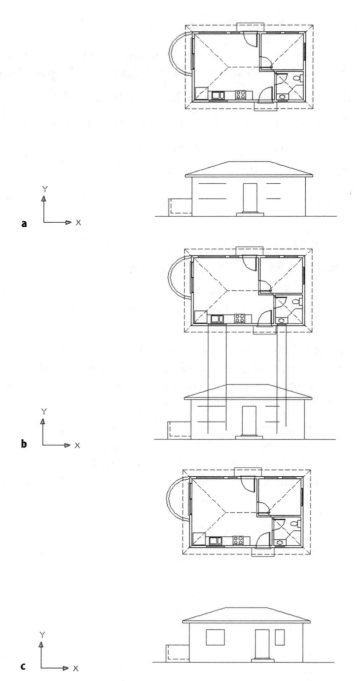

FIGURE 8.21: Erased lines (a), dropped lines (b), and the revised rear elevation (c)

6. You need to save the User Coordinate System (UCS) you used to work on this elevation so that you can quickly return to it in the future, from the World Coordinate System, or any other UCS you may be in. Type **ucs** ⌐ **s** ⌐. For the UCS name, type **rear_elev** ⌐. This will allow you to recall it if you need to work on this elevation again.

You can save any UCS in this way. The World Coordinate System is a permanent part of all drawings, so it never needs saving.

7. You also can save the view to be able to quickly recall it. Choose View ➤ Named Views. The View Control dialog box comes up. The View command can also be started by typing **v** ⌐.

8. Click New. The New View dialog box appears.

9. In the New Name text box, type **rear_elev**. Select the Current Display radio button and click OK. Back in the View Control dialog box, rear_ elev appears in the list of views. Click OK again. Now you can restore the drawing to its original orientation with the front elevation below the floor plan and right side up.

Any view of your drawing can be named and saved, then recalled later. When you have done this, you can quickly restore a previously used view of your drawing.

10. Click and hold down the UCS icon on the Standard toolbar. The UCS flyout toolbar opens.

11. Move the cursor down to the UCS World button, then release the mouse button. This sets the World UCS—the original and default UCS—as the current UCS. Now you need to re-orient the drawing to the plan view in the World UCS.

12. Choose View ➤ 3D Views ➤ Plan View ➤ Current UCS. This zooms to extents and displays a plan view of the drawing with the *X* and *Y* positive directions in their default orientation.

We created a new UCS as a tool to flip the drawing upside down without changing its orientation with respect to the World Coordinate System. You'll get a chance to use UCSs in another way in Appendix A, *A Look at Drawing in 3D*. But for now, we'll use it again to create the right and left elevations.

Making the Left and Right Elevations

The left and right elevations can be generated using techniques similar to those you have been using for the front and back elevations. You need to be able to transfer the heights of building components from the front elevation to one of the side elevations. To do this, we'll make a copy of the front elevation and rotate it 90°, then line it up so we can transfer the heights to the right elevation. It's really quite easy.

1. Use Realtime Zoom to zoom out slightly, then zoom into a view of the floor plan and front elevation. Pan the drawing so that the floor plan and front elevation are on the left part of the drawing area. You need to transfer the height data from the front elevation to the right elevation. To insure that the right elevation is the same distance from the floor plan as the front elevation, we'll use a 45° line that extends down and to the right from the rightmost and lowest lines in the floor plan.

2. Be sure Polar Tracking is on and set to 45°. Also make sure that the Otrack button on the Status bar is toggled on. Then set the Quadrant and Endpoint Osnaps to running and be sure Midpoint Osnap is not running.

3. Start the Line command. Move the crosshair cursor to the right edge of the outside arc of the balcony in the floor plan. Hold it there for a moment. A cross will appear at the Quadrant point. Don't click yet.

4. Move the crosshair cursor to the lower-right corner of the step and hold it there until a cross appears at that point. Don't click yet.

5. Now move the crosshair cursor to a point directly to the right of the corner of the step and directly under the right quadrant point of the balcony (Figure 8.22a). Vertical and horizontal tracking lines appear and intersect where the crosshair cursor is positioned, and a small × appears at the intersection. A tracking tooltip will also appear.

6. When all this has happened, click. A line is started at this point.

7. Move the crosshair cursor down, away from this point, and to the right at a negative 45° angle (or a positive 315° angle). When the 315° polar tracking path appears, type 35' ↵. Press ↵ again. The diagonal reference line is completed (Figure 8.22b).

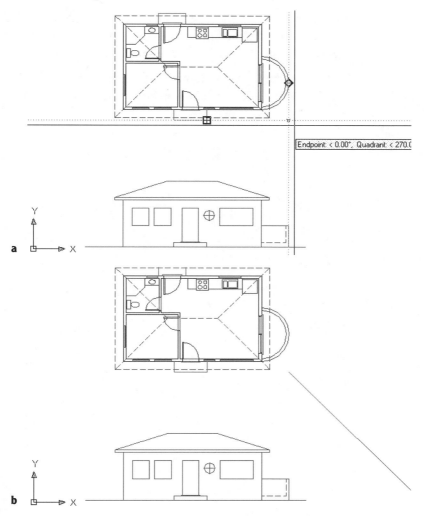

FIGURE 8.22: Starting a diagonal reference line with tracking points (a), and the completed diagonal line (b)

8. Turn off Quadrant as a running Osnap.

9. Start the Copy command and select the entire front elevation and nothing else, then press ↵.

10. For the base point, select the left endpoint of the ground line, then press ↵.

11. For the second point, pick the Intersection Osnap and place the cursor on the diagonal line. When the × symbol appears, click. Then

move the cursor to the ground line of the front elevation. An × will appear on the diagonal line where the ground line would intersect it if it were longer (Figure 8.23a).

12. Click to locate the copy. Zoom out to include the copy, then Zoom Window to include the floor plan and front elevations (Figure 8.23b).

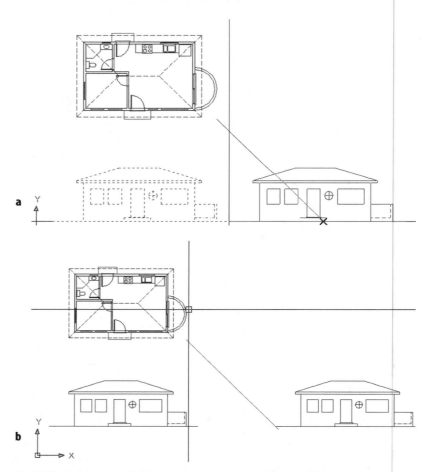

FIGURE 8.23: Making a copy of the front elevation (a) and adjusting the view (b)

13. Start the Rotate command and select this copy of the front elevation, then press ↵. Pick Intersection Osnap and click on the intersection of the diagonal line with the ground line. For the angle of rotation, type 90 ↵ (Figure 8.24a).

14. Start the Move command and, when prompted to select objects, type p ↵ ↵. The rotated front elevation will be selected. For the base point, click a point in a blank space to the right of the upper endpoint of the ground line of the rotated elevation. For the second point, move the cursor down using Polar Tracking until the top of the ground line is lower than the bottom line of the front step in the plan view, then click.

15. Zoom out and Zoom Window to adjust the view (Figure 8.24b).

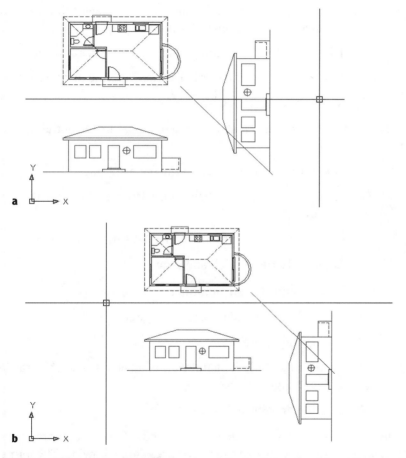

FIGURE 8.24: Rotating the copy of the front elevation (a) and the moved copy with the view adjusted

T I P   If you're working on a small monitor, you may have to do some extra zooming in and out that isn't mentioned in these steps.

The rest of the process for creating the right elevation is straightforward and uses routines you have just learned. Here's a summary of the steps:

1. Set up a new UCS for the right elevation. (Type ucs ⏎ z ⏎ 90 ⏎.) Use the Plan command to rotate the drawing to the current UCS.

2. Drop lines from the floor plan across the height lines, which you will produce from the copied elevation.

3. Trim these lines as required and add any necessary lines.

4. Erase the copy of the front elevation, and the diagonal transfer line.

5. Name and save the UCS and view.

The left elevation can be created from a mirrored image of the right elevation. Here are the steps:

1. Mirror the right elevation to the opposite side.

2. Set up a UCS for the left elevation. Use Plan to rotate the drawing to the current UCS.

3. Revise the elevation to match the left side of the cabin.

4. Name and save the UCS and view.

When you have completed all elevations:

1. Return to the World Coordinate System.

2. Call up the Plan view.

3. Zoom out slightly for a full view of all elevations. The drawing will look like Figure 8.25a.

4. Save the drawing as Cabin08c.

Once an elevation has been drawn, it may be rotated to the same orientation as the front elevation and moved to another area of the drawing. The four elevations for the cabin could all be displayed next to each other, as in Figure 8.25b.

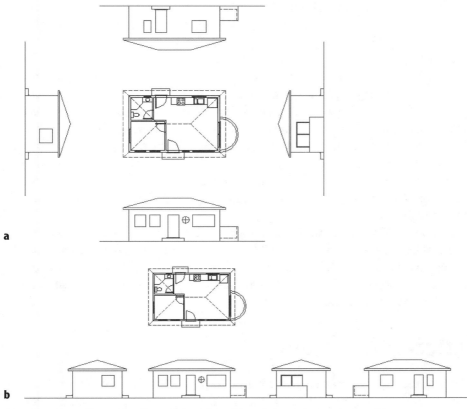

a

b

F I G U R E   8 . 2 5 :   The finished elevations (a), and the elevations in line (b)

Drawing Scale Considerations

This last view brings up several questions: How will these drawings best fit on a page? How many pages will it take to illustrate these drawings? What size sheet should be used? At what scale will the drawing be printed? In traditional hand drafting, the first line could not be drawn without answers to some of these questions. You have completed a great deal of the drawing on the computer without having to make decisions about scale and sheet size because in AutoCAD you draw in real-world scale or full-scale. This means that when you tell AutoCAD to draw a 10-foot line, it draws it 10 feet long. If you inquire how long the line is, AutoCAD will tell you that it is 10 feet long. Your current view of the line may be to a certain scale, but that changes every time you zoom in or out. The line is stored in the computer as 10 feet long.

Decisions about scale need to be made when you are choosing the sheet size, putting text and dimensions on the drawing, or using hatch patterns and non-continuous linetypes. Since we have a dashed linetype in the drawing, we had to make a choice about scale in Chapter 6, *Using Layers to Organize Your Drawing*, when we assigned a linetype scale factor of 24 to the drawing. That number was chosen because when the drawing consisted of only the floor plan and the view was zoomed as large as possible while still having all objects visible, the scale of the drawing was about ½" = 1'-0". That scale has a true ratio of 1:24, or a scale factor of 24. We will get further into scale factors and true ratios of scales in the next chapter.

If you look at your Cabin08c drawing with all elevations visible on the screen, the dashes in the dashed lines look like they may be too small, so you may need to increase the linetype scale factor. Don't worry about that now. Beginning with the next chapter, and right on through the end of the book, we will need to make decisions about scale each step of the way.

Interior Elevations

Interior elevations are constructed using the same techniques you have learned for the exterior elevations. Lines are dropped from a floor plan through offset height lines and then trimmed away. Interior elevations usually include fixtures and built-in cabinets and shelves, and are used to show finishes. Each elevation will consist of one wall and may include a side view of items on an adjacent wall if the item extends into the corner. Not all walls are shown in elevation—usually just the ones that require special treatment or illustrate special building components. You might use one elevation to show a wall that has a window and to describe how the window is treated or finished, then assume that all other windows in the building will be treated in the same way unless noted otherwise. A few examples of interior wall elevations are shown in Figure 8.26. Try to identify which walls of the cabin each one represents.

In the next chapter, you will learn how to use hatch patterns and fills to enhance floor plans and elevations.

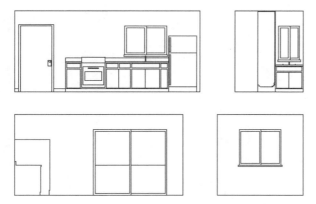

FIGURE 8.26: Samples of interior elevations of the cabin

If You Would Like More Practice...

▶ Exterior elevations: Bring up Cabin08c and move the right, left, and rear elevations around so they fit in a line, as in Figure 8.25b.

▶ Interior elevations: For some practice with interior elevations, try drawing one or two elevations, using Figure 8.26 as a guide. You can measure the heights and sizes of various fixtures in your own home or office as a guide. Save what you draw as Cabin8d.

Are You Experienced?

Now you can...

☑ **draw an exterior elevation from a floor plan**

☑ **use grips to copy objects**

☑ **add detail to an elevation**

☑ **set up, name, and save a User Coordinate System and a new view**

☑ **transfer height lines from one elevation to another**

☑ **copy, move, and rotate elevations**

CHAPTER 9

Working with Hatches and Fills

Hatches can be abstract patterns of lines, solid *fills*, or they can resemble the surfaces of various building materials. To give texture to an AutoCAD drawing, a drafter will hatch in areas or fill them in with a solid color. Solid fills in a drawing can give a shaded effect when printed using a half-screen, resulting in a look quite different from the solid appearance in the Auto-CAD drawing on the screen.

In a floor plan, the inside of full-height walls are often hatched or filled to distinguish them from low walls. Wooden or tile floors can be hatched to a parquet or tile pattern. In a site plan, hatches are used to distinguish between areas with different ground covers, such as grass, gravel, or concrete. When working with elevations, almost any surface can be hatched to show shading and shadows, and realistic hatch patterns can be used to illustrate the surfaces of concrete, stucco, or shingles. Hatches and fills are widely used in details as a tool to aid in clear communication.

To learn how to hatch and fill areas, you will start with some of the visible surfaces in the front elevation of the cabin. Then you will move to the floor plan and hatch the floors and put hatch patterns and fills in the walls. The *Hatch command* will be used for all hatching and filling. It is a complex command with many options.

A key part of a hatch pattern is the boundary of the pattern. The area being hatched is defined through a complex procedure in which AutoCAD searches the drawing for lines or objects to serve as the hatch boundary.

Hatching the Front Elevation

Hatches and fills generally need to be on their own layers so they can be frozen without also making other objects invisible. We will begin the exercise by creating new layers for the hatches and assigning colors to them.

1. Open the Cabin08a drawing. It should contain the floor plan and front elevation only. Turn off any running Object Snaps and turn off the UCS icon.

T I P   To get the best visual effect from putting hatch patterns on the front elevation, change the background color for the drawing area to white. Choose Tools ➢ Options and click the Display tab. Click the Colors button and make the change.

2. Set up three new layers as follows:

Layer Name	Color
Hatch-elev-brown	42
Hatch-elev-gray	Light gray (8)
Hatch-elev-black	Black (White) (7)

3. Make the Hatch-elev-gray layer current. Now, any new objects we create will be assigned to this layer.

4. Click the Hatch icon on the draw toolbar. The Boundary Hatch dialog box comes up (Figure 9.1). You will use this dialog box to choose a pattern, set up the pattern's properties, and determine the method of specifying the boundary of the area to be hatched. The Quick tab should be active. If it's not, click the tab. Predefined and ANSI31 should be displayed on the Type and Pattern drop-down lists, respectively. If not, open the lists and select those options.

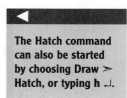

The Hatch command can also be started by choosing Draw ➤ Hatch, or typing h ↵.

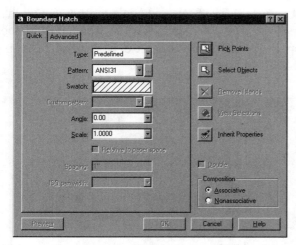

FIGURE 9.1: The Boundary Hatch dialog box

5. Move to the right of the Pattern drop-down list and click the Browse button. The Hatch Pattern Palette dialog box comes up (Figure 9.2). Of the four tabs, ANSI will be active and the ANSI31 pattern will be highlighted.

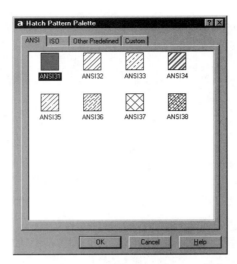

FIGURE 9.2: The Hatch Pattern Palette dialog box

6. Click the Other Predefined tab. Find the AR-RROOF pattern and click it, then click OK. Back in the Boundary Hatch dialog box, note that AR-RROOF has replaced ANSI31 in the Pattern drop-down list. A new pattern is displayed in the Swatch preview box, which is below the Pattern list (Figure 9.3). The Scale and Angle settings can be changed in their drop-down lists, which are below the Swatch preview box. In the Angle drop-down list, the preset angle of 0.00 is fine, but you need to adjust the Scale setting.

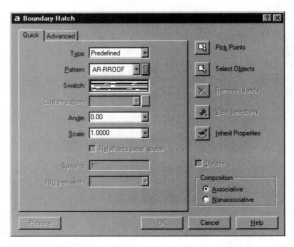

FIGURE 9.3: The Boundary Hatch dialog box with the AR-RROOF pattern chosen

7. In the Scale drop-down list, delete 1.0000 and type **6**. The Scale drop-down list contains preset scale factors that range from 0.2500 to 2.0000. To set the scale to 6, you have to type it in. Once you do that, however, 6 is added to the drop-down list and will be displayed as 6.0000 the next time you bring up the dialog box.

8. Move to the upper-right corner of the dialog box and click the Pick Points button. Return to the drawing.

9. In the elevation view, click the middle of the roof area. The lines that form the boundary of the roof area ghost, forming an outline of the area to be hatched (Figure 9.4).

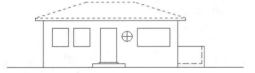

FIGURE 9.4: The roof's boundary is selected.

10. Right-click and pick Preview from the bottom of the shortcut menu that appears. In the preview drawing, take a look at how the hatch will appear, then right-click to return to the Boundary Hatch dialog box.

11. Click OK. You are returned to the drawing. The hatch is now placed in the roof area (Figure 9.5).

FIGURE 9.5: The finished hatch pattern in the roof area

12. Zoom into a view of just the front elevation. Notice how the appearance of the hatch pattern changes with the new view.

Looking at Hatch Patterns

Let's take a short tour through the available patterns.

1. Start the Hatch command.

2. In the Boundary Hatch dialog box, be sure that the Quick tab is active. Then click the Browse button that is next to the Pattern drop-down list. The Hatch Pattern Palette dialog box comes up.

3. Make the Other Predefined tab active if it is not already. Look at the display of hatch patterns. There are 11 patterns whose names begin with *AR-*, including the one that we just used. These patterns have been designed to look like architectural and building materials, hence the AR prefix. In addition to the roof pattern we just used, there are several masonry wall patterns, a couple of floor patterns, and one pattern each for concrete, shakes, and sand.

4. Scroll down the display and observe the other non-AR patterns. They are geometrical patterns, some of which use conventions to represent various materials.

5. Click the ANSI tab and take a look at a few of the ANSI patterns. These are abstract line patterns developed by the American National Standards

Works by Kappe Architects

A San Francisco Bay Area Residence

Ron Kappe of Kappe Architects designs residential and public buildings. In May 2001 he finished the design for a house to be built in Marin County, California. Mr. Kappe contributed drawings and photographs of this house for this color insert. We have chosen the drawings that we think best illustrate the design as a whole, and the ways in which AutoCAD has been used in the design development and construction document phases of the project.

The Overall Drawings

The following four drawings show views of the entire building. They include a floor plan, an exterior elevation, a section, and a photograph taken at the construction site. The last three illustrations are all of approximately the same view. As you can see from the section, the house is sited on a sloping hillside. The building's various rooms sit at multiple elevations, so it takes several floor plans to show all the levels.

Drawings and renderings were prepared by Jason Baggs at Kappe Architects.

Plate 1

The floor plan shown here has the structural grid (see Chapter 10, *Controlling Text in a Drawing*) externally referenced into the drawing.

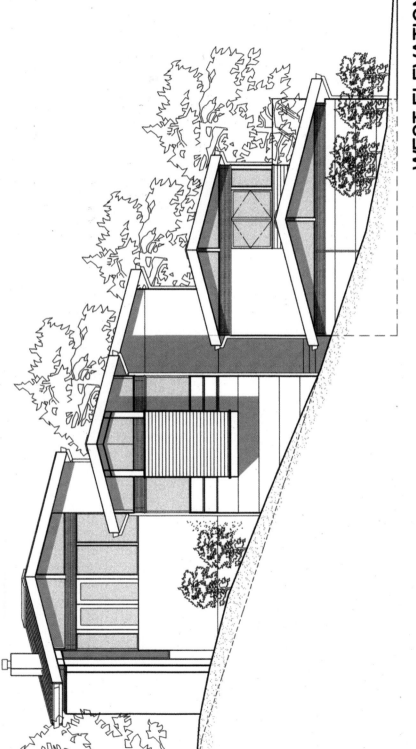

The west elevation shows the various levels stepping down the hillside. The residence will have commanding views of San Francisco and the bay.

Plate 2

WEST ELEVATION

Plate 3

This digital photo of the building under construction shows the steel framing in parts of the house, and wood framing in other parts. When the construction is complete, much of the framing will be exposed to the interior spaces.

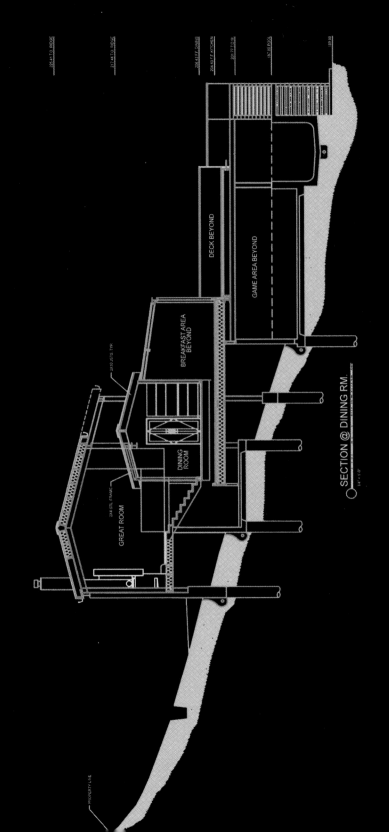

SECTION @ DINING RM.
1/4" = 1'-0"

GREAT ROOM

DINING ROOM

BREAKFAST AREA BEYOND

DECK BEYOND

GAME AREA BEYOND

2X10 JSTS. TYP.

2X4 STL. FRAME

PROPERTY LINE

225.41 T.O. RIDGE

217.44 T.O. RIDGE

208.43 F.F. DINING

204.43 F.F. KITCHEN

201.77 T.O.W.

192.70 POOL

189.66

Plate 4

This view is of a building section that is cut through the great room on top, and down through the adjoining kitchen, pantry and breakfast nook. Further down the slope, an exterior set of stairs and a bridge over the lap pool create a dramatic entry.

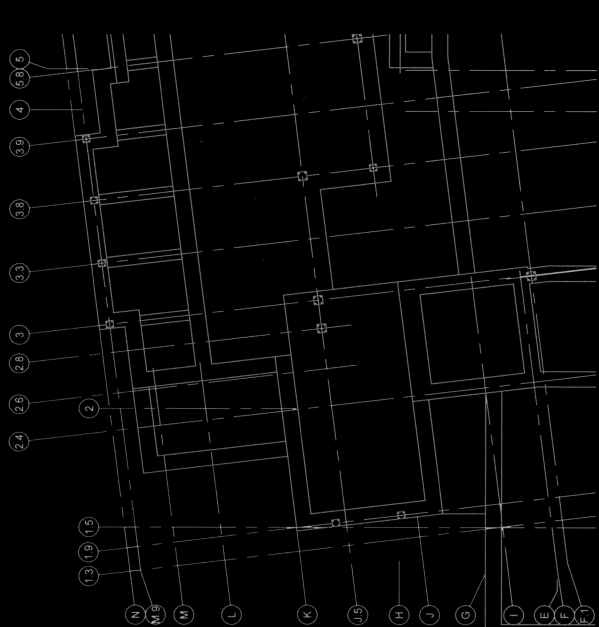

The Excerpted Drawings

For the next four illustrations, we have focused on a portion of the building that includes the kitchen, pantry, dining room, and the great room. For this area, there is a foundation plan, floor plan, reflected ceiling plan, and a roof plan. All of these drawings are based on the floor plan and have different combinations of layers visible.

Plate 5

The foundation plan shows the pier and grade beam structural support for the split-level rooms above.

Plate 6

The floor plan for some of the split-level rooms. The main entry is to the right into a foyer with glass stairs ascending to the great room. That room overlooks the kitchen and breakfast nook and steps down to the formal dining room to the left. The stairwell descends to the garage below.

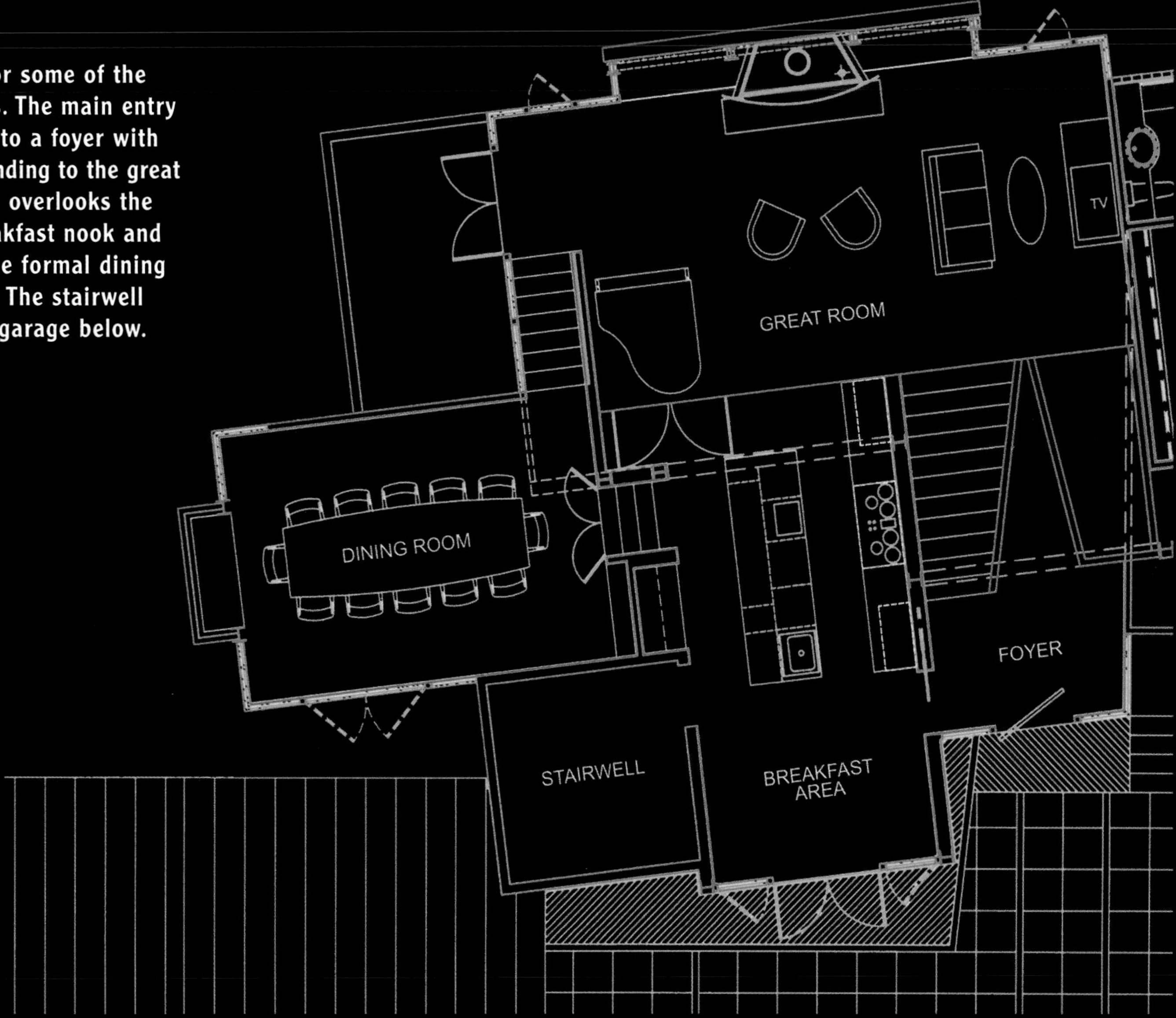

TV

GREAT ROOM

FOYER

BREAKFAST AREA

STAIRWELL

DINING ROOM

Plate 7

The reflected ceiling plan shows the location of ceiling light fixtures, exposed steel beams, and skylights over the kitchen and breakfast area.

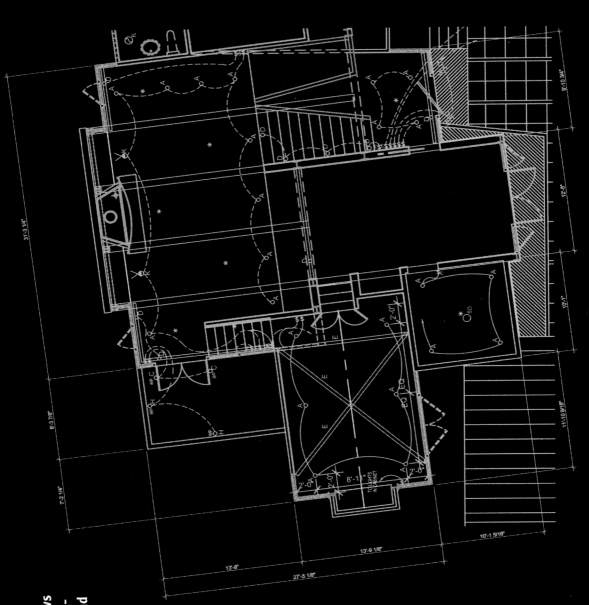

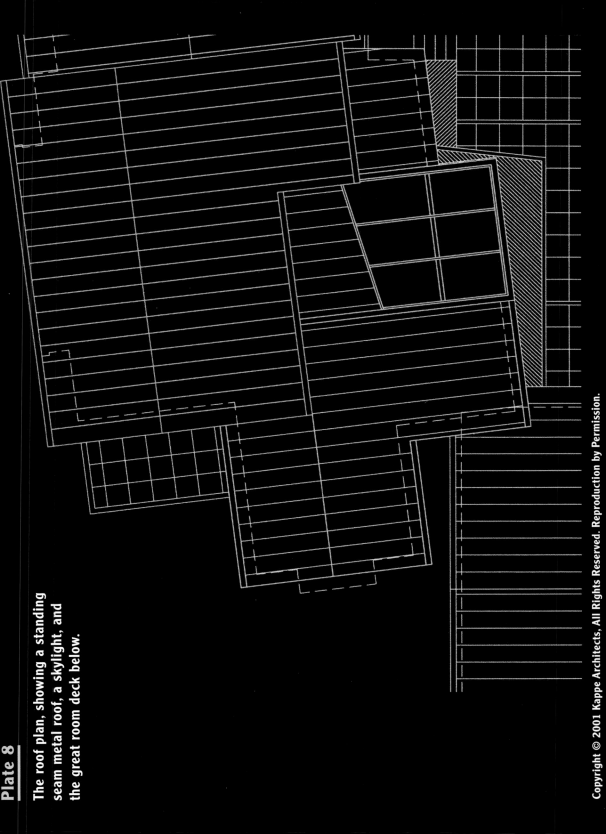

Plate 8

The roof plan, showing a standing seam metal roof, a skylight, and the great room deck below.

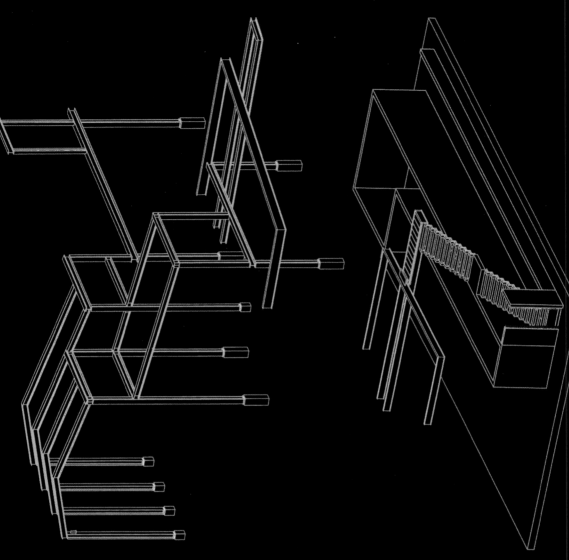

Other Drawings

For this particular job, 3D studies were done for specific features in design. The 3D models were created in AutoCAD by Jason Baggs.

Plate 9

A steel frame is used for the great room and will be exposed to the interior space, so a partial 3D study of these beams was constructed to see how the structure would define the space. The large horizontal steel rectangles will contain picture windows to frame views of the city and the bay.

Plate 10

This partial 3D model shows the dramatic entrance to the residence, again framed in steel, which includes stairs and a glass-and-steel bridge that spans the swimming pool. The model was created to study the arrangement of these building elements.

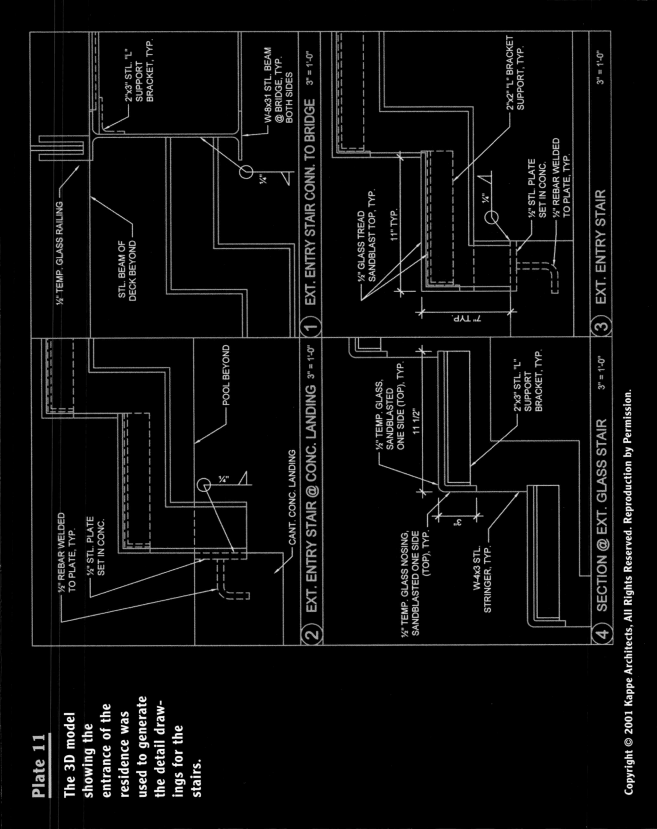

Plate 11

The 3D model showing the entrance of the residence was used to generate the detail drawings for the stairs.

½" TEMP. GLASS RAILING

STL. BEAM OF DECK BEYOND

2"x3" STL. "L" SUPPORT BRACKET, TYP.

W-8x31 STL. BEAM @ BRIDGE, TYP. BOTH SIDES

¼"

1 EXT. ENTRY STAIR CONN. TO BRIDGE 3" = 1'-0"

½" GLASS TREAD SANDBLAST TOP, TYP.

11" TYP.

7" TYP.

2"x2" "L" BRACKET SUPPORT, TYP.

½" STL. PLATE SET IN CONC.

½" REBAR WELDED TO PLATE, TYP.

¼"

3 EXT. ENTRY STAIR 3" = 1'-0"

POOL BEYOND

½" REBAR WELDED TO PLATE, TYP.

½" STL. PLATE SET IN CONC.

CANT. CONC. LANDING

¼"

2 EXT. ENTRY STAIR @ CONC. LANDING 3" = 1'-0"

½" TEMP. GLASS, SANDBLASTED ONE SIDE (TOP), TYP.

11 1/2"

½" TEMP. GLASS NOSING, SANDBLASTED ONE SIDE (TOP), TYP.

3"

W-4x3 STL. STRINGER, TYP.

2"x3" STL. "L" SUPPORT BRACKET, TYP.

4 SECTION @ EXT. GLASS STAIR 3" = 1'-0"

A Corporation Yard Headquarters

Here are three renderings of a 3D model of a city's corporation yard headquarters in northern California, out of which are run the city's public works projects, such as street repair, parks maintenance, etc. The model and renderings were generated in 3D Studio Max from AutoCAD drawings, by David Cookman and Tylor Bohlman.

Plate 12

A view of the southeast entry to the office headquarters.

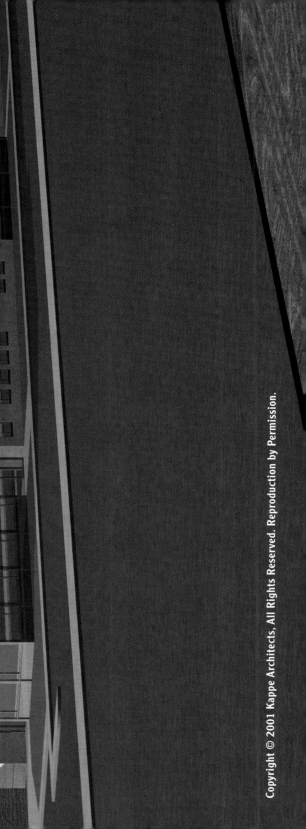

Plate 13

A view of the northeast entrance to the corporation yard shops and storage building.

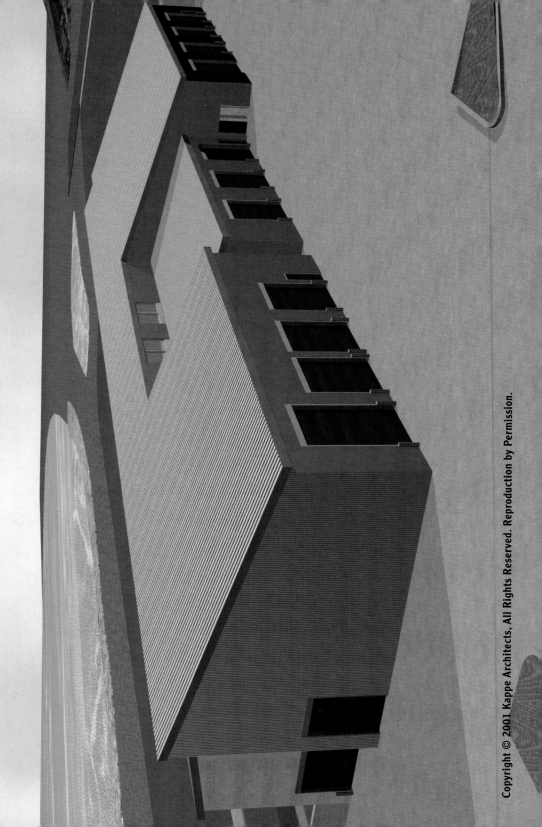

Plate 14

A view of the northwest side of the corporation yard.

This page shows CabinH2B.dwg with both white and black backgrounds. The colors assigned to layers have been adjusted to work with the opposite backgrounds.

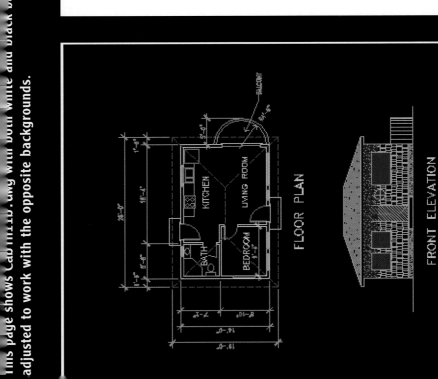
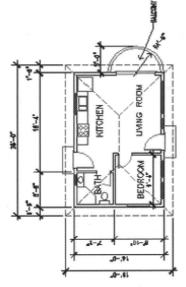
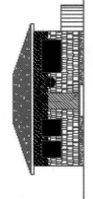

Plate 16

Finally, we have two renderings of the cabin that were done by following the instructions in Appendix A, *A Look at Drawing in 3D*. In the second one, the 3D-Glass layer has been turned off so you can see through the interior of the cabin.

Institute and are widely used by public and private design offices in the United States.

6. Click the ISO tab. These are also abstract line patterns developed by another organization, the International Standards Organization. The Custom tab will be empty unless custom hatch patterns have been loaded into AutoCAD.

7. Click Cancel in the Hatch Pattern Palette dialog box. Click Cancel again to close the Boundary Hatch dialog box.

As you work with hatch patterns, you will need to adjust the scale factor for each pattern so the patterns will look right when the drawing is printed. The AR patterns are drawn to be used with the scale factor set approximately to the default of one-to-one (displayed as 1.0000), and should only need minor adjustment. However, the pattern you just chose for the roof is an AR pattern, and its scale factor needed to be changed to 6.0000. The AR-RROOF pattern is somewhat anomalous compared to the rest of the AR patterns and requires this unusually large adjustment.

T I P   When using one of the AR patterns, leave the scale factor at 1.0000 until you preview the hatch; then you can make changes. This rule also applies to the 14 ISO patterns displayed on the ISO tab of the Hatch Pattern Palette dialog box.

For the rest of the patterns, you will need to assign a scale factor that imitates the true ratio of the scale at which you expect to print the drawing. The table below gives the true ratios of some of the standard scales used in architecture and construction.

T A B L E   9 . 1 :   Standard Scales and Their Corresponding Ratios

Scale	True Scale Factor
1" = 1'-0"	12
½" = 1'-0"	24
¼" = 1'-0"	48
⅛" = 1'-0"	96
1/16" = 1'-0"	192

Some confusion arises from the fact that the scale is traditionally written by mixing inches with feet in the expression. For example, the third scale in the table, commonly called "quarter-inch scale," shows that a quarter inch equals one foot. A True Ratio of this scale would have to express the relationship using the same units, as in ¼" = 1'-0". Simplifying this expression to have no fractions, you would translate it to, say, 1" = 48". This is how you arrive at the True Scale Factor of 48, or True Ratio of 1:48.

As you continue through this chapter, take special note of the various scale factors used for different hatch patterns.

Hatching the Rest of the Front Elevation

You will apply hatches to the foundation, front door, and front wall. Then we'll work with some special effects.

Using a Concrete Hatch on the Foundation

For the foundation hatch, keep the Hatch-elev-gray layer current.

1. To represent the top of the foundation, draw lines from the upper-left and upper-right corners of the step to the edges of the building (Figure 9.6a).

2. Start the Hatch command. Then click the Browse button next to the Pattern drop-down list in the Boundary Hatch dialog box.

3. Activate the Other Predefined tab. Find and select the AR-CONC pattern and click OK.

4. Open the Scale drop-down list and select 1.0000.

5. Click Pick Points. Then, in the drawing, click once in each rectangle representing the foundation. The borders of these areas will ghost.

6. Right-click, then click Preview, right-click, and then click OK. The concrete hatch pattern is applied to the foundation surfaces (Figure 9.6b).

After you select the Pick Points button in the Boundary Hatch dialog box, pick a point in the area to be hatched, and AutoCAD finds the boundary of that area and displays it in ghosted form.

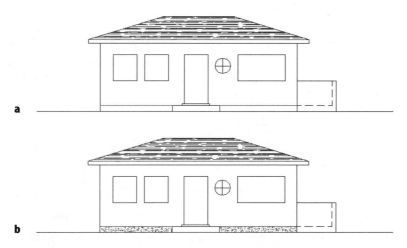

F I G U R E 9 . 6 : The front elevation with foundation lines drawn (a), and the resulting hatches in place (b)

Hatching the Front Door and Wall

For the front door, we'll use a standard hatch pattern: ANSI31. This is the default pattern when you first use the Hatch command, but now the default pattern is the last one used.

1. Start the Hatch command and select the Browse button.

2. Activate the ANSI tab. Select ANSI31 and click OK.

3. In the Scale text box, type 18. Then click Pick Points.

4. Click the middle of the door. The edges of the door and door sill ghost.

5. Right-click, and then click Preview. Observe the preview, right-click, then click OK. The door is hatched (Figure 9.7).

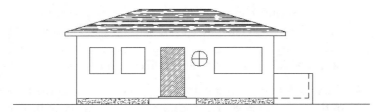

F I G U R E 9 . 7 : Hatching the door

6. Change the current layer to Hatch-elev-brown.

7. Start the Hatch command and go through the same process to apply a hatch to the wall. This time you will use the AR-RSHKE pattern, which looks like wooden shingles (often called shakes). Here is a summary of the steps:

   A. Click the Browse button.

   B. Activate the Other Predefined tab, select the AR-RSHKE pattern, and click OK.

   C. Set the Scale to 1 and click Pick Points.

   D. Pick any place on the front wall that's not inside a window.

   E. Right-click, click Preview, right-click, then click OK.

The wall is hatched (Figure 9.8).

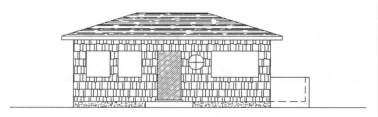

FIGURE 9.8: The hatching of the front wall is completed.

Using a Solid Fill Hatch

The windows will be hatched with a solid fill. It operates the same way as the other hatches you have been using, except that you don't have a choice of scale or angle.

1. Make Hatch-elev-black the current layer.

2. Start the Hatch command. Then click the Browse button. Make sure the Other Predefined tab is active and select the first pattern: SOLID. Click OK. Back in the Hatch Boundary dialog box, note that the text boxes for Scale and Angle are not available. These don't apply to solid fills.

3. Click Pick Points. In the drawing, select a point in the middle of each of the four windows. The round window will have to be clicked four times because of the mullions (the separators between the panes).

4. Right-click, click Preview, right-click, then click OK. The windows have a solid black (or white) fill (Figure 9.9).

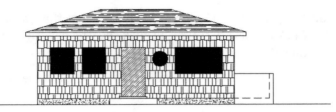

FIGURE 9.9: The windows with a solid fill hatch

Special Effects

To finish the front elevation, you will learn how to show shading and work a little with a curved surface.

Applying Shading to a Surface

When shaded surfaces are illustrated on an exterior elevation, they give a three-dimensional quality to the surface. We'll put some additional hatching at the top portion of the wall to illustrate the shading caused by the roof overhang.

You need to hatch the top 2'-6" of the wall with the same hatch that was put on the front door. To determine the boundary line of the hatch, you need to turn off the layer that has the shake pattern. Then you will create a guideline to serve as the lower boundary of the hatch.

1. Be sure the Hatch-elev-black layer is still current. Then turn off the Hatch-elev-brown layer.

2. Offset the soffit line of the roof down 2'-6" (Figure 9.10a).

3. Start the Hatch command. In the Boundary Hatch dialog box, click the Inherit Properties button. You are returned to the drawing. The cursor is now a pick box accompanied by a paintbrush, telling you that AutoCAD is in Select Hatch Mode.

4. Choose the hatch pattern on the door. The command window will display the name, scale, and rotation of the hatch pattern you picked. Now, the prompt is Select internal point:.

5. Pick a point on the wall above the offset line but not inside the door or windows. Click the door above the offset line. The boundary lines ghost (Figure 9.10b). Press ↵.

6. In the Boundary Hatch dialog box, change the scale from 18 to 16. Click Preview, press ↵, and click OK. The pattern is applied to the upper part of the wall.

7. Turn on the Hatch-elev-brown layer and erase the offset guideline. The drawing will look like Figure 9.10c.

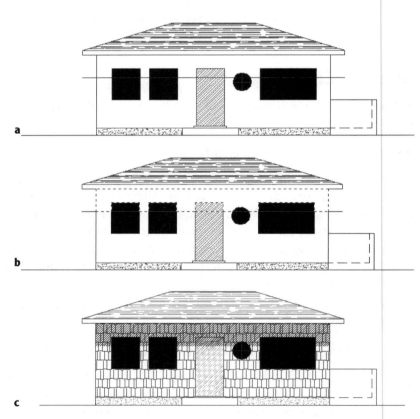

FIGURE 9.10: Applying a hatch to a shaded area: drawing a guideline (a), finding the hatch boundary (b), and the resulting effect (c)

You erased the offset guideline because there is no edge on the wall at the bottom of the shaded area. And you used the Inherit Properties button to set up a hatch pattern exactly like one already present in the drawing. You can also use the List command on hatch patterns to find out the name, scale, and rotation of an existing pattern, as well as the layer the hatch is on.

Indicating a Curved Surface

The curved outside wall of the balcony appears as a rectangle in the front elevation. We need to use a pattern that will increase in density in the X direction as we move around the curve. Vertical straight lines will do the job if we space them properly. We'll use the floor plan to help us to do that.

1. Make the Hatch-elev-brown current. Use Realtime Zoom to zoom the view out until you can see the balcony in the floor plan.

2. Use the Line command with Quadrant Osnap to start a line from the right extremity of the outside balcony wall. Use Endpoint Osnap to end the line at the top-right corner of the balcony in the elevation (Figure 9.11).

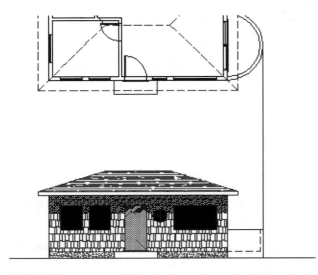

FIGURE 9.11: A line is dropped from the balcony in the floor plan to the elevation.

3. Turn off the Headers, Roof, and Steps layers. Use Zoom Window to zoom into the lower half of the balcony in the floor plan. Set Endpoint Osnap to be running, then use Center Osnap to draw a line from the center point of the balcony arc down to the lower-right corner of the building (Figure 9.12a).

Here's the plan: If we create a series of equally spaced radii across the lower-right quadrant of the balcony, vertical lines dropped from these radii will give us a graduated spacing to indicate the curved surface of the balcony wall in elevation. The Polar Array tool helps us do that.

 1. At the Command: prompt, click the Array button on the Modify toolbar. This brings up the Array dialog box. At the top are two radio buttons. Click the Polar Array radio button.

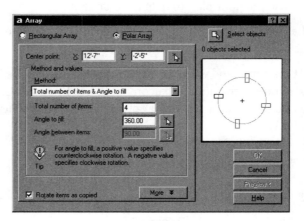

2. In the upper right, click the Select Objects button, select the line from the center of the balcony to the corner of the building, and then press ↵.

 3. Just to the right of the Center Point X and Y coordinate text boxes, click the Pick Center Point button.

4. Back in the drawing, use Center Osnap to select the center of the balcony arcs.

5. In the dialog box, note the Method drop-down list box. It should say "Total number of items & Angle to fill." If it does, move to step 9. If not, open the drop-down list and select that option.

6. In the Total Number of Items text box, enter **10**, but don't press ↵ yet.

7. In the Angle to Fill text box, enter **90** ↵.

8. In the lower-left corner of the dialog box, make sure a check mark is in the Rotate Items as Copied box. Then click the Preview button. The preview should look like Figure 9.12b. If it does, click the Accept button. The line is arrayed around the lower half of the balcony (Figure 9.12b).

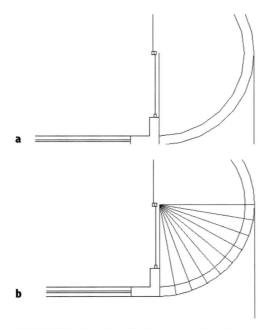

FIGURE 9.12: The line drawn from the center of the balcony (a), and the results of the Polar array (b)

9. Set Endpoint Osnap to running. Then use grips again to copy/move the dropped line to the endpoint of each line that was just arrayed. Here is a summary of the steps:

   A. Click the dropped line to activate grips.

   B. Click the grip on the upper endpoint.

   C. Right-click and select Move from the shortcut menu that appears.

   D. Right-click again and select Copy from the menu. This activates the Copy options for the Move command.

   E. Click each spoke line (like the spoke of a wheel) on its outer end-point. Don't copy the line to the vertical spoke line you first drew.

   F. Type x ⏎, then press Esc to remove the grips.

The results will look like Figure 9.13a. Now you have all the lines you need to complete the task. To finish, get rid of what you no longer need.

1. Erase all the spoke lines and the original dropped line (Figure 9.13b).

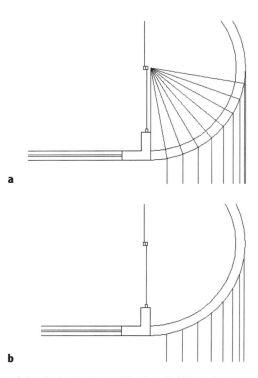

FIGURE 9.13: The drop line is copied to the ends of the spoke lines (a), and the spoke lines and first dropped line are erased (b).

2. Turn on the Headers, Roof, and Steps layers. Zoom Previous, then zoom in close to the elevation of the balcony.

3. Erase the two dashed lines that represent the floor and inside wall of the balcony.

4. Start the Trim command and select the line representing the top edge of the balcony wall, and the ground line. Press ↵. Type f ↵ to activate the Fence selection option.

5. Draw a horizontal line that crosses over the eight vertical lines extending above the balcony, then press ↵. The eight lines are trimmed down to the balcony, and the Trim command is still running.

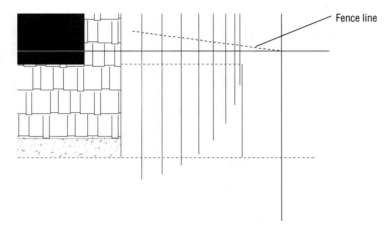

Fence line

6. Click the three lines that extend below the ground line. Click them below the ground line. Then press the Shift key and click the five lines that need to be extended to the ground line. Press ↵ to end the Trim command (Figure 9.14).

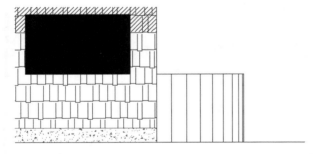

FIGURE 9.14: The balcony in elevation after erasing, extending, and trimming lines

Modifying a Hatch Pattern

You won't know for sure if the hatch patterns will look right until you print the drawing, but you can at least see how they look together now that you've finished hatching the elevation.

1. Zoom Previous and use Realtime Pan to have both the floor plan and elevation on the screen (Figure 9.15a). The roof hatch could be a little denser. You can use the *Modify Hatch command* to change the hatch scale.

2. Double-click the roof's hatch pattern.

3. In the Hatch Edit dialog box, change the scale from 6.000 to 4.000.

4. Click OK. The roof hatch pattern is denser now (Figure 9.15b).

5. Save this drawing as Cabin09a.

By double-clicking several kinds of objects, you activate a dialog box for editing them. We'll point them out along the way.

a

b

FIGURE 9.15: Full view of the drawing with the hatching completed for the front elevation (a), and the same view with the roof hatch modified (b)

You can use the Modify Hatch command to change the pattern, scale, or angle of an existing hatch.

If you worked on putting more detail in the front elevation in the previous chapter, and saved this as Cabin08b, you can go through the exercise again with that drawing. Then you can see how more detail and hatch patterns enhance the way the elevations appear. Figure 9.16 shows the front elevation with hatch patterns and more detail in the door and windows. If you have the time to do any hatching on this drawing, save your work as Cabin09b.

FIGURE 9.16: Cabin09b with the front elevation hatched

Using Hatches in the Floor Plan

In the floor plan, hatches can be used to fill in the walls or to indicate various kinds of floor surfaces. We'll start with the floors.

Hatching the Floors

So far you have used only predefined hatch patterns—the 72 patterns that come with AutoCAD. There is also a *user-defined pattern*, which is a series of parallel lines that can be set at any spacing and angle. If you want to illustrate square floor tile, the user-defined pattern also has a Double option, which uses two sets of parallel lines, one perpendicular to the other, resulting in a tiled effect.

The User-Defined Hatch Pattern

You'll use the user-defined pattern for a couple of rooms, then return to the pre-defined patterns.

1. With Cabin09a open, zoom into the floor plan and be sure the Headers and Doors layers are visible. The header lines can be used to help form a boundary line across an entryway to a room and to keep the hatch pattern from extending to another room.

2. With the floor plan in full view, zoom into the bathroom and freeze the Roof layer. Even if the roof lines are dashed, they will still form a boundary to a hatch.

3. Create a new layer called Hatch-plan-floor. Assign it color 142 and make it current. (If you have only 16 colors, choose any color.)

4. Start the Hatch command. Be sure the Quick tab is active.

5. Open the Type drop-down list and select User-defined. The list closes and User-defined replaces Predefined as the current Pattern Type. The Pattern and Scale drop-down lists are not available, but the Spacing text box is.

6. In the Spacing text box, change 1" to 9". Click the check box next to Double to activate it. Then click Pick Points.

7. Back in the drawing, be sure no Osnaps are running. Then click a point in the bathroom floor, not touching the fixture lines or the door. Click the floor between the door swing and the door, being careful to not touch the door.

8. Right-click and choose Preview from the shortcut menu. The tiled hatch pattern should fill the bathroom floor and stop at the header, while not going onto the door or fixtures. If the tile pattern looks OK, right-click again, then click OK (Figure 9.17).

Note that in the user-defined pattern, there is no scale factor to worry about. You simply set the distance between lines in the Spacing text box.

 W A R N I N G   If you can't get the Hatch command to hatch the desired area, some of the lines serving as the hatch boundary may not have been drawn accurately. This may prevent AutoCAD from being able to find the boundary that you intend to use. Zoom into the areas where objects meet and check to see that they really do meet where they should.

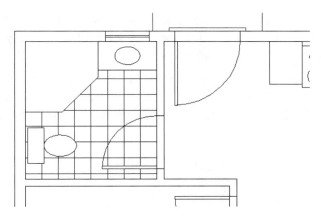

FIGURE 9.17: The tiled hatch pattern in place

Controlling the Origin of the Hatch Pattern

Often a designer will want to lay out the tile pattern such that the pattern is centered in the room. To do this, the tiles are set to start in the center of the room and move out to the edges, where they are cut to fit. We'll use the *Snapbase* setting to set this up in the bedroom.

1. Use Realtime Pan to slide the drawing up until the bedroom occupies the screen. Use Realtime Zoom to zoom out if you need to.

2. Turn Otrack on (on the Status bar) and set Midpoint Osnap to be running.

3. Type **snapbase** ↵. Place the cursor at the midpoint of the inside wall line on the left. A cross (called a *tracking point)* will appear inside the triangular Midpoint Osnap symbol. Don't click. Move to the wall line at the upper part of the room and do the same thing. Then move the cursor straight down until it is positioned directly to the right of the first acquired tracking point. When the cursor is positioned properly, two tracking lines and a tooltip are displayed (Figure 9.18a). Click. This sets the origin of any subsequently created hatch patterns at the center of the room.

4. Start the Hatch command. The User-defined Pattern Type is still current and the spacing is set to 9".

5. Change the spacing to 12". Be sure Double is still checked, then click Pick Points.

6. In the drawing, pick a point anywhere in the middle of the bedroom and between the door swing and the door, similar to what you did in the bathroom. Right-click and select Preview on the menu.

7. Inspect the drawing to see if the hatch looks all right, then right-click again. Click OK. The hatch of 12" tiles is placed in the bedroom (Figure 9.18b). Note how the pattern is centered left to right and top to bottom.

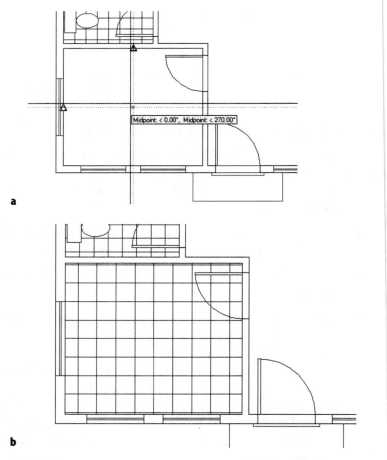

a

b

FIGURE 9.18: Hatching the bedroom: the two tracking lines (a), and the finished, centered hatch (b)

The default setting for Snapbase is 0,0 or the origin of the drawing. Each time you change this setting, all subsequent hatch patterns will use the new setting as their origin. For most hatches, the origin isn't important, but if you need to control the location of tiles or specific points of other hatch patterns, you can reset the Snapbase setting before you create the hatch.

Finishing the Hatches for the Floors

To finish hatching the floors, you'll use a parquet pattern from the set of predefined patterns in the living room and kitchen, and another user-defined pattern on the balcony.

1. Use Realtime Pan and Zoom to adjust the view so it includes the living room, kitchen, and balcony.

2. Start the Hatch command and set the current Pattern Type to Predefined.

3. Use the Browse button and activate the Other Predefined tab. Select the AR-PARQ1 pattern. Set the scale to 1 and be sure the angle is set to zero. Then click Pick Points.

4. Click anywhere in the living room. Then click between each of the door swings and doors for the front and back doors. Check the ghosted boundary line to be sure that it follows the outline of the floor.

5. Right-click, then choose Preview from the menu. The squares look a little small.

6. Right-click again. Reset the scale to 1.33.

7. Click Preview. This looks better. Right-click and click OK. The parquet pattern is placed in the living room and kitchen (Figure 9.19).

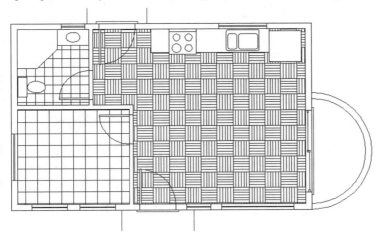

FIGURE 9.19: The parquet hatch in the living room and kitchen

8. Type **snapbase** ↵. The Midpoint Osnap should still be running. Pick the threshold line that extends across the sliding glass door opening near its midpoint.

9. Restart the Hatch command and set User-defined to be the pattern type.

10. Click the check mark in the Double box to uncheck it. Set the spacing to 0'6". Click Pick Points.

11. Click anywhere on the balcony floor.

12. Right-click, then choose Preview. Right-click again and click OK. The balcony floor is hatched with parallel lines that are 6" apart (Figure 9.20).

With the floors complete, the only components left to hatch are the walls.

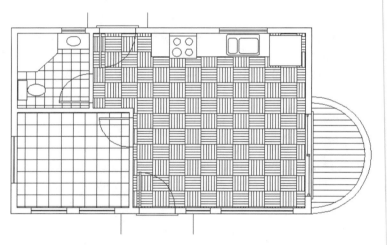

FIGURE 9.20: The user-defined hatch on the balcony floor

Hatching the Walls in the Floor Plan

A solid fill is often used for full-height walls but not for low walls. The interior and exterior walls of the cabin are all full height and will be hatched with a solid fill. Then you'll use a regular predefined pattern for the low balcony wall.

1. Zoom and pan to a full view of the floor plan.

2. Create a new layer called Hatch-plan-wall. Assign it the same color that you are using for the Walls layer and make this new layer current.

3. Start the Hatch command. Set the type to Predefined. Open the Pattern drop-down list and select the Solid pattern from the list.

4. Click Pick Points. In the drawing, click the 10 areas inside the wall and between the door and window jamb lines.

5. Right-click, then choose Preview from the menu and look at the drawing. The fill will look a little odd because the blue boundaries of the wall line are ghosted. Check to be sure all 10 areas in the wall are properly filled, then right-click again.

6. Click OK. The walls now have a solid fill.

7. Restart the Hatch command and click Pattern.

8. Select ANSI31 for the pattern and enter a scale of 24.

9. Select Pick Points and pick a point between the two balcony arcs.

10. Right-click, choose Preview, right-click again, and then click OK. A diagonal crosshatch pattern is placed on the balcony wall (Figure 9.21).

This completes the exercises for setting up and placing hatch patterns.

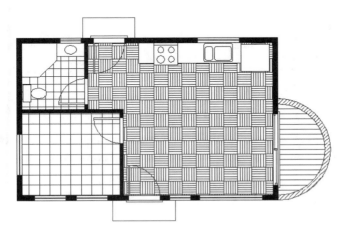

FIGURE 9.21: The hatched balcony wall

Modifying the Shape of Hatch Patterns

The final exercise in this chapter will be a demonstration of how hatches are *associative*. This characteristic means that a hatch pattern will automatically update when you modify the part of a drawing that is serving as the *boundary* for the pattern. You will be changing the current drawing, so before you begin making those changes, save the drawing as it is.

1. Zoom out and pan to get the floor plan and front elevation in the view. Thaw the Roof layer.

2. Save this drawing as Cabin09c. You'll use the Stretch command to modify this drawing.

3. Turn off the Hatch-elev-gray layer. Zoom into the front elevation.

 4. Click the Stretch button on the Modify toolbar.

5. Pick a point above and to the right of the ridge of the roof in elevation. Drag a window down and to the left until a crossing selection window encloses the ridgeline of the roof (Figure 9.22a). Click to complete the window. Then press ↵ to finish the selection process.

6. For the base point, choose a point in the blank area to the right of the elevation.

7. Hold the cursor directly above the point you picked so that the Polar tracking line and tooltip appear, then type 3' ↵. The roof is now steeper (Figure 9.22b).

8. Turn on the Hatch-elev-gray layer (Figure 9.22c). The hatch pattern has expanded to fill the new roof area.

9. Zoom Previous. Save this drawing as Cabin09d.

Hatches are a necessary part of many drawings. You have seen a few of the possibilities AutoCAD offers for using them in plans and elevations.

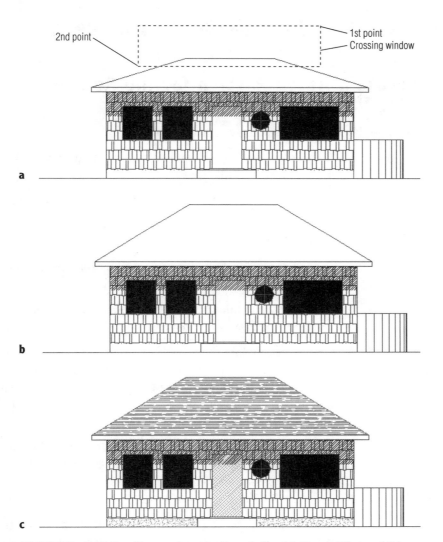

FIGURE 9.22: The crossing selection window (a), the modified roof (b), and the adjusted hatch pattern (c)

If You Would Like More Practice...

Create a Hatch Pattern for the Roof in Plan View

In doing this, make these changes and additions:

1. Make the Roof layer current and change its linetype from Dashed to Continuous. Turn off all other layers.

2. Put a chimney in the roof approximately as shown in Figure 9.23a. Here are the dimensions:

   ▶ Rectangle is 2'-8" by 3'-0".

   ▶ Circle has an 8" radius. It is centered horizontally and its lower quadrant point is set 4" up from the lower edge of the rectangle.

3. Create a new layer called Hatch-plan-roof. Assign the same color you are using for the Roof layer. Make this new layer current.

   Now apply the AR-RSHKE pattern to each quadrant of the roof, changing the rotation angle by 90° for each adjacent area. Use a scale of 1.0000. When you pick the quadrant with the chimney, pick a point in the quadrant that is outside the chimney rectangle. The result should look like Figure 9.23b.

   Double-click the hatch in the quadrant that contains the chimney. In the Hatch Edit dialog box, click the Advanced tab to make it active. In the Island Detection area, select the Outer option, then click OK. Now the hatch pattern does not appear in the circle.

   Move the chimney rectangle and circle to a different location in the quadrant and see the results (Figure 9.23c). The hatch adjusts. What happens if you move the chimney lines to a different quadrant? To a location completely off the roof?

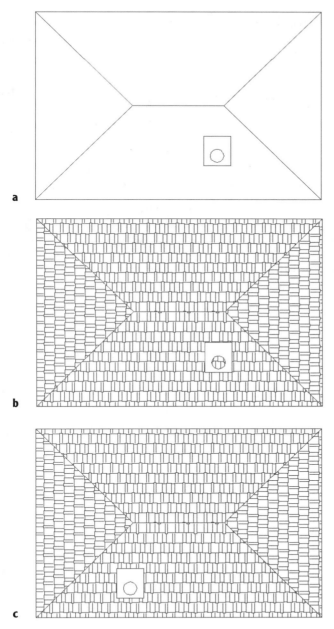

F I G U R E 9 . 2 3 : The roof with continuous lines and with a chimney (a), the new hatch for the roof (b), and the roof hatch with Island Detection adjusted and chimney moved (c)

Are You Experienced?

Now you can...

- ☑ create a predefined hatch pattern and apply it to a drawing

- ☑ set up and apply user-defined hatch patterns

- ☑ create a polar array of a line

- ☑ use lines to indicate a curved surface

- ☑ modify the scale of a hatch pattern

- ☑ modify the shape of a hatch pattern

- ☑ control the origin of a hatch pattern

CHAPTER 10

Controlling Text in a Drawing

- ▶ Setting up text styles
- ▶ Placing new text in the drawing
- ▶ Modifying text in a drawing
- ▶ Working with grid lines
- ▶ Managing single-line and multiline text

Y ou will have many uses for text in your drawings, including titles of views, notes, and dimensions. Each of these may require a different height, orientation, and style of lettering. In order to control the text in your drawing, you will need to learn how to do three basic operations:

▶ Determine how the text will look by setting up text styles.

▶ Specify where the text will be located and enter it into the drawing.

▶ Modify the text already in your drawing.

AutoCAD offers two types of text objects: single-line and multiline text. Single-line text makes a distinct object of each line of text, whether the line is one letter or many words. This type of text is useful for titles of drawings, titles of views within a drawing, room labels, and short notes. Dimensions and longer notes are done with multiline text. AutoCAD treats a whole body of multiline text as one object, whether the text consists of one letter or many paragraphs.

The two types of text share the same text styles, but each has its own command for placing text in the drawing. When you modify text, you can use the same commands for either type of text, but the commands operate differently for multiline than for single-line text. Any text used in *dimensioning*—a process by which you indicate the sizes of various components in your drawing—is handled slightly differently from other text and will be covered in Chapter 11, *Dimensioning a Drawing*.

We will progress through this chapter by first looking at the process of setting up text styles. Then we will start placing and modifying single-line text in the cabin drawing. Finally we'll look at the methods of creating and controlling multiline text.

Setting Up Text Styles

In AutoCAD, a text style consists of a combination of a style name, text font, height, width factor, oblique angle, and a few other, mostly static settings. These text style properties will be specified with the help of a dialog box that comes up when you start the *Style command*. You will begin by setting up two text styles—one for labeling the rooms in the floor plan and the other for putting titles on the two views. You will need a new layer for text.

1. Open the Cabin09c drawing.

2. Create a new layer named Text1. Assign it a color and make it current.

3. Freeze the Hatch-plan-floor and Hatch-plan-wall layers. Be sure all other layers are thawed and turned on. Your drawing should look like Figure 10.1.

FIGURE 10.1: The Cabin09c drawing with the Hatch-plan-floor and Hatch-plan-wall layers frozen

Text and Drawing Scale

When you set up text styles for a drawing, you have to determine how high the text letters need to be. To make this determination, you first need to decide the scale at which the final drawing will be printed.

In traditional drafting, you could ignore the drawing scale and set the actual height that each kind of text needed to be. This was possible because, while the drawing was drawn to a scale, the text didn't have to conform to that scale and was drawn full size. In AutoCAD, a feature called *layouts* makes it possible to set the height of text in the same way—that is, at the height at which it will be printed. You will learn about using layouts in Chapter 13, *Using Layouts to Set Up a Print*. In that chapter, text will be placed on layouts; here we will demonstrate how text is used without layouts. We'll place it in the cabin drawing, where the drawing is actual size, but the text has to be much larger than actual size because both the drawing and its text will be scaled down by the same factor in the process of printing the drawing.

We will use a final scale of this drawing of ⅛" = 1'-0". This scale has a true ratio of 1:96 and a scale factor of 96 (see Table 9.1 in Chapter 9, *Working with Hatches and Fills*). If you want text to be ⅛"-high when you print the drawing at ⅛-inch scale, multiply ⅛" by the scale factor of 96 to get 12" for the text height. You can check that calculated text height by studying the floor plan for a moment and

◄

A *layout* is a drawing environment that has been overlaid on the drawing of your project. The layout and the drawing are part of the same file.

noting the sizes of the building components represented in the drawing. You can estimate that the room label text should be about half as high as the front step is wide, or 1 foot high.

Defining a Text Style for Room Labels

Now that you have a good idea of the required text height, it's time to define a new text style. Each new AutoCAD .dwg file comes with one predefined text style named Standard. You will add two more.

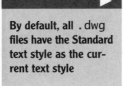

You can also start the Style command by choosing Format ➤ Text Style from the pull-down menus.

1. Type st ⏎. This starts the Style command and brings up the Text Style dialog box (Figure 10.2). In the Style Name area, you will see the default Standard text style.

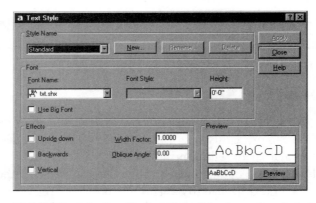

FIGURE 10.2: The Text Style dialog box, where text styles are set up

By default, all .dwg files have the Standard text style as the current text style

2. Click New. The New Text Style dialog box comes up. There is a Style Name text box with Style1 in it, highlighted. When you enter a new style name, it will replace Style1.

3. Type Label ⏎. The New Text Style dialog box closes and, in the Text Style dialog box, Label appears in the Style Names drop-down list. You have created a new text style named Label. It has settings identical to those of the Standard text style, and it is now the current text style. Now you will change some of the settings for this new style.

4. Move down to the Font area and click the Font Names drop-down list to open it. A list of *fonts* appears; the number of choices depends on what software is installed on your computer.

5. Scroll through the list until you find romans.shx, then click on it. The list closes, and, in the Font Name text box, the romans.shx font replaces the txt.shx font that was previously there. In the Preview area in the lower-right corner, a sample of the romans.shx font replaces that of the txt.shx font.

6. Press the Tab key to jump to the next text box. The Height setting is highlighted at the default of 0'0".

7. Type 12, then press Tab again. A height of 1'-0" replaces the default height.

8. You won't need to change any of the other parameters that define the new Text Style. They can all stay at their default settings.

9. Click Apply in the upper-right corner of the dialog box. The Label text style is saved with the current drawing, and becomes the current text style.

A *font* is a collection of text characters and symbols that all share a characteristic style of design and proportion.

N O T E   The current text style is similar to the current layer. All text created while a text style is current will follow the parameters or settings of that text style.

When you define a new text style, you first name the new style. This has the effect of making a copy of the current text style settings, giving them the new name and making the new text style current. Then you change the settings for this new style and save the changes by clicking Apply.

Defining a Second Text Style

Before you close the dialog box, define another text style.

1. Click New.

2. In the New Text Style dialog box, type **Title** and click OK. A new text style called Title has been created and is now the current text style. Its

font, height, and other settings are a copy of the Label text style. Now you will make changes to these settings to define the Title text style.

3. Click the current font, romans.shx. The drop-down list of fonts opens. Scroll up one font and click romand.shx. The list closes and romand.shx is displayed as the chosen font.

4. Tab once to move to the Height text box and type 18, then Tab once more. The height is converted to 1'-6".

 T I P   If you press ↵ after typing in the height, the new style is automatically applied, meaning it is saved and made the current text style. Don't do this if you need to change other settings for the style.

5. Click Apply, then click Close.

Of the many fonts available in AutoCAD, you will use only a few for your drawings. Some are set up for foreign languages or mapping symbols. Others would appear out of place on architectural or technical drawings. Later in this chapter, you'll have a chance to experiment with the available fonts.

Look back at Figure 10.2 for a moment, and note that the Standard text style has a height of 0'-0". When the current text style has a height set to 0, you are prompted to enter a height each time you begin to place single-line text in the drawing. The default height will be ³⁄₁₆" (or 0.20 for decimal units and 2.5 for metric). Multiline text will use the default height of ³⁄₁₆" unless you change it.

Now that you have two new text styles, you can start working with single-line text.

Using Single-Line Text

Your first task is to put titles in for the floor plan and front elevation, using the new Title text style.

Placing Titles of Views in the Drawing

The titles need to be centered approximately under each view. If we establish a vertical guideline through the middle of the drawing, we can use it to position the text.

Romans.shx and *Romand.shx* are frequently used fonts in AutoCAD. Romans (formally named roman simplex) is usually applied to notes in the drawing. Romand (duplex) is like a boldface version of Romans, and can be used for titles. The more complex roman fonts—romanc and romant—are used for titles of drawing sheets and other larger text.

1. Pan the drawing up to create a little more room under the front elevation.

2. Set up your Osnaps and Status bar such that Polar and Osnap are on and Endpoint and Midpoint Osnaps are running. Drop a line from the midpoint of the ridgeline in the floor plan, down through the front elevation, to a point near the bottom of the screen.

3. Offset the bottom line of the front step in the floor plan down 4'.

4. Choose Draw ➤ Text ➤ Single Line Text. This will start the Dtext command—the command used for single-line text.

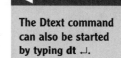

The Dtext command can also be started by typing dt ↵.

5. The bottom line of text in the Command window reads, `Specify start point of text or [Justify/Style]:`. The line above it displays the name of the current text style and the style's height setting. The bottom line is the actual prompt, with three options. By default, the Justification point is set to the lower-left corner of the text. You need to change it to the middle of the text to be able to center it on the guideline.

6. Type j ↵. All the possible justification points appear in the prompt.

7. Type c ↵ to choose Center as the justification.

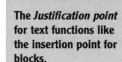

The *Justification point* for text functions like the insertion point for blocks.

8. Hold down the Shift key and click the right mouse button. A menu of Osnap options appears on the screen next to where the cursor had just been positioned.

The Osnap Cursor menu (Shift+right-click) contains all the Object Snap options; an Osnap Settings option, which opens the Osnap Settings dialog box to allow you to set running Osnaps; and a Point Filters menu.

9. Select Intersection on the menu and pick the intersection of the guideline and the offset line.

10. For the rotation, press ⏎ to accept the default angle of 0°. An "I" cursor will be positioned at the intersection (Figure 10.3).

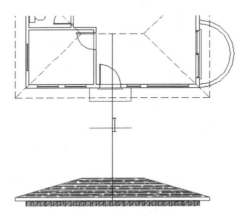

FIGURE 10.3: The text cursor sits on the guidelines.

11. With Caps Lock on, type **floor plan** ⏎. The text is at the intersection as you type it (but not centered yet), and the cursor jumps down to allow you to type another line (Figure 10.4a)

12. Press ⏎ again to end the Dtext command. The text is centered relative to the vertical guideline and sits on the offset line (Figure 10.4b).

13. Offset the ground line of the elevation down 4'. Start the Dtext command again and repeat steps 4–12 above, this time entering **front elevation** (again with Caps Lock on). When finished, erase the offset lines and the vertical guideline. Your drawing will look like Figure 10.5.

You specified a location for the text in two steps: First, you set the justification point of each line of text to be centered horizontally; then you used the Intersection Osnap to position the justification point at the intersection of the two guidelines. We will discuss justification in more depth a little later in this chapter.

Next you will move to the interior of the cabin floor plan and place the room labels in their respective rooms.

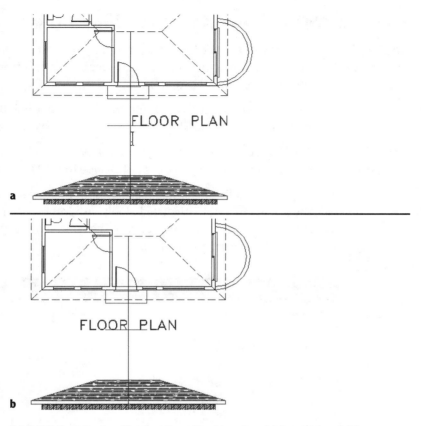

a

b

FIGURE 10.4: The first line of text is entered (a), and placed (b).

FLOOR PLAN

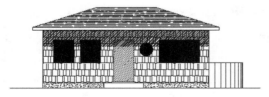

FRONT ELEVATION

FIGURE 10.5: The drawing with the titles complete

Placing Room Labels in the Floor Plan

Text for the room labels will use the Label text style, so you need to make that style current before you start placing text. You can accomplish this from within the Dtext command by using the Style option.

1. Pan the drawing down and zoom into the floor plan. Click the Polar and Osnap buttons on the Status bar to turn these features off.

2. Start the Dtext command. At the prompt, type s ↵ to choose the Style option. The prompt reads Enter style name or [?] <Title>:.

3. Type ? ↵ ↵ to see a list of defined text styles. In the text screen, you see Label, Standard, and Title listed along with information about the parameters of each style (Figure 10.6). At the bottom of the text screen, you can see the Dtext prompt again.

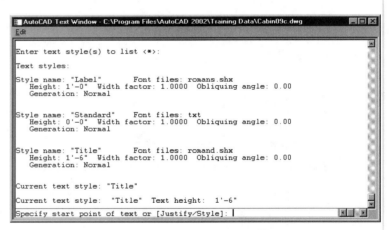

F I G U R E   1 0 . 6 : The text screen listing the defined text styles

4. Type s ↵ again. Then type **label** ↵ to make Label the current text style.

5. Press F2 to close the text screen and return to the drawing.

6. Pick a point in the kitchen a couple of feet below and to the left of the oven.

7. Press ↵ at the Rotation prompt. The text cursor appears at the point you picked.

8. With Caps Lock on, type **kitchen** ↵ **living room** ↵ **bedroom** ↵ **bath** ↵ ↵. The Dtext command ends. You will have four lines of text in the kitchen and living room area (Figure 10.7).

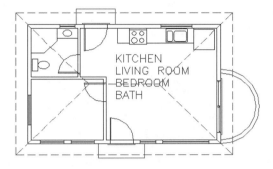

FLOOR PLAN

FIGURE 10.7: The four room labels placed in the cabin

For this text, you used the default Left justification, and each line of text was positioned directly below the previous line at a spacing set by AutoCAD. In many cases, it is more efficient to type in a list of words or phrases first, and then move the text to its appropriate location. That's what we are doing for this text.

Moving Text

We will eyeball the final position of this text because it doesn't have to be exactly centered or lined up precisely with anything. It should just sit in the rooms in such a way that it is easily readable.

1. Click anywhere on the text that says "BATH." One grip appears, at the justification point of the text.

2. Click the grip to activate it. The BATH text is attached to the cursor and moves with it (Figure 10.8a). The Stretch command automatically starts. Since text can't be stretched, the Stretch command functions like the Move command.

3. Be sure that Ortho, Polar, Osnap, and Otrack are turned off. Move the cursor to the bathroom and click a location to place the word in such a way that the letters—while they may be on top of the door swing and the roof line—don't touch any fixtures or walls (Figure 10.8b). The Move command automatically ends when you complete a move.

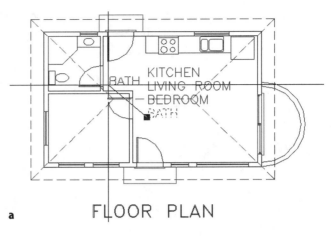

a

FLOOR PLAN

b

FLOOR PLAN

FIGURE 10.8: Moving the BATH text (a), and the new location (b)

4. Press Esc to remove the grip. Then select the BEDROOM text.

5. Click the grip for the newly selected text.

6. Pick a point in the bedroom so that the BEDROOM text is positioned approximately at the center of the bedroom and crossing only the roof line. Press Esc to remove the grip.

7. Repeat this process to move the LIVING ROOM and KITCHEN text into their appropriate locations (Figure 10.9). You may not have to move the KITCHEN text.

FLOOR PLAN

FIGURE 10.9: The BEDROOM, LIVING ROOM, and KITCHEN text moved to their positions

As you have seen, text is easily moved around the drawing. Often, however, you will be unable to position it without it sitting on top of a line or other object. In the cabin, three of the room labels are crossing the roof line, and BATH is crossing a door swing. You need to erase parts of these lines around the text. To do this, you'll use the Break command.

Breaking Lines

The *Break command* chops a line into two lines. When working with text that is sitting on a line, you will usually want a gap left between the lines after the break. The Break command provides this option as well as others.

1. Be sure no Osnaps are running, then click the Break button on the Modify toolbar.

2. Move the cursor near the roof line that crosses through the LIVING ROOM text. Place the pickbox on the roof line just above the text and click. The line ghosts and the cursor changes to the crosshair cursor.

3. Put the crosshair cursor on the roof line just below the text and pick that point. The line is broken around the text and the Break command ends.

4. Press ↵ to restart the Break command and do the same operation on the roof line that crosses the BEDROOM text.

The Break command can also be started by choosing Modify ➢ Break, or typing **br** ↵.

5. Press ↵ again and break the roof line around the BATH text. The arc representing the door swing is part of the door2_6 block and, as such, cannot be broken. You must explode the block to be able to break the arc.

6. Select the Explode button on the Modify toolbar and select the bathroom door. Then press ↵. The door2_6 block is exploded.

7. Zoom in closer to the bathroom. Start the Break command and select two points on the arc to break it around the BATH text. Zoom previous to get a full view of the floor plan (Figure 10.10).

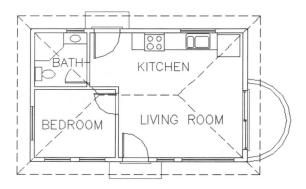

FLOOR PLAN

F I G U R E   1 0 . 1 0 : Lines are broken around the room labels.

A CLOSER LOOK AT THE BREAK COMMAND

You should use your own judgment to determine how far away from the text a line has to be broken back. You have to strike a balance between making the text easy to read and keeping what the broken line represents clear. In the bathroom, you were directed to keep the text away from any fixtures because if any lines of the fixtures had to be broken to accommodate the text, this might have made it difficult for a viewer to recognize that those lines represent a shower or a toilet.

Continued on next page

Other Options for the Break Command:

1. Normally, when you select a line to be broken, the point where you pick the line becomes the beginning of the break. If the point where the break needs to start is at the intersection of two lines, you must select the line to be broken somewhere else than at a break point. Otherwise, AutoCAD won't know which line you want to break. In that case, after selecting the line to break, type **f** ↵. You will be prompted to pick the first point of the break, and the command continues. Now that AutoCAD knows which line you want to break, you can use Intersection Osnap to pick the intersection of two lines.

2. The Break command can also be used to break a line into two segments without leaving a gap. You might want to do this to place one part of a line on a different layer from the rest of the line. To break the line this way, after specifying the first point of the break, type **@** ↵. This will force the second break point to be at the same place as the first one. If you're using Osnaps, you can snap to the same point twice to accomplish the same thing.

3. When you create a gap in a line for text, the line will have a gap in it even when the text layer is turned off. This will be a problem for the bath door swing and the roof line. We'll attend to it in the last few chapters of the book.

Using Text in a Grid

AutoCAD provides a grid of dots, which you worked with in Chapter 3, *Setting Up a Drawing*. The grid is a tool for visualizing the size of the drawing area and for drawing lines whose geometry conforms to the spacing of the dots. Many floor plans have a separate *structural* grid, created specifically for the project, and made up of lines running vertically and horizontally through key structural parts of the building. At one end of each grid line, a circle or hexagon is placed and a letter or number is centered in the shape to identify it. This kind of grid is usually reserved for large, complex drawings, but we will put a small grid on the cabin floor plan to learn the basic method for laying one out.

1. Create a new layer called Grid. Assign it a color and make it current.

2. Type z ↵ .6x ↵ to make more room around the floor plan.

3. Offset the upper roof line up 10'. Offset the left roof line 10' to the left. Offset the lower roof line down 2'. Offset the right roof line to the right 4'. Pan and zoom as necessary.

4. Set Endpoint and Perpendicular Osnaps to be running. Then start the Line command.

5. Draw lines from the upper-left and upper-right corners of the exterior walls up to the horizontal offset line. Then draw lines from the left upper and lower corners of the exterior walls to the vertical offset line on the left (Figure 10.11).

F I G U R E   1 0 . 1 1 : The first grid lines

6. Now you need to draw grid lines through the middle of the interior walls. Zoom into the bathroom area and draw a short guideline across the interior wall between the bathroom and bedroom, where this wall meets the exterior wall (Figure 10.12).

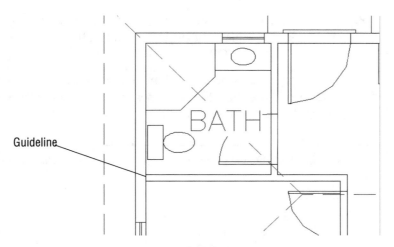

FIGURE 10.12: A guideline for drawing a grid line through one of the interior walls

7. Use Realtime Zoom and Pan to set up the view so that it contains the bathroom and the offset roof lines above and to the left of the floor plan.

8. Draw two vertical lines and one horizontal line from the middle of the interior walls out to the offset roof lines. Use Midpoint Osnap and pick one of the jamb lines, or the guideline, to start each line from the middle of a wall (Figure 10.13).

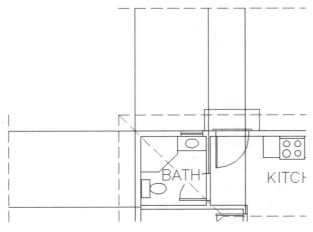

FIGURE 10.13: Drawing the grid lines

9. Erase the guideline you drew in step 6, then zoom out to a view that includes the floor plan, the grid lines, and all the offset roof lines (Figure 10.14a).

10. Use the Extend command to extend the seven grid lines to the right or down, and use the offset roof lines on those sides of the floor plan as boundary edges (Figure 10.14b).

 T I P   When erasing the guideline, use a regular selection window to select it.

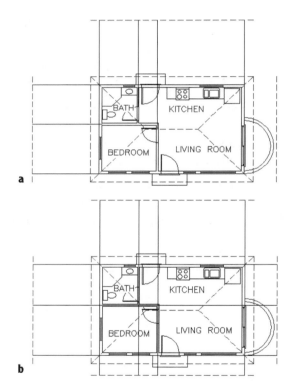

FIGURE 10.14: Zoomed view for completing the grid lines (a), and the completed grid lines (b)

This completes the grid lines. To finish the grid, you need to add a circle with a letter or number in it to the left, or upper, end of the lines. We'll use letters across the top and numbers running down the side.

1. Erase the four offset roof lines. Zoom out a little.

2. Choose Draw ➤ Circle ➤ 2 Points, then pick the upper end of the left-most vertical grid line.

3. Type @2'<90 ↵. A circle 2' in diameter is placed at the top of the grid line (Figure 10.15a).

4. Click the KITCHEN text. A grip will appear.

5. Click the grip and type c, for copy, and press ↵.

6. Select the Center Osnap and click the circle on the grid. The KITCHEN text is placed on the circle with the lower-left corner of the text at the center of the circle (Figure 10.15b). Press Esc to clear the grip.

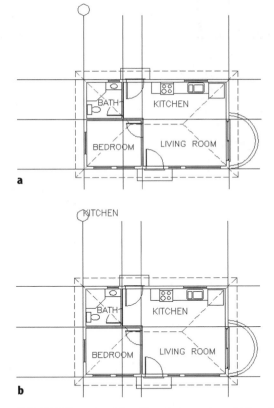

FIGURE 10.15: The circle on the grid line (a), and the KITCHEN text copied to the circle (b)

7. Click the copy of the KITCHEN text that is now on the grid. Then click the Properties button on the Standard Properties toolbar. The Properties dialog box comes up and Text is displayed on the drop-down list at the top, telling you that you have selected a text object. Be sure the Categorized tab is active.

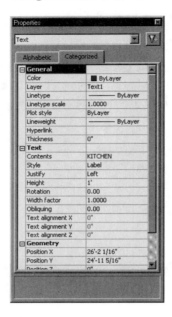

This may seem like a roundabout method for generating letters for the grid symbols, but the exercise is meant to show you how easy it is to use text from one part of the drawing for a completely different text purpose. It's a handy technique, as long as you want to use a font that has been chosen for a previously defined text style. Several of the exercises in the book are designed to illustrate an important feature, though there may be faster ways to accomplish the same goal in Auto-CAD. I'll warn you when I'm doing this.

8. Use the Categorized tab of this dialog box to change the KITCHEN text as follows:

   A. Change the Layer from Text1 to Grid.

   B. Change the Contents from KITCHEN to the letter *A*.

   C. Change the Justify setting from Left to Middle.

For each change, follow these steps in the Properties dialog box:

1. First, click the category in the left column that needs to be changed. If the setting is on a drop-down list, an arrow will be highlighted in the right column.

2. Click the down arrow to open the list. In the case of the KITCHEN text, just highlight it, as there is no drop-down list.

3. Click the new setting, or type it in.

4. When finished, close the dialog box and press Esc to remove the grip.

The KITCHEN text changes to the letter *A*, is centered in the grid circle, and moves to the Grid layer (Figure 10.16).

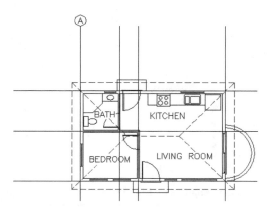

FIGURE 10.16: The grid circle with the letter *A*

You used the Insertion Osnap on the KITCHEN text to position its justification point at the center of the circle. Then you modified the justification point from the Left position (which is actually short for Lower Left) to the Middle position (short for Center Middle). The Middle position is the middle of the line of text, horizontally and vertically. So what we did had the effect of centering the text in the circle. Let's look at Text Justification briefly.

Text Justification

Each line of single-line text is an object. It has a justification point, which is similar to the insertion points on blocks. When drawing, you can use the Insert Osnap to precisely locate the justification point of text (or the insertion point of blocks), and thereby control the text's position on the drawing. When you use the Dtext command, the default justification point is the lower-left corner of the line of text. At the Dtext prompt (`Specify start point of text or [Justify/Style]:`), if you type j ↵, you get the prompt, `Enter an option [Align/Fit/Center/ Middle/Right/TL/TC/TR/ML/MC/MR/BL/BC/BR]:`. These are your justification options.

Most of these options are represented in Figure 10.17. The dots are in three columns—left, center, and right—and four rows—top, middle, lower, and base. The names of the justification locations are based on these columns and rows. So you have, for example, TL for Top Left, MR for Middle Right, etc. The third row down doesn't use the name Lower. It simply goes by Left, Center, and Right. Left is the default justification position, so it's not in the list of options. The Middle position will sometimes coincide with the Middle Center position, but not always. For example, if a line of text has *descenders*—lowercase letters that drop below the base line—the Middle position will drop below the Middle Center position. Finally, the lowest row, the *Base row*, sits just below the letters at the lowest point of any descenders.

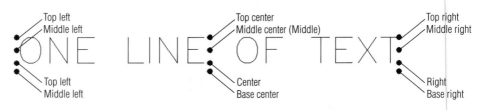

FIGURE 10.17: The justification points on a line of text

Finishing the Grid

To finish the grid, you need to copy the grid circle with its text to each grid line, then change the text.

1. Be sure Endpoint Osnap is still running. Then, at the Command: prompt, select the letter *A*, then click the circle. Grips appear.

2. Click the grip at the bottom of the circle to activate it.

3. Right-click and select Move, then right-click again and select Copy to activate the copy option.

4. Pick the top end of each vertical grid line. Then right-click and select Enter (Figure 10.18).

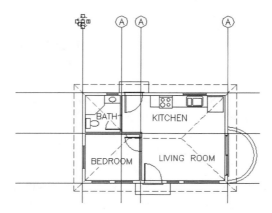

FIGURE 10.18: The grid circle and letter are copied to the top of all three vertical lines.

5. Move back to the original grid circle and select the grip on the right side of the circle to activate it.

6. Repeat steps 3 and 4 to copy the original grid circle and letter to the left end of each horizontal grid line.

7. Press Esc to remove the grips. Now you'll use the Text Edit command to change the text in each circle.

8. Be sure Caps Lock is on. Type **ed** ↵. Select the letter *A* in the second grid circle from the left on the top row. The Edit Text dialog box comes up.

This command can also be started by choosing Modify ➤ Object ➤ Text ➤ Edit from the pull-down menus.

9. With Caps Lock on, type **b** ↵. The *A* changes to *B*.

10. Click the *A* in the next circle to the right, then type **c** ↵. The *A* changes to *C*.

11. Repeat this process for the remaining four grid circle letters, changing them to *D, 1, 2,* and *3*. Press ↵ to end the Edit Text command. The letters and numbers are all in place, and the grid is complete (Figure 10.19).

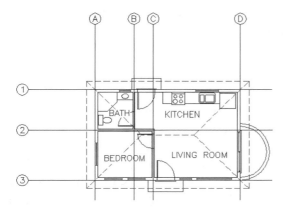

FIGURE 10.19: The completed grid

12. Zoom to Extents, then zoom out a little to get a view of the entire drawing with the grid completed (Figure 10.20).

13. Save this drawing as Cabin10a.

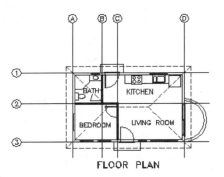

FIGURE 10.20: The Cabin10a drawing

Often it is easier to copy existing text and modify it than to create new text; and grips are a handy way to copy text. The Edit Text command (technically called Ddedit) gives you a quick way to modify the wording of short lines of text, ones that consist of a word or a few letters. The Properties dialog box is very useful for changing all aspects of a line of text.

For the next exercise with text, you get a chance to set up some more new text styles, place text precisely, and use the Ddedit command again to modify text content. This will all be done as you develop a title block for your drawing.

Creating a Title Block and Border

The first step in creating a title block and border for the cabin drawing is deciding on a sheet size for printing the final drawing. Because many people have access to an 8.5×11-inch format printer, we will use that sheet size. If we print the drawing at a scale of ⅛" = 1'-0", will it fit on the sheet?

To answer that question, we have to ask ourselves: How big of an area will fit on an 8.5×11-inch sheet at 1" = 8'-0" scale? The answer is really quite simple: If every inch on the sheet represents 8', you multiply each dimension of the sheet in inches by 8' per inch. For this sheet, you multiply 8.5"×8' per inch to get 68'. And you multiply 11"×8' per inch to get 88'. So the 8.5×11" sheet represents a rectangle with dimensions of 68'×88' at a scale of 1" = 8'-0" (usually called *eighth-inch scale*). That should be plenty of room for your cabin drawing. This is the information we need to start creating the title block.

Drawing the Border

The border of the drawing will be set in from the edge of the sheet.

1. Create a new layer called Tblk1. Leave the default color assigned and make this layer current.

2. Start the Rectangle command (it was used in Chapter 4, *Gaining Drawing Strategies: Part 1*, to make the doors).

3. At the prompt, type **0,0** ↵. Then type **68',88'** ↵. A rectangle is drawn that extends off the top of the screen (Figure 10.21a).

4. Use Realtime Zoom to zoom out until the entire rectangle is visible in the drawing area (Figure 10.21b). You need to fit the drawing into the rectangle as if you were fitting it on a sheet of paper—the easiest and safest way to do this is to move the rectangle over to the drawing.

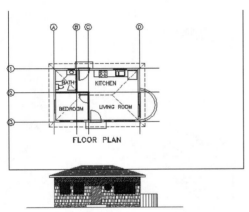

a

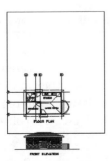

b

FIGURE 10.21: Creating the rectangle (a), and zooming out to include the entire rectangle (b)

5. At the Command: prompt, click the rectangle to turn on the grips. Grips appear at the corners of the rectangle.

6. Click the lower-left grip. Press the spacebar once. Then move the rectangle over the drawing (Figure 10.22a).

Once a grip has been activated and the Stretch command begins, pressing the spacebar toggles you through the other four commands available, in this order: Move, Rotate, Scale, Mirror.

7. When the rectangle is approximately in the position shown in Figure 10.22b, click. Then press Esc to turn off the grips. The rectangle is positioned around the drawing and represents the edge of the sheet.

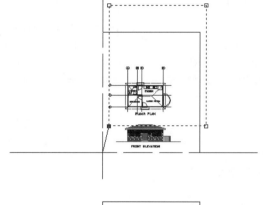

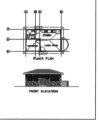

FIGURE 10.22: Moving the rectangle with grips (a), and the results (b)

8. You need a border set in from the edge. Offset the rectangle 3' to the inside. (With a scale of 1" = 8'-0", which is another way of expressing the scale of ⅛" = 1'-0", each 1'-0" on the drawing will represented by ⅛" on the sheet. So a 3' offset distance will create an offset of ⅜" on the printed sheet.)

9. Double-click the inside rectangle. This brings up the Properties window.

10. In the list of Geometry settings in the Properties window, change the Global Width from 0" to 3". Close the Properties dialog box and press Esc to remove the grips.

11. Zoom to Extents, then zoom out a little to create a view in which the drawing with its border nearly fills the screen. You now have a border for the drawing (Figure 10.23). The outer rectangle represents the edge of the sheet of paper, while the thicker, inner rectangle is the drawing's border.

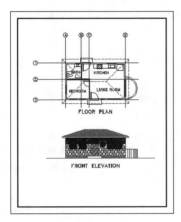

FIGURE 10.23: The drawing with its border

Constructing a Title Block

The *title block* is a box that contains general information about a drawing, such as the name of the project, the design company, and the date of the drawing. It will be set up in the lower-right corner of the border and will use the same special line—the *polyline*—that was used in the Rectangle command.

Polylines

We first used the Rectangle command in Chapter 4 for drawing the doors. At that time, it was mentioned that rectangles created with the Rectangle command were made up of a polyline whose four segments were grouped as one object. In step 10 of the previous section, you saw that these segments could have varying widths.

There is also a *Polyline command,* nicknamed the Pline command, which allows you to draw continuous straight and curved line segments of varying widths, with all segments behaving as if they were one object.

When you explode a polyline using the Explode command, the segments lose any width they had and become independent lines. The ability of a polyline to have a width makes it useful in constructing title blocks. We'll use the Pline command to draw the various lines that make up the title block. Then we'll fill in the text.

1. Zoom into a view of the lower third of your drawing, including the bottom of the border. Be sure Endpoint and Perpendicular Osnaps are running.

2. Pick the Polyline icon on the Draw toolbar. The `Specify start point:` prompt appears in the Command window.

You can also start the Polyline command by typing pl ↵ or by choosing Draw ➤ Polyline from the pull-down menus.

3. Click Polar on the Status bar to turn Polar Tracking on. Then select the Temporary Tracking Point Osnap. Click the lower-left corner of the border and hold the cursor directly above that point. When the vertical tracking path appears along the left boundary line, type 12' ↵. This starts a polyline on the left side of the border 12' above the lower-left corner.

4. Notice the bottom two lines in the Command window. The upper one tells you the current width set for polylines. The lower one displays the options for the Polyline command, with the default option being to pick a second point. You need to set the line width.

5. Type w ↵, then type 3 ↵ ↵. This sets the starting and ending width of polyline segments to 3". The original Polyline command prompt returns, and you can pick a point to define the line segment (Figure 10.24a).

6. Hold the crosshair cursor on the right side of the border. When the perpendicular icon appears on the border line, click. Then press ↵. The first polyline segment is drawn (Figure 10.24b). The 3" width setting will stay until you change it, and will be saved with the drawing file.

7. Restart the Polyline command. Choose the Midpoint Osnap and start a new segment at the midpoint of the line you just drew.

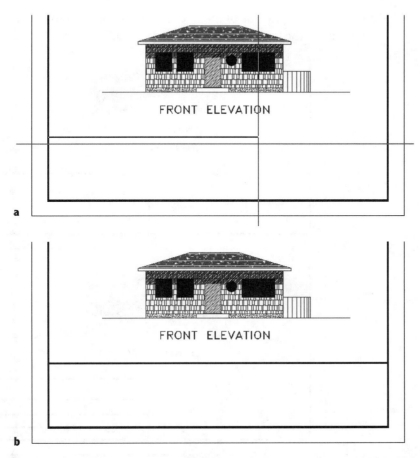

FIGURE 10.24: Drawing a polyline: setting the width (a), and completing the segment (b)

8. Move to the bottom of the border near its midpoint. When the running Perpendicular Osnap is activated, click. The left edge of the title block is drawn (Figure 10.25a). Press ↵ to end the Polyline, or Pline, command.

9. Trim the left half of the first Pline drawn back to the Pline just drawn.

10. Offset the horizontal Pline down 4'. Then offset this new line down 3'. Then offset this new line down 2'-6" (Figure 10.25b).

11. Start the Pline command. Using Midpoint Osnap, start a Pline at the midpoint of the third horizontal line down. Then end the segment at the bottom of the border, taking advantage of the running Perpendicular Osnap. Press ↵ to end the Pline command.

12. Trim the right side of the line just above the bottom of the border, back to the line you just drew (Figure 10.25c).

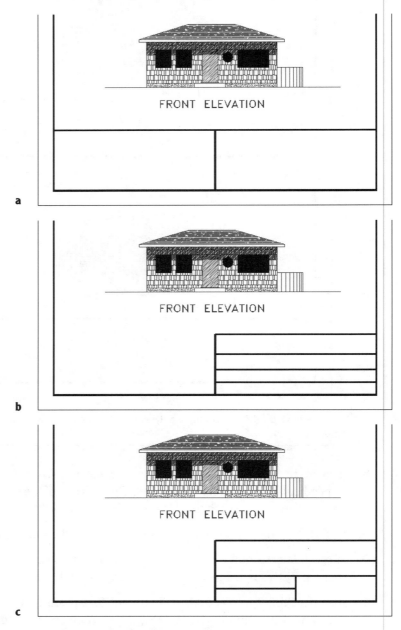

FIGURE 10.25: Building the title block: the left edge (a), the horizontal lines (b), and the last line trimmed (c)

The lines for the title block are almost done. Some of the Plines may look wider than others. This almost certainly is caused by the monitor distorting the picture at the current view. By zooming in, you can assure yourself that everything is correct.

1. Zoom into a close view of the title block. Notice that the intersection of the outer lines in the upper-left corner doesn't seem clean.

2. Zoom into that corner using a zoom window (Figure 10.26a). The lines don't intersect in a clean corner. They need to be joined.

3. Type **pe** ↵ to start the Polyline Edit command and select one of the two lines. You must place the pickbox on the edge of the polyline to select it, not in the middle of it.

4. Type **j** ↵. Then select the other Pline and press ↵. The corner is corrected (Figure 10.26b). Type **x** ↵ to end the Pedit command.

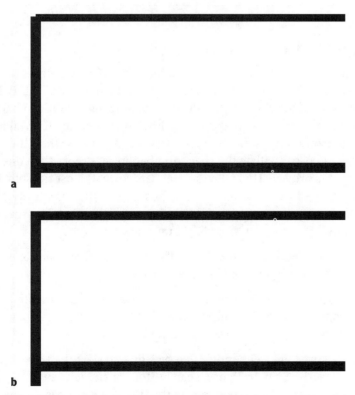

FIGURE 10.26: Zoomed into the upper-left corner (a), and the corner corrected (b)

5. Zoom Previous once. Then use Realtime Zoom to zoom out just enough to see the Front Elevation text at the top of the screen (Figure 10.27).

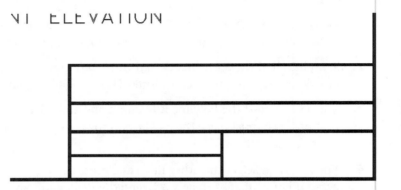

FIGURE 10.27: The completed lines of the title block after zooming out

Putting Text in the Title Block

The title block has five boxes that will each contain distinct pieces of information. The large one at the top will contain the name of the project. Below that will be the name of the company producing the drawing—your company. (If you don't have a company name, make one up.) Below that on the left will be the initials of the person—you—who drew this drawing, and below that, the date. In the lower-right corner will be the sheet number, in case more than one sheet is required for this project. This follows a standard format. Most title block layouts will contain this information and more, depending on the complexity of the job.

You need to put labels in some of the boxes to identify what information will be shown there. For this, you need to set up a new text style.

1. Choose Format ➤ Text Style. The Text Style dialog box appears. The Label text style should still be current.

2. Click New and type **Tblk-label** and click OK. Leave the font set to romans.shx, but change the height to 8". Then click Apply & Close. Tblk-label is the current text style.

3. Be sure Caps Lock is on, then type **dt** ↵ to start the Dtext command. Click the Snap to None Osnap button. Then pick a point in the upper-left corner of the upper box of the title block. It doesn't have to be the perfect location now; you can fix it after you see the text.

If you press ↵ after changing the height, the Apply button ghosts out. Pressing ↵ at this point has the same effect as clicking the Apply button.

4. Press ↵ at the rotation prompt. Type **project:** ↵ ↵. PROJECT: will be placed in the upper box (Figure 10.28a).

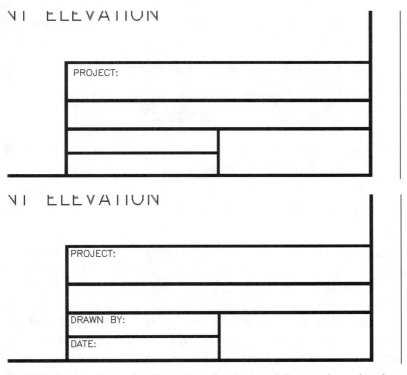

FIGURE 10.28: One line of text placed (a), and the text changed to the correct wording (b)

5. If necessary, move this text to the upper-left corner, as far as possible, while still allowing it to be readable. It will help if Polar and Osnap are temporarily turned off.

The closer you zoom in, the more precisely you will be able to fine-tune the location of the text. Then you need to zoom out to check how it looks.

T I P If you have running Osnaps and need to have them off for one pick, you can click the Snap to None Osnap button. This cancels all running Osnaps for the next pick. If you need running Osnaps turned off for several picks, click the Osnap button on the Status bar. Click it again when you want the running Osnaps to become active.

6. Use the Copy command to copy this text to the bottom two boxes on the left, using the Multiple option and the endpoint of the horizontal lines above each of the boxes as the base and displacement points.

This will keep each piece of text in the same position relative to the upper-left corner of each box.

7. Type **ed** ↵ to start the Ddedit command. Then click the upper of the two copies of text. The Edit Text dialog box appears with PROJECT: highlighted.

8. Type **drawn by:** and click OK. Pick the lower copy of text. The Edit Text dialog box returns.

9. Type **date:** and click OK. Press ↵ to end the Ddedit command. The text is changed and three of the boxes have their proper label (Figure 10.28b).

The Ddedit command is a quick way to change the wording of text and make spelling corrections. You have to change one line at a time, but the command keeps running until you stop it.

The next area to work on is the lower-right box. This is where the sheet number is located, and it is usually displayed in such a way that the person reading the drawing can tell not only the page number of the current sheet, but also the number of sheets being used for the project. We will create a new text style for this box.

1. Start the Style command. In the Text Style dialog box, click New.

2. Type **Sheet_No** and click OK. For the font, select romand.shx. Change the height to 1'-3". Click Apply, then click Close. Sheet_No is now the current text style.

3. You will need to center the text horizontally in the box. This will require breaking the horizontal line running across the top of this box at the upper-left corner of the box. To do this, click the Break button on the Modify toolbar. Then select the line to break at a point where no other lines are touching it.

4. Type **f** ↵ to select the first point of the break. Then use the running Osnap to pick the upper-left corner of the box.

5. At the Enter second break point: prompt, type **@** ↵. This forces the second point to coincide with the first point, and the line is broken without leaving a gap.

6. Start the Dtext command and type **j** ↵. Then type **tc** ↵. Select Midpoint Osnap and pick a point on the line across the top of the box.

7. Press ↵ at the rotation prompt. With Caps Lock on, type **sheet no.:** ↵ **1 of 1** ↵ ↵. (When you get to the *of*, turn Caps Lock off.) For clarity, leave a double space after the first *1* and before the second *1*. The text is inserted into the box and is centered horizontally (Figure 10.29a).

8. With Polar Tracking on, use the Move command to move the text down and center it vertically in the box (Figure 10.29b). Remember, when you select the text to move it, you have to pick each line because they are two separate objects.

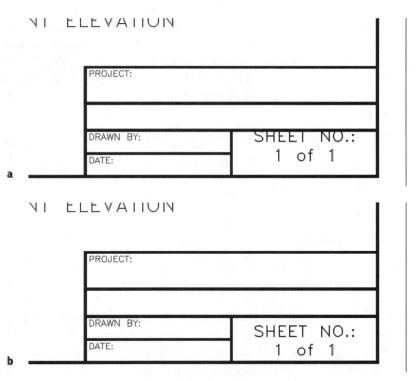

FIGURE 10.29: The text after being inserted (a), and after centering vertically (b)

Now it's time for you to experiment. Use the same techniques you just went through to fill in the text for the other four boxes. Feel free to try other fonts, but you will have to adjust the height for each text style so that the text fits in its box. Some guidelines for height follow.

Box	Recommended Height of Text
PROJECT:	2'-6"
COMPANY:	1'-3"
DRAWN BY:	1'-0"
DATE:	1'-0"

You will have to set up a new style for each new font or height you choose, unless you set up a style with a height of 0'-0". In that case, you will be prompted for the height each time you start to place text in the drawing. This is the recommended way to operate for the top two boxes because it will give consistency to the text even when heights vary. You might try several fonts, then come back to this technique at the end. I also recommend that you use a relatively simple font for the text in the Drawn By and Date boxes, something a little larger and possibly bolder than the labels in those boxes.

Try these fonts:

- ▶ romant.shx or romanc.shx
- ▶ any of the swis721 series
- ▶ Times New Roman
- ▶ Technic
- ▶ SansSerif
- ▶ CityBlueprint or CountryBlueprint
- ▶ Arial

In the top two boxes, the text can be centered vertically and horizontally if you draw a line diagonally across the box, choose Middle as a justification for the text, and use Midpoint Osnap to snap to the diagonal line when you start the text. For the Drawn By and Date boxes, centering the text horizontally is not advisable because the label text already in the boxes takes up too much space. However, you can use the diagonal line to center it, then move the text to the right until it makes a good fit. Using Polar Tracking will keep the new text vertically centered.

Be careful in your use of running Osnaps as you position text. If you are eyeballing the final location, it is best to have no running Osnaps. On the other hand, if you are precisely locating justification points by snapping to lines and other objects, you might try having the following Osnaps running: Endpoint, Intersection, Perpendicular, and Insertion, with Midpoint optional.

When you finish, your title block should look something like Figure 10.30. In this sample, romant.shx font was used for a style that was set to zero height, then applied to the top two boxes at the recommended heights. The romand.shx font was used for the Drawn By and Date boxes, also at the recommended height.

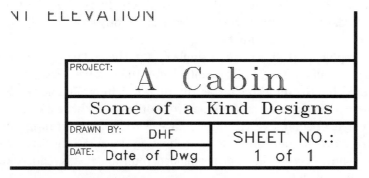

FIGURE 10.30: The completed title block

If you are going to design your own company title block, be ready to spend a little time setting it up and deciding which fonts will give the look that best reflects the image you want to project. You can then use this title block on all your subsequent projects.

Zoom to Extents, then zoom out a little to view the entire drawing. Save this drawing as Cabin10b (Figure 10.31).

The final part of the chapter will introduce you to multiline text, which you will also work with as you learn about dimensions in the next chapter.

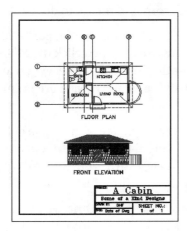

FIGURE 10.31: The latest version of the cabin drawing

Using Multiline Text

Multiline text (often referred to as *Mtext*) is a more complex form of text than single-line text. It can be used the same way single-line text has been used in this chapter, and it can do more. If you have several lines of text, or if you need certain words within a line of text to appear differently than the adjacent words, multiline text is the best thing to use.

A paragraph of multiline text is a single entity. The text will wrap around and the length of a line can be easily modified after the text has been placed in the drawing. Within the multiline text entity, all text is fully editable and behaves as if it were in a word processor. A special word or letter of the text can be given its own text style or color. Everything you have learned about defining a new text style also applies to multiline text, as both kinds of text use the same text styles. Just as polylines become lines when exploded, multiline text is reduced to single-line text when exploded.

Dimensions use multiline text, and any text that is imported into an AutoCAD drawing from a word processing document or text editor will become multiline text in the drawing. In this section, you will learn how to place a paragraph of multiline text in the cabin drawing and then modify it. In Chapter 11, you will work with dimension text and text with leader lines, both of which use multiline text. We will start by adding a note in the lower-left corner of the drawing, using Multiline Text.

> Use the Explode command to turn multiline text into single-line text, to unblock objects in a block reference, and to convert a polyline into a regular line or a series of regular lines. Click the Explode button on the Modify toolbar to start the command.

1. Click the Make Object's Layer Current button on the left end of the Object Properties toolbar. Then click the FRONT ELEVATION text to make the Text1 layer current. Zoom into the blank area to the left of the title block in the lower-left corner of the cabin drawing.

> You can also start the Multiline Text command by typing t ↵, or by choosing Draw ➢ Text ➢ Multiline Text from the pull-down menus.

2. Click the Osnap button on the Status bar to the Off position. This will temporarily disable any running Osnaps. Then click the Multiline Text button on the Draw toolbar. At the Command window, you are shown the name of the current text style and height, and are prompted to specify a first corner.

3. Select a point near the left borderline in line with the top of the title block. The prompt now reads, `Specify opposite corner or [Height/Justify/Line spacing/Rotation/Style/Width]:`. These are all the options for the Multiline Text command.

4. If the current style is Label, go on to step 5. Otherwise type s ↵ for the style option and type **label** ↵.

5. Drag open a window that fills the space between the left border and the left side of the title block. This defines the length of line for the multiline text (Figure 10.32). Click to finish the window.

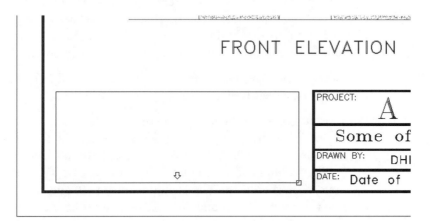

FIGURE 10.32: Making a Multiline Text window

6. The Multiline Text Editor dialog box opens, and you can see a long blank area with a flashing cursor in it. This is where you will type the text. In the drop-down lists at the top, you can see the font and height of the current text style.

7. Type in the following text, using single spacing and pressing Enter only at the end of the first line and at the end of each note:

GENERAL NOTES:

1. All work shall be in accordance with the 1990 Ed. Uniform Building Code and all local ordinances.

2. Roof can be built to be steeper for climates with heavy snowfall.

The Multiline Text Editor dialog box can be resized to accommodate more lines of text and a greater line length.

3. Solar panels available for installation on roof.

4. All windows to be double-paned.

When finished, press OK. The text is placed in the drawing (Figure 10.33a). The window you specified was only used to define the line length. Its height does not control how far down the text will come, as that is determined by how much text you enter.

8. Double-click anywhere on the new text. The Multiline Text Editor dialog box comes back up.

9. Move the cursor to the upper-left corner of the window containing the text and in front of the *G* in the first word. Hold down the left mouse button and drag it to the right and down until all the text is highlighted. Release the mouse button. Be sure the Character tab is active, then change the Text Height from 1' to 9" and click OK. The text is redrawn smaller and now makes a better fit within the space available (Figure 10.33b).

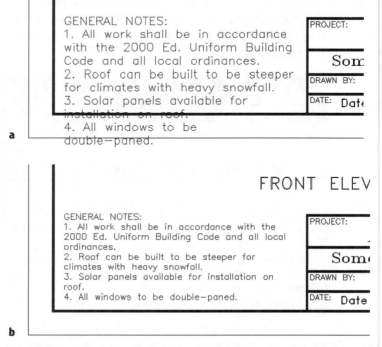

FIGURE 10.33: Mtext in the drawing (a), and modified to be smaller (b)

10. Double-click the Mtext again. The Multiline Text Editor dialog box comes up and displays the text you just clicked.

11. Highlight all the text again. In the Fonts drop-down list at the left side of the Character tab, select SansSerif as the current font. The selected text changes to the new font.

12. Click OK. The Mtext in the drawing has become more compact and there is room for more notes (Figure 10.34).

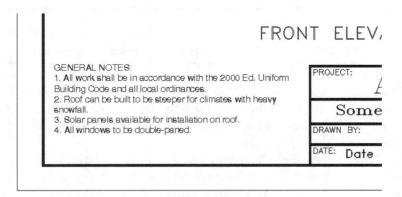

FIGURE 10.34: The results of a font modification

The SansSerif is a TrueType font supported by Windows. When used in Auto-CAD drawings, it can be italic or boldface. To see how to change individual words within the text, we will underline and boldface the Uniform Building Code text.

1. Double-click the Mtext again. The Multiline Text Editor dialog box appears again.

2. Use the same technique as earlier to highlight just the Uniform Building Code text. Then click the Bold (B) and Underline (U) buttons on the Character tab. The selected text is underlined and boldfaced.

3. Click OK. The text is redrawn with the changes (Figure 10.35).

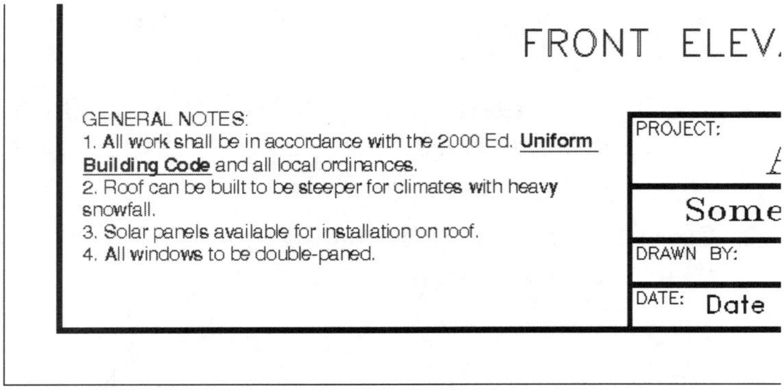

FIGURE 10.35: The Mtext with individual words modified

Individual words can also be italicized and given a different color or height than the rest of the Mtext, by using the other tools at the top of the Multiline Text Editor dialog box. You are encouraged to experiment with all these tools to become familiar with them.

The length of a line can be easily altered to make the Mtext fit more conveniently on the drawing. Let's say you've decided to put your company logo to the left of the title block. You need to squeeze the text into a narrower space. You have some extra room at the bottom, so you should be able to do it.

1. At the Command: prompt, select the text. Four grips appear at the corners of the body of Mtext.

2. On the Status bar, be sure Polar is on and Osnap and Otrack are off. Then click the upper-right grip to activate it.

3. Slowly move the cursor to the left, stopping periodically until the defining rectangle appears. When the bottom of the rectangle gets close to the bottom line of the border, you will have moved about a third of the way to the left borderline (Figure 10.36a).

4. Click the mouse button, then press Esc. The text is squeezed into a narrower space but still fits on the page (Figure 10.36b).

5. Zoom to Extents, then zoom out a little to a view of the whole drawing (Figure 10.37). You won't be able to read the Mtext at this magnification, but it will look fine when you print your drawing.

6. Save this drawing as Cabin10c.

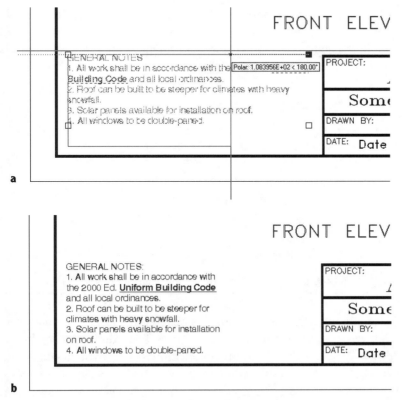

FIGURE 10.36: Modifying the Mtext line length with grips (a), and the results (b)

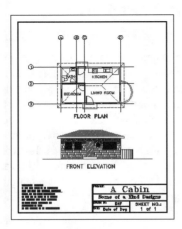

FIGURE 10.37: The full drawing

Mtext has justification points similar to those of single-line text, and they behave the same way. The default justification point for Mtext, however, is the upper-left corner of the body of text, and the available options are for nine points distributed around the perimeter of the body of text and at the center (Figure 10.38).

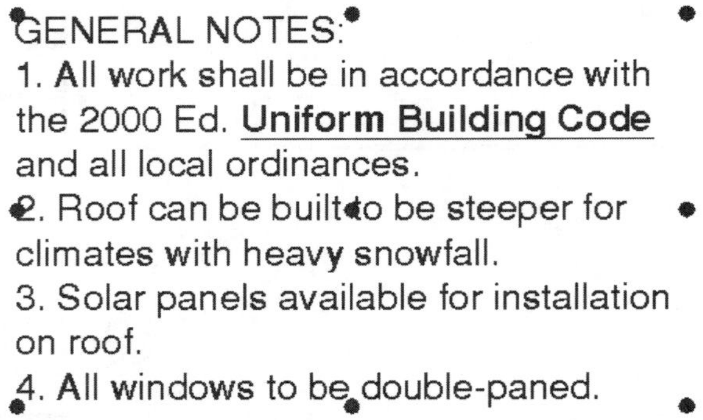

GENERAL NOTES:
1. All work shall be in accordance with the 2000 Ed. **Uniform Building Code** and all local ordinances.
2. Roof can be built to be steeper for climates with heavy snowfall.
3. Solar panels available for installation on roof.
4. All windows to be double-paned.

FIGURE 10.38: Justification points for Mtext

This completes the exercises for this chapter. If you want to play around with the Mtext, it can be edited with the Multiline Text Edit dialog box by choosing Modify ➢ Object ➢ Text ➢ Edit and selecting the text you need to edit.

With both Mtext and single-line text, you can add special characters—degree symbol, diameter symbol, etc.—that are not included in most font character packages. You will have a chance to do this in the next chapter.

FEATURES OF THE MULTILINE TEXT EDITOR

Here's a brief summary of the various features of the Mtext Editor.

Import Text button: Used to import a word processing or text file into an AutoCAD drawing. The maximum size allowable is 16k, so the smallest Word document possible is too large; you can, however, use files in Text Only or RTF formats. The Import Text button uses a Select File dialog box that views only files having the .txt or .rtf extensions. You can bring in text files with other extensions if you enter the full filename with its extension, and if they are not larger than 16k. Text comes in as Mtext and uses the current text style, height setting, and layer. If there are complex code fields for such things as tabs, multiple margin indents, etc., the imported file may not retain these.

Continued on next page

On the **Character tab:**

Font drop-down list—Sets the font for selected text.

Height drop-down text box—Sets the height for selected text.

Bold, Italic, and Underline buttons—Change selected text.

Undo button—Undoes the last editing action.

Fraction button—Converts selected text into any of three styles of stacked fraction. Use one of three symbols to specify the fraction bar: "/" for horizontal, "#" for slanted, and "^" for none.

Text Color drop-down list—Changes the color of a selected portion of text.

Symbol button—Imports symbols (such as diameter, degree, etc.) that are not available in the font you are using.

The **Properties tab** contains four drop-down lists:

Style—Changes the text style of the Mtext currently in the editor.

Justification—Changes the justification of the Mtext currently in the editor.

Width—Changes the line length of the Mtext currently in the editor. Choose a width or enter one.

Rotation—Rotates the Mtext in the editor. Choose an angle or enter one.

The **Line Spacing tab** contains two drop-down lists:

Type—Controls the style of spacing between lines. The At Least option adjusts the spacing to accommodate larger letters. The Exactly option holds a constant spacing regardless of character size.

Spacing—Specifies the distance between lines as an absolute distance or as a fraction of the default Single spacing. Choose a spacing or enter a distance within parameters.

The **Find/Replace tab** contains two drop-down lists, two buttons, and two check boxes:

Text To Find—Enter the word or string of words to be changed, or choose a previously entered word or string of words.

Binoculars button—Click to start a search for the specified text.

Text To Replace—Enter or choose the word or string of words that will replace the found text.

Replace button—Click to perform the replacement operation.

Match Case—When checked, it forces AutoCAD to match text by upper/lowercase as well as by spelling.

Whole Word—When checked, it forces AutoCAD to find only whole words that match.

If You Would Like More Practice...

For more practice using single-line text:

1. Close all drawings, then bring up Cabin04c-addon.dwg.

2. Bring in the Title and Label text styles from the Cabin10a drawing while it is closed, using Design Center.

3. Add Labels to the features that were added on.

   ▶ Use the Title text style to identify the addition as GARAGE.

   ▶ Use the Label text style to give the features the following names: WALKWAY, STORAGE, OFFICE, and CAR.

For more practice using Mtext:

1. Open Cabin10c and zoom into the blank space between the structural grid and the top border.

2. Create a new text style called Description that uses the Times New Roman font and a height of 12".

3. Start up Mtext and specify a rectangle for the text that covers the width of the sheet between the borders, and occupies the space above the structural grid.

4. Enter the following text exactly as shown here, errors and all:

   This is a design for a small vaction cabin. It contains approximately 380 square feet of living space and includes one bedrooms and one bath. It can be adopted to provide shelter in all climates and can be modified to allow constuction that uses local building materials. Please sund all inquiries to the manufacturer.

5. Double-click the new text and make these changes:

   ▶ Correct all spelling errors.

   ▶ Change "square feet" to "sq. ft."

   ▶ Make the following words bold: "one bedroom," "one bath," "all climates," and "local building materials."

   ▶ Italicize the last sentence.

   ▶ See if you can modify the shape of the defining rectangle so the text fits in the space in the upper-left corner.

Are You Experienced?

Now you can...

- ☑ set up text styles
- ☑ place single-line text in a drawing for titles and room labels
- ☑ create a grid for a drawing
- ☑ modify single-line text
- ☑ construct a title block and place text in it
- ☑ place Mtext in a drawing
- ☑ modify Mtext in several ways

CHAPTER 11

Dimensioning a Drawing

- ▶ Setting up a dimension style
- ▶ Dimensioning the floor plan of the cabin
- ▶ Modifying existing dimensions
- ▶ Modifying existing dimension styles

Dimensions are the final ingredient to be added to your drawing. To introduce you to dimensioning, we are going to follow a pattern similar to the one we used in the previous chapter on text.

Dimension Styles

Dimension styles are similar to text styles, but are more complex. They are set up the same way, but there are many parameters that control the various parts of dimensions, including the dimension text.

Before you start setting up a dimension style, you need to make a few changes to your drawing to prepare it for dimensioning.

1. Open Cabin10c and zoom into the upper half of the drawing.

2. Create a new layer called Dim1. Assign it a color and make it current.

3. Freeze the Grid layer.

4. Set Endpoint Osnap to be running.

5. Set the Status bar so that only the Osnap and Model buttons are in the on position.

6. Right-click any button on any toolbar on the screen to bring up the on-screen toolbar menu. Click Dimension. The Dimension toolbar comes up on the drawing area in the form of a floating toolbar.

7. Move the Dimension toolbar to the top center of the drawing area, being careful to avoid docking it. (You learned about moving toolbars around on the screen in Chapter 1, *Getting to Know AutoCAD*.) Your drawing will look like Figure 11.1.

Making a New Dimension Style

Each dimension has several components: the dimension line, arrows or tick marks, extension lines, and the dimension text (Figure 11.2). The appearance and location of these components is controlled by an extensive set of variables that is stored with each drawing file. You will work with these variables through a series of dialog boxes that have been designed to make setting up a dimension style as easy and trouble-free as possible. Remember that AutoCAD has been designed to be useable by drafters from many trades and professions, each of which has its own standards for drafting. To satisfy these folks' widely varied needs, AutoCAD dimensioning features have many options and settings for controlling the appearance and placement of dimensions in drawings.

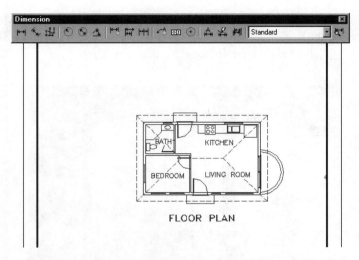

FIGURE 11.1: The floor plan of `Cabin10c` with the Dimension toolbar centered at the top of the drawing area

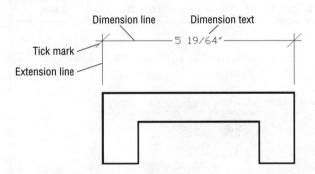

FIGURE 11.2: The parts of a dimension

Naming a Dimension Style

Every dimension variable has a default setting, and these as a group comprise the default Standard dimension style. As in defining text styles, the procedure is to make a copy of the Standard dimension style and rename the copy—in effect, making a new style that is a copy of the default style. Then you make changes to this new style so it has the settings you need to dimension your drawing.

1. Click the Dimension Style button on the Dimension toolbar. The Dimension Style Manager dialog box comes up (Figure 11.3). On the top left in the Styles list box, Standard is listed.

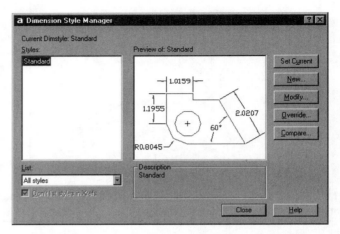

FIGURE 11.3: The Dimension Style Manager dialog box

2. Click the New button on the right side of the dialog box. The Create New Dimension Style dialog box appears.

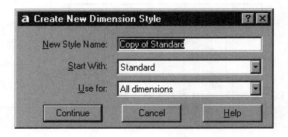

3. In the New Style Name text box, Copy of Standard is highlighted. Type **DimPlan** but don't press ↵ yet. Notice that Standard is in the Start With drop-down list just below. Because it is the current and only dimension style in this drawing, the new dimension style you are about to define will begin as a copy of the Standard style. This is similar to the way in which new text styles are defined (Chapter 10, *Controlling Text in a Drawing*). The Use For drop-down list allows you to choose the kinds of dimensions to which the new style will be applied. In this case, it's all dimensions, so we don't need to change this.

4. Click the Continue button. The Create New Dimension Style dialog box changes into a large dialog box with the same name, but with DimPlan added to the title bar (Figure 11.4). It has six tabs. You have created a new dimension style that is a copy of the Standard style, and now you will make the changes necessary to set up DimPlan to work as the main dimension style for the floor plan of the cabin.

5. Be sure the Lines and Arrows tab is active (on top). If it's not, click it.

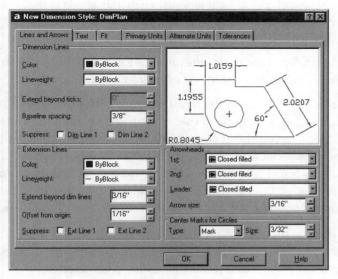

FIGURE 11.4: The New Dimension Style dialog box with DimPlan as the current style and Lines and Arrows as the active tab

Using the Lines and Arrows Tab

You will use the Lines and Arrows tab to control the appearance of the dimension and extension lines, the arrowheads, and the center marks.

1. In the Arrowheads area, click the down arrow in the upper drop-down list to open the list of arrowheads.

2. Click Architectural Tick. The drop-down list closes with Architectural Tick displayed in the first and second drop-down lists. In the preview window above, a graphic displays the new arrowhead type.

3. In the Arrow Size text box, use the down scroll arrow to change 0'-0 ³⁄₁₆" to 0'-0 ⅛".

4. Move to the Dimension Lines area. Change the Extend Beyond Ticks setting from 0" to ³⁄₃₂" by highlighting the 0 and typing the new setting. This will extend the dimension line past the tick mark a short distance.

5. In the Extension Line area, use the down scroll arrow to change the Extend Beyond Dim Lines setting from 0'-0 ³⁄₁₆" to 0'-0 ⅛". This controls how far the extension line will extend beyond the dimension line.

Before saving these changes, make some more modifications to the DimPlan style.

Making Changes in the Text Tab

The settings in the Text tab control the appearance of dimension text and how it is located relative to the dimension and extension lines.

1. Click the Text tab on the New Dimension Style dialog box. There are three areas with settings that affect the appearance and location of dimension text. Look ahead to Figure 11.5 for a graphic of the Text tab. The preview window appears in all tabs and is updated automatically as settings are modified. Move to the Text Appearance area in the upper-left corner of the dialog box where there are five settings that control how the text looks. We are concerned about only two of them.

2. Click the Browse button that sits at the right end of the Text Style drop-down list. The Text Style dialog box opens. Set up a new text style called Dim that has the following parameters:

   ▶ Romand.shx font

   ▶ 0'-0" height

   ▶ 0.8000 width factor

   ▶ All other settings at their default

   If you need a reminder on creating text styles, refer to Chapter 10. Apply this text style to make it current, then close the Text Style dialog box.

3. Back in the Text tab, open the Text Style drop-down list and select the new Dim style from the list.

4. Change the Text Height setting from ³⁄₁₆" to ³⁄₃₂".

5. Move down to the Text Placement area. These settings determine where the text is located, vertically and horizontally, relative to the dimension line. There are two settings to change.

6. Open the Vertical drop-down list and select Above. At this setting, the text will sit above the dimension line and not break the line into two segments. Set the Offset From Dim Line setting to ⅟₃₂".

7. Now move to the Text Alignment area. There are three radio buttons that control whether dimension text is aligned horizontally or with the direction of the dimension line. The ISO Standard option varies text alignment depending on whether the text can fit between the extension lines. Only one of the buttons can be active at a time. Horizontal should already be active. Click the Aligned with Dimension Line button. Notice how the appearance and location of the text has changed in the preview window. This finishes our work in this tab. The settings should look like Figure 11.5.

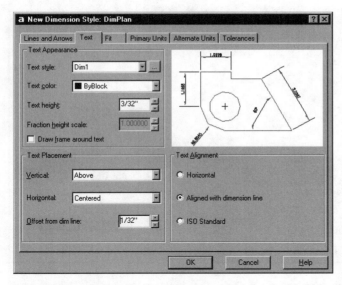

FIGURE 11.5: The Text tab with settings for the DimPlan style

There are four more tabs with settings, but we'll be making changes in only two of them: Fit and Primary Units.

Working with Settings in the Fit Tab

The settings in the Fit tab control the overall scale factor of the dimension style and how the text and arrowheads are placed when the extension lines are too close together for both text and arrows to fit.

1. Click the Fit tab on the New Dimension Style dialog box. Look ahead to Figure 11.6 to see a graphic of the Fit tab.

2. In the upper-left corner, in the Fit Options area, click the Text radio button.

3. In the Text Placement area, click the Over the Dimension Line, Without a Leader radio button.

4. Make no changes in the Fine Tuning area for now. Move to the Scale for Dimension Features area. Be sure Use Overall Scale Of radio button is active. Set the scale to 96. (Use the highlight-and-type-in method described in step 4 of an earlier section, "Using the Lines and Arrows Tab.") The settings in the Fit tab should look like Figure 11.6.

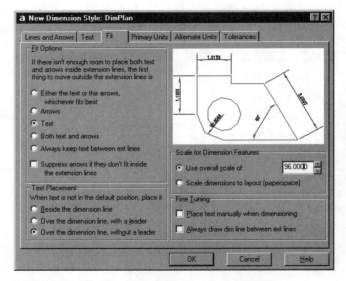

FIGURE 11.6: The new settings in the Fit tab

Setting Up the Primary Units Tab

In the preview window, you may have noticed that the numbers in the dimension text maintained a decimal format with four decimal places, rather than the feet and inches format of the current Architectural units. Dimensions have their own units setting, independent of the basic units for the drawing as a whole. In the next tab, you will set the dimension units.

1. Click the Primary Units tab and take a peek ahead at Figure 11.7 to see how it's organized. There are two areas: Linear and Angular

Dimensions. Within each of these areas are a few settings and one or two nested areas.

2. In the Linear Dimensions area, starting at the top, make the following changes:

    A. Change the Unit Format setting from Decimal to Architectural.

    B. Change the Fraction Format setting to Diagonal.

    C. In the Zero Suppression sub-area, uncheck 0 Inches.

N O T E Zero Suppression controls (a) whether or not the zero is shown for feet when the dimensioned distance is less than one foot, and (b) whether or not the zero is shown for inches when the distance is a whole number of feet. For the Cabin drawing, we will suppress the zero for feet, but we will show the zero for inches. So 9" will be shown as 9", and 3' will be shown as 3'-0".

3. In the Angular Dimensions area, leave Decimal Degrees as the Units Format and change Precision to two decimal places, as you did for the basic drawing units in Chapter 3, *Setting Up a Drawing*. For now, leave the Zero Suppression sub-area as it is. After these changes, the Primary Units tab will look like Figure 11.7.

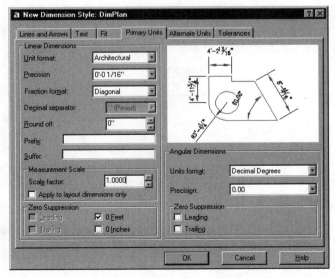

FIGURE 11.7: The Primary Units tab after changes have been made

The last two tabs, Alternate Units and Tolerances, are advanced settings that we don't need to change. It's time to save these setting changes to the new Dim-Plan dimension style and begin dimensioning the cabin.

1. Click the OK button at the bottom of the New Dimension Style dialog box. You will be returned to the Dimension Style Manager dialog box (Figure 11.8). DimPlan is displayed with a gray swatch in the Styles list box, along with Standard. In the lower-right corner of the dialog box, in the Description area, the following information is presented about the new style: the name of the original style that the new style is based on and the changes that were made to the original style to create the new style.

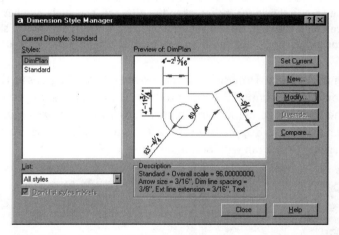

FIGURE 11.8: The Dimension Style Manager dialog box with DimPlan listed

2. Click DimPlan to highlight it in a dark blue. Then click the Set Current button. Finally, click the Close button. You are returned to your drawing, and the Dimension toolbar now displays DimPlan in the Dim Style Control drop-down list. This indicates that DimPlan is now the current dimension style.

You have made changes to 16 settings that control dimensions. This is not too many, considering that there are more than 50 dimension settings. Here is a summary of the changes you've made to make the dimensions work with the cabin drawing:

Tab	Setting	Default Setting	DimPlan
Lines and Arrows	Arrowheads	Closed Filled	Architectural Tick
	Arrowhead size	$3/16$"	$1/8$"
	Dim Line Extension	0"	$3/32$"
	Ext. Line Extension	$3/16$"	$1/8$"
Text	Text Style	Standard	DimPlan
	Text Height	$3/16$"	$3/32$"
	Text Vertical Justification	Centered	Above
	Offset from Dim Line	$3/32$"	$1/32$"
	Text Alignment	Horizontal	Aligned with Dimension Line
Fit	Fit Options	Either—whichever is best	Text
	Text Placement	Beside Dim line	Over Dim line, no leader
	Overall scale	1.0000	96.0000
Primary Units	Unit Format	Decimal	Architectural
	Fraction Format	Horizontal	Diagonal
	Zero Suppression	Feet, Inches	Feet only
	Angular Precision	No decimal places	Two decimal places

You will change a few more settings throughout the rest of this chapter as you begin to dimension the cabin in the next set of exercises.

Placing Dimensions on the Drawing

Upon returning to your drawing, it should still look almost exactly like Figure 11.1, and it should have the following:

- ▶ A new layer called Dim1, which is current
- ▶ A new dimension style called DimPlan, which is current and is now displayed in the drop-down list on the Dimension toolbar

▶ The Grid layer frozen

▶ Endpoint Osnap running

▶ On the Status bar: Ortho, Polar, and Otrack off

▶ A new text style called Dim, which is current

Horizontal Dimensions

First, you will dimension across the top of the plan, from the corner of the building to the center of the interior wall, then to the other corner. Then you'll dimension the roof.

1. Click the Linear button at the left end of the Dimension toolbar to activate the Dimlinear command. The prompt reads `Specify first extension line origin or <select object>:`.

2. Pick the upper-left corner of the cabin walls. The prompt changes to `Specify second extension line origin:`. At this point, zoom into the bathroom area until you can see the wall between the bathroom and kitchen, as well as the back wall, close up.

3. Type .x ↵ to start point filters.

4. Activate Midpoint Osnap and click the upper jamb line of the bathroom door opening when the triangle appears at the jamb's midpoint (Figure 11.9).

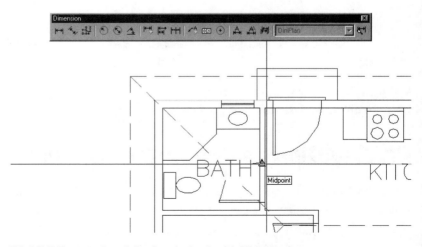

F I G U R E 1 1 . 9 : Selecting the jamb with Midpoint Osnap

5. Click the upper-left corner of the cabin walls again. The dimension appears in ghosted form attached to, and moving with, the cursor (Figure 11.10a). Notice that the right extension line starts just outside the outer wall line. This is the result of using the point filters.

6. Use Realtime Pan to pan the drawing down until there's room to place the dimension. Move the cursor until the dimension line is about 3' above the back step. Click to place it (Figure 11.10b).

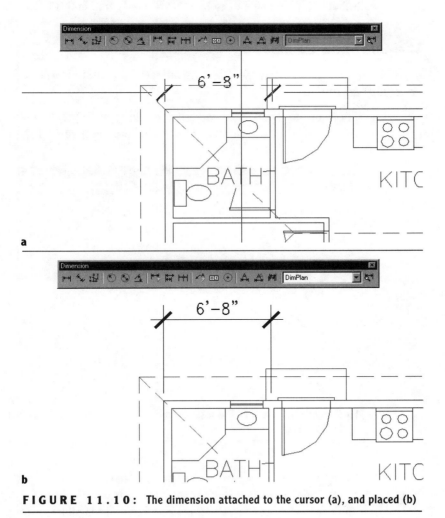

FIGURE 11.10: The dimension attached to the cursor (a), and placed (b)

Your first dimension is completed.

When dimensioning walls, you usually dimension to the outside of the exterior ones and to the center of the interior ones. The next dimension will run from the right side of the first dimension to the right corner.

> **N O T E**   Studs are the vertical 2"×4" or 2"×6" members in the framing of a wall. When dimensioning buildings that have stud walls, architects usually make the dimensions show the distance to the face of the stud for the outside walls, but we are not able to go into that level of detail in this book.

The Continue Command

AutoCAD has an automatic way of placing adjacent dimensions in line—the *Continue command*.

1. Zoom out and pan until you have a view of the upper wall and roof line, with space above them for dimensions (Figure 11.11).

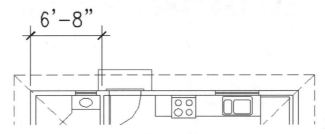

FIGURE 11.11: The result of zooming and panning for a view of the top of the floor plan

2. Select the Continue button on the Dimension toolbar. The prompt reads Specify a second extension line origin or [Undo/ Select] <Select>:. All you need to do here is pick a point for the right end of the dimension—in this case, the upper-right corner of the walls.

3. Click the upper-right corner of the house. The second dimension is drawn in line with the first (Figure 11.12). Note that the same prompt has returned to the Command window. You could keep picking points to place the next adjacent dimension in line, if there was need of one. Press Esc to cancel the Continue command.

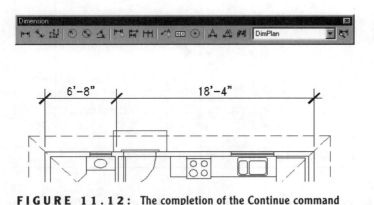

FIGURE 11.12: The completion of the Continue command

With the Continue command, you can dimension along a wall of a building very quickly, just by picking points. AutoCAD assumes that the last extension line specified for the previous dimension will coincide with the first extension line of the next dimension. If the extension line you need to continue from is not the last one specified, press ↵ at the prompt, then pick the extension line you want to continue from, and continue the command.

Another automatic routine that can be used with linear dimensions is called Baseline.

The Baseline Command

The *Baseline command* gets its name from a style of dimensioning called baseline, in which all dimensions begin at the same point (Figure 11.13). Each dimension is stacked above the previous one. Because of the automatic stacking, you can use the Baseline command for overall dimensions. AutoCAD will stack the overall dimension a set height above the incremental ones.

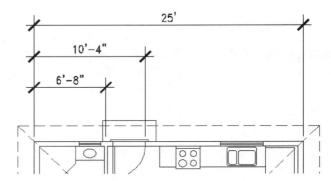

FIGURE 11.13: Example of baseline dimensions

 1. Pick the Baseline button on the Dimension toolbar. The prompt reads `Specify a second extension line origin or [Undo/Select] <Select>:`, just like the first prompt for the Continue command.

2. Press ↵ to choose the Select option.

3. Pick the extension line that extends from the upper-left corner—the first extension line of the first dimension.

4. Pick the upper-right corner of the walls, then press Esc to cancel the Baseline command. The overall dimension is drawn above the first two dimensions (Figure 11.14). (The Baseline command will keep running until you cancel it, just like the Continue command.)

The Baseline command assumes the baseline is the first extension line of the last dimension. For the cabin, that would be the extension line that extends to the center of the interior wall. You want the baseline to be the extension line above the upper-left corner of the walls, so press ↵ to select that extension line to be the baseline.

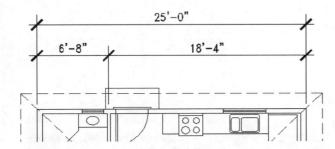

FIGURE 11.14: The completion of the overall dimension with the Baseline command

It would be nice to have a dimension for the roof spaced the same distance above the overall dimension as the overall dimension is spaced above the incremental dimensions. The Baseline command can help you do this.

1. Start the Baseline command again and press ↵ for the Select option.

2. Pick the extension line for the upper-left corner of the walls as the baseline.

3. Pick the upper-right corner of the roof. A dimension is placed above the overall dimension (Figure 11.15a). Press Esc to cancel the Baseline command. To finish it, you need to move the left extension line of this last dimension to the upper-left corner of the roof.

4. Click the text of the roof dimension. Grips appear in five places on the dimension, and the dimension ghosts (Figure 11.15b).

5. Click the grip at the bottom of the left extension line to activate it.

6. Click the upper-left corner of the roof, then press ↵. The extension line moves, and the dimension text is updated to display the full length of the roof (Figure 11.15c).

This completes the horizontal dimensions for the back wall.

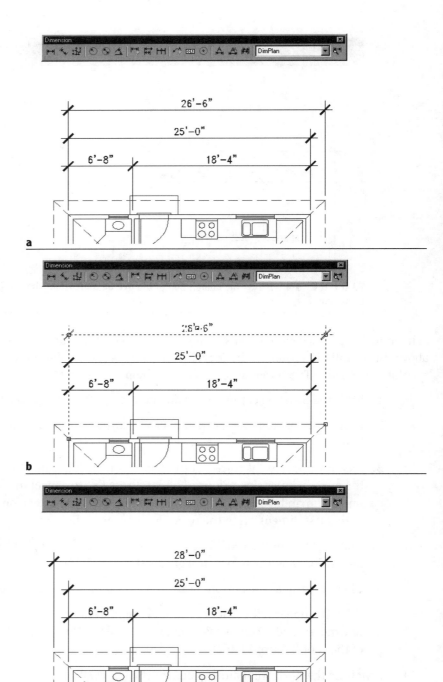

FIGURE 11.15: The result of the second use of the Baseline command (a), starting grips to modify the dimension (b), and the result (c)

Vertical Dimensions

Because the Linear command can be used for vertical and horizontal dimensions, you can follow the same steps as above to do the vertical dimensions on the left side of the floor plan. The only difference from the horizontal dimensioning is that there is no jamb line that can be used with point filters to establish the center of the interior wall between the bedroom and bathroom. You will draw a guideline—the same one you drew in the last chapter to help make the grid. The following steps will take you through the process of placing the first vertical dimension. Then you'll be able to finish the rest of them by yourself.

1. Pan and zoom to get a good view of the left side of the floor plan, including the space between the roof and the border (Figure 11.16).

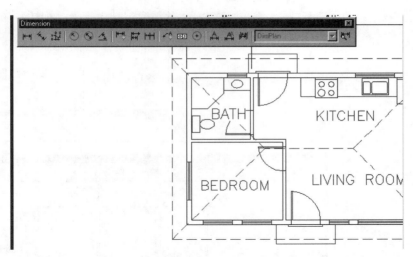

FIGURE 11.16: The result of zooming and panning for a view of the left side of the floor plan

2. Draw a guideline between the two horizontal interior wall lines where they meet the exterior wall (Figure 11.17a). Endpoint Osnap should be running, and you should be able to do this without having to zoom in.

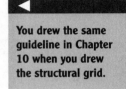

You drew the same guideline in Chapter 10 when you drew the structural grid.

3. Click the Linear button. Then pick the upper-left corner of the walls.

4. Type .y ↵ to start the point filters. Pick Midpoint Osnap and move the cursor to the short guideline you just drew. When the triangle appears on the line, click the mouse.

5. Click again on the upper-left corner of the walls to complete the point filter process. The vertical dimension appears in ghosted form, attached to the cursor.

6. Move the dimension line to a point about 3' to the left of the roof line and click. The first vertical dimension is drawn (Figure 11.17b).

7. Erase the short guideline from between the interior walls.

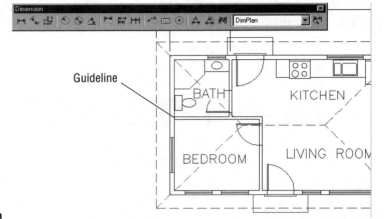

a

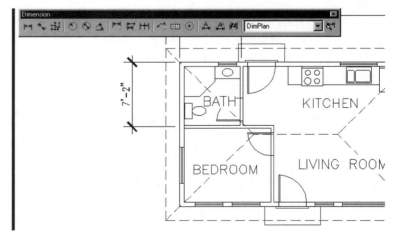

b

F I G U R E   1 1 . 1 7 :   A guideline is drawn to help find the center of an interior wall (a), and the first vertical dimension is placed (b).

Finishing the Vertical Dimensions

The rest of the vertical dimensions are placed using the same procedure as was used to complete the horizontal dimensions. Here is a summary of the steps:

1. Use the Continue command to dimension the bedroom.

2. Use the Baseline command to place an overall dimension.

3. Use the Baseline command to place a roof dimension to the left of the overall dimension.

4. Use grips to move the first extension line of the roof dimension to its corner.

Refer back through the previous section if you need more detailed instructions. The completed vertical dimensions will look like Figure 11.18.

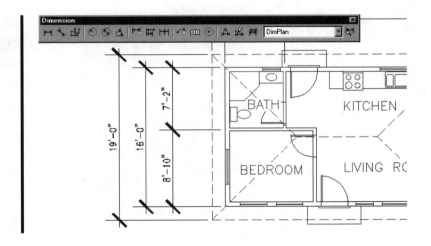

F I G U R E   1 1 . 1 8 : The completed vertical dimensions

The next area to dimension will be the balcony.

1. Pan to a view of the balcony. Include some space below and to the right of it.

T I P   When you have a floating toolbar on the screen, using the Zoom Window command doesn't take into account the area that the floating toolbar takes up. When you can, it's better to use Realtime Pan and Zoom to adjust your view in this situation.

2. Start the Linear command and pick the lower-right corner of the building walls.

3. Use Quadrant Osnap and pick near the rightmost edge of the outside balcony wall.

4. When the dimension appears, move it a couple of feet below the bottom roof line and place it there (Figure 11.19).

This will be enough on vertical and horizontal linear dimensions for now. Let's take a look at some other kinds of dimensions.

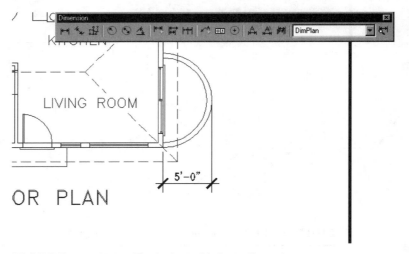

FIGURE 11.19: The horizontal balcony dimension

Other Types of Dimensions

AutoCAD provides tools for placing radial and angular dimensions on the drawing, and for placing linear dimensions that are neither vertical nor horizontal. You'll use the Radial command to dimension the inside radius of the balcony.

Radial Dimensions

On the Dimension toolbar, there are icons for Radius and Diameter dimensions. They both operate the same way and are controlled by the same settings.

Radius   Diameter

T I P The icons on the toolbars don't really look like buttons until you move the pointer cursor onto them. In this book, we refer to them as both icons and buttons.

1. Click the Osnap button on the status bar to temporarily disable any running Osnaps.

2. Click the Radius Dimension button to start the Dimradius command.

N O T E Most of the commands used for dimensioning are prefaced with a "dim" when you enter them at the command line, and that is the actual name of the command. For example, when you click the Radius Dimension button on the Dimension toolbar, or choose Dimension ➢ Radius on the menu bar, you will see _dimradius in the Command window to let you know that you have started the Dimradius command. The same command can be started by typing **dimradius** ↵ or **dra** ↵ (the shortcut alias).

3. Click the inside arc of the balcony a slight distance above the midpoint. The radius dimension appears in ghosted form. Its angle of orientation is determined by where you pick the arc. The dimension text then stays attached to the cursor (Figure 11.20).

4. Notice that the tick mark used for linear dimensions is used here also. We must have an arrowhead for the radial dimension. Press Esc to cancel the command.

We will have to alter the dimension style to specify an arrowhead for radial dimensions.

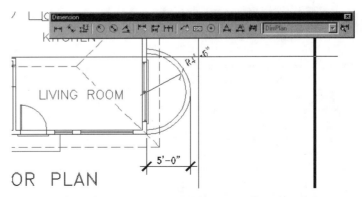

FIGURE 11.20: The radius dimension initially positioned in the arc

Parent and Child Dimensioning Styles

The DimPlan dimension style you set up at the beginning of this chapter applies to all dimensions and is called the *parent* dimension style. But you can change settings in this dimension style for particular types of dimensions, such as the radial type, for example. This makes a *child* dimension style. The child version is based on the parent version, but has a few settings that are different. In this way, all your dimensions will be made using the DimPlan dimension style, but radial dimensions will use a child version of the style. Once you create a child dimension style from the parent style, you refer to both styles by the same name, and you call them a dimension style *family*.

1. Click the Dimension Style button on the Dimension toolbar to bring up the Dimension Style Manager dialog box. It will look like Figure 11.21.

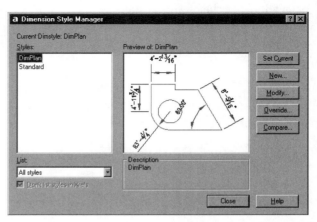

FIGURE 11.21: The Dimension Style Manager dialog box with DimPlan current

2. Be sure DimPlan is highlighted in the Styles list. Then click the New button. The Create New Dimension Style dialog box will come up.

3. Open the Use For drop-down list and select Radius Dimensions. Then click the Continue button. The Dimension Style dialog box gets larger and now has the six tabs you worked with earlier. Its title bar now includes Radial, and the preview window shows a radial dimension.

4. Activate the Lines and Arrows tab. Then move to the Arrowheads area and open the second Arrowhead drop-down list.

5. Select Right-Angle. Notice how the preview window now illustrates a radial dimension with a right-angle arrowhead.

6. Click the Text tab.

7. In the Text Placement area, open the Vertical drop-down list and select Centered.

8. Click OK to close the New Dimension Style: DimPlan: Radial dialog box.

9. In the Dimension Style Manager dialog box, notice the Style list. Radial is now a sub-style of DimPlan. Radial is referred to as a "child" style of the "parent" style DimPlan. Click Close to close the Dimension Style Manager dialog box.

10. Click the Radius button on the Dimension toolbar.

11. Click the inside arc of the balcony at a point about 15° above the right quadrant point. The radius dimension appears in ghosted form, and it now has an arrow instead of a tick mark.

12. Move the cursor to the outside of the balcony, and place the dimension text so that it looks similar to Figure 11.22.

When placing the radial dimension, you have control over the angle of the dimension line (by where you pick the arc) and the location of the dimension text (by where you pick the second point).

The balcony also needs to be given a name in the drawing, like the other rooms.

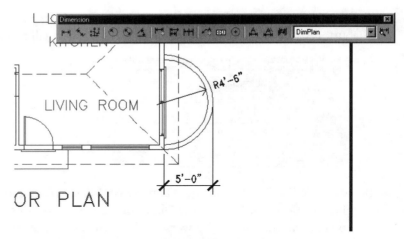

FIGURE 11.22: The radius dimension for the balcony

Leader Lines

Use the *Leader command* to draw an arrow to the balcony and place the text outside the arcs. Before you do that, the Leader Line dimension also requires an adjustment of a few dimension style settings.

1. Click the Dimension Style button on the Dimension toolbar.

2. With DimPlan highlighted, click New.

3. In the New Dimension Style dialog box, open the Use For drop-down list and click Leaders and Tolerances. Then click Continue.

4. Activate the Lines and Arrows tab, then move to the Arrowheads area and open the Leader drop-down list. Click Right-Angle.

5. Click the Text tab. In the Text Placement area, change Above to Centered. Then click OK.

TIP   If you wanted the Balcony label text to be in the same text style as the room labels, you could change the Text Style in the Text Appearance area of the Text tab to the Label text style.

6. Notice how Leader is now a Child Style, along with Radial, in the Styles list. Click Close. Another child DimPlan dimension style is created that is identical to the regular DimPlan style except for the two settings you just changed.

7. Click the Quick Leader button on the Dimension toolbar.

8. Click the Osnap button on the Status bar to temporarily disable running Osnaps, if it's not already in the off position.

9. Pick a point inside the balcony just below the radial dimension line.

10. Drag the line to the outside of the balcony, making the line approximately parallel to the radius dimension line, and pick a point (Figure 11.23a).

11. Press ↵. Then, at the `Specify text width <0">:` prompt, press ↵ again. At the next prompt, with Caps Lock on, type **balcony** ↵. The prompt changes to read `Enter next line of annotation text:`. Now you can enter multiple lines of text for the leader. Press ↵. The leader line is completed, and the word BALCONY is placed at the end of the line (Figure 11.23b).

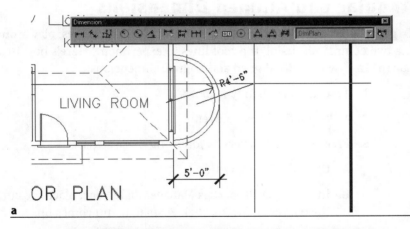

a

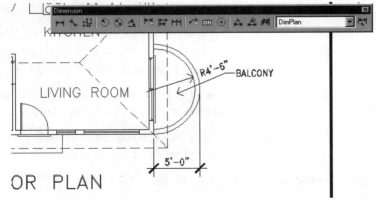

b

FIGURE 11.23: The leader line being drawn (a), and the completed leader (b)

N O T E   If the angle of the leader line is steeper than 15°, a short horizontal line called a *dogleg* or *hook line* is added between the leader line and the text.

12. Zoom to Extents, then zoom out a little and pan to view the whole drawing with dimensions.

13. Save this drawing as Cabin11a.

This exercise got you started using the Leader command. Later in this chapter, in the section on modifying dimensions, you will get another chance to work with leader lines and their text. Next, I will introduce you to two more types of dimensions.

Angular and Aligned Dimensions

To get familiar with the Aligned and Angular dimension types, play around with the two commands, using the roof lines to experiment. Here's how to set up Cabin11a to work with Aligned and Angular dimensions:

1. Type **undo** ↵, then type **m** ↵.

2. Make the Roof layer current.

3. Freeze all other layers by following these steps:

   A. Click the Layers button.

   B. In the Layer Properties Manager dialog box, place the cursor on the 0 layer and right-click. A small menu comes up.

   C. Click Select All on the menu. Then click one of the light bulbs in the On column.

   D. Click OK in the warning box. The light bulb changes to a snowflake for all the layers, indicating that they have been turned off.

   E. Click again on the Roof layer to highlight it. Then click the Roof layer's light bulb to turn it (and the Roof layer) back on.

   F. Click OK to close the dialog box and return to the drawing. Everything has disappeared except the roof lines.

4. Zoom in to a closer view of the roof.

5. Create a new layer called Dim2. Keep the black/white color and make it current.

6. Set Endpoint Osnap to be running. Now you are ready to dimension.

Aligned Dimensions

Aligned dimensions are linear dimensions that are not horizontal or vertical. They are placed in the same way that horizontal or vertical dimensions are placed with the Linear command. You can also use the Baseline and Continue commands with aligned dimensions.

Use the *Aligned command* to dimension a hip line of the roof. Try it on your own. Follow the prompts. It works just like the Dimlinear command, except that the dimension is not displayed on the drawing until you finish the command.

 Start the Aligned command by clicking the Align button on the Dimension toolbar.

Angular Dimensions

The angular dimension is the only basic dimension type that uses angles in the dimension text instead of linear measurements. Generally, tick marks are not used with angular dimensions, so you'll need to create another child dimension style for this type of dimension. Follow the steps listed previously in this chapter for setting up the Radial and Leader child styles. The only change you need to make is on the Lines and Arrows tab: Replace the Architectural Tick with the Right-Angle arrowhead.

 Try making an angular dimension on your own. You can start the *Angular command* by clicking the Angular button on the Dimension toolbar. Follow the prompts and see if you can figure out how this command works.

Figure 11.24 illustrates angular and aligned dimensions on the roof.

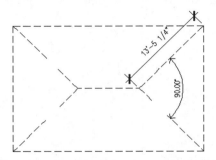

FIGURE 11.24: The roof with angular and aligned dimensions

When settings for a dimension style are changed, dimensions created when that style was current will be automatically updated to reflect the changes. You'll do more modifications of dimensions in the next section.

You have been introduced to the basic types of dimensions—linear, radial, leader, and angular—and some auxiliary dimensions—baseline, continue, and aligned—that are special cases of the linear type. The Baseline and Continue dimensions can also be used with angular dimensions.

The final part of this chapter will be devoted to teaching you a few methods for modifying various parts of dimensions.

Modifying Dimensions

Several commands and grips can be used to modify dimensions, depending on the desired change. You can:

- ▶ Change the dimension text content.
- ▶ Move the dimension text relative to the dimension line.
- ▶ Move the dimension or extension lines.
- ▶ Change the dimension style settings for a dimension or a group of dimensions.
- ▶ Revise a dimension style.

The best way to understand how modifications of dimensions are achieved is by making a few yourself. Here's how to set up:

1. Type **undo** ↵, then type **b** ↵. This undoes all steps since you saved the drawing as Cabin11a.

2. Zoom and pan until your view of the floor plan is similar to Figure 11.25.

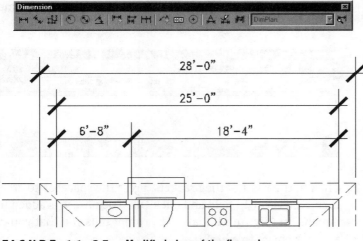

FIGURE 11.25: Modified view of the floor plan

Modifying Dimension Text

Any aspect of the dimension text can be modified. We'll look at how the content is changed first.

Editing Dimension Text Content

To change the content of text for one dimension, or to add text before or after the actual dimension, use the Ddedit command. (You used this command in Chapter 10 to modify text.) We'll change the text in the horizontal dimensions for the roof and walls.

> **1.** Type **ddedit** ↵. Then select the horizontal roof dimension at the top of the drawing. The Multiline Text Editor dialog box appears. The angle brackets in the editing box represent the existing text in the dimension,

28'-0". You can highlight the brackets and enter a new dimension, or enter new text before or after the brackets.

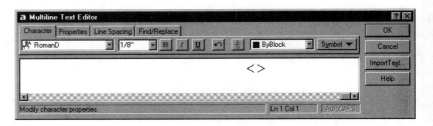

2. Click to the right of the brackets, press the spacebar to create a space, then type **verify in field** and click OK. The phrase is added to the dimension (Figure 11.26a). The prompt tells you that you can select another object to edit.

3. Click the dimension just below the roof dimension.

4. In the Multiline Text Editor dialog box, click to the right of the angle brackets again. Then click the Symbol button in the upper-right corner. A drop-down list gives three special characters and some other choices.

5. Select Plus/Minus. The ± symbol is now in the edit window.

6. Click OK. The dimension now has a ± after it (Figure 11.26b). Press ⏎ to end the Ddedit command.

If you need to change the text of several dimensions at once, use the Dimedit command.

1. Click the Dimension Edit button on the Dimension toolbar.

2. At the `Enter type of dimension editing [Home/New/Rotate/ Oblique] <Home>:` prompt, type **n** ⏎ to replace the existing text or add to it.

3. In the Multiline Text Editor dialog box, highlight the angle brackets.

4. Type **Unknown** and click OK.

5. In the drawing, click the 6'-8" and 18'-4" dimensions. Then press ⏎.

6. The two dimensions now read Unknown (Figure 11.26c).

Next, you'll learn about moving the dimension text.

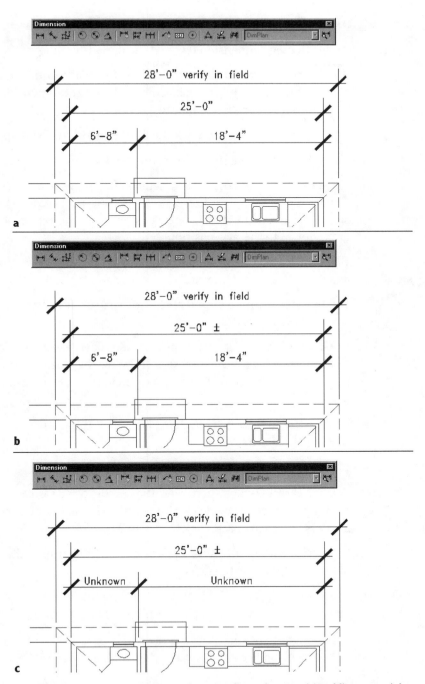

FIGURE 11.26: Adding a phrase to dimension text (a), adding a special character (b), and editing more than one dimension text at a time (c)

Moving Dimension Text Around

You can use grips to move dimension text and the dimension line.

1. Zoom into a view of the right side of the floor plan until you have a view that includes the entire balcony and its three dimensions, as well as the entire right cabin wall.

2. At the Command: prompt, click the 5'-0" dimension. Grips appear.

3. Click the grip on the right tick mark to activate it.

4. Move the cursor up until the dimension text is above the balcony. Then click again to fix it there. Press Esc (Figure 11.27a). The dimension, line, and text move to a new position, and the extension lines are redrawn to the new position.

5. Click the leader line. Then click the word BALCONY. Two grips appear on the leader line, and one appears on the text.

6. Hold down the Shift key and click the two grips near the text. Then release the shift button.

7. Click one of the two activated grips. Then move the cursor down to reposition the leader and text slightly below the Quadrant point of the balcony arcs. Then click to fasten them there. Press Esc (Figure 11.27b).

8. Be sure Osnap is turned off, then click the 4'-6" radial dimension. Three grips appear.

9. Click the grip at the arrowhead.

10. Select Nearest Osnap. Then move the cursor to the inside arc and below the just relocated leader line until the radial dimension line displays in a clear space. Pick that point.

11. With grips still on the radial dimension, click the grip in the middle of the dimension text.

12. Drag it down and to the right until it clears the leader line and its text. Then click again to fix it there. Press Esc (Figure 11.27c).

To finish the changes to the balcony, you need to suppress the left extension line of the 5'-0" dimension because it overlaps the wall and header lines.

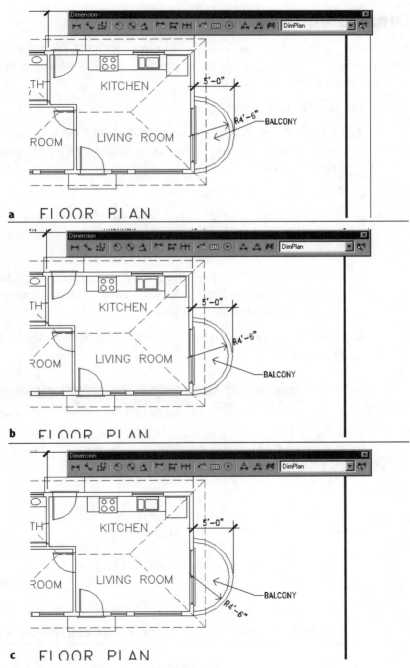

a   FLOOR PLAN

b   FLOOR PLAN

c   FLOOR PLAN

FIGURE 11.27: Moving the balcony dimensions with grips: the linear dimension (a), the leader (b), and the radial dimension

Dimension Overrides

Suppression of the left extension line will be done with the Properties command, which allows you to change a setting in the dimension style for one dimension without altering the style settings.

1. Turn off the Headers layer.

2. Click the Properties button on the Standard toolbar. If necessary, drag the Dimensioning toolbar far enough to the right to clear the Properties window.

3. Click the 5'-0" dimension.

4. In the Properties dialog box, move to the Lines and Arrows heading and click the + sign to the left of it. The settings of the Lines and Arrows tab appear.

5. Click Ext line 1. Then click the down arrow in the right column to open the drop-down list. Click Off. The left extension line on the linear balcony dimension is suppressed.

6. Close the Properties dialog box. Press Esc to remove the grips (Figure 11.28).

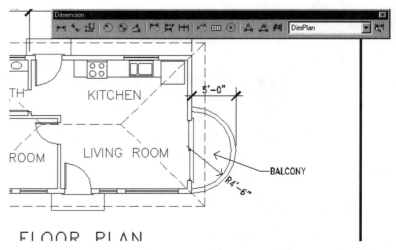

FIGURE 11.28: The 5'-0" dimension with the left extension line suppressed

The bedroom needs a horizontal dimension. Because space outside the floor plan is tight, you'll place the dimension inside the bedroom and suppress both extension lines with an override to the current dimension style.

1. Pan the drawing over until the bedroom is fully in view.

2. Open the Dimension Style Manager dialog box and click the Override button.

3. Activate the Lines and Arrows tab. In the Extension Lines area, move to the bottom where it says Suppress and put a check mark in the Ext Line 1 and Ext Line 2 check boxes. Then click OK.

4. In the Dimension Style Manager dialog box, click Close.

5. Click the Linear button on the Dimension toolbar.

6. Activate running Osnaps. In the bedroom, pick the lower-left inside corner, then pick the lower-right inside corner. The dimension appears in ghosted form, attached to the cursor.

7. Suppress the running Osnaps for one pick. Then move the dimension up to a position below the BEDROOM text and above the lower wall, and click to fix it there. The dimension is placed, and both extension lines are suppressed (Figure 11.29).

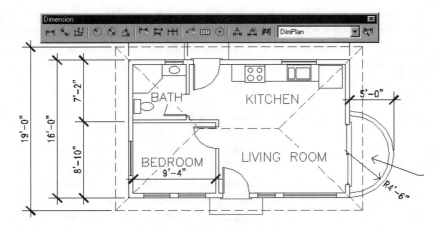

FIGURE 11.29: The completed bedroom dimension

8. Open the Dimension Style Manager dialog box. In the Styles list, the current style is the sub-style under DimPlan called <style overrides>. We can delete this style now, as it is no longer needed.

9. Click DimPlan in the list. Then click the Set Current button. A warning window appears. You are warned that the override settings will be deleted if you make DimPlan the current dimension style. Click OK. The style overrides are deleted.

10. Click Close to close the dialog box.

T I P   If you set a style override that you later decide should be incorporated into the parent dimension style, highlight Style Overrides in the Styles list, right-click, and then click Save to Current Style on the small menu that appears.

To illustrate how dimension style overrides work, we have suppressed extension lines in two dimensions without having to alter the dimension style. Extension lines are usually the thinnest lines in a drawing. It is usually not critical that they be suppressed if they coincide with other lines because the other lines will overwrite them in a print. In the bedroom, for example, if the extension lines were not suppressed, they would be overwritten by the wall lines.

However, in the first example, the left extension line of the 5'-0" dimension for the balcony coincides with the line representing a header. If the Headers layer were turned off, the extension line of this dimension would have to be suppressed or moved so it would not be visible spanning the sliding door opening. Also, if you dimension to a non-continuous line, the extension line that coincides with that line should be suppressed.

Dimensioning Short Distances

When you have to dimension distances so short that the text and arrows (or tick marks) can't both fit between the extension line, a dimension style setting determines where they are placed. To see how this works, you'll redo the horizontal dimensions above the floor plan, this time dimensioning the distance between the roof line and wall line, as well as the thickness of the interior wall. When we set up the DimPlan dimension style before, the setting changes that we made in the Fit tab then will help us now.

1. Zoom and Pan to a view of the upper portion of the floor plan so that the horizontal dimensions above the floor plan are visible (Figure 11.30).

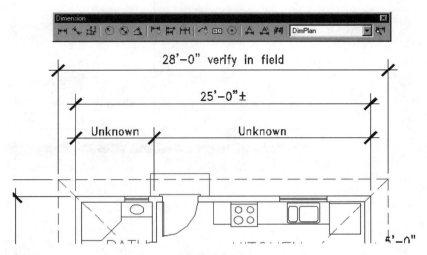

F I G U R E   1 1 . 3 0 :   The new view of the upper floor plan and its dimensions

2. Use the Erase command to erase the four dimensions that are above the floor plan. Each dimension is a single object, so you can select them with four picks, or one crossing window.

3. Activate the running Osnaps, then select the Linear button and pick the upper-left corner of the roof. Then pick the upper-left corner of the wall lines. Place the dimension line about 3' above the upper roof line (Figure 11.31a).

4. Select the Continue button. Click the upper end of each interior wall line, then click the upper-right corner of the wall lines, and, finally, click the upper-right corner of the roof (Figure 11.31b). Press Esc to cancel the Continue command.

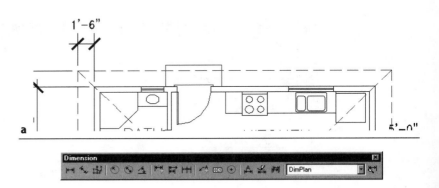

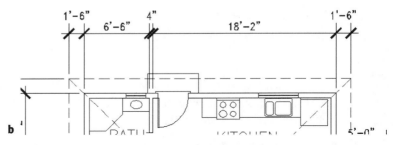

FIGURE 11.31: The first dimension is placed (a), and the other dimensions (b)

5. Click the Baseline button. Press ↵ and then pick the left extension line of the 1'-6" dimension on the left end.

6. Click the upper-right corner of the roof. The overall dimension is placed a set distance above the lower dimensions (Figure 11.32a). Press Esc to cancel the Baseline command.

Because some of the dimension text in the lower dimensions was placed higher than normal, the overall dimension needs to be raised to clear that text.

1. Click the overall dimension. Grips appear. Click the grip at the intersection of the right extension line and the dimension line to activate it.

2. Click the Snap to None Osnap button, then move the cursor up until the dimension line clears the higher text of the lower dimensions and click. Press Esc. The text of the two 1'-6" dimensions crosses over the outer extension lines (Figure 11.32b).

3. You can move dimension text with grips. Click the right 1'-6" dimension. Grips appear. Click the grip right in the middle of the text. Put Polar on and Osnap off. Then move the text to the left until it clears the extension line and click to place it.

4. Click the 1'-6" dimension on the left and repeat step 3, this time moving the text to the right.

5. When the text is where you want it, press Esc twice to clear the grips (Figure 11.32c).

This concludes the exercises for dimensions in this chapter. The current drawing won't be used in future chapters, so feel free to experiment with the dimensioning commands you have just learned. When you finish a drawing session, before you save, it is a good habit to Zoom to Extents and then zoom out a little so all visible objects are on the screen. This way, the next time you bring up this drawing, you will have a full view of it at the beginning of your session.

1. Click the X in the upper-right corner of the Dimension toolbar to close it.

2. Zoom to Extents, then zoom out a little to a full view of the cabin (Figure 11.33).

3. Save this drawing to your training folder as Cabin11b.

4. Take a break. You deserve one!

5. Turn for a moment to the next to last page in the color insert to see two samples of the Cabin11b drawing in color. One has a white background and the other a black one.

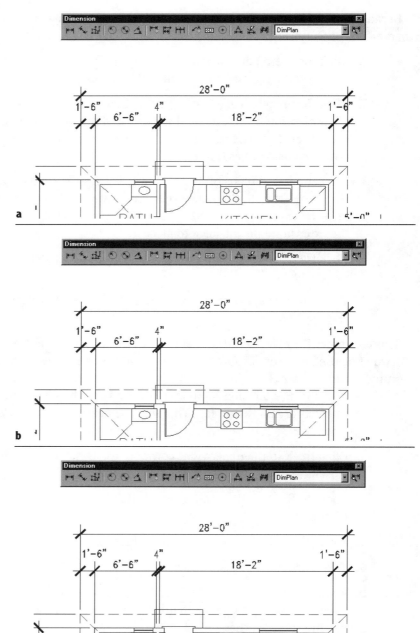

FIGURE 11.32: The overall dimension is placed using Baseline (a), raised using grips (b), and the 1'-6" dimensions are moved to clear the extension lines (c).

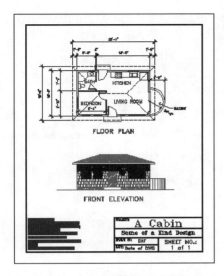

FIGURE 11.33: The full view of the cabin drawing with dimensions complete

Working successfully with dimensions in your drawing requires an investment of time to become familiar with the commands and settings that control how dimensions appear, how they are placed in the drawing, and how they are modified. The exercises in this chapter have led you through the basics of the dimensioning process. For a more in-depth discussion of dimensions, refer to *Mastering AutoCAD 2002* by George Omura (Sybex, 2001).

The next chapter will introduce you to external references, a tool for viewing a drawing from within another drawing.

If You Would Like More Practice...

Try dimensioning the garage addition to the cabin that was shown at the end of Chapter 4, *Gaining Drawing Strategies: Part 1* (Cabin04b-addon.dwg). Use the same techniques and standards of dimensioning that you used in this chapter to dimension the cabin. In other words:

▶ Dimension to the outside edges of exterior walls and to center lines of interior walls.

▶ Use the DimPlan dimension style that you set up and used in this chapter. Close all files that you used in this chapter and open Cabin04b-addon. Then use Design Center to bring over the DimPlan dimension style, the Dim text style, and the Dim1 layer.

▶ If you added text to this drawing and saved it in the practice exercise in Chapter 10, use this drawing (Figure 11.34).

▶ When finished, save this drawing as Cabin11b-addon.

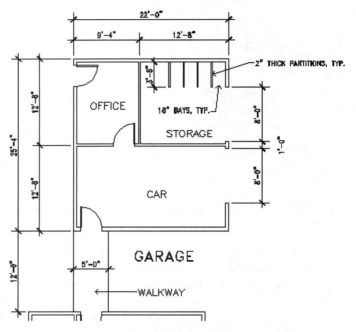

FIGURE 11.34: The walkway and garage dimensioned

Are You Experienced?

Now you can...

- ☑ create a new dimension style
- ☑ place vertical and horizontal dimensions in a drawing
- ☑ use radial, aligned, and angular dimensions
- ☑ create leader lines for notes
- ☑ modify dimension text
- ☑ override a dimension style
- ☑ modify a dimension style

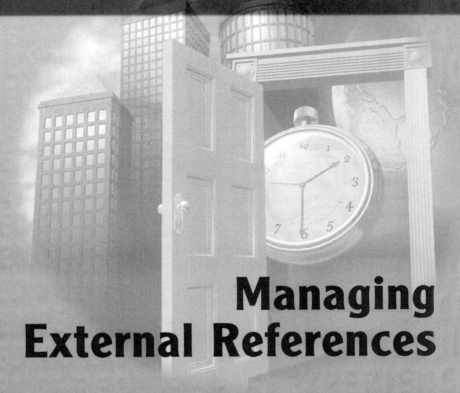

CHAPTER 12

Managing External References

- ▶ Understanding external references
- ▶ Creating external references
- ▶ Modifying external references
- ▶ Converting external references into blocks

he floor plan of a complex building project may actually be a composite of several AutoCAD files that are linked together as external references to the current drawing. This enables parts of a drawing to be worked on at different workstations (or in different offices) while remaining linked to a central host file.

External references are .dwg files that have been temporarily connected to the current drawing and are used as reference information. The externally referenced drawing is visible in the current drawing. Its layers, colors, linetypes, and visibility can be manipulated, and its objects can be modified. But it is not a permanent part of the current drawing.

External references are similar to blocks in that they both behave as single objects and are inserted into a drawing in the same way. But blocks are part of the current drawing file and external references are not.

Blocks can be exploded back to their component parts, but external references cannot. In Chapter 7, *Grouping Objects into Blocks*, you were able to modify the window block and, in so doing, update all instances of the window block in the drawing. This was done without having to explode the block. With an external reference—usually called an *Xref*—the same mechanism can be applied. To manage external references, you need to learn how to set up an Xref, manipulate its appearance in the host drawing, and update it.

Before you set up the Xref, you will create a site plan for the cabin. Then you will Xref the cabin drawing into the site drawing (Figure 12.1). In this figure, the lines of the cabin floor plan comprise the Xref, and the rest of the objects are part of the host drawing. After these exercises, we will look at a few ways that external references are used in design offices.

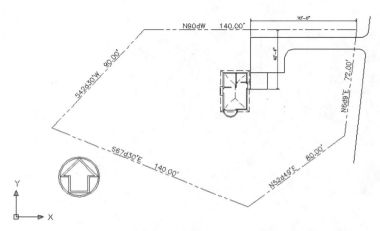

FIGURE 12.1: The site plan with the cabin as an external reference

Drawing a Site Plan

The site plan you will use has been simplified so that you can draw it with a minimum of steps and get on with the external referencing. Essential elements are:

- ▶ Property lines
- ▶ Access road to the site
- ▶ North arrow
- ▶ Indication of where the building is located on the site

The first step is to draw in the property lines.

Using Surveyor Units

Property lines are drawn using surveyor units for angles and decimal feet for linear units. In laying out the property lines, you will use relative polar coordinates, so you will enter coordinates in the format *@distance<angle* where the distance is in feet and hundredths of a foot, and the angle is in surveyor units to the nearest minute.

Surveyor Units

Surveyor units, called *bearings* in civil engineering, describe the direction of a line from its beginning point. The direction (bearing) described as a deviation from the north or south toward the east or west, is given as an angular measurement in degrees, minutes, and seconds. The angles used in a bearing can never be greater than 90°, so bearing lines must be headed in one of the four directional quadrants: northeasterly, northwesterly, southeasterly, or southwesterly. If north is set to be at the top of a plot plan, then south is down, east is to the right, and west is to the left. Thus, when a line from its beginning goes up and to the right, it will be headed in a northeasterly direction. And when a line from its beginning goes down and to the left, it is headed in a southwesterly direction, etc. A line that is headed in a northeasterly direction with a deviation from true north of 30 degrees and 30 minutes is shown as N30d30'E in AutoCAD notation.

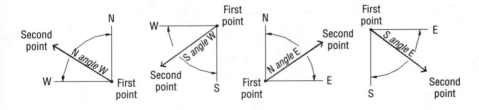

With the surveyor unit system, a sloping line that has an up-and-to-the-left direction would have a down-and-to-the-right direction if you started from the opposite end. So in laying out property lines it is important to move in the same direction (clockwise or counterclockwise) as you progress from one segment to the next.

Laying Out the Property Lines

You will set up a new drawing, and then start at the upper-right corner of the property lines and work your way around counterclockwise.

1. Open Cabin11a from your training folder. Choose File ≻ Save As to save the drawing as Cabin12a.

2. Click the New button on the Standard toolbar. In the Create New Drawing dialog box, click Start from Scratch, then click OK.

3. From the menu bar, select Format ≻ Units. In the Drawing Units dialog box, change the precision in the Length area to two decimal places (0.00).

4. In the Angle area, open the Type drop-down list and select Surveyor's Units. Then change the precision to the nearest minute (N0d00' E). Click OK. You will need an area of about 250' × 150' for the site plan.

5. Open the Format menu again and pick Drawing Limits. Press ↵ to accept the default 0.00,0.00 for the lower-left corner. Type **250,150** ↵. Don't use the foot sign.

6. Right-click the Snap button on the Status bar, then click Settings. Change the Snap Spacing to 10.00 and the Grid to 0.00. Then click the Grid check box to turn the grid on. Click OK.

7. In the drawing, type z ↵ a ↵. Then zoom to .85× to see a blank space around the grid (Figure 12.2).

> We are using Decimal linear units in such a way that one decimal unit represents one foot. The foot symbol (') is used only with Architectural and Engineering units.

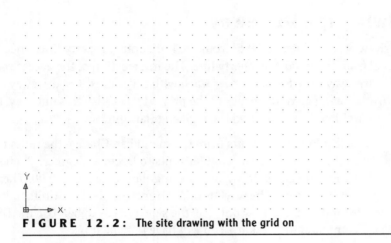

FIGURE 12.2: The site drawing with the grid on

8. Create a new layer called Prop_line. Assign it a color and make it current.

9. Start the Line command. For the first point, type **220,130** ↵. This will start a line near the upper-right corner of the grid.

10. Be sure Snap is turned off. Then type:

    @140<n90dw ↵

    @90<s42d30'w ↵

    @140<s67d30'e ↵

    @80<n52d49'e ↵

    c ↵

The property lines are completed (Figure 12.3).

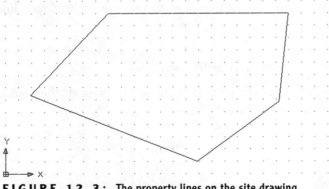

FIGURE 12.3: The property lines on the site drawing

Drawing the Driveway

The driveway is 8' wide and set 5' from the horizontal property line. The access road is 8' from the parallel property line. The intersection of the access road line and the driveway lines forms corners, each with a 3' radius. The driveway extends 70' in from the upper-right corner of the property. Let's lay this out now. First, switch to Architectural units and Decimal angular units.

1. Select Format ➤ Units from the menu bar. Change the units to Architectural and the angular units to Decimal degrees. Then set the Length precision to ¹⁄₁₆" and the angular precision to 0.00. Then click OK. Because of the way AutoCAD translates decimal units to inches, your drawing is now only ¹⁄₁₂ᵗʰ the size it needs to be. (Use the Distance command to check it.) You will have to scale it up.

2. Click the Scale button on the Modify toolbar.

3. Type all ↵ ↵. For the base point, type 0,0 ↵.

4. At the Specify scale factor or [Reference]: prompt, type 12 ↵. Then click Grid on the Status bar to turn the grid off.

5. Zoom to Extents, then zoom out a little. The drawing looks the same, but now it's the right size. Check it with the Distance command, which you encountered in Chapter 7.

6. Offset the upper, horizontal property line 5' down. Offset this new line 8' down.

7. Offset the rightmost property line 8' to the right (Figure 12.4a).

8. Create a new layer called Road. Leave the default color assigned to it and make the Road layer current.

9. Use the Property button to move the driveway and road lines to the Road layer.

10. Extend the driveway lines to the access road line. Trim the access road line between the driveway lines.

11. Fillet the two corners where the driveway meets the road, using a 3' radius (Figure 12.4b).

> **The Scale command can also be started by choosing Modify ➤ Scale from the menu bar, or by typing sc ↵.**

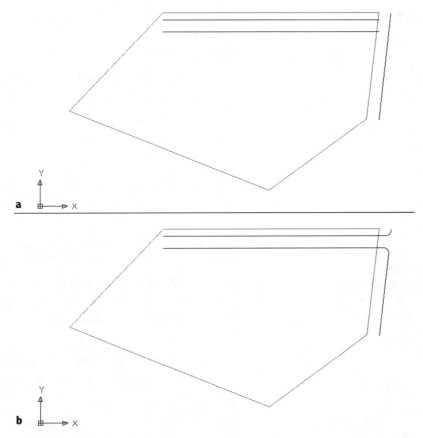

FIGURE 12.4: Offset property lines (a), and the completed intersection of the driveway and access road (b)

Finishing the Driveway

A key element of any site plan is information that shows how the building is positioned on the site relative to the property lines. Property lines are staked out by surveyors. Then the building contractor takes measurements off the stakes to locate one or two corners of the building. In this site, you need only one corner because we are assuming the cabin is facing due west. A close look at Figure 12.1 will reveal that the end of the driveway lines up with the outer edge of the back step of the cabin. Below the driveway is a square patio, and its bottom edge lines up with the bottom edge of the back step. So the bottom corner of the back step coincides with the lower-left corner of the patio. This locates the cabin on the site (Figure 12.5).

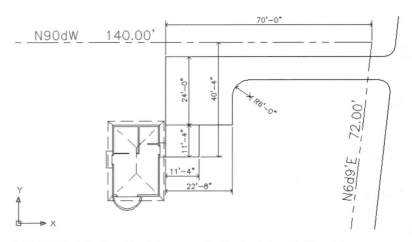

FIGURE 12.5: The driveway and patio lined up with the cabin

Imagine the site being on a bluff of a hill overlooking land that falls away to the south and west, offering a spectacular view in that direction. To accommodate this view, we will want to change the orientation of the cabin when we Xref it into the site drawing.

1. On the Status bar, turn Polar on. Then draw a line from the upper-right corner of the property lines straight up to a point near the top of the screen.

2. Offset this line 70' to the left. This will mark the end of the driveway.

3. Draw a line from the lower endpoint of this offset line down a distance of 40'-4". Then, using Polar Tracking, continue this line 11'-4" to the right.

4. Offset the 40'-1" incline 11'-4" to the right. Offset the newly created line 11'-4" to the right as well.

5. Offset the upper driveway line 24' down. These are all the lines you need to finish the site plan (Figure 12.6a).

6. Finish the driveway and patio by using the Trim, Fillet, and Erase commands as you have in previous chapters. The radius of the corner to fillet is 6'. See Figure 12.6b.

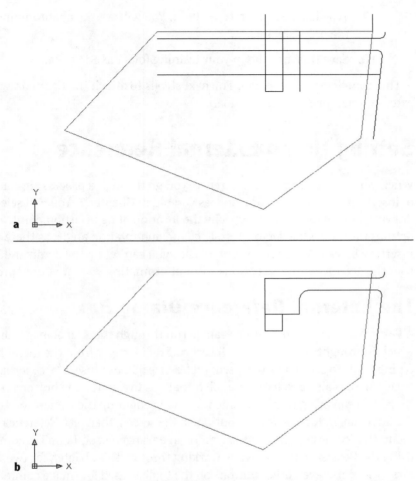

FIGURE 12.6: The offset lines (a), and the finished driveway and patio (b)

7. Make the 0 layer current, then draw a north arrow and place it in the lower-left corner.

8. Open the Layer Control dialog box and change the linetype for the Prop_line layer to Phantom. (You will have to load it; see Chapter 6, *Using Layers to Organize Your Drawing*.)

9. Type **ltscale** ↵, then type 100 ↵. You will see the phantom linetype for the property lines.

10. Save this drawing in your training folder as Site12a.

This completes the site plan. The next step is to attach the Cabin drawing as an external reference into the site plan.

Setting Up an External Reference

When you set up an external reference, you go through a process similar to that of inserting a block into a drawing, as you did in Chapter 7. You will select the drawing to be referenced and specify the location of its insertion point. There are options for the *X* scale factor, *Y* scale factor, and rotation angle, as there are for inserting blocks. And here, as with blocks, you can set up the command so that it uses the defaults for these options without prompting you for your approval.

The External Reference Dialog Box

All external reference operations can be run through the Xref Manager dialog box, which is brought up by selecting Insert ➤ Xref Manager from the menu bar, or by typing **xr** ↵. To set up a new external reference, choose Insert ➤ External Reference. There is also a Reference toolbar that has five command buttons related to Xrefs. You can bring it up the same way you brought up the Dimension toolbar in the last chapter: Right-click any button on the screen, then pick Reference from the menu that comes up. But unless you're an advanced user, I don't recommend using the Reference toolbar while working through this chapter, for two reasons. First, there are seven other buttons on the toolbar used for Image commands that allow you to import raster drawings into AutoCAD, an operation not covered in this book. Second, the toolbar does not include all of the Xref commands we will be covering. If you have already brought this toolbar up, click the X in the upper-right corner to remove it.

1. With Site12a as the current drawing, create a new layer called Cabin. Use the default color of White/Black and make the Cabin layer current.

2. Choose Insert ➤ External Reference from the menu bar. The Select Reference File dialog box appears.

3. Locate the Training Data folder (or the folder your training files are stored in) and select Cabin12a.dwg. Then click Open. The External Reference dialog box comes up.

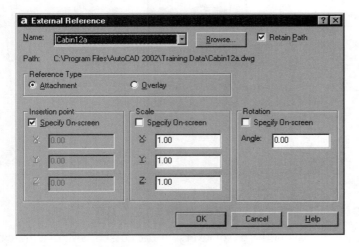

The file being referenced, Cabin12a, is displayed in the drop-down list at the top of the dialog box, with the full path of the file's location just below. The bottom half contains three options for the insertion process, which are like those in the Insert dialog box that you used for inserting blocks in Chapter 7. Note that only the insertion point is specified on-screen. The Scale and Rotation options are preset to use the default settings. If they are not set up this way, click the appropriate check boxes so they are.

1. Click OK. A technical AutoCAD message appears that doesn't concern us right now.

2. Click OK to close it. You return to your drawing and the cabin drawing appears and moves with the crosshair cursor.

3. Pick any point within the property line and to the left of the patio to be the insertion point. The Xref drawing is attached and appears in the site plan (Figure 12.7).

The attached Xref appears exactly as it did when it was the current drawing. When we use this file as part of a site plan, we don't want all of the information in Cabin12a to be visible. In fact, we want most of the information invisible. We will accomplish this by freezing many of the layers in the Xref drawing.

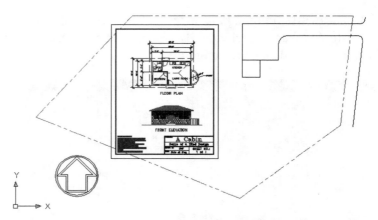

FIGURE 12.7: The Cabin12a drawing attached to the Site12a drawing

Controlling the Appearance of an Xref

Xref layers will be part of the list of layers for the current, or host, drawing. But the name of the Xref file is added to the front of the layer's previous name, separated from the layer's previous name by a vertical bar (|).

1. Click the Layer button on the Object Properties toolbar. The Layer Properties Manager dialog box comes up. Layers from the Xref drawing all have *Cabin12a* and a vertical bar before the name of the layer, as in Cabin12a|Balcony.

2. Click the Save State button near the upper-right corner. The Save Layer States dialog box comes up.

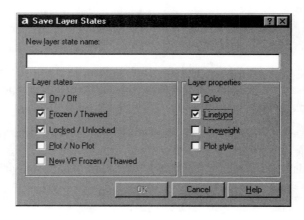

3. In the New Layer State Name text box, enter **as is** but don't press ↵ yet.

4. In the Layer States area, be sure check marks are in the On/Off, Frozen/Thawed, and Locked/Unlocked boxes.

5. In the Layer Properties area, be sure the Color and Linetype boxes have check marks.

6. Click OK. Now we can make a few changes.

7. Freeze all layers beginning with Cabin12a *except:*

Cabin12a|Balcony

Cabin12a|Roof

Cabin12a|Steps

Cabin12a|Walls

Here's how to do this:

▶ Click the Cabin12a|Dim1 layer.

▶ Hold down the Shift key and click the Cabin12a|Windows layer.

▶ Hold down the Ctrl key and click the last three layers listed above to deselect them. The Cabin12a|Balcony layer was not originally selected.

▶ Click one of the sun icons for a highlighted layer.

8. Click OK to close the dialog box and view the drawing (Figure 12.8).

We are freezing layers here rather than turning them off because we don't expect them to be made visible again for quite a while.

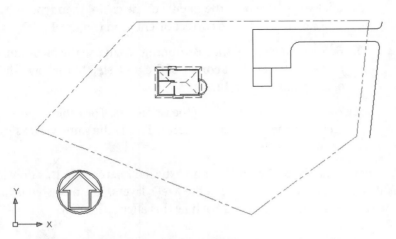

FIGURE 12.8: The site plan with most of the cabin layers frozen

You can resize the Layer Properties Manager dialog box to display more layers at a time. Depending on the size of your screen and your screen resolution, you might be able to view all Xref layers at once.

Because we want the visible parts of the cabin to read as a unit, we will assign the same color to all the thawed cabin layers. Let's make those changes now.

1. Click the Layer button again and highlight the Cabin12a|Balcony layer. Then hold down the Ctrl key and click the other three cabin layers listed in step 7 above. Change the color of one of the selected layers to a dark green. The rest of the selected layers will also change to a dark green. Click OK.

2. Repeat steps 2–5 in the previous set of steps, except, in step 3, enter Xref as the Layer State Name.

3. Click OK. The cabin is now all one color.

Moving and Rotating an Xref

Now the cabin needs to be moved and rotated to its position next to the patio.

1. Zoom into a view where the cabin and the left side of the patio are visible.

2. Start the Rotate command and click the cabin. The entire cabin is selected. Press ↵.

3. Click anywhere near the middle of the cabin, then type –**90** ↵. The cabin is rotated to the correct orientation (Figure 12.9a).

4. Be sure Endpoint Osnap is running. Then use the Move command to move the lower-right corner of the back step to the lower-left corner of the patio (Figure 12.9b).

5. Zoom Previous to a view of the whole site. The cabin is oriented correctly on the site (Figure 12.10). This is the same view as in Figure 12.1.

You have established Cabin12a as an external reference in this drawing and modified the appearance of some of the Xref's layers. The next step is to make some revisions to Cabin12a and see how this affects the Xref.

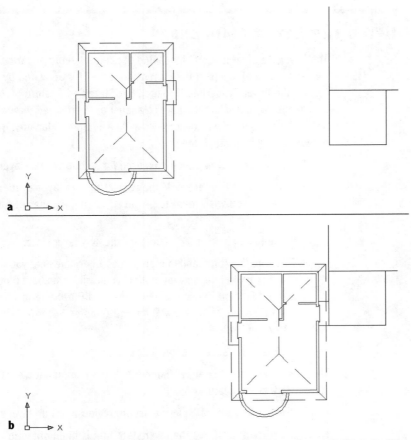

FIGURE 12.9: The cabin rotated (a), and positioned next to the patio (b)

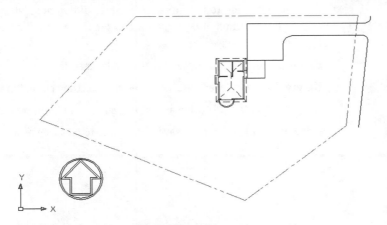

FIGURE 12.10: The cabin Xref is located on the site drawing.

USING THE LAYER MANAGER

The Layer Manager is a tool for saving the current setup of various *properties* and *states* of layers in the current drawing. It is activated by two buttons in the Layer Properties Manager, Set State and Restore State. All the operations for controlling the Layer Manager are performed through the use of two dialog boxes, Save Layer States and Layer States Manager. Here's how to work your way through them:

The **Save Layer States** dialog box, used for setting up new layer states.

► In the Layer Properties Manager, set up the layer properties and states as you wish them to be saved, then click the set Save State button.

► In the dialog box, enter a name for the new layer state.

► There are five states and four properties. Check the ones you want to be saved as part of the new layer state. (You will learn about Plot/No Plot, New VP Frozen/Thawed, Lineweight, and Plot Style in Chapter 13, *Using Layouts to Set Up a Print* and Chapter 14, *Printing an Auto-CAD Drawing*.)

► Click OK. This saves the new layer state.

The **Layer States Manager** dialog box is used to manage existing layer states. Here are its features:

Layer States list box: Displays a list of previously set up layer states.

Restore button: Restores the layer state that is highlighted in the Layer State list box.

Edit: Returns you to the Save Layer State dialog box, where you can change the selection of layer modes and properties to be included in the highlighted saved layer state.

Rename: Changes the name of the saved layer state.

Delete: Deletes a layer state. This does not affect the current layer setup.

Import: Imports a .las file as a new layer state in the current drawing.

Export: Exports the chosen saved layer state to be saved as a .las file.

Modifying an Xref Drawing

You can modify Cabin12a either by making it the current drawing or by using a special modification command while the host drawing is current. We'll start by bringing up Cabin12a and making an addition to it. Then we'll make Site12a current again and modify Cabin12a as an Xref. Before we do anything, however, we need to change a setting so that the new layer states and the changes we have made to the layers of the Xref are saved with the host file.

1. Type **visretain** ↵. If the value in the angle brackets is set to 1, press ↵. Otherwise, type 1 ↵ to set the value to 1. This will allow you to save the layer settings of the Xref layers and the new layer states with the current file.

2. Choose File ➢ Save As to save the current file as Site12b.

3. Click Window on the menu bar. At the bottom of the menu, Cabin12a should be displayed next to 1.

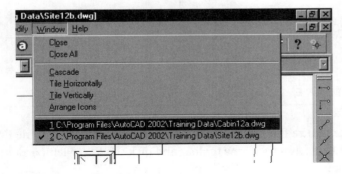

4. Select Cabin12a.dwg to make it the current drawing. Notice how the wall, roof, balcony, and steps in the floor plan of this drawing retain their original colors and are not dark green.

Modifying an Xref by Making It the Current Drawing

Because we found such a spectacular site for the cabin, we want to add a deck around what was originally the front door and is now the west-facing entrance.

1. Zoom into the area that includes the floor plan and the area between it and the front elevation.

2. Create a new layer called Deck. Assign it a color and make it current. Next, give yourself some room to make this revision.

3. Turn off the following layers:

- ▶ Dim1
- ▶ F-elev
- ▶ Tblk1
- ▶ Text1
- ▶ Any Hatch layers that aren't already frozen

4. The drawing will look like Figure 12.11. Use the Pline command to draw a deck across the front of the cabin that extends down 10'. (The Polyline command was introduced in Chapter 10, *Controlling Text in a Drawing*.)

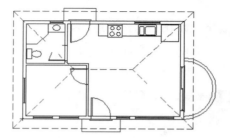

FIGURE 12.11: The view with selected layers frozen

5. Make sure the Endpoint Osnap is running. Then select the Polyline button from the Draw toolbar and pick the lower-left corner of the cabin walls to start the Pline.

6. Type w ↵. Then type 0 ↵ ↵ to reset the Pline width to zero.

7. Be sure Polar is clicked on. Then hold the crosshair cursor straight down below the first point picked and type 10' ↵.

▶

The command window shows the polyline width currently set to 3", from when you drew the border and title block in Chapter 10.

8. Click the Otrack button on the Status bar to turn Otrack mode on. Hold the crosshair cursor on the lower-right corner of the cabin walls for a moment, until a cross appears. When it does, begin moving the crosshair cursor directly down, while staying on the tracking path. A small × will appear at the intersection of the vertical tracking path and the horizontal polar tracking line, as well as a Polar & Endpoint tooltip (Figure 12.12a). When you see the small × and tooltip, click once to establish the second line segment. A horizontal line is drawn that parallels the front wall of the cabin and is 10' below it.

9. Finally, pick the lower-right corner of the cabin walls to complete the outline of the deck. Press ↵ to end the Pline command.

10. Offset this polyline 6" to the inside (Figure 12.12b). When a polyline is offset, all segments are automatically offset together and filleted to clean up the corners. (The fillet radius is zero for this operation, even if it's currently set to a non-zero value.) This concludes the modifications we will make to the Cabin12a drawing. Now we can return to the Site12b drawing.

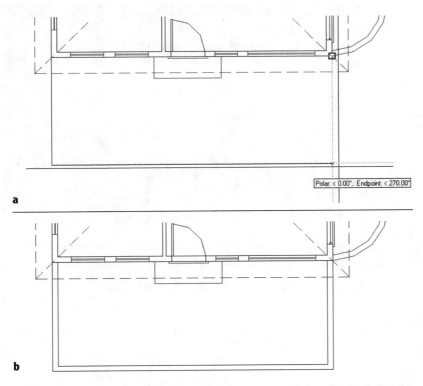

FIGURE 12.12: The vertical tracking path (a), and the offset deck line (b)

11. It is important to save the file at this point. Keep the name as Cabin12a, otherwise the Xref in the Site12b drawing will not be updated to include the deck. This is a revision to the Cabin12a drawing that has been externally referenced into the Site12b drawing. Save Cabin12a, then choose Window ➤ Site12b to switch back to the site drawing.

    A host drawing reads the latest saved version of a drawing that is externally referenced to it.

12. On the pull-down menus, choose Insert ➤ Xref Manager. The Xref Manager dialog comes up.

Once an External Reference has been set up, you will use this dialog box to control the linkage between the Xref and the host drawing. We need to update the Cabin12a Xref to reflect the changes we made to the Cabin12a drawing.

1. In the list of Xref files, click Cabin12a to highlight it. All the buttons on the right side of the dialog box are now available.

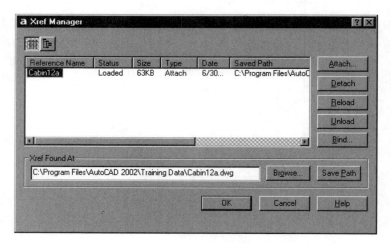

2. Click the Reload button, then click OK. You are returned to the Site12a drawing; the new deck has been added (Figure 12.13).

3. Save this drawing. It's still called Site12b.

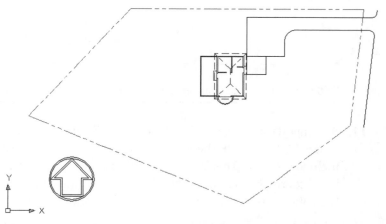

FIGURE 12.13: The Site12b drawing with the revised Xref of the cabin

In this exercise, you have seen how a host drawing is updated when the drawing that is externally referenced is made current, modified, and updated as an Xref. You also saw how the appearance of objects in the Xref drawing can be controlled from the host drawing by working with the Xref layers. This is a good example of the power of layers. They can be set up one way in the actual drawing and another way in the Xref of that drawing in a host file. In fact, you can Xref the same drawing into any number of host files and have the layer characteristics of visibility, color, and linetype be different in each host file, and saved as such with each host file. Xref is a powerful feature of AutoCAD, and you will learn more about the possible applications of this tool toward the end of this chapter.

Modifying an Xref from within the Host Drawing

In Chapter 7, we used the In-place Xref and Block Edit command to update the window block. The same tool can be used here for editing an Xref while the host drawing is the current drawing. You can't create a new layer with this tool, but many of the regular editing commands are available when you use it. We'll make a few modifications related to the new deck to illustrate this feature.

1. Use the Window menu to switch to Cabin12a. Then close this file. (Choose File ➤ Close.) Site12b will return to the drawing area. Make the 0 layer current.

2. Zoom into the cabin floor plan on the site plan (Figure 12.14a). We need to erase the old front step and fill in the roof lines that were broken out to make room for the room label text.

3. On the pull-down menus, choose Modify ➤ In-place Xref and Block Edit ➤ Edit Reference. You are prompted to select the Xref to edit.

4. Click anywhere on the cabin; it's all one object for now. The Reference Edit dialog box comes up. It lists Cabin12a as the selected Xref, and there is a preview window to illustrate the Xref drawing.

5. Click OK. At the Select nested objects: prompt, click on the six roof hip lines that need repair, the roof ridge line, and the three lines that make up what was formerly the front step. Then press ⏎. The Command: prompt returns to the command window. The Refedit toolbar appears.

> **The roof lines needing repair may appear normal in this view because they are dashed. As you select them, you will see that they are broken.**

You are now free to use many of the Draw and Modify commands on the objects that we just selected.

6. Use the Erase command to erase the three lines of the front step and the three broken roof line segments that connect to the ridgeline.

7. Use the Fillet command with a radius of zero to extend the three remaining broken roof line segments to the ridgeline (Figure 12.14b).

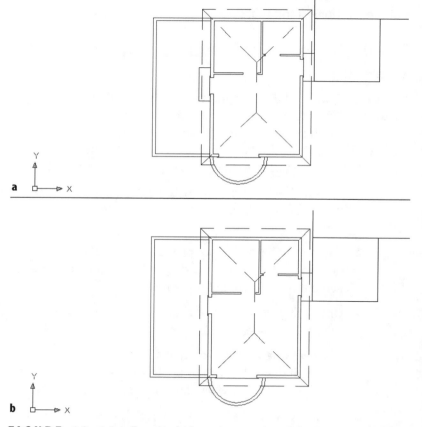

FIGURE 12.14: Zooming in for a close-up view of the Xref cabin (a), and the Xref cabin with the step erased and the roof lines filled in

T I P   The right fillet will require you to use the ridgeline as one of the lines to fillet, rather than the unbroken hip line, because the latter line was not selected to be part of the Xref edit in step 5.

8. Move to the Refedit toolbar. On the far right end of the toolbar, click the Save Back Changes to Reference button. When the warning dialog box comes up, click OK.

9. Zoom to Extents, then zoom out a little to a view of the whole (Figure 12.15). Save this drawing. It is still named Site12b.

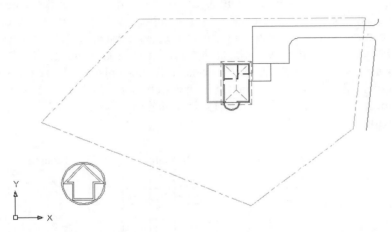

FIGURE 12.15: The Site12b drawing with the revised Xref of the cabin

In this exercise, you have seen how a host drawing is updated when its external reference is changed, and how the appearance of objects in the Xref drawing can be controlled from the host drawing by working with the Xref layers. You also saw how modifications can be made to objects in the Xref from the host drawing by using the In-place Xref Edit tool. A drawing can serve as an external reference in several host drawings at the same time and have a different appearance in each one. The results of in-place Xref editing, however, must be saved back to the original drawing in order to be viewed in the Xref. So in this case when you open Cabin12a, the front step will be missing. Also, the roof hip lines will be drawn over the room label text, as they were before they were broken in Chapter 10. In-place Xref editing is usually done only when the results are meant to be permanent changes in the original source drawing. We only used it in this case to show you how the feature works.

Applications for Xrefs

There are many different uses for external references. I will describe two common applications for Xrefs to illustrate their range.

Let's suppose you are working on a project as an interior designer and a subcontractor to the lead architect. The architect can give you a drawing of a floor plan that is still undergoing changes. You would load this file onto your hard disk, in a specially designated folder, then Xref it into your drawing as a background—a drawing to be used as a reference to draw over. You can now proceed to lay out furniture, partitions, etc., while the architect is still refining the floor plan. At an agreed-on time, the architect will give you a revised version of the floor plan. You will overwrite the one you have on your computer with the latest version. Then you can reload the Xref into your furniture layout drawing and the newer version of the floor plan will now be the background. In this example, the lead architect may also be sending the same versions of the floor plan to the structural and mechanical engineers and the landscape architect, all of whom are working on the project and using the architect's floor plan as an Xref in their respective host drawings (Figure 12.16).

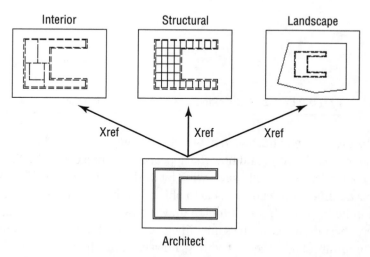

FIGURE 12.16: A single floor plan as an Xref to three subcontractors

Xrefs are often used when parts of a different job are being done in an office where a network is in place. Suppose a project involves work on several buildings that are all on the same site. By using Xrefs, each building can be externally referenced to the site plan. This keeps the site plan drawing file from getting too large, and allows the project work to be divided up to different workstations, while the project manager can open the host site plan and keep track of progress on the whole project (Figure 12.17).

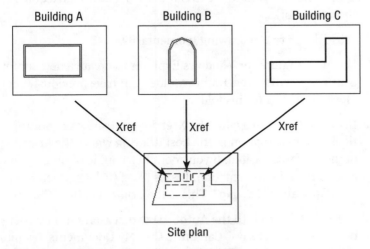

FIGURE 12.17: Three buildings as Xrefs to a single site plan

Additional Features of External References

You have seen how properties of layers in an Xref can be changed and how modifications to an Xref can be made. A few other features of external references deserve mention.

The Xref Path

When you attach an Xref to the host drawing, AutoCAD stores the name of the Xref and its path.

N O T E   **The path of a drawing file is the name of the drive, folders, and subfolders where a file is stored, followed by the name of the drawing.**
`C:\Program Files\AutoCAD 2002\Training Data\Site12b.dwg` **is the path of the current drawing file.**

Each time you bring up the host drawing, AutoCAD searches for any Xrefs saved with the host file and brings them up in the host drawing. If the Xref drawing is moved to a new folder after the Xref has been attached, AutoCAD won't be able to find the Xref and can't bring it up. To avoid that situation, you must update the host drawing with the new path to the Xref file. We'll go through a quick exercise to illustrate how this works.

1. Close the Site12b drawing momentarily.

2. Use My Computer or Windows Explorer to create a new subfolder called Xref within the Training folder you have previously set up. Move Cabin12a to this folder.

3. Bring up Site12b again. The Xref does not show up, but there's a little line of information in the host drawing where the insertion point of the Xref was located. If you zoom in a couple of times, you will be able to read the information. It says "Xref C:\1-My Documents\Training Data\Cabin12a.dwg." This is the original path of the Xref.

4. Press F2 to switch to the AutoCAD text screen for a moment and note the line that says "Can't find C:\1-My Documents\Training Data\ Cabin12a.dwg." AutoCAD is unable to find the Xref because the path has changed. Press F2 again.

5. Bring up the Xref Manager dialog box. In the large box where Xrefs are listed, the path is listed for each Xref under the heading Saved Path. You can slide the scroll bar to the right to see the full path. Notice also that in the Status column for this Xref, it says "Not Found."

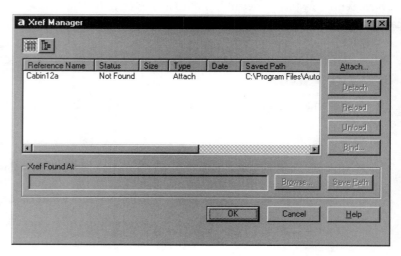

6. Click the Cabin12a Xref to highlight it.

7. Next to the Xref Found At text box, click Browse. Find Cabin12a in the new Xref folder. Highlight it and click Open.

8. Back in the Xref Manager dialog box, the path has been updated for Cabin12a. Click OK. Zoom Previous. The Xref is restored in your drawing.

 W A R N I N G   When you're working with a lot of Xrefs, it is important to be very careful where you store files that are acting as Xrefs to other files.

Binding Xrefs

On occasion, you will want to permanently attach an Xref to the host drawing. If you send your drawing files to a printing service to be plotted, having to send a whole set of files that are Xrefs can make things complicated. Also, for archiving finished work, it's better to reduce the number of files. There may also be occasions when the Xref has been revised for the last time and no longer needs to be a separate file. In all these situations, you will use the *Bind command* to convert an external reference into a block that will be stored in the host drawing.

1. Open the External Reference dialog box and highlight the Cabin12a Xref.

2. Click the Bind button. The Bind Xrefs dialog box comes up.

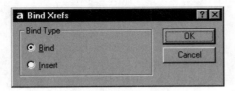

The two options in the Bind Type area have to do with how layers are treated when an Xref is bound to the host drawing. The default is Bind. It sets the Xref layers to be maintained as unique layers in the host drawing. With the Insert option, layers that have the same name in the two drawings will be combined into one layer. None of the layers in Cabin12a have the same name as any layers in Site12b. Let's use the Insert option.

3. Change the Bind Type to Insert and click OK. The Xref disappears from the list of Xrefs.

4. Click OK. Your drawing looks unchanged.

5. Click on the cabin, then type li ↵. The text screen shows that the cabin is now a block reference.

6. Press F2 and click the Layer button on the Object Properties toolbar. The cabin's layers have all become layers in the Site12b drawing, and no longer have the Cabin12al prefix.

7. Click OK, then choose Insert ➤ Block. In the Insert dialog box, open the Name drop-down list. Cabin12a is listed here as a block, along with the window and two door blocks that you created in Chapter 7. There are a couple of other blocks on the list. These blocks are used by the dimensions in the drawing.

8. Close the drop-down list by clicking a blank portion of the dialog box. Then click Cancel again to return to your drawing. The cabin is now a permanent part of the Site12b drawing. If you need to make changes to the drawing, you can explode it and use the modify commands to make those changes. Or you can use the In-place Xref and Block Edit tools that you used previously in Chapter 7 to modify the window block, and again in this chapter to modify the roof lines and erase the front step.

9. Save this drawing as Site12c.

This has been a quick tour of the basic operations that are used to set up and control external references. There are more features and commands for working with Xrefs than have been covered here, but you now know enough to start working with them.

Other Features of Xrefs

What follows are a few additional operations and features that you may find useful when you delve more deeply into external references. Play around a little and see what you can do.

▶ Externally referenced drawings can have drawings externally referenced to them. These are called *nested* Xrefs. There is no limit to the number of levels of nested Xrefs that a drawing can have.

▶ You can't explode an Xref, but you can detach it from the host. The Detach command is a button on the Xref Manager toolbar.

▶ Large, complex drawings that are Xreferenced often have their insertion points coordinated in such a way that all Xrefs are attached at the 0,0 point of the host drawing. This helps keep drawings aligned properly. By default, any drawing that is Xreferenced into a host drawing uses 0,0 as its insertion point. But you can change the coordinates of the insertion point with the *Base command*. With the drawing you want to change current, type **base** ↵ and enter the coordinates for the new insertion point.

▶ You can limit which layers and, to some degree, which objects in a drawing are Xreferenced in the host drawing by using *Indexing* and *Demand Loading*.

▶ A host drawing can be Xreferenced into the drawing that has been Xreferenced into the host. This is called an *overlay* and is an option in the Attach Xref dialog box. Overlays ignore nested Xreferences.

▶ If you freeze the layer that was current when an Xref was attached, the entire Xref is frozen. If you turn off this same layer, it has no effect on the visibility of the Xref.

▶ The Unload button in the External Reference dialog box lets you deactivate Xrefs without detaching them from the host file. They stay on the list of Xrefs and can be reloaded at any time with the Reload button. This can be a time-saver in complex drawings.

If You Would Like More Practice...

In this chapter you Xreferenced the cabin drawing into the site drawing, as a landscape architect who was designing the development plan for the site might have done. If you were the lead architect, you might want to Xref the landscape architect's site plan into your cabin drawing. Try doing this.

▶ Open Cabin07b.

▶ Attach Site12a to Cabin07b as an Xref.

▶ Change the Site12a layers to a dark green.

▶ Rotate the UCS 90° around the *z* axis (as you did in Chapter 8, *Generating Elevations*).

▶ Use the Plan command to position the drawing correctly.

▶ Change the Ltscale to 100.

▶ Use In-place Reference Editing to change the driveway or patio in the Xref.

Are You Experienced?

Now you can...

☑ **draw a basic site plan**

☑ **use Surveyor units to lay out property lines**

☑ **attach an external reference**

☑ **control the appearance of an external reference by modifying layers**

☑ **use Visretain to save Xref layer changes**

☑ **revise a drawing that is externally referenced**

☑ **modify an Xref from the host drawing**

☑ **update an Xref path**

☑ **bind an Xref to a host file**

CHAPTER 13

Using Layouts to Set Up a Print

- ▶ Putting a title block in a Layout

- ▶ Setting up viewports in a Layout

- ▶ Aligning viewports

- ▶ Controlling visibility in viewports

- ▶ Setting up a text style for a Layout

- ▶ Adding text in a Layout

In the previous chapter, we introduced external references, which are useful and powerful tools. Although the commands for Xrefs are a little tricky, the overall concept is fairly straightforward—in effect, you are viewing another drawing from within the current drawing. In contrast, the concept of the *Layout* display mode is a little difficult to understand, but the commands are fairly simple. While external references help you combine several drawings into a composite, Layouts allow you to set up and print several views of the same file. The Layout is a view of your drawing as it will sit on a sheet of paper when printed. (The Layouts feature was added to AutoCAD with version 2000.)

Each Layout has a designated printer and paper size for the print. You adjust the positioning of the drawing and the scale of the print. The part that is hard to understand is the way two scales are juxtaposed in the same file: the scale of the drawing on the printed paper (usually a standard scale used by architects, such as ¼" = 1'-0") and the scale of the Layout, which is almost always 1:1, or the actual size.

One way to visualize how a Layout works is to think of it as a second drawing, or a specialized layer, that has been laid over the top of your current drawing. Each Layout that you create will have one or more *viewports*—special windows through which you will view your project at a scale to be printed. The layouts are usually at a scale of 1:1 (actual size), and will contain some of the information that you originally put with the building lines, such as the border and title block, notes, the scale, north arrow, etc.

Think for a moment about drawing the floor plan of a building on a traditional drafting table. You draw the building to a scale such as ⅛" = 1'-0". Then, on the same sheet of paper, you print out a note using letters that are, say, ⅛" high. If you look at those letters as being on the same scale as the building, they would measure 1' high, and that's what we've been doing on the cabin drawing so far. But in traditional drafting, you don't think that way; instead, you work with two scales in the drawing without thinking about it. So a letter is ⅛" high (actual size) and a part of the building that measures ⅛" on the paper is thought of as being 1' long (at a scale of ⅛" = 1'-0"). Layouts are designed to let you juggle two or more scales in a drawing in the same way, in order to set the drawing up to be printed.

Setting Up Layouts

We will begin working with Cabin11a, the drawing we used for basic dimensioning in Chapter 11. This drawing is essentially complete and ready to print. You will print it in the next chapter, just as it is (Figure 13.1), without using Layouts.

For now, you will modify this drawing and create a Layout for it to get a basic understanding of what Layouts are and how they are activated and set up. Then, in the next chapter, you'll print this same drawing a second time, both with and without a Layout.

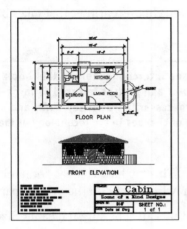

FIGURE 13.1: Cabin11a **ready to print**

In setting up a new Layout, we will use an 8.5" × 11" sheet.

1. Open Cabin11a. Notice the border of the drawing and the rectangle just outside the border that represents the edge of the sheet of paper on which the print will be made. You will recall from Chapter 10, *Controlling Text in a Drawing*, that when you constructed the border and title block for this drawing, you had to make a calculation to determine that the size of the border for a scale of ⅛" = 1'-0". This was based on a rectangle 68' wide by 88' high, which you then offset 3' to make the border. With Layouts, you don't have to make this kind of calculation; you draw the border actual size.

2. Create a new layer called Tblk-L1. Assign it a color and make it current.

3. Look at the lower-left corner of the drawing area. On the Model tab, you will see two Layout tabs. Click the Layout1 tab. After a moment,

This chapter has been designed so readers can benefit by following along even if they don't have a printer hooked up to their computer, or if their printer isn't the one referred to in the text.

the Page Setup – Layout1 dialog box comes up. It has two tabs. Click the Plot Device tab to make it active if it isn't already (Figure 13.2a). This is where you associate the new Layout with a printing device. The example shows an HP LaserJet printer in the Plotter Configuration area, but yours may be different. If your computer is linked to more than one printer, make sure you choose a printer that takes 8.5" × 11" paper.

N O T E   *Print* and *plot* are used interchangeably in this book, as are *printer* and *plotter*. In the past, *plot* and *plotter* referred to large-format devices and media, but that's not necessarily true today. *Print* and *printing* are more widely used now because of changes in the technology of the large-format devices.

4. Click the Layout Settings tab. This tab has six areas containing settings that control how the drawing will fit on the printed paper.

5. In the Paper Size and Paper Units area, be sure the Paper Size drop-down list is set to Letter 8 ½ × 11 in. Below that, the Printable Area for the chosen printing device is displayed. This shows the maximum area your printer can print on an 8.5" × 11" sheet of paper and thus gives you an idea of how close to the edge of the paper the printer will print. Jot down the Printable Area. In this example, it's 7.94 × 10.48 inches.

6. Move to the Drawing Orientation area and select Portrait.

7. The Plot Area contains five radio buttons for selecting what is to be plotted. Some are disabled. Be sure that Layout is selected.

8. In the Plot Scale area, the scale to be used is 1:1. If it's not already selected, open the Scale drop-down list and select 1:1 from the 26 preset scale choices.

9. We'll ignore the Plot Options area for now. The Layout Settings tab should look like Figure 13.2b.

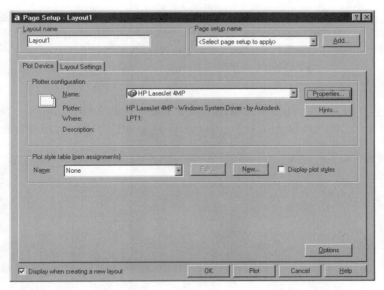

FIGURE 13.2: The Page Setup – Layout1 dialog box with the Plot Device tab active (a), and with the Layout Settings tab active (b)

10. In the upper-right corner of the Page Setup – Layout1 dialog box, in the Page Setup Name area, click Add. The User Defined Page Setups dialog box comes up. In the New Page Setup Name text box at the top, type **Cabin11a-L1**. Then click OK. Your setting changes are named and saved.

11. Click OK to close the Page Setup – Layout1 dialog box. You are returned to your drawing and Layout1 is displayed (Figure 13.3).

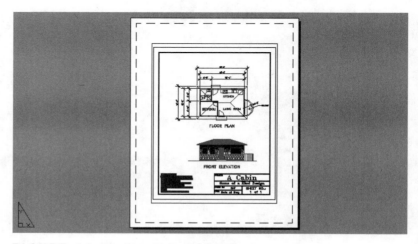

FIGURE 13.3: Layout1 for Cabin11a

The drawing area now displays a white sheet of paper resting on a gray background. The drawing of the cabin is centered on the paper with its border and outer rectangle. We'll be changing this in a moment. Outside this rectangle, there is another rectangle. This is a viewport, and it was automatically created when you set up Layout1. The viewport is a new AutoCAD object that creates a hole, or window, in the Layout so that you can see through the Layout to the drawing of the building. You can think of the building as residing "underneath" the Layout. Finally, near the outer edge of the white rectangle is a rectangle of dashed lines. This represents the 7.94" × 10.48" printable area of our printer.

Look to the lower-left corner of the drawing area at the Model and Layout tabs. Note that the Layout1 tab is now the active tab.

1. Click the Model tab. A view of Cabin11a, without Layout1, appears.

2. Click the Layout1 tab. The Layout returns.

Throughout the book so far, you have been drawing in the Model tab (sometimes called *Model space*). You have put some information—some of the text, the title block, and the border—on the Model tab that is usually put on the Layout if you're using the Layout feature. Notice the triangle in the lower-left corner of the drawing area. This icon indicates that your cursor is currently residing on the active Layout. In this setup, you cannot select any part of the cabin to work on, and any new objects you create will be on the Layout. To work on the cabin itself, you need to move the cursor to Model space. There are two ways of doing that. One is to click the Model tab. This temporarily removes the Layout, and you are left with just the drawing or *model*. The other way is to switch to the Model space while a Layout is active. We'll try this latter method now.

As the term *Model space* implies, the lines and other Auto-CAD objects that make up the components of the cabin are often referred to as a *model*. This distinguishes them from other AutoCAD objects, such as the title block and border, that reside on a Layout.

1. Move the crosshair cursor around and notice that it can be placed at any point on the Layout. You can move the cursor over the cabin, but you can't select any part of the cabin drawing.

2. On the far right end of the Status bar, click Paper. The Paper button changes to become the Model button. Continue moving the cursor around the drawing area. The cursor becomes a crosshair only when it is placed inside the viewport surrounding the cabin drawing (Figure 13.4). Otherwise the cursor changes to a pointer arrow, as it does when it is placed on the toolbars and menus. When the cursor is within the viewport, the lines of the crosshair extend only to the edge of the viewport. This is the boundary of where you may pick points to draw when working on the cabin.

When you activate Model space while a Layout is active, it is like opening a window and reaching through the opening to touch the drawing of the building behind the window.

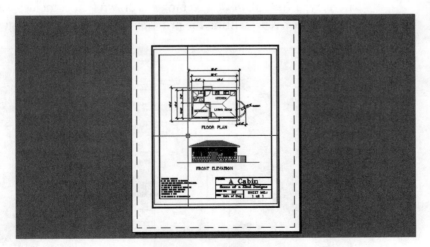

FIGURE 13.4: The crosshair cursor in Model space with Layout active

N O T E   If the lines of your crosshair cursor don't normally extend to the edges of the drawing area, choose Tools ≻ Options and select the Display tab. In the lower-left corner, where it says Crosshair Size, push the slidebar all the way to the right and press Apply. The new setting will be 100 and the crosshair lines extend to the drawing area edges.

Once Layouts are set up, you will find it practical to make the Model tab active when making major changes to the drawing. This will temporarily disable the Layout and make it invisible. To make minor changes to the cabin (or other buildings), leave the Layout tab active and click the Paper button on the Status bar to make Model space active while the Layout is still visible.

You need to transfer the title block and border from Model space to Layout. We'll start by drawing a new border on the Layout.

Drawing a Border on a Layout

The border for a Layout is drawn at the actual size that it will be when it is printed, as the Layout is the actual size of the paper to be used, in this case, 8.5" × 11".

1. Click the Model button on the Status bar. This moves the crosshair cursor back to the Layout.

2. Start the Rectangle command and type 0,0 ↵. Then type the Printable Area number that you jotted down in step 5 above. For the example here, type **7.94,10.48** ↵. A rectangle is drawn that coincides with the dashed lines representing the printable area of the sheet (Figure 13.5).

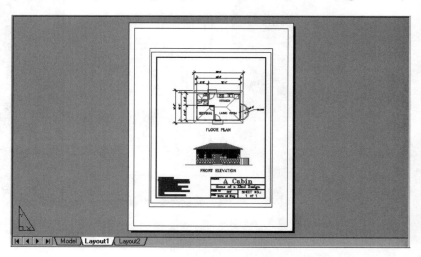

F I G U R E   1 3 . 5 : Layout1 with a rectangle drawn on the boundary of the printable area

3. We want the border to be set in from the rectangle you just drew by about ⅛". Offset the new rectangle ⅛" to the inside.

4. Erase the outer rectangle. The dashed lines become visible again. The border should be a line ¹⁄₃₂" wide.

5. Click the new rectangle, then activate the Properties window. Change the Global Width from 0 to ¹⁄₃₂. Close Properties and press Esc to clear the grips. The lines of the offset rectangle are now ¹⁄₃₂" wide and will serve as the new border (Figure 13.6).

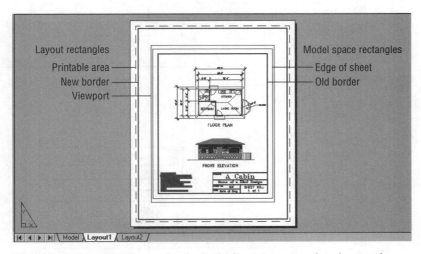

FIGURE 13.6: The new border in the Layout, among a lot of rectangles

There are a lot of rectangles around the drawing of the cabin, but you will be removing some of them soon. You have a border and a rectangle in Model space, the second of which indicates the edge of the sheet of paper. These will both be removed. But first you need to put a title block in the Layout, connected to the border that you just created. Let's look at the title block you've already drawn.

6. Click the Model tab. Layout1 is temporarily deactivated and you are back in the Model space. Take note of the title block.

Designing a Title Block for a Layout

The original title block was drawn to a size that could be plotted at ⅛" scale, so its dimensions are quite large (Figure 13.7a). You will need to make the size of the new title block much smaller to make it fit on the border that you just drew.

How much smaller? The dimensions of the new title block drawn at actual size are shown in Figure 13.7b.

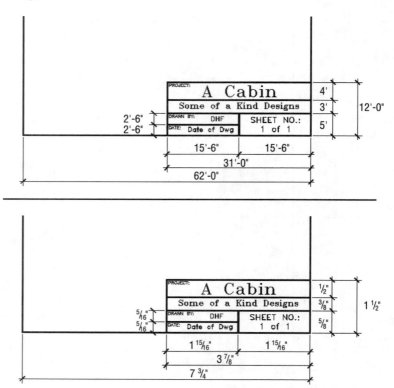

FIGURE 13.7: The original dimensions of the cabin title block (a), and the new, actual-size dimensions in the Layout (b)

The text, too, has to be made smaller to fit into the new title block. The following is a chart showing the heights of the various text used in the two title blocks:

Text	Original Title Block	Layout1 Title Block
A Cabin	2'-6"	$5/16$"
Some of a Kind Design	1'-3"	$5/32$"
DHF	1'-0"	$1/8$"
Date of Dwg	1'-0"	$1/8$"
SHEET NO.: 1 of 1	1'-3"	$5/32$"
PROJ.:, DRAWN BY:, DATE:	8"	$1/12$"

This may seem complicated at first, but think about the discussion we had near the beginning of this chapter in which we talked about using two scales in the same drawing. Traditional drafting uses a scale for the lines that represent the building. The text, title block, and border are drawn at actual size. In CAD drafting without Layouts, you have the convenience of being able to draw the building at full size; but you have to draw the text, title block, and border larger than they will eventually be in the finished plot because there is only one scale for the drawing. With Layouts, you can return to the method used by traditional drafters. The Layout is the part of the drawing where you put everything that relates to the actual size of the sheet, and Model space is where the building lines and objects representing building components reside. You'll see shortly how the two spaces work together to make a complete drawing.

Let's get back to this title block and finish making one on the Layout. You need to look at the change of size of the title block and text from the original title block to the new one. Because Cabin11a is set up to be printed at a scale of ⅛" = 1'-0", the text, border, and title block have all been drawn larger than their actual size by the scale factor of ⅛" scale. And what is the scale factor of ⅛" scale? It's the true ratio of the scale and is found by dividing the smaller number on one side of the equation into the larger number on the other side of the equation. If you divide ⅛" into 1'-0" (or 12"), you will get the scale factor, 96. We did this in Chapter 10. The text, border, and title block are all 96 times larger in the original than they need to be in Paper space, where they will be actual size.

After scaling the original title block down by a factor of 96, you will have a new title block that will be actual size. Then you will need to put it in the Layout and attach it to the border. You can easily do the scaling and the moving after using the AutoCAD's cut-and-paste tools.

Cutting and Pasting in AutoCAD

When you use the Windows cut-and-paste tools that have been customized to work with AutoCAD, the objects that are cut (or copied) can have an insertion point and can be inserted as a block back into the drawing or into another drawing. With Layout1 deactivated, the Cabin11a drawing is visible on the screen.

1. Right-click anywhere on the screen and select Copy with Base Point from the shortcut menu. Use the Endpoint Osnap and pick the lower-left of the title block as the base point. Use a regular selection window to select the title block and all of its text, but not the border. (Selection windows were described in Chapter 6, *Using Layers to*

Organize Your Drawing, when you were selecting the kitchen and bathroom fixtures to move them onto the Fixtures layer.) Press ↵.

2. Click the Layout1 tab again, click the Paper button on the status bar, then erase the original border and title block, and the outer rectangle representing the edge of the sheet—all of which were created in the original Cabin11a drawing. The two rectangles and the original title block disappear (Figure 13.8a).

3. Click the Model button (on the Status bar) to move the cursor back to Layout1.

4. Right-click the screen and select Paste as Block from the menu bar. Part of the image of the title block appears in the drawing, attached to the cursor. It's huge; you can see only the end of one line. Remember that we drew the original title block and border in a scaled-up fashion so that they would match the drawing's scale. The original scale factor we used to scale it up was 96 for ⅛" scale, so we'll use the reciprocal of that to scale it down.

5. Use the Nearest Osnap and pick a point anywhere on the left half of the bottom borderline as the insertion point. Now we'll use the scale command to scale down the title block.

6. Start the Scale command. Select the large polyline by clicking its edge, then press ↵. At the `Specify base point:` prompt, move the cursor to the center of the bottom edge of the polyline. When the Endpoint Osnap symbol appears there, click. Then type **1/96** ↵ (Figure 13.8b). The title block is now the correct size.

7. Start the Move command. Be sure Polar is on. Using the Endpoint and Perpendicular Osnaps, move the title block to the right until the right end of the top line in the title block (Endpoint) meets the right side of the border (Perpendicular). This will position the title block correctly on the border (Figure 13.8c).

8. Use the Explode command to explode the title block. Then use the Properties button to move the title block lines and its text to the Tblk-L1 layer. This completes the transfer of the title block from Model space to Layout1.

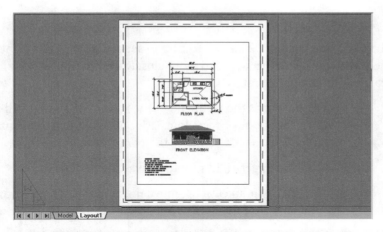

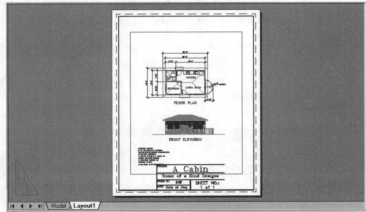

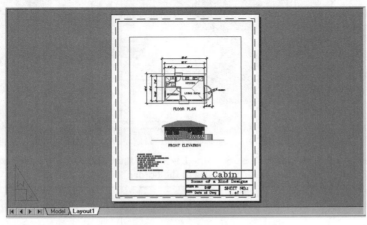

FIGURE 13.8: Removing the title block and border rectangles (a), pasting the title block into Layout1 (b), and positioning it correctly (c)

Adjusting a Viewport

The last step in using the Layout feature to set up Cabin11a to print is to adjust the size of the default viewport to more closely fit into the border, and to set the scale of the cabin drawing to ⅛" = 1'-0".

1. The button at the right end of the status bar should still read Paper. Click the viewport rectangle. Grips appear. Click the Osnap and Polar buttons on the Status bar to temporarily deactivate them.

2. Click the upper-right grip to activate it.

3. Turn off Polar and Osnap, move the cursor to a point near the upper-right corner of the border, but still inside of it, then click.

4. Click the lower-left grip. Then move, as in step 3, to a point close to the lower-left corner of the border and click to set it.

5. Press Esc to remove the grips. The viewport is now about as large as it can be on the page (Figure 13.9). To complete the last step, you need to adjust the scale of the cabin drawing to be ⅛" = 1'-0" and make the viewport border invisible.

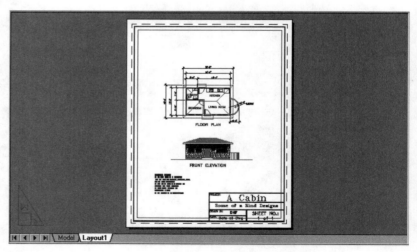

FIGURE 13.9: The Layout1 of the Cabin11a drawing with the viewport enlarged to nearly the size of the border

6. Create a new layer called Vports-L1. Assign it a color that really stands out, such as purple. Don't make this new layer current.

T I P   It's useful to assign a color to the Vports-L1 layer that will stand out in your drawing, so you are reminded that the viewports, while an essential part of the drawing, are usually designed to be invisible.

7. Click the viewport to select it. Then click the Properties button on the Standard toolbar.

8. In the Properties dialog box, Viewport should be in the drop-down list at the top. In the list of properties, click Layer. Then open the drop-down list next to Layer and select Vports-L1.

9. Close the Properties dialog box and press Esc to remove the grips. The viewport is now on the Vports-L1 layer.

10. Click Paper on the Status bar to move to Model space, then type z ↵. Type **1/96xp** ↵. The cabin drawing is reset to a scale of 1:96, or ⅛" = 1'-0".

11. Use Realtime Pan to pan the drawing so it fits properly within the new border.

12. Click Model on the Status bar to return to Paper space.

13. Click the viewport to select it. Right-click and, on the shortcut menu, click Display Locked. Choose Yes on the little flyout menu to place a check mark next to it if there isn't one already. This locks the viewport at the scale you just set.

14. Tblk-L1 should be current. Freeze the Vports-L1 layer (Figure 13.10). The drawing looks very much like the original Cabin11a before Layouts were introduced, but we now have the title block and border on a Layout at 1:1 scale.

Locking a viewport is an important step and will be discussed in the next section.

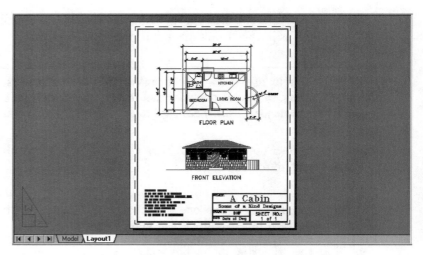

FIGURE 13.10: Cabin11b with the title block and border on Layout1

Switching between Model Space and a Layout

Let's look at our drawing for a moment to see what happens when you switch from Model space to a Layout. Currently, Layout1 is active.

1. Start the Erase command and pick the top dimension to erase. Try to select something on the front elevation. You will find that you cannot pick anything in the cabin drawing. The only objects you can select are the title block and the borderlines, which are on Layout1. When Layout1 is current, only objects on the Layout can be chosen. The triangle icon in the lower-left corner of the drawing area is visible when a Layout is current. Press Esc to cancel the Erase command.

2. Click Paper on the Status bar. Paper changes to Model, and the triangular Paper space icon disappears.

N O T E   When a Layout is active, the Paper/Model button on the Status bar controls whether the current Layout or Model space portion of the drawing is active, i.e., accessible. If Model space is active, the Status bar always displays the Model button. If you click the Model button when Model space is active, the last current Layout becomes active, and the button on the Status bar changes to the Paper button.

3. Restart the Erase command and try to select objects in the cabin drawing again. This time you are able to choose anything within the viewport except the title block and its text.

N O T E The cursor always resides in the active portion of the drawing. Work can be done in only one of the two portions (Model space or a Layout) at any given time.

4. Try to select the viewport boundary line, the border, or the title block. You can't choose anything on the Layout when Model space is current. Cancel the Erase command.

N O T E The viewports in Layouts are called *floating* viewports because they can be moved around. They always reside in the Layout portion of the drawing. There is another kind of viewport in AutoCAD called a *tiled* viewports, which is fixed and exists only in Model space. For brevity, in this chapter, we will refer to floating viewports as viewports.

5. Click the Model tab. The Layout disappears, and you now view your drawing without a title block or border. We transferred them to Layout1, so they are no longer visible when the Model tab is active.

6. Zoom into the front door of the elevation, then click the Model button on the Status bar. Layout1 returns with the previous view of the cabin that you had when Layout1 was most recently active.

7. Click the Model tab again. Zoom to Extents. Click the Layout1 tab.

8. Click Paper in the Status bar. Now use zoom window to zoom into the front door again. Because the viewport is locked for scale, Auto-CAD switches to the viewport (or to *Paper space*) to make the zoom, then switches back to *Model space*.

9. Zoom Previous, then save this drawing as Cabin13a.

N O T E When a Layout tab is active, this is sometimes referred to as being "in Paper space." Conversely, when the Model tab is active, this is called being "in Model space." When a Layout is active (i.e., when you are in Paper space) you can switch to Model space, while keeping the Layout visible, by clicking the Paper button on the Status bar. The button will change to the Model button, and you can work on the portion of your drawing that is visible in the viewport. Then you can click the Model button and switch back to the Layout (or Paper space).

Picturing your drawing as two drawings in one is still a useful way to understand Layouts, and will help you to understand how Layouts and Model space work together.

Once you have set up a title block, border, and viewport in a Layout, you can deactivate the Layout and work on your drawing from within Model space. Then, when you are ready to plot it out, reactivate the Layout. The orientation and magnification of your drawing relative to the Layout border will be preserved. You can also work on your drawing while the Layout is active by clicking the Paper button (as mentioned in the Note above). However, once you have zoomed Model space to a scale in the viewport, you don't want to zoom while in Model space because that changes the relationship between Model space and the Layout that you set up by zooming to ¹⁄₉₆xp. The ¹⁄₉₆xp zoom must be preserved so that the drawing plots at the correct scale.

This is why it was important to lock the viewport, as you did in step 13 in the previous section titled "Adjusting a Viewport." If you want to zoom into your drawing while a layout is visible and when you are in Model space, lock the viewport. AutoCAD will automatically switch to the layout to zoom, then switch back to Model space. That way, the 1/*scale factor*xp zoom won't be affected.

> **When you zoom to ¹⁄₉₆xp, you are using the zoom option called *n*XP in the command window. The *n* represents the reciprocal of the scale factor. It's the "paper space" partner of the *n*X zooming option that you have used in previous chapters.**

N O T E   When a Layout is active, you can also switch back and forth between the Layout and Model space by typing **ps** ↵ or **ms** ↵.

This may seem like too much work to be worth the effort for a small drawing like this one, but be patient. As you start working on larger drawings, you will see what Layouts can do for you.

Working with Multiple Viewports in a Layout

The previous exercises introduced you to Layouts and taught you how they work. I used the example of a single viewport within a border and title block, all of which were on Layout1. This is the way Layouts are used much of the time, even in large projects or on large sheets. A title block is developed for a project. Each sheet in a set of drawings is a .dwg file with a title block on a Layout and one viewport, which encompasses most of the area inside the border, where you view the building components in Model space. But this is certainly not the only way Layouts are used. At times, more than one viewport will be used within a border, or a drawing file will have more than one viewport. The rest of the exercises in this chapter will lead you through an exploration of the advantages and techniques of using multiple viewports and Layouts.

Setting Up Multiple Viewports

You'll start by creating a new Layout with two viewports using the Layout Wizard. Then you'll adjust the views of the cabin on the Layout sheet. To give ourselves room to work, we'll use a sheet of 11" × 17" paper.

1. Using Cabin13a, create a new layer called Tblk-L2, assign it a color, and make it current. If you have a Layout2 tab in the lower-left corner of the drawing area, right-click it and select Delete from the shortcut menu. Then, with Layout1 enabled and active, go to the pull-down menus and choose Insert ➢ Layout ➢ Layout Wizard. The Create Layout dialog box appears, and Begin is in the title bar (Figure 13.11a). On the left side, a list of the steps for creating a new Layout is displayed, and an arrow points at Begin. In a text box on the bottom right of the dialog box, Layout2 is highlighted as the name of the new Layout.

2. Leave Layout2 in the box and click Next. The dialog box now displays a list of printers on the right. The pointer on the left is now pointing at Printer (Figure 13.11b). If you have DWF ePlot (optimized for plotting).pc3 in the list of printers, or any printer that takes an 11" × 17" sheet of paper, highlight it and click Next again.

3. As the pointer indicates, the next step is to specify paper size. Open the drop-down list near the upper-right corner and select ANSI B (11.00 × 17.00 Inches). Then click Next again.

4. In the Orientation step, select Landscape, if it isn't already selected. Click Next again.

5. The next step is to choose a predrawn title block, or pick None and make your own. Click a few choices to see how they look in the preview port. We will make our own, so when you're finished browsing, highlight None. Then click Next.

6. Now you will set up viewports in the new Layout (Figure 13.11c). Open the Viewport Scale drop-down list and select ⅛" = 1'-0". (Don't select 1:8.) In the Viewport Setup area, there are four choices. Since we want two viewports side by side, we'll use the Array option. Click Array. The Array specification boxes become enabled below the Viewport Setup area. Change the number of rows to 1, and leave the other three boxes as they are. Then click Next.

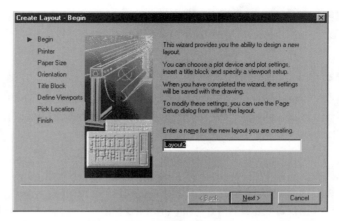

a

b

c

F I G U R E   1 3 . 1 1 :   Three pages in the Layout Wizard: Begin (a), Printer (b), and Define Viewports (c)

7. Now the pointer is indicating Pick Location. Click the Select Location button on the right. You are returned to the drawing and Layout2 is displayed at the correct orientation. You are prompted to Specify first corner. This means that you need to create a window in the Layout that will encompass the area to be taken up with the new viewports. Make a window similar to the one in Figure 13.12a.

8. Back in the Create Layout dialog box, click Finish. In the drawing, two identical viewports are drawn with the cabin drawing in each one, both displayed at a scale of ⅛" = 1'-0" (Figure 13.12b).

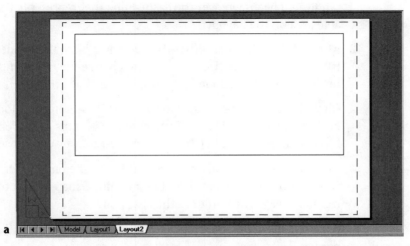

a

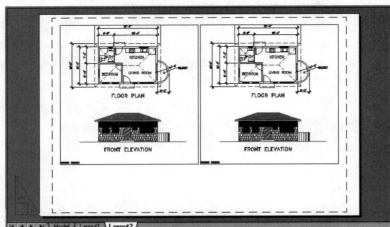

b

FIGURE 13.12: Windowing the viewport area in Layout2 (a), and the new viewports (b)

We'll work on the viewports in a moment, but first we need to create a border and title block for Layout2.

1. Right-click the Layout2 tab and choose Page Setup from the menu. In the Page Setup – Layout2 dialog box, be sure the Layout Settings tab is active. In the Paper Size and Paper Units area, note the Printable Area for the current printer and jot it down. Click OK.

2. Start the Rectangle command. Type **0,0** ↵. Then enter as coordinates the two numbers that define the printable area. For example, if the printable area is 15.66" × 10.60", you would type **15.66,10.6** ↵. A rectangle will be drawn over the dashed line that represents the printable area on the Layout.

3. As you did for Layout1, offset this rectangle ⅛" to the inside. Erase the outer rectangle. Use Properties to change the width of the polyline of the new rectangle to ¹⁄₃₂" (Figure 13.13a).

4. Click the Layout1 tab to switch to Layout1. Be sure the Model/Paper button on the Status bar is displaying Paper. If it's not, click the button to change it. Then right-click and select Copy with Base Point.

5. Click the Osnap button on the Status bar to the on position to activate the running Osnaps. Use the Endpoint Osnap to pick the lower-right corner of the border as the base point.

6. Use a regular selection window to select the title block without the border. Press ↵.

7. Click the Layout2 tab to switch back to Layout2. Choose Edit ➤ Paste and pick the lower-right corner of Layout2's border as the insertion point. The title block has been copied from Layout1 to Layout2 (Figure 13.13b).

8. Use the Properties button to move the title block objects onto the Tblk-L2 layer.

Now we're ready to work on the viewports.

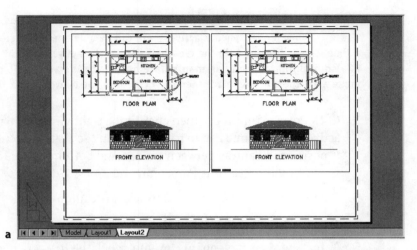

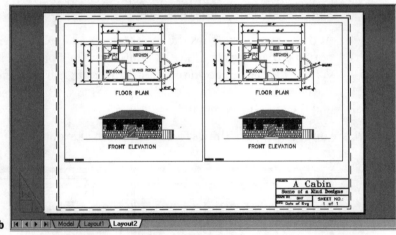

FIGURE 13.13: The new border for Layout2 (a), and the copied title block from Layout1 (b)

Aligning Viewports

We want the floor plan to be displayed in the left viewport and the front elevation to be displayed in the right viewport. We also want the titles of these two views to line up with each other horizontally. To accomplish this, we will need to perform some steps in Model space and some on the Layout, so we'll be switching back and forth while keeping Layout2 visible.

1. Click Paper on the Status bar to switch to Model space. Then move the cursor onto the viewports. The one that is active is the one where the crosshair cursor is visible.

T I P When Model space is active, there can be only one active viewport at a time. This is the one with the crosshair cursor. The active viewport's border is also highlighted. You can manipulate objects in the active viewport. To make a viewport active, place the arrow cursor in the viewport and click.

2. Click Polar to turn it on, then click in the right viewport to make it active. Use Realtime Pan to pan the drawing so that the front elevation is positioned halfway between the top and bottom of the 11" × 17" sheet. End the Realtime Pan command.

3. Type mvsetup ↵. Then type a ↵ to select the Align option.

4. Type h ↵ to select the Horizontal option.

5. At the Specify basepoint: prompt, click the Insert Osnap. Then click the FRONT ELEVATION text.

6. At the next prompt, click the Insert Osnap again. Click the left viewport and then click the FLOOR PLAN text. The floor plan in the left viewport is panned down so that its title is aligned with the title of the front elevation in the right viewport (Figure 13.14). Press Esc to end the Mvsetup command.

There are one or two more things to do to finish the Layout.

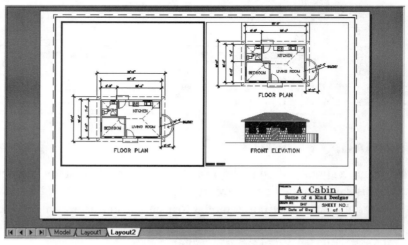

F I G U R E   1 3 . 1 4 : The text in the two viewports is aligned.

Finishing the 11" x 17" Drawing

We want to make the floor plan in the right viewport invisible, and we want to add the Mtext that was in the lower-left corner of the original drawing (Cabin11a) to the lower-left corner of Layout1. We'll use grips to adjust the right viewport.

1. Click the Model button on the Status bar to move the cursor back to the Layout (or back to Paper space).

2. Click the right viewport. Grips will appear at its corners.

3. Turn off the running Osnaps. Click the upper-right grip to activate it.

4. Move the crosshair cursor down along the right edge of the right viewport until the horizontal line of the crosshair sits between the floor plan and the elevation, then click. The viewport now only extends to just above the elevation.

5. Click the lower-right grip. Move it up slightly so that the top of the note text in the lower-left corner of the viewport is no longer visible, then click. Press Esc. Now the right viewport displays only the front elevation (Figure 13.15).

6. If necessary, select the left viewport and adjust it in the same way so only the floor plan is visible.

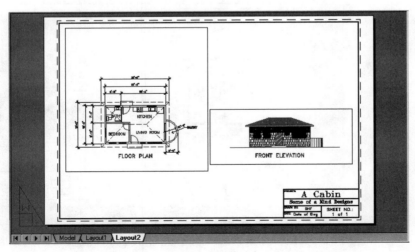

FIGURE 13.15: The right viewport showing only the front elevation after adjustments

To finish this drawing, you need to place the note text in the lower-left corner. You will accomplish this by creating a third viewport.

1. Choose View ➢ Viewports ➢ 1 Viewport.

2. Pick two points in the lower-left corner to create a square viewport. The entire Model space drawing appears in the viewport (Figure 13.16a).

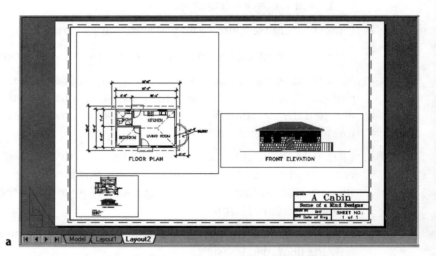

FIGURE 13.16: A third viewport is created (a), and the results of panning and zooming the view (b)

3. Click the Paper button to switch to Model space.

4. Be sure the new viewport is active. If not, click it, then pan the drawing in the new viewport until the note text is in the middle of the viewport. Press Esc to cancel Realtime Pan.

5. Type z ↵. Then type **1/96xp** ↵. The text is now the right size.

6. Do any additional panning necessary to get the text positioned in the corner near the border. If necessary, click the Model button to switch back to the viewport, then use grips to resize the Layout, and use Move to move it.

7. Click the Model button to switch to the Layout, if you haven't already (Figure 13.16b).

8. Create a new layer called Vports-L2 and assign it a color. Don't make this new layer current. Click OK.

9. With the Layout active, select the three viewports. Then pick the Properties button and move the viewports onto the Vports-L2 layer. Close the Properties dialog box and press Esc to remove the grips.

10. As you did in Layout1, click a viewport, right-click and choose Display Locked ➤ Yes to lock the display of the viewport. Repeat this for the other two viewports.

11. With the Tblk-L2 layer current, freeze the Vports-L2 layer (Figure 13.17).

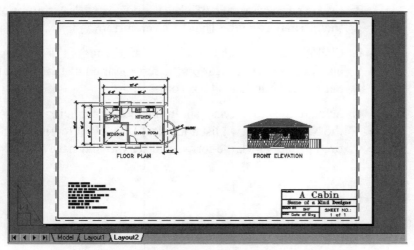

FIGURE 13.17: The completed 11" × 17" drawing with Layout2

12. Click the Layout1 tab to view the smaller Layout sheet. Click the Model tab to view the original drawing without its border and title block. Click the Layout2 tab again. All three views are of the same drawing.

13. Save this drawing to your training folder as Cabin13b.

Now you have two prints set up in Layouts, both based on the same drawing in Model space. There is room for more views in the larger of the two, possibly another elevation or a detail, but we're going to move on to a larger drawing.

Setting Up Viewports in Different Scales

In the next set of exercises, you will create a new Layout for a 30" × 42" sheet for the site plan you created in Chapter 12, *Managing External References*. Then you will create several viewports that have drawings of different scales. Because the site plan has the cabin drawing Xreferenced into it, you will also have a chance to see how external references are handled in a drawing that is using Layouts.

Setting Up a Layout for a 30" x 42" Drawing

To set up a 30" × 42" Layout, you will use almost the same procedure you used earlier. The title block will be different, but you won't take the time to fill in a complete title block; you'll just indicate its location in the drawing.

1. Close Cabin13b, then open Site12b.

2. Create new layers called Tblk-L1 and Vports-L1. Assign colors to them. Then make the Tblk-L1 layer current.

3. Click the Layout1 tab in the lower-left corner of the drawing area. A blank Layout will appear on the screen for an instant. Then the Page Setup – Layout1 dialog box comes up.

4. Activate the Plot Device tab. In the Plotter configuration area, open the Name drop-down list and select DWF ePlot (optimized for plotting).pc3, or any large-format plotter you may have set up to use.

5. Click the Layout Settings tab. In the Paper Size and Paper Width area, open the Paper Size drop-down list and scroll down to ARCH E1 (30.00 × 42.00 Inches). Select that size. Jot down the Printable Area setting (in the example, it's 40.60 × 29.54 Inches).

6. Drawing Orientation should be Landscape; Plot Area should be Layout; Plot Scale should be 1:1. When these are set, click Add in the upper-right corner of the dialog box. Enter **Site12b-L1**. Then click OK. Click OK again to close the Page Setup dialog box. You will be returned to your drawing. Layout1 is displayed. There is a viewport whose boundary is set in from the edge of the sheet. Site12b is zoomed to Extents within the viewport (Figure 13.18).

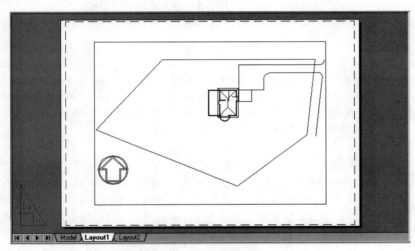

FIGURE 13.18: Site12b within Layout1

7. Use the Rectangle command to draw a rectangle from 0,0 to the point you jotted down in step 5 (in the example, 40.60,29.54).

8. Offset the rectangle ⅛" to the inside. Zoom into a corner, then erase the outer rectangle and Zoom Previous to a full view of the Layout (Figure 13.19a).

9. Click the border rectangle to turn on the grips. Hold down the Shift key and select the two grips on the left side to activate them. Be sure Polar is on and the running Osnaps are off. Click one of the two active grips. Hold the cursor directly to the right of the selected grips and type 1 ↵. The left side of the border is moved 1" to the right, leaving room for a binding on the left edge of the sheet. Press Esc. Sheets of large sizes usually have their title blocks on a vertical strip on the right side. We will draw a guideline to indicate the title block.

10. Offset the border rectangle 4" to the inside. Then explode the new rectangle. Erase the top, bottom, and left lines of this new rectangle. Then use the Extend command to extend the remaining line up and down to the rectangle that will serve as the border (Figure 13.19b).

T I P   Don't worry about the fact that the left side of the title block almost coincides with the right edge of the viewport. This is a coincidence. It makes it a little more difficult to pick the lines, but you know techniques now that can help you with this problem.

11. Start the Pedit command (type **pe** ↵) and select the rectangle that is the new border. Use the Width option to change the width of the borderline to ¹⁄₁₆". Type ↵ ↵ to stop and restart the Pedit command. Then pick the new line that represents the left side of the title block. When asked if you want to make this line into a polyline, press ↵ to accept the default of Yes. Use the Width option again and set this line to the same width as you used for the border. You now have a border and title block area set up in Layout1 and are ready to work with the viewports (Figure 13.19c).

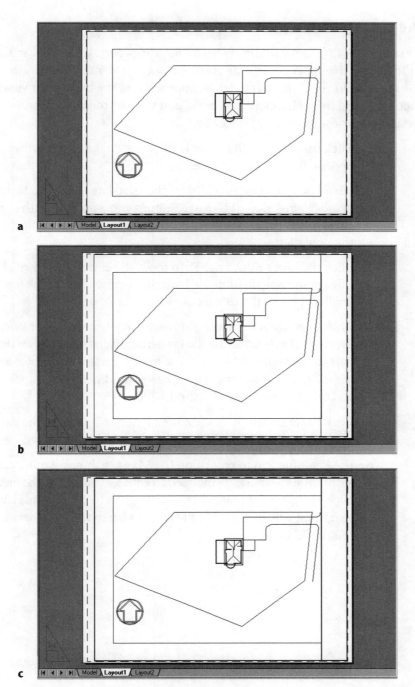

FIGURE 13.19: Creating the new title block and border: the border rectangle (a), the strip for the title block (b), and the finished title block and border (c)

Adjusting a Viewport for the Site Plan

On the 30" × 42" sheet, we already have a large viewport. We'll move it and resize it to fit into the upper two-thirds of the Layout in order to view the site plan at ⅛" scale. Then you'll make smaller viewports across the bottom for views of the floor plan and front elevation at ¼" scale, and the bathroom at 12" scale. Let's resize and reposition the larger viewport first.

1. Click the viewport in Layout1. Grips appear. Click the grip on the upper-left corner to activate it.

2. Turn Polar and Osnap off. Press the spacebar once. The Move command begins. Move the crosshair cursor to a point near the upper-left corner, just inside the border, then click. The viewport is moved to the upper left.

3. Click the lower-right grip. Then move the cursor to a point about one third of the way up from the bottom boundary line to the top boundary line, next to the title block (Figure 13.20a).

4. Click to position the second corner of the viewport. Then click the Properties button and use the Properties dialog box to move the viewport to the Vports-L1 layer. Close the Properties dialog box. Finally, press Esc to remove the grips. The viewport is resized, repositioned, and on its proper layer (Figure 13.20b).

5. Click Paper on the Status bar, then type z ↵ 1/96xp ↵. The site plan gets slightly smaller and looks like it will fit in the resized viewport.

6. Use Realtime Pan to reposition the Site12a drawing more centrally within the viewport. If you need to enlarge the size of the viewport, click Model on the Status bar and use grips to stretch the viewport to a size that will allow you to fit the site plan in the viewport at ⅛" scale (Figure 13.20c).

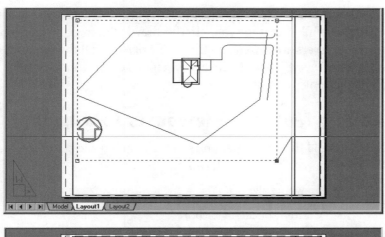

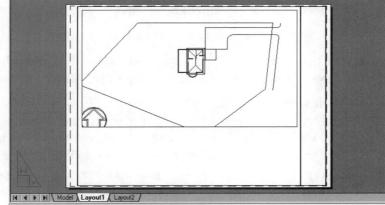

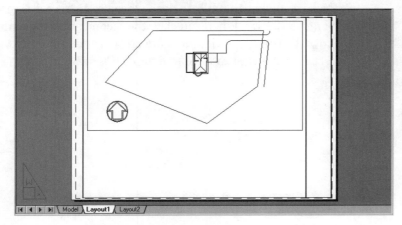

FIGURE 13.20: Adjusting a viewport with grips on (a), after the adjust-ment (b), and after the zoom (c)

The view of the site plan is just like the drawing before Paper space was activated. Remember that the cabin in this drawing is an external reference. Many of the cabin layers are frozen and the visible ones are all the same color, except the new deck. This will have to change when we set up other viewports for the floor plan and front elevation.

Adding Multiple Viewports to a Layout

Now we'll add three new viewports to the empty space below the first viewport, then modify each of them in terms of:

▶ Viewport size

▶ Content of each viewport

▶ Scale of objects within each viewport

▶ Visibility and color of layers within each viewport

We'll create the three viewports together, then modify them individually, starting with the leftmost viewport where we'll place the floor plan of the cabin.

1. Be sure that the Model/Paper button on the Status bar is set to Paper. Then set the Vports-L1 layer to be current. Choose View ➤ Viewports ➤ 3 Viewports. At the [Horizontal/Vertical/Above/Below/Left/ Right] <Right>: prompt, type **V** ↵. You will be prompted to Specify first corner or[Fit]:. This means you need to make a window that the three new viewports will fit inside of, side by side.

2. Make a window that fills the open area below the existing viewport (Figure 13.21a). When you click the second point to define the window, the three new viewports are created and each has a view of the Site12a drawing zoomed to Extents (Figure 13.21b).

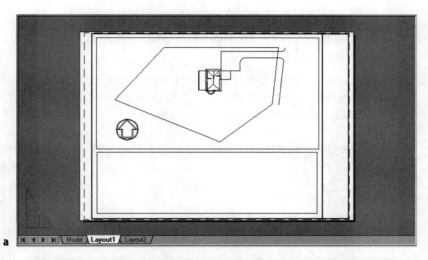

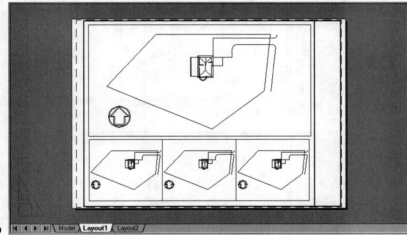

FIGURE 13.21: Windowing the area in which to insert the viewports (a) and the inserted viewports (b)

3. Click the Model/Paper button on the Status bar to move to Model space and click in the leftmost viewport. The UCS icon appears in all viewports. Click and hold down the UCS button on the Standard toolbar. The UCS flyout toolbar comes up. Move the cursor down to the Z Axis Rotate UCS button and release. Then type –90 ↵. Then choose View ➢ 3D Views ➢ Plan View ➢ Current UCS. The site plan is rotated 90° counterclockwise. The cabin is now oriented the way it was before being inserted as an external reference into the site plan (Figure 13.22a).

4. Pan the cabin to the middle of the viewport, then zoom its view to ¼" scale by typing z ↵ 1/48xp ↵. The floor plan fills the viewport (Figure 13.22b). Pan again if necessary.

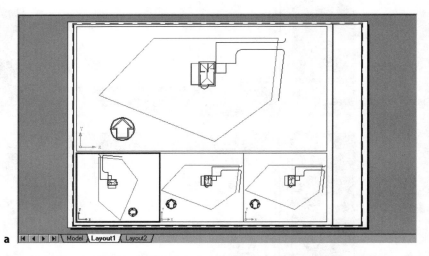

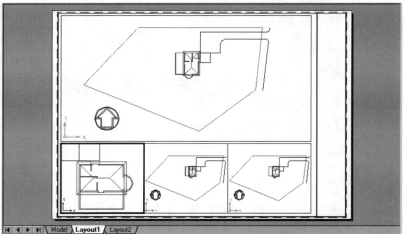

FIGURE 13.22: The left viewport with a rotated site plan (a), and the floor plan zoomed to ¼" scale in the viewport (b)

N O T E The visibility of the UCS icon can be controlled in each viewport and in Paper space by choosing View ➤ Display ➤ UCS Icon, and then clicking On. When the check mark next to On is visible, the UCS icon is displayed. When the Layout is active, the icon is a triangle and sits outside the Layout.

To complete this view, you'll need to do a few things. You need to resize the viewport and pan the view so everything that you want to see is visible. You also need to determine which layers you want visible in this viewport and freeze the ones whose objects you don't want to see. We'll work with the layers first because we need to make all the objects to be displayed visible in order to tell how big the viewport needs to be.

Controlling Layers in Viewports

You can control which layers are visible in each viewport, so two viewports can have a different combination of layers visible. The way this is done is to first thaw all frozen layers and make sure all layers are turned on. Then, with Model space current, you make a viewport active and freeze the layers you don't want visible in that viewport. When finished, you move to the next viewport and freeze layers you don't want visible in that viewport. In this situation, you'll eventually have to reset the visibility of the layers in all viewports.

1. On the Layout1 tab, be sure that Model space is active and the lower-left viewport is current. Then click the Layers button on the Object Properties toolbar. When the Layer Properties Manager dialog box opens, click and drag the right edge of the dialog box to the right to widen it enough to see the Current column on the far right.

2. Thaw all currently frozen layers and turn on all layers. (Right-click any layer, then choose Select All on the menu that appears in the drawing area. All layers are highlighted. Then click a snowflake in the Freeze column and a turned-off light bulb in the On column. All layers are thawed and turned on. Scroll back to the top and click the Cabin layer. The rest of the layers are de-selected.) Now that all layers are visible, you need to go down the list of layers. When you see a layer that needs to be frozen in the current viewport, click the sun in the Current column for that layer. The smaller viewport is current, so let's start with the layers for that one.

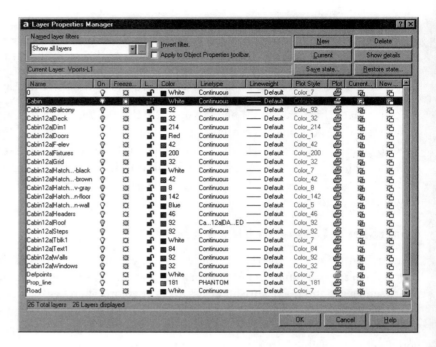

3. Move down the list and click the sun in the Current column for these layers:

   ▶ The following Cabin12al layers: Dim1, F-elev, Roof, Tblk1, Text1, and all the hatch layers *except* Hatch-plan-wall

   ▶ Prop-line and Road layers

   Click OK when finished. You are returned to your drawing (Figure 13.23a). The smaller viewport looks OK, but it needs resizing. All the layers are visible in the other two small viewports and in the larger one. Let's set the layers for the larger viewport now.

4. Click the larger viewport to make it active. Then click the Layers button again. In the Layer Properties Manager dialog box, go down the list again, clicking the suns in the Current column, as you did before, to make the following layers invisible in this viewport: all Cabin12al layers except Balcony, Deck, Roof, Steps, and Walls. Click OK when finished. The drawing in this viewport is what we want (Figure 13.23b).

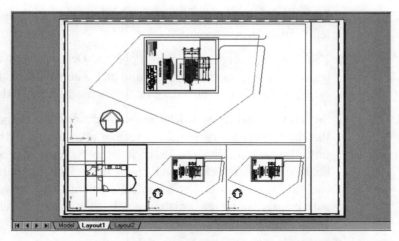

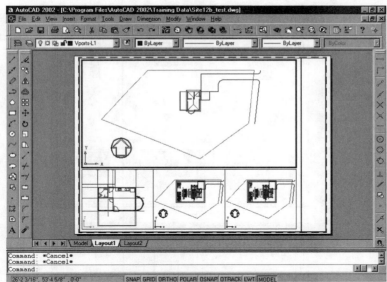

FIGURE 13.23: Layer changes made in the smaller left viewport (a), and in the larger viewport (b)

Now you need to adjust the size and view of the smaller left viewport so the structural grid will be fully displayed. You're going to stretch the viewport up to a point where it will overlap the larger viewport, so, while the larger viewport is active, move the north arrow to the other side of the site plan to get it out of the way.

1. Start the Move command and select the north arrow. Press ↵. Click the middle of the arrow and click again to place it in a clear space in the lower-right corner of the larger viewport.

2. Switch to Layout1 (or Paper space). Click the small viewport on the left to make grips appear.

3. Click the upper-right grip. With Polar and Ortho off, move the cursor up and to the right at about 45°, and pick a point just below the property line and click (Figure 13.24a). Press Esc to remove the grips.

4. Switch to Model space. Click the lower-left viewport to make it active. Use the Pan command to move the floor plan around in the viewport until the deck and the grid are completely visible. Leave some room below the deck for text. Press Esc to end the Pan command. Switch back to Paper space and do a final adjustment of the viewport's size with grips, making it as small as possible while still showing everything (Figure 13.24b). Press Esc to remove the grips.

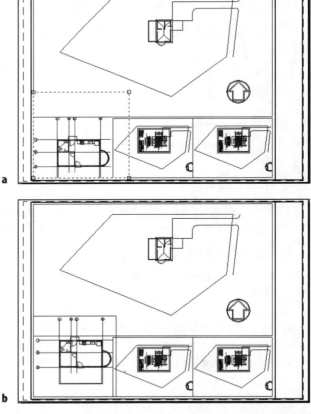

FIGURE 13.24: Stretching the viewport with grips in the Layout (a), and panning the view in Model space (b)

The layers are now set up so they are visible in all viewports (the Freeze column), except where frozen in particular viewports (the Current column). The other two small viewports have all layers visible, because we have yet to make these viewports current and work on them. Let's move to those viewports now and set them up using the procedures we've just used for the first two.

1. Switch to Model space. Click the smaller viewport that's in the middle to make it active. Then click the Layers button. Freeze all layers in the Current column, except the following layers:

   ▶ Cabin

   ▶ Cabin12a|F-elev

   ▶ Cabin12a|Hatch-elev-black

   ▶ Cabin12a|Hatch-elev-brown

   ▶ Cabin12a|Hatch-elev-gray

   Click OK to return to the drawing.

2. Click the Z Axis Rotate UCS icon on the standard toolbar. (Because it was recently used, it has replaced the UCS icon.) Then type **−90**. Choose View ➤ 3D Views ➤ Plan View ➤ Current UCS. Pan the front elevation to the middle of the viewport. Then type z ↵ **1/48xp** ↵. Pan the drawing again until the ground line approximately lines up with the bottom line of the deck in the floor plan on the left.

3. Move to the Layout and resize the viewport so that it includes the entire front elevation and nothing more (Figure 13.25).

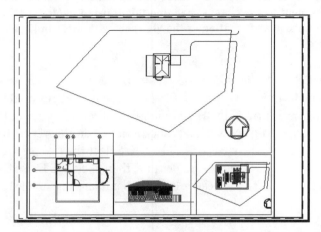

FIGURE 13.25: The front elevation in the middle small viewport

4. Now move to the viewport in the lower-right corner and make adjustments to display the bathroom at a scale of 1" = 1'-0". Follow these steps:

   A. To work on the fourth viewport, switch to Model space and activate the right small viewport.

   B. Use the Z Axis Rotate UCS icon and the Plan View command to rotate the drawing 90° counterclockwise, as you've done for the other two small viewports.

   C. In the Current column of the Layer Properties Manager dialog box, freeze the following layers: all the Cabin12al layers, except for Doors; Fixtures; Hatch-plan-floor; Hatch-plan-wall; Headers; Walls; and Windows; and all layers not prefaced by Cabin12a except the Cabin and 0 layers.

   D. Zoom to 1/12xp.

   E. Pan the drawing until the bathroom is centered in the viewport. Try to line up the bottom bathroom wall with the ground line in the front elevation.

   F. Switch to the Layout (click the Model button) and adjust the size and position of the viewport. Try to make the right and bottom boundary lines of the viewport coincide with the right and bottom edges of the wall lines. Zoom in close if you need to.

N O T E   Once a viewport is zoomed to a scale with 1/*scale factor*xp, the final adjustment has two steps: panning the drawing in Model space, and adjusting the size and location of the viewport with grips in Layout (or in Paper space).

   G. Switch to Model space and repair the bathroom door using the same technique we used in Chapter 12, when we repaired the roof hip lines. Turn off the Hatch-plan-floor layer temporarily. Choose Modify ➤ In-place Xref and Block Edit ➤ Edit Reference, then click an object in the viewport. Click OK. Select the two pieces of the door swing and the left header line, then click OK. Erase the small swing line. Use the header line as a boundary line and extend the swing to it. Save changes back to the reference file. Turn the Hatch-plan-floor layer back on.

H. Switch back to Layout, then zoom out to a full view of the Layout. Be sure Polar is on. If necessary, move any of the small viewports horizontally to space them evenly on the layout. Then select a viewport and right-click. Choose Display Locked ➤ Yes to place a check mark next to Yes. Do this for each of the four viewports.

The results should look something like Figure 13.26.

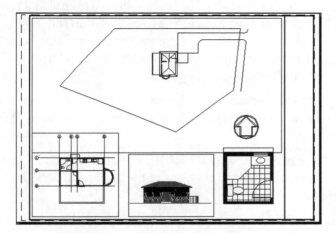

FIGURE 13.26: All viewports completed

TIP Since viewports are usually made to be invisible, it isn't important to line them up evenly. Viewports can overlap each other as long as the objects viewed in the viewports do not overlap.

Adding Text to Paper Space

Now you'll add titles to the views in a style that matches the style of the front elevation title. Underneath each title we will put the scale of the view.

1. Switch to Model space. Make the viewport containing the front elevation active. Then thaw the Cabin12a|Text1 layer in the Current column. The FRONT ELEVATION text appears.

T I P   If the GENERAL NOTES or the FLOOR PLAN text also appears, you can stretch the viewport to hide it the next time you are in Paper space.

2. Create a new layer called Text-L1. Assign it the same color as the Cabin12a|Text1 layer and make it current.

3. Create a new text style called Title-L1. (Remember, the Style command is started by choosing Format ➤ Text Style on the menu bar.) We want the new style to be identical to the Title text style we used in Model space, but the height has to be adjusted for use in a Layout. It was 1'-6" high in Model space. The front elevation is now at ¼" scale. If you divide 1'-6" by 48, you have the Paper space text height: ⅜". Assign this text style the romand.shx font and a ⅜" height. Click Apply, then click Close.

4. Switch to Paper space. Then choose Draw ➤ Text ➤ Single Line Text from the menu bar. Type j ↵, then type c ↵. To activate point filters, type .y ↵.

5. Select the Insert Osnap and click the FRONT ELEVATION text. Select the Midpoint Osnap and click one of the horizontal deck lines in the floor plan.

6. Press ↵ for the Rotation prompt. With Caps Lock on, type **floor plan** ↵ ↵. The floor plan title is placed on the drawing. Zoom in to see it better (Figure 13.27a).

7. With Polar on, copy this text down ¾". Use the Properties button to change this text to ¼" high and to SCALE: ¼" = 1'-0" (Figure 13.27b). Leave a space before and after the = sign.

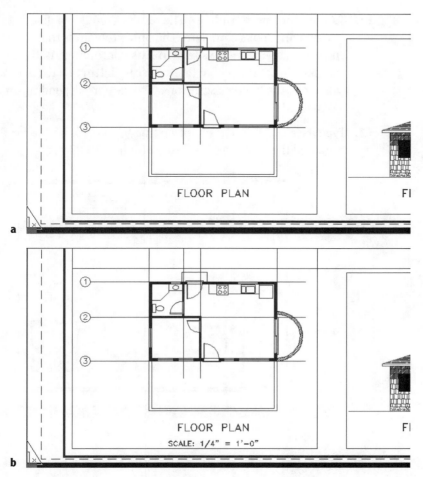

a

b

FIGURE 13.27: A title is placed on the floor plan (a), and a scale is added (b).

8. Zoom Previous. Use Copy and the Insertion Osnap to copy the scale to the front elevation.

9. With Polar on, use the Copy command with the Multiple option to copy both the view title and the scale from the floor plan to the bathroom viewport. Then turn Polar off and place the second copy of the text under the site plan.

10. Choose Modify ➢ Object ➢ Text ➢ Edit to start the Ddedit command. Use this command to change the titles to BATHROOM and SITE PLAN, and to change the scales to 1" = 1'-0" and ⅛" = 1'-0", respectively.

11. Turn off the Vports-L1 layer. The results should look like Figure 13.28a. The drawing looks complete. The only problem is that the roof lines and property line in the site plan look continuous. With Paper space, you need to set the global linetype scale setting to 1. Then AutoCAD will adjust the linetype scale for each viewport, depending on the scale it's zoomed to.

12. Type ltscale ↵ 1 ↵. The phantom linetype is now visible for the site plan, and the roof lines are dashed (Figure 13.28b).

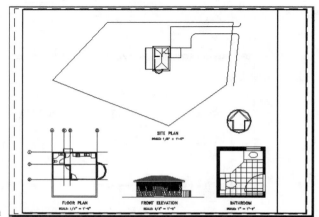

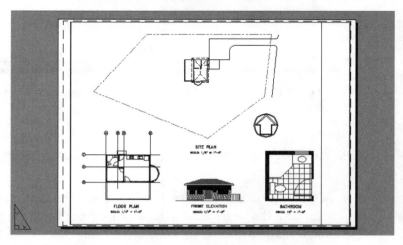

FIGURE 13.28: The 30" × 42" drawing complete with titles and scales of views (a), and with the ltscale setting adjusted for Paper space (b)

You added one line of text on the Layout, then copied and changed it to make six more lines of the text.

If you have been using a black Model space background, some of your colors may appear faded on the Layout. Feel free to assign darker colors to the layers.

As you have just seen, text and lines on a Layout can be put on top of viewports. The viewport is like a window through which you can view the Model space drawing, but the window has a transparent surface, like glass or cellophane, on which you can place text or other AutoCAD objects.

A layer can have some objects on a Layout and some in Model space. But arranging the drawing like this is not a good habit to get into because it can make the drawing harder to manage.

Turning Off Viewports

Beyond controlling the visibility of layers in each viewport, you can also turn off a viewport so that all Model space objects within it are invisible.

1. Turn on the Vports-L1 layer for a moment.

2. Select the three small viewports, then click the Properties button.

3. In the Properties dialog box, under Misc, click On. Then open the drop-down list next to On and click No. Close the Properties dialog box. Then press Esc to remove the grips. All selected viewports go blank, and all that is visible are their borders and the text on the Layout (Figure 13.29).

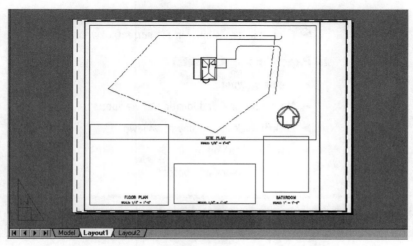

FIGURE 13.29: Layout1 with the smaller viewports turned off

4. Reselect the three small viewports and use Properties to turn them back on. Turn off the Vports layer again. Your drawing should look like Figure 13.28b.

5. Save this drawing as Site13.

Being able to turn viewports off can be an advantage for a complex drawing with many viewports, or one with a lot of information in each viewport. Remember that even though all four views in this drawing are based on one drawing, AutoCAD is drawing at least part of that drawing in each viewport. In a complex drawing, this can slow down the computer, so it's handy to be able to temporarily turn off any viewports you aren't working on. It's also an easy way to check which objects are on Model space and which are on the Layout (or on Paper space).

We will work with the viewports and Layouts again in the next chapter where you will round out your knowledge of AutoCAD by learning the principles of plotting and printing AutoCAD drawings.

WHAT YOU DO IN MODEL SPACE AND PAPER SPACE (LAYOUTS)

Here's a partial list of some of the things you do in the two environments.

In Model Space

▶ Zoom to a scale in a viewport (1/*scale factor*xp).

▶ Work on the building (or the project you are drawing).

▶ Make a viewport current.

▶ Control layer visibility in the current viewport.

In Paper Space (Layouts)

▶ Create viewports.

▶ Modify the size and location of viewports.

▶ Lock/Unlock the display in a viewport.

▶ Turn viewports on or off.

▶ Add a title block and border.

If You Would Like More Practice...

Create a second layout for Site13 that is similar to Layout2 in Cabin13b (Figure 13.30). Use the Layout Wizard to create the Layout. Then copy the border and title block from Layout2 of Cabin13b and the title and scale of the site plan from Layout1 of Site 13. Here's an outline of the steps.

► Layout Wizard:

1. Delete Layout2, then choose Insert ➢ Layout ➢ Layout Wizard.

2. Layout name: Replace Layout2 with **B-size**.

3. Printer: DWF ePlot (optimized for plotting).pc3.

4. Paper size: ANSI B (11.00 × 17.00 inches).

5. Orientation: Landscape.

6. Title Block: None.

7. Viewport setup: Single.

8. Viewport scale: ⅟₁₆" = 1'-0".

9. Location: Make a rectangle that covers the printable area except for the bottom 2".

► In the B-size layout:

1. Switch to Model space.

2. Freeze all Cabin12al layers except Balcony, Deck, Roof, Steps, and Walls.

3. Switch back to Paper space.

► Copy Title block and border from Cabin13b:

1. Open Cabin13b.

2. Select border and title block, then right-click.

3. Select Copy with Base Point.

4. For base point, type **0,0** ↵.

5. Use the Window menu to switch to Site13b.

6. Right-click, then select Paste from the menu.

7. For insertion point, type 0,0 ↵.

▶ Copy site plan view title and scale from Layout1:

1. Switch to Layout1.

2. Click SITE PLAN and SCALE: ⅛" = 1'-0" text.

3. Right-click and choose Copy with Base Point.

4. Use the Insert Osnap and select the insert point of SITE PLAN.

5. Switch to the B-size Layout.

6. Right-click, and select Paste.

7. Click the blank area to the left of the title block to place text.

8. Use the Scale command to reduce the text by half.

9. Double-click the SCALE text to change it to ¹⁄₁₆" = 1'-0".

10. Right-click the Layout1 tab and select Rename.

11. Change Layout1 to 30 × 42.

12. Save this drawing as Site13-extra.

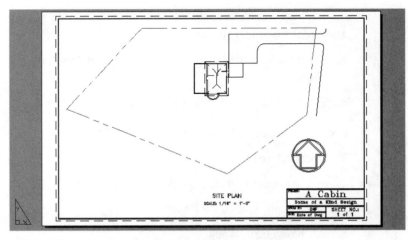

FIGURE 13.30: A second layout for Site13

Are You Experienced?

Now you can...

- ☑ create a Layout
- ☑ draw a border and title block on a Layout
- ☑ set up viewports on Layouts
- ☑ cut and paste in AutoCAD
- ☑ zoom to a scale in a viewport
- ☑ lock the display of a viewport
- ☑ align viewports
- ☑ control layer visibility in individual viewports
- ☑ control the visibility of viewport boundaries
- ☑ use the Layout Wizard
- ☑ set up a text style for Layouts
- ☑ add text to a Layout
- ☑ turn viewports off and on

CHAPTER 14

Printing an AutoCAD Drawing

F irst of all, with today's equipment, there is no difference between printing and plotting. Printing used to refer to smaller-format printers, and plotting used to refer to pen plotters, most of which were for plotting large sheets. But the terms are now used almost interchangeably. Pen plotters have a few extra settings that other printing devices do not have. Otherwise, as far as AutoCAD is concerned, the differences between plotters and laser-jet, ink-jet, dot-matrix, and electrostatic printers are minimal. So in this book, printing and plotting mean the same thing.

Getting your drawing onto paper can be very easy or very hard, depending on whether your computer is connected to a printer that has been set up to print AutoCAD drawings, and whether AutoCAD has been configured to work with your printer. If these initial conditions are met, printing can be handily managed with the tools you will learn in this chapter. If you do not have the initial setup, you will need to get some help to either set up your system to make AutoCAD work properly with your printer, or to find out how your system is already set up to print AutoCAD drawings.

We will be using a couple of standard setup configurations between AutoCAD and printers to move through the exercises. You may or may not be able to follow each step to completion, depending on whether you have access to an 8.5" × 11" laser-jet or ink-jet printer, a larger format printer, or both.

We have four drawings to print:

▶ Cabin11a: a drawing with Model space only, to be printed on an 8 ½" × 11" sheet at ⅛" scale

▶ Cabin13a: the same drawing as Cabin11a, except with the title block and border on Layout1, to be printed from Layout1 on an 8.5" × 11" sheet at a scale of 1:1

▶ The 11" × 17" drawing in Cabin13b, to be printed on an 11" × 17" sheet from a Layout

▶ Site13, to be printed on a 30" × 42" sheet from a Layout

Even if your printer won't let you print in all these formats, I suggest you follow along with the text anyway. You'll at least get to preview how your drawing would look if printed in these formats, and you will be taking large strides toward learning how to set up and run a print for your drawing. The chapter is written to give you the basic principles for printing whether or not you have access to a printer.

The Plot Dialog Box

The job of getting your AutoCAD file onto hard copy can be broken down into five tasks. You will need to tell AutoCAD:

- ▶ The printing device you will use
- ▶ The lineweight assigned to each object in your drawing
- ▶ The portion of your drawing you are printing
- ▶ The sheet size you are printing
- ▶ The scale, orientation, and placement of the print on the sheet

Most of these tasks will be handled through the Plot dialog box.

1. Open Cabin11a. Zoom to Extents, then zoom out a little (Figure 14.1). This drawing is not quite ready to print.

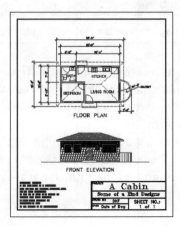

FIGURE 14.1: Cabin11a zoomed to Extents, then zoomed out a little

 2. Click the Plot button on the Standard toolbar. The Plot dialog box appears. This dialog box is a near duplicate of the Page Setup dialog box that you worked with in Chapter 13, *Using Layouts to Set Up a Print*. It has the same two tabs: Plot Device and Plot Settings (called Layout Settings in the Page Setup dialog box). Be sure the Plot Settings tab is active here (Figure 14.2).

The Plot dialog box can also be brought up by choosing File ➢ Print, by pressing Ctrl+P, or by typing plot ↵ or print ↵.

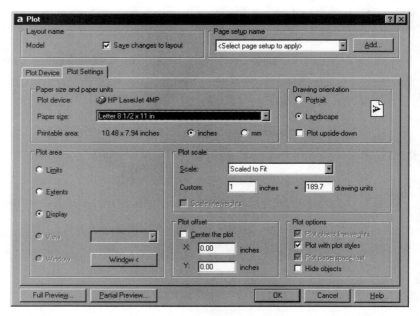

FIGURE 14.2: The Plot dialog box with the Plot Settings tab active

You worked in the same dialog box when you set up Layouts. When we get to the point in this chapter where we are printing Layouts, you'll find that much of the setup work has already been done. But before we do, let's take a quick tour of this dialog box. Then we'll start setting up to print.

Most of the work you have to do in this dialog box is on the Plot Settings tab. There are six areas of settings on this tab. Some of the buttons and boxes won't be activated. I'll mention others only in passing, as their functions are for more advanced techniques than those covered in this book.

Paper Size and Paper Units

In the Paper Size and Paper Units area, the current Plot Device is displayed at the top (in this case it's the HP LaserJet 4MP). Just below that is the Paper Size drop-down list. It will contain paper sizes that the current plot device can handle. Below that is the Printable Area of the selected paper size on the selected plot device. We used this data to set up Layouts in the previous chapter.

1. Click the Plot Device tab to make it active (Figure 14.3).

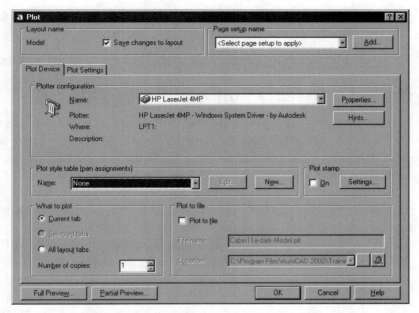

FIGURE 14.3: The Plot dialog box with the Plot Device tab active

2. In the Plotter Configuration area at the top of the dialog box, the Name drop-down list contains the various printing devices to which AutoCAD has been configured, with the current one, the HP LaserJet 4MP, displayed. Just below the list, the name of the driver and port are displayed for the selected printer. The Properties button to the right opens up the Plotter Configuration Editor, which has three tabs of data specific for the current printer. Most of these will already be set up by your Windows operating system. The other areas in the lower part of the Plot Device tab contain more advanced tools for:

   ▶ Selecting a previously named and saved plot style table, or creating a new one

   ▶ Controlling which tabs, and how many copies, are printed

   ▶ Directing AutoCAD to make and save the print as a file, rather than sending it to a printer

If you find yourself repeatedly using the same setup for the same printer, you will need to get at least a little familiar with these areas, but we won't be using these features in this book. We will, however, come back to the Plot Device tab when we set up prints for large-format drawings in the last half of this chapter.

3. Click the Plot Settings tab to make it active, so we can finish our tour.

Drawing Orientation and Plot Scale

To the right of the Paper Size and Paper Units area of the Plot Settings tab on the Plot dialog box is the Drawing Orientation area. The settings here are self-explanatory. The radio buttons serve as a toggle between the Portrait and Landscape orientation, and the Plot Upside-down check box serves as an on/off toggle.

Moving down, we come to the Plot Scale area, where you control the scale of the plot. The Scale drop-down list contains 33 preset scales to choose from, including Custom and Scaled to Fit. With this latter choice selected, AutoCAD will take whatever area you have chosen to print and automatically scale it so that it will fit on the selected page size. Some of the scales in the list are displayed as pure ratios, such as 1:50. Others are shown in their standard format, such as ¼" = 1'-0". Below the drop-down list is a pair of text boxes for setting up a custom scale. When a preset scale is chosen, these text boxes display the true ratio of the current scale.

To set up a custom scale, you enter a plotted distance in the Inches text box. Then, in the Drawing Units text box, enter the distance that, in your drawing, will be represented by the distance that you have entered in the Inches text box. The Inches distance will be an actual distance on the plotted drawing, while the Drawing Units distance is the distance the plotted units represent. For ¼" scale (¼" = 1'-0") you could enter several combinations:

Inches	Drawing Units
¼	1'
1	4'
1	48

Layouts are plotted at a scale of 1:1. We'll come back to this and other scale issues as we prepare a drawing for printing.

Plot Offset and Plot Options

Below the Plot Scale area are two small areas: Plot Offset and Plot Options. The Plot Options area has four miscellaneous on/off settings that don't concern us now. In the Plot Offset area, there are two text boxes and a check box. Place a check mark in the Center the Plot box to center the plot on the printed sheet. If it is not checked, by default, AutoCAD will place the lower-left corner (or the Origin) of the area you have specified to plot at the lower-left corner (or Origin) of the printable area of the current paper size. By changing the settings in the X and Y text boxes, you can move the drawing horizontally or vertically to fit on the page as you wish. When the Center the Plot check box is checked, the X and Y text boxes display any movement from the lower-left corner of the sheet that was necessary to center the drawing.

Just as each drawing has an origin (0,0 point), each plotter creates an origin for the plot. Usually it's in the lower-left or upper-left corner, but not always. When the plot is being made, the printer first locates the origin and starts the print there, moving outward from the origin. If the origin is in the lower-left corner, the print may come out looking like Figure 14.4a. If the origin is the upper-left corner, the print will look like Figure 14.4b.

By using the X Origin and Y Origin settings in the Plot Offset area, you can make one margin wider for a binding. To center your drawing on the page, place a check mark in the Center the Plot box (Figure 14.4c).

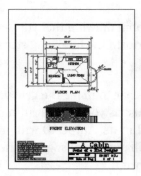 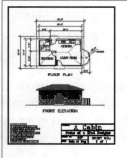 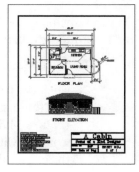

a   b   c

FIGURE 14.4: A print with its origin in the lower-left corner (a), in the upper-left corner (b), and with the drawing centered (c)

T I P   Usually, 8.5" × 11" format printers are configured to the portrait orientation. If your drawing is also that orientation, the origin of the plot will be in the lower-left corner. If your drawing is in the landscape orientation, the plot origin will move to the upper-left corner of the page because the plot has been rotated to fit on the page.

Setting the material to be printed accurately on the page will be a result of trial and error, and getting to know your printer well. We will return to this area shortly, when we get ready to print.

Plot Area

On the left side of the Plot area, there are five radio buttons for the five ways to specify what to print in your drawing. We have already decided which layers will be visible when the print is made, and by freezing the layers whose objects we don't want to print. Now we must decide how to designate the area of the drawing to be printed. As we go through the options, it will be useful to think about the choices with regard to two printing possibilities: printing the whole drawing and printing just the floor plan.

To illustrate how these options work, we will make a couple of assumptions. First, the Scaled to Fit option is selected in the Scale drop-down list in the Plot Scale area, so AutoCAD will try to fill the sheet with the drawing. Second, the drawing will be in portrait orientation.

Limits

Do you remember the drawing limits for the cabin drawing that you set in Chapter 3, *Setting Up a Drawing*? As a refresher, perform the following steps:

1. Select Cancel to cancel the plot.

2. Click the Grid button on the status bar to make the grid visible. It's still there, around the floor plan, just as you first set it in Chapter 3 (Figure 14.5a). When you print to Limits, AutoCAD will print only what lies within the limits, and it will push what's within the limits to the corner that is the origin of the print.

3. Click the Plot button again. In the Plot dialog box, click Limits in the Plot area, and be sure Portrait is selected in the Drawing Orientation area. Then click the Full Preview button in the lower-left corner (Figure 14.5b). This print won't work here because the limits don't cover the entire drawing. Also, the limits are in Landscape orientation, so the portion of the drawing to be printed doesn't fit properly on the paper. Printing to Limits can be a good tool for setting up a print, but you will usually reset the limits from their original defining coordinates to new ones for the actual print.

4. Right-click and choose Exit from the shortcut menu. Cancel the plot, then press F7 to turn off the grid.

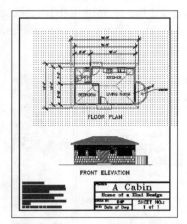

a

b

FIGURE 14.5: The grid showing the limits of Cabin11a (a), and a pre-view of the drawing printed to Limits (b)

Extents

When you select the Extents option, AutoCAD tries to fill the sheet with all visible objects in the drawing. If you print Cabin11a using the Extents method of selecting

You can use the Full Preview option to view how the drawing will print for Extents and the three following printing options.

what to print, the results would look like Figure 14.6. This is a good method to use if the border has been drawn with the same proportions as the printable area of the sheet. It was in this case because you offset a rectangle that represented the sheet to make the border, but the rectangle that represented the sheet was also printed, and we didn't want that. You would have to erase the outer rectangle before printing to Extents.

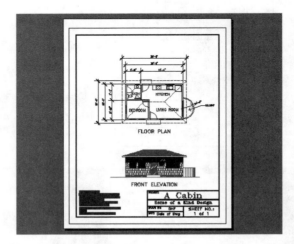

FIGURE 14.6: The Cabin11a drawing printed to Extents

Display

The Display option will print what's currently on the screen, including the blank area around the drawing. With both drawing and sheet in portrait orientation, and with the origin in the lower-left corner of the sheet, the plot would look like Figure 14.7. The dashed lines represent the edge of what was the drawing area on the screen. The drawing doesn't fit well on the sheet with this option. It's oriented correctly, but it's forced to be too small on the sheet. The blank space in the drawing area on the left and right of the print is brought into the print with this option, and that's what creates the misfit. Printing to Display is a good method if the drawing is in landscape orientation and is proportional in size to the drawing area, and if the printer is also set to landscape orientation.

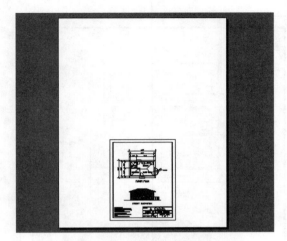

FIGURE 14.7: The Cabin11a drawing printed to Display

View

When printing to View, you tell AutoCAD to print a previously defined view that was saved with the drawing. Right now the View radio button is grayed out because we haven't defined and saved any views yet. We'll save a view, and then we'll see what the print will look like.

1. If the Plot dialog box is still on the screen, cancel it. Choose View ➤ Named Views. The View control dialog box comes up.

2. Click the New button. In the New View dialog box, type **plot1**. Click the Define Window button. Then move to the right and click the Define View Window button.

3. Back in the drawing, make a window around the left half of the floor plan, not including the dimensions, as in Figure 14.8a.

4. Click OK. The saved view, called plot1, is listed in the Views list box of the View dialog box.

5. Click OK to return to the drawing. Then click the Plot button and continue reading along.

Now, to plot the plot1 view of this drawing, click the View button in the Plot area of the Plot dialog box. Then move to the right and select plot1 from the drop-down list of saved views. At the settings for scale and orientation we have been using, the print will look like Figure 14.8b. This is a valuable tool for setting up partial prints of a drawing.

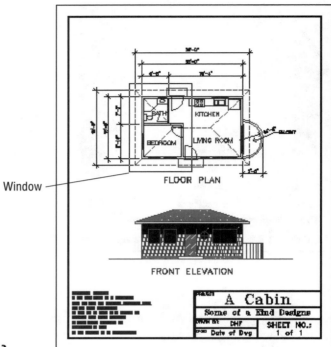

Window

a

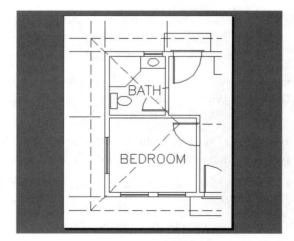

b

F I G U R E   1 4 . 8 : Using a window to define a view (a), and the print to this view (b)

Window

Using a window to define the area of a plot is the most flexible of the five methods being described. It's like using a zoom window in the drawing. To select this option, click the rectangular Window button. In your drawing, make a window around the area you want to print. AutoCAD will print only what is in the window you made, regardless of how it fits on the sheet. This method is similar to the View method we just discussed. The difference lies in the fact that the View method prints a previously defined view (one that was possibly defined by a window, but could also be defined in other ways), and the Window method prints what is included in a window that you define as you are setting up the plot. The window used by the Window method can't be saved and recalled at a later time.

These are the five ways to specify what to print. We'll use the Window option in the first exercise that follows.

We have taken a quick tour of the Plot dialog box, and we still have a drawing, Cabin11a, to print. Let's print it. As we set up the print, refer back to this section for explanation of the steps, if necessary.

Printing a Drawing

Our task is to print Cabin11a.dwg at a scale of ⅛" = 1'-0" on an 8.5" × 11" sheet. In this exercise, we will use the default system printer, which is set up for an 8.5" × 11"–format laser-jet printer. If you have an 8.5" × 11"–format printer, you should be able to follow the steps. If you don't have a printer, you can still get familiar with printing by following along with the steps in the book.

The first step is to assign lineweights to the visible layers.

Determining Lineweights for a Drawing

Look at the Cabin11a drawing as a whole. We need to decide on weights for the various lines. The floor plan is drawn as if a cut were made horizontally through the building just below the tops of the window and door openings. Everything that was cut will be given a heavy line. Objects above and below the cut will be given progressively lighter lines, depending on how far above or below the cut the objects are located. In this system, the walls, windows, and doors will be heaviest. The roof, headers, fixtures, and steps will be lighter. For emphasis, we'll make the walls a little heavier than the windows and doors. In the front elevation, the hatch pattern will be very light and the outline of the various components will be heavier, for emphasis. Text and the title block information will use the default lineweight. These are general guidelines; weights will vary with each drawing.

We will use four lineweights for this drawing:

Weight	Thickness In Inches
very light	0.005
light	0.008
medium	0.010
heavy	0.014

There are 15 layers in Cabin11a that are visible in the drawing as it is presently set up. Their lineweights will be assigned as follows:

Layer	Lineweight
Balcony	light
Dim1	very light
Doors	medium
F-elev	medium
Fixtures	light
Hatch-elev-42	very light
Hatch-elev-black	very light
Hatch-elev-gray	very light
Headers	light
Roof	very light
Steps	light
Tblk1	medium
Text1	medium
Walls	heavy
Windows	medium

When we look at the lineweights presently assigned to these layers, and at the thickness we need these lineweights to be, we can generate a third chart that will show us what lineweight needs to be assigned to each group of layers:

Thickness	Layers
0.005	Dim1, all visible hatch layers, Roof
0.008	Balcony, Fixtures, Headers, Steps
0.010 (default)	Doors, F-elev, Tblk1, Text, Windows
0.014	Walls

Now it's time to assign the lineweights to the layers in the drawings.

1. Click Cancel to close the Plot dialog box. Then click the Layers button on the Object Property toolbar. The Layer Properties Manager dialog box comes up.

2. Click the Dim1 layer to highlight it. Hold down the Ctrl key and click the three Hatch-elev layers and the Roof layers to select them. Then release the Ctrl key.

3. In the Lineweight column, click one of the highlighted Default words. The Lineweight dialog box comes up.

N O T E   If the lineweights listed in the Lineweight dialog box are in millimeters, cancel to get back to your drawing and type **lw** ↵. Then, in the Lineweight Settings dialog box, click the Inches radio button in the Units for Listing area and click OK.

4. Click 0.005". Then click OK. The Lineweight dialog box disappears. In the Layer Properties Manager dialog box, the five highlighted layers now have a lineweight of 0.005" assigned to them.

5. Click on the Balcony layer near the layer's name.

6. Hold down the Ctrl key and click on Fixtures, Headers, and Steps.

7. Click one of the highlighted Default words. The Lineweight dialog box reappears.

8. Click 0.008". Then click OK. The newly highlighted layers now have a lineweight of 0.008" assigned to them.

9. You can leave Default as the linetype for the Doors, Windows, and Text1 layers because the thickness they need is the default thickness of 0.010". Click the Walls layer and use the same procedure to assign it the thickness of 0.014".

10. Click OK to close the Layer Properties Manager dialog box.

11. Type lw ↵ to open the Lineweight Settings dialog box.

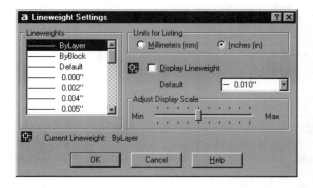

Notice the Default drop-down list on the right side, where 0.010" is displayed. This tells you that the default lineweight thickness is 0.010", which is what we are assuming.

12. Click Cancel to close the dialog box.

The lineweights have been assigned. When the print is complete, you can judge whether these lineweight assignments are acceptable or if they need to be adjusted. In an office, a lot of time is invested in developing a lineweight standard that can be used in most drawings.

Setting Up the Other Parameters for the Print

Now that we have set the lineweights, it's time to move to the Plot dialog box and complete the setting changes we need to make in order to print this drawing. We will use the Window option to select what we will print.

1. Click the Plot button on the Standard toolbar.

2. In the Plot dialog box, be sure the Plot Settings tab is active. Check the Paper Size and Paper Units area to be sure you have the correct printer listed as the Plot Device and 8.5 × 11 as the selected paper size. Then move down to the Plot Area and click the Window button.

3. In the drawing, disable any running Osnaps. To start the window, pick a point outside the border, as close to the lower-left corner of the border as you can without touching it.

4. To complete the window, click a point above and to the right of the border, also as close to the border as you can without touching it. Back in the Plot dialog box, the Window radio button in the Plot Area will be selected.

5. Move to the right side of the dialog box. Be sure Portrait is selected in the Drawing Orientation area at the top.

6. In the Plot Scale area, open the Scale drop-down list and select ⅛" = 1'0". Notice that the text boxes next to Custom now read 1 and 96, the scale factor for ⅛" scale.

7. In the Plot offset area, click the Center the Plot check box.

This completes the setup for the first plot. Before we waste paper, let's preview how it will look as a result of our setup changes.

Previewing a Print

There are two ways of previewing a plot: Partial and Full. In the Partial Preview method, AutoCAD very quickly generates a diagram of what will be printed. The

Full Preview method shows you exactly what you are going to get. We'll do both for this plot.

1. In the lower-left corner of the Plot dialog box, click the Partial Preview button. The Partial Plot Preview dialog box comes up (Figure 14.9). At the top is a diagram of the sheet being plotted. The white area is the actual sheet of paper. The dashed line near the perimeter is the printable area boundary. The blue rectangle is your drawing. The red triangle indicates the origin of the plot.

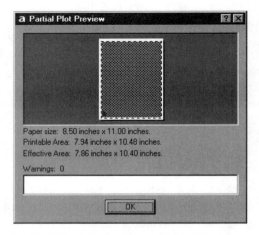

FIGURE 14.9: The Partial Plot Preview dialog box

The middle of the dialog box lists information on the paper size, the printable area, and the effective area (the actual area taken up by the drawing). At the bottom, a warning box will alert you if your drawing doesn't fit on the page properly.

Everything looks fine in this preview.

2. Click OK to close the dialog box.

3. Click the Full Preview button. The computer takes a moment to calculate the plot, then displays a full view of your drawing as it will fit on the page (Figure 14.10a).

4. Right-click and, on the shortcut menu, select Zoom Window.

5. Make a window that encloses the bathroom and a couple of the dimensions. You have to left-click and hold down the mouse button, drag open

the window, and then release. The new view displays the lineweights you have set up (Figure 14.10b).

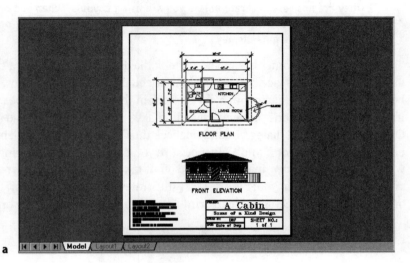

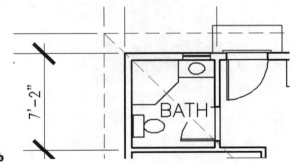

FIGURE 14.10: The full preview of Cabin11a, ready to print (a) and the zoomed-in view showing the lineweights

6. Right-click and select Zoom Original, to return to the first preview view.

7. Right-click again and select Exit to return to the Plot dialog box. If your print was oriented correctly on the sheet, you are ready to print. If not, recheck the setup steps for errors.

8. At the bottom of the Plot dialog box, click OK. The computer will begin calculating the print and eventually send it to the printer.

9. After the print is done, save this drawing as Cabin14a.

N O T E   You can change a setting in the Lineweight Settings dialog box to be able to see lineweights in your drawing before you preview a plot, but they are not very accurate unless you are using Layouts. When you print from Model space, you have to preview the drawing in the Plot dialog box to see how the lineweights display.

When your print comes out, it should look like Figure 14.10a. Take a close look at the border. Is the space outside the border equal on the left and right, or top and bottom? It should be, if you put a check mark in the Center the Plot box. If not, or if you need to widen one of the margins to make room for a binding, go to the Plot Offset area of the Plot dialog box and uncheck the Center the Plot check box. Then change the settings for *X* and *Y*. Just be sure you don't move the drawing to a point where one of the border lines gets lopped off. It takes a little trial and error. The Preview features will help you. Figure 14.11 illustrates what you will see in the Partial and Full Previews when you try to print Cabin11a with the landscape orientation.

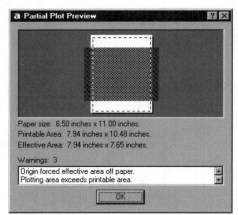

FIGURE 14.11: The Partial Preview (a), and Full Preview (b) of Cabin11a set up to be printed in the wrong orientation

Check the lineweights of the various components on the print. You may have to make adjustments for your particular printer.

Next you'll plot a similar drawing that uses Layouts for its border and title block.

Printing a Drawing Using Layouts

As a comparison to the previous exercise, we'll print a drawing that has a Layout set up. When a Layout tab has been set up properly and is active, you print at a scale of 1:1. The elements of the drawing on the Layout are then printed actual size, and the Model space portion of the drawing is printed at the scale to which the viewport has been zoomed.

1. Open Cabin13b. Be sure the Layout1 tab is active. This drawing is similar to Cabin11a. The only difference in appearance is that this one displays the dashed lines just outside the border, and the sheet is resting on the gray background with a shadowing effect, similar to how a Full Preview appears (Figure 14.12). These differences are the result of this drawing having a Layout that contains the title block and border, with a viewport through which the model of the cabin is seen. The viewport is on a layer that's been frozen, so you can't see its border. (For a review of Layouts and viewports, see Chapter 13.)

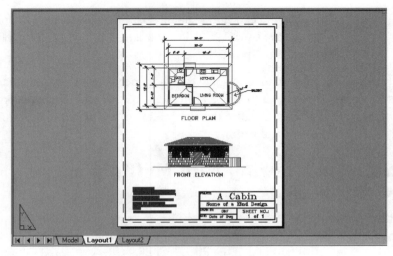

FIGURE 14.12: The Cabin13a drawing ready for printing

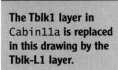

The Tblk1 layer in Cabin11a is replaced in this drawing by the Tblk-L1 layer.

2. Open the Layer Properties Manager dialog box and set the lineweights for the layers as you did for Cabin11a. Then click OK.

3. Start the Plot command. The Plot dialog box appears. Be sure the Plot Settings tab is active. All the parameters you set for the last print will still be in effect, so you have to determine what settings need to be changed to accommodate Paper Space.

4. We are using the same printer, paper size, and orientation as before, so those stay the same.

5. Notice that in Plot area the top radio button is labeled Layout instead of Limits. Layout is also the active button. AutoCAD has sensed that this drawing has Layouts set up, and made this change automatically.

6. In the Plot Scale area, the scale has been set to 1:1. This is what we want.

7. In the Plot Offset area, the Center the Plot check box is grayed out; it is not needed when using a Layout to plot.

8. There are no changes to make. Because Layout1 has been set up for printing when it was created, all the settings in the Plot dialog box are automatically taken care of.

9. In the Print Preview area, select Full Preview. Your preview should look like Figure 14.10a.

10. Right-click and exit to the dialog box. Click OK to start the print. If you don't have a printer, or if you are just following along, click Cancel to cancel the print at this point.

This exercise was intended to show you that once a Layout has been created, most of the setup work for printing is already done for you. This greatly simplifies the printing process because the parameters of the print are determined before the Print command begins.

Printing a Drawing with Multiple Viewports

Multiple viewports in a Layout don't require any special handling. The print will be made with the Layout active at a scale of 1:1. For the next print, you will use a different printer—one that can handle larger sheet sizes. If you don't have access to a large-format printer, you can still configure AutoCAD for one and preview how the print would look. In fact, that's what we did in Chapter 13, in order to set up Layout2, so this task is already completed.

Printing with a Large-format Printer

The procedure here varies little from the one you just followed to print Layout1.

1. Save the current drawing to your training directory as Cabin14b, but don't close it yet.

2. This drawing has two Layout tabs. We just printed Layout1. Layout2 consists of an 11" × 17" drawing in landscape orientation. You'll print this one, so be sure Layout2 is active (Figure 14.13).

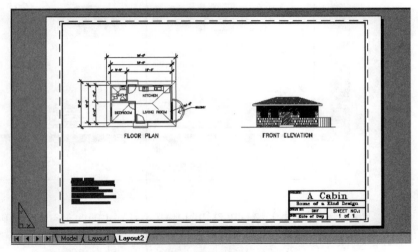

FIGURE 14.13: Cabin13b with the Layout2 tab active

3. Check the Layer Properties Manager dialog box to see that the lineweight assignments you made for Layout1 are still there.

4. Click the Plot button on the Standard toolbar to start the Plot command.

5. In the Plot dialog box, make sure the Plot Settings tab is active. Look in the Paper Size and Paper Units area. The plot device is now listed as DWF ePlot (optimized for plotting).pc3, or that of your own large-format plotter. Also the paper size has been set for 11 × 17. This was all done when you set up Layout2 in the previous chapter.

6. Note the orientation of the drawing. It's now Landscape.

7. In the rest of the dialog box, the settings are the same as they were for Layout1. There are no changes to be made. Again, by setting up a Layout, all parameters for printing are done in advance.

8. Select the Full Preview button. The preview looks fine (Figure 14.14).

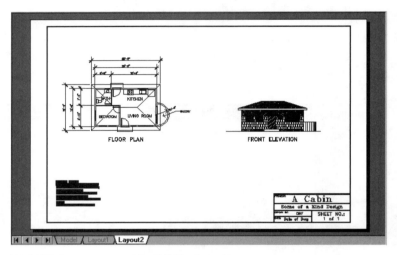

F I G U R E   1 4 . 1 4 :   The Full Preview of Layout2

9. Press ↵ or Esc to cancel the preview. If you have a large-format printer configured and can plot this drawing on an 11" × 17" sheet, click OK to start the print. Otherwise, click Cancel.

10. Resave this drawing as Cabin14b.

For the last exercise in this chapter, you will set up a print for Site13, using the large-format printer.

Printing the Site Plan

The site plan was also set up with a Layout and based on a 30" × 42" sheet in landscape orientation. As in the last two prints, we shouldn't have to do much to print this drawing. Follow along even if you can't make the print.

1. Open Site13. The Layout1 tab should be active. If it's not, click it to activate it.

2. Type lw ↵. In the Lineweight Settings dialog box, put a check mark in the Display Lineweight box and click OK.

3. Open the Layer Properties Manager dialog box and assign to the Prop_line layer a lineweight of 0.055. Click OK to close the dialog box. Click OK again.

4. While in Paper Space, zoom into a view of the place where the driveway meets the property line. Include the top borderline in the view to see the contrast in lineweights (Figure 14.15). The borderline has a thickness because it is a polyline assigned a width of ¹⁄₁₆" or 0.0625.

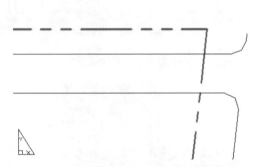

FIGURE 14.15: Zooming in to check the lineweights

5. Zoom previous, then start the Plot command. The Plot dialog box comes up. There are no changes that need to be made.

6. Click Full Preview. You see how the print sits on the sheet. We want the margins to be the same on the top and bottom, and the right margin to be as small as possible so that there is extra room on the left side for the binding strip.

7. Press ↵ or Esc to return to the Plot dialog box. In the Plot Offset area, change the X setting from 0.00 to 0.15.

8. Click Full Preview again. The drawing is positioned fairly well but the right margin may be partially lopped off (Figure 14.16a).

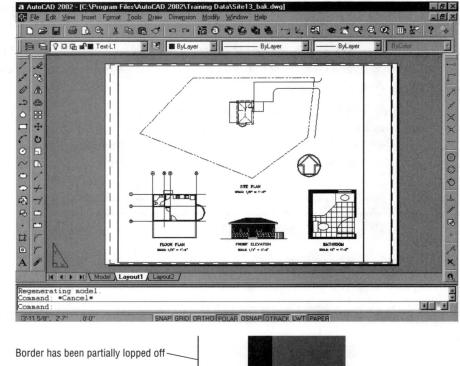

a

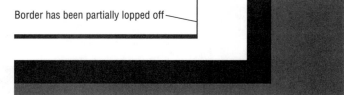

b

FIGURE 14.16: The plot preview after adjusting the *X* value in the Plot Offset area (a) and zooming in to check the border (b)

9. Right-click and select Zoom Window, then click and drag a Zoom window around the lower-right corner of the border (Figure 14.16b). The right border has been partially cut off. We'll have to readjust the *X* value in the Plot Offset area.

10. Right-click again and choose Exit. Change the *X* setting to 0.09. Click Full Preview again. Right-click and select Zoom Window again. Zoom into the corner and confirm that the border is now OK. Right-click and select Zoom Original to return to the Full Preview (Figure 14.17).

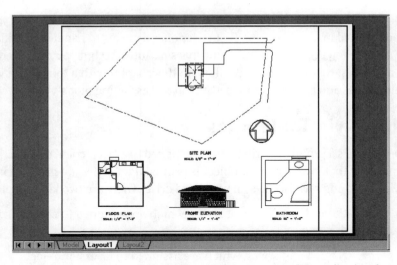

FIGURE 14.17: The Full Preview of the site plot after readjusting the
X value to 0.09

11. Feel free to make minor adjustments to the Origin settings. You could
    also use the Stretch command to move the left side of the border to the
    right in order to gain a little more space for the binding. Because the
    border so closely fits the printable area, we could move the drawing
    on the sheet only a little more than ⅛" without lopping off the right
    side, so the results are barely noticeable. Normally you make these
    adjustments when you set up the Layout.

12. When you are finished making adjustments, return to the Plot dialog
    box. Click OK to start the print, or Cancel to cancel it.

13. Save this drawing as Site14a.

   The last section in this chapter will consist of a discussion on a more advanced
feature of plotting—plot styles.

A Few Words about Plot Styles

So far in this chapter, we have assigned lineweights to layers. We have assumed
that any printer was monochromatic and was converting all colors in the Auto-
CAD drawing to black. Laser-jet printers usually are monochromatic, but they
may print the lighter colors in your drawing as screened. If you have access to a
large-format ink-jet plotter, you may have the option to print in monochrome or

color. And you may have objects in your drawing that are one color, and you want them printed in another color. Plot styles offer a means to handle these kinds of situations. You don't have to use plot styles in AutoCAD but you may need to work on a drawing that uses them. We'll finish this chapter with a tour of the various dialog boxes and procedures for setting up and assigning plot styles.

Plot Style Table Files

A *plot style* is a group of settings that is assigned to a layer, color, or object. It determines how that layer, color, or object is printed. Plot styles are grouped into Plot Style Tables and saved as files on your hard drive. There are two kinds of plot styles:

▶ Color-dependent plot styles, which are assigned to colors in your drawing

▶ Named plot styles, which are assigned to layers or objects

Leave AutoCAD for a moment and use Windows Explorer to go to the place where AutoCAD is installed; it's usually C:\Program Files\AutoCAD 2002. Open the subfolder called Plot Styles. Figure 14.18 shows the contents of the Plot Styles folder. There are 14 plot style table files already set up. Eight of them are Color-dependent Plot Style Table files, with the extension .ctb, and six are Named Plot Style Table files, with extension .stb. Finally, there is the shortcut to the Add-a-Plot Style Table Wizard, which you use to set up custom plot style tables. Close Windows Explorer and return to AutoCAD.

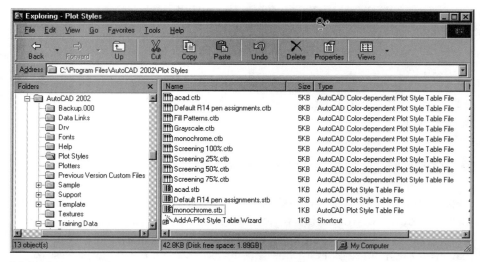

FIGURE 14.18: The contents of the Plot Styles folder

How Plot Style Table Files are Organized

Plot style table files are assigned to a drawing and contain all the plot styles needed to control how that drawing is printed. Color-dependent plot styles control printing parameters through color, so there are 255 of them in each color-dependent plot style table, one for each color. Named plot style tables, on the other hand, have only as many plot styles as are necessary, possibly only two or three. Let's look at a plot style table and see how it's organized.

1. In AutoCAD, choose File ➤ Plot Style Manager. The Plot Styles dialog box comes up. It is very much like the Windows Explorer view of Auto-CAD's Plot Style. In fact, it is another view of the same folder. Your view may have large icons and may not display all the details.

2. Double-click acad.ctb. The Plot Style Table Editor comes up with acad.ctb in its title bar (Figure 14.19). The Editor has three tabs. The General tab displays information and presents a Description text box for our input, if we desire.

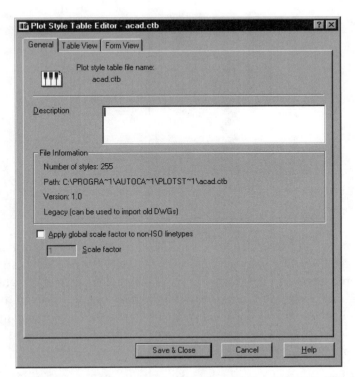

FIGURE 14.19: The General tab of the Plot Style Table Editor for the acad.cbt file

3. Click the Table View tab. Now we see the actual plot styles across the top and the plot style properties listed down the left side. This tab organizes the information like a spreadsheet (Figure 14.20). Use the scroll bar to assure yourself that there are 255 plot styles here. Notice that there are 12 properties for each plot style. This tab displays the plot style information in a way that gives you an overview of the table as a whole.

FIGURE 14.20: The Table View tab of the Plot Style Table Editor for the acad.cbt file

4. Move on to the Form View tab. The same information is organized in a slightly different way (Figure 14.21). Here the plot styles are listed in the box on the left. One or more plot styles can be highlighted at a time. The properties of the highlighted styles are shown on the right. This view is set up to modify the properties of chosen plot styles. Notice that the first property, Color, has Use Object Color assigned for all plot styles.

5. Close this Plot Style Table and open monochrome.ctb. Click the Table View tab. Now look at the Color property. All plot styles have the color Black assigned (Figure 4.22).

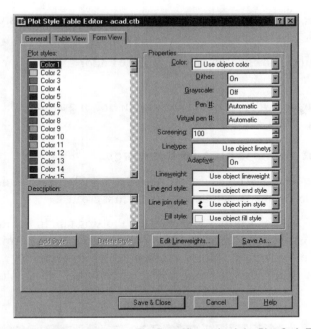

FIGURE 14.21: The Form View tab of the Plot Style Table Editor for the `acad.cbt` file

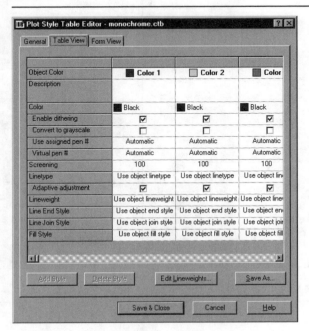

FIGURE 14.22: The Table View tab of the Plot Style Table Editor for the `monochrome.cbt` file

6. Open acad.sbt and monochrome.sbt to see how few plot styles they contain.

7. Close all windows of the Plot Style Table Editor and close the Plot Style Manager.

The monochrome.cbt will print all colors in your drawing as black, but won't change them in the AutoCAD file.

Assigning Plot Style Tables to Drawings

Each drawing can be assigned only one kind of plot style table file: color-dependent or named. This is determined when the drawing is first created.

1. Choose Tools ➤ Options and click the Plotting tab. In the upper-right corner of the tab are the two radio buttons that control which type of plot style a drawing will accept, color-dependent or named (Figure 14.23). New drawings will accept only the type of plot style that is selected here.

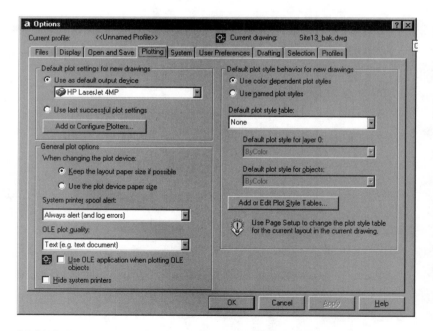

FIGURE 14.23: The Plotting tab of the Options dialog box

2. Below the radio buttons is the Default Plot Style Table drop-down list. Here you can select a plot style table file (of the type that is selected by the radio buttons) to be automatically assigned to new drawings. One of the options is None.

3. Close the Options dialog box.

N O T E Even though the type of plot style for a new drawing is fixed in the Options dialog box, two utility commands let you switch the type of plot style a drawing can have, and assign a different one. They are the *Convertpstyles* and the *Convertctb* commands.

Throughout this book, all the drawings that you created (or downloaded) were set up to use color-dependent plot styles, so we can assign this type of plot style to the drawing. Usually this is done by assigning a particular plot style to a Layout or to Model space. To finish our tour, and this chapter, we'll assign one of the available plot style table files to the Cabin14b drawing and use the Full Preview option to see the results.

1. Make Cabin14b the current drawing, if it isn't already.

2. Click Layout1 to make it current, if it isn't already.

3. Start the Plot command, then click the Full Preview button. The LaserJet assesses each color and determines what shade of gray to print it (Figure 14.24). Some colors are printed as black, others as various shades of gray.

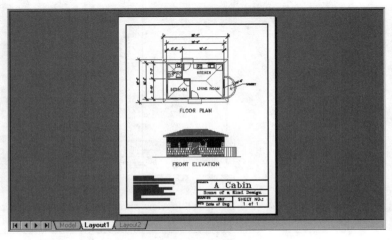

FIGURE 14.24: The Full Preview of Layout1 as is

4. Exit the Full Preview display, then click the Cancel button to cancel the plot.

5. Right-click the Layout1 tab, then select Page Setup.

6. Click the Plot Device tab. Notice that in the Plot Style Table (Pen Assignments) area, None is selected. No plot style table file has been assigned to this layout.

7. Open the drop-down list.

All the available .ctb (color-dependent plot style table) files are listed. You can choose one or click the New button to the right and create your own. Once one is chosen, you can click Edit to modify it and make a new plot style out of it.

8. Select monochrome.ctb, then click OK.

9. Click Full Preview (see Figure 14.25). All lines and filled areas in the drawing are solid black.

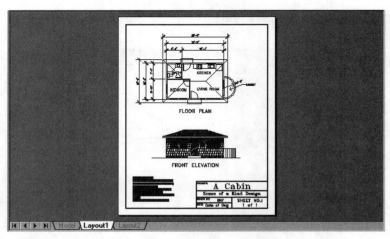

FIGURE 14.25: The Full Preview with the monochrome.cbt plot style table assigned to Layout1

10. Exit Full Preview.

11. Repeat steps 5–10 and select a different .cbt file from the Plot Style Table drop-down list. (I recommend trying Screening 50%.cbt.) When you get back to the Full Preview, you will see the difference.

12. Exit the Plot dialog box and close the drawing without saving any changes.

This has been a quick tour of and introduction to the Plot Style feature that helps control how your drawing will plot, and completes the chapter on plotting. Getting consistently good output from your AutoCAD drawings involves an investment of time by you, or the office CAD Manager/IT (Information Technologist), to set up the best configuration of your printers and AutoCAD. As you have seen, layouts provide a very good tool for setting up plots, once the configuration is right.

Are You Experienced?

Now you can...

☑ **set up a drawing to be printed**

☑ **assign lineweights to layers in your drawing**

☑ **select the area of your drawing to print**

☑ **choose a sheet size to print your drawing on**

☑ **control the orientation and origin of the print**

☑ **set the scale of the print**

☑ **preview a print**

☑ **print a Layout**

☑ **navigate through the Plot Style features**

CHAPTER 15

Making the Internet Work With AutoCAD

AutoCAD 2002 contains a set of tools that make it easier to use with the Internet. They range from simple utilities to send AutoCAD files with your e-mail to software that supports online meetings where AutoCAD files can be modified by participants in real time.

Icons on the Standard toolbar represent several of the tools.

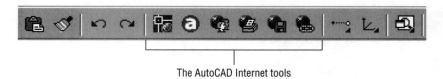

The AutoCAD Internet tools

In this chapter, we will be looking at the features accessed through these icons, as well as a few others.

The AutoCAD Today Window

The AutoCAD Today window offers three tools:

► An alternative to either the Startup or the Open File dialog box

► A special bulletin board for inter-office or intra-office communication

► A portal to a Web site maintained by Autodesk, called Autodesk Point A

We'll look at each of these features in a moment. The AutoCAD Today window opens, by default, when you start up AutoCAD. If your workstation is set up in such a way that this window does not come up when you boot up the program, you can still bring it up any time by clicking on the Today button on the Standard toolbar. Let's do that now and take a tour of this window.

1. Click the Today button on the Standard toolbar to bring up the AutoCAD Today window (Figure 15.1).

The window is divided into three parts, corresponding to the three features listed above.

► The upper two-thirds of the window is called My Workplace. It includes a section called My Drawings on the left and one called Bulletin Board on the right.

► The lower third of the window is a banner that will link you to Autodesk's Web site, which is called Point A.

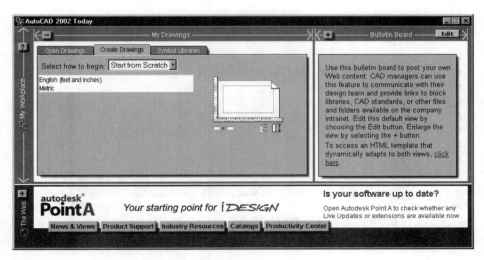

FIGURE 15.1: The AutoCAD 2002 Today window

2. If you go to the upper-left corner of the Today window and click on the ? that sits on the up arrow for My Workplace, AutoCAD displays a Welcome to the Today Window screen that gives an overview of the areas that we will discuss below.

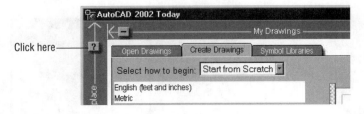

Let's take a look at the My Drawings area first.

My Drawings

This area is an enhancement of the traditional Startup dialog box. It has every option that feature provided, and more.

1. In My Workplace area, click the middle tab, called Create Drawings.

2. On this tab, open the drop-down list (Figure 15.2).

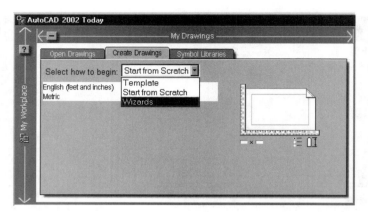

FIGURE 15.2: The My Workplace area with the Create Drawings tab in front and the drop-down list open

The three options on the drop-down list are the same as three of the four options in the Startup dialog box. When you choose one of these options, the Create Drawings tab changes its display to reflect your choice.

3. Choose Template on the list. The Create Drawings tab now displays the list of .dwt files in the AutoCAD Template folder (Figure 15.3).

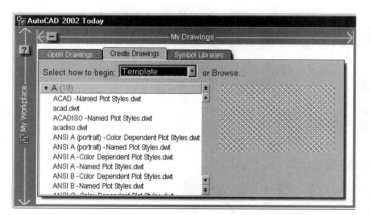

FIGURE 15.3: The Create Drawings tab with Template chosen in the Select How to Begin drop-down list

4. Click the Open Drawings tab, which has several tools for locating the file you want. The drop-down list offers four ways of sorting previously open files (Figure 15.4).

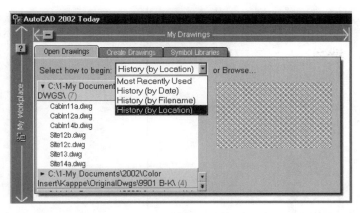

FIGURE 15.4: The drop-down list on the Open Drawings tab

5. Click Browse on the Open Drawings tab. The Select File dialog box comes up (Figure 15.5). Here you have the folder navigation tools to locate your file, and, on the left, a series of icons that are shortcuts to specific, predefined places. At the top are the standard History, My Documents, and Favorites icons.

FIGURE 15.5: The Select File dialog box

6. Scroll down to the bottom of the list on the left. There are four Internet sites at your disposal and the shortcut to the Desktop.

Clicking the icon for Point A, Buzzsaw, RedSpark, or FTP begins a connection to the Internet and, if you are already signed up, directly to the site. We'll look at the first three of these later on in this chapter.

7. As we continue our tour of AutoCAD Today, click the Symbol Libraries tab. This tab displays a list of symbol libraries for various trades (Figure 5.6). Each of the original library names is linked to an AutoCAD drawing that is stored in the AutoCAD 2002\Sample\DesignCenter folder, and contains a set of blocks that make up the particular library. When you click on a library, Design Center opens to the .dwg linked to that library, and you can drag blocks from the library into the current drawing.

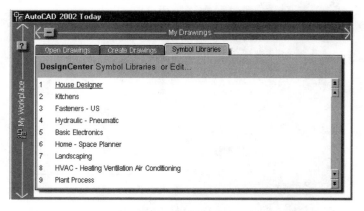

F I G U R E   1 5 . 6 : The Symbol Libraries tab in My Drawings

8. Click Edit on the Symbol Libraries tab. This brings up the Edit Design-Center Symbol Libraries dialog box (Figure 15.7). Here you can change the order in which the libraries are listed, delete or add library names, and choose a different .dwg file to be linked to a library.

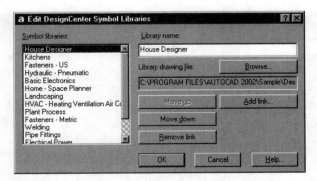

FIGURE 15.7: The Edit DesignCenter Symbol Libraries dialog box

The My Drawings area is a tool to help you get access to your drawings and template files. It does not offer a link to the Internet except indirectly through the Select File dialog box.

The Bulletin Board

To the right of the My Drawings area is the Bulletin Board. This is a place to display intra-office announcements and notices and is usually controlled by the CAD or IT manager. Before it is customized, it looks like Figure 15.8.

FIGURE 15.8: The original Bulletin Board

1. Click on the + button at the top. The Bulletin Board opens horizontally to cover the entire width of the Today window and hide the My Drawings area (Figure 15.9). Explanatory text tells how to customize this area and put material from the Internet on it.

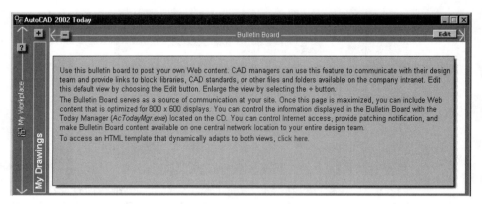

FIGURE 15.9: The maximized Bulletin Board

2. Click the – button at the upper-left corner of the maximized Bulletin Board to close it back to its normal size.

3. Click the Edit button in the upper-right corner. A dialog box comes up that lets you put your own message on the Bulletin Board (Figure 15.10). Click the Browse button and select the file you wish to substitute. It can be any of the following types of files:

▶ Microsoft Word .doc

▶ HTML

▶ ASCII

▶ Rich Text Format (RTF)

▶ GIF

▶ JPG

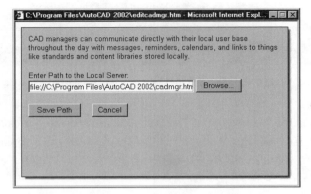

FIGURE 15.10: The dialog box for customizing the Bulletin Board

4. When the file and its path are displayed in the Enter Path to the Local Server text box, click the Save Path button. Your text will replace the original Bulletin Board text (Figure 15.11).

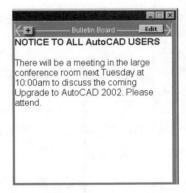

FIGURE 15.11: The Bulletin Board with a custom message

We'll finish the tour with a look at the bottom portion of the Today window.

Autodesk Point A

As you move down to the bottom of the Today window, you will see the area called The Web (Figure 15.12). This is a *portal*, or gateway, to an array of resources for AutoCAD users and design professionals. It's the Autodesk Point A Web site.

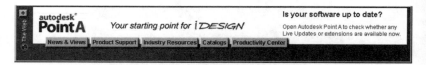

FIGURE 15.12: The Web area with the Point A portal

The five buttons along the bottom of The Web area are the categories of resources available through this Web site. Clicking any of the buttons connects you to the Internet through your Internet service provider and opens Point A to that category. You can also open the Point A home page.

1. Click the + button in the upper-left corner of The Web area. This connects you to the Internet, expands The Web area downwards, and displays the Point A home page (Figure 15.13). There is general information displayed and the combination of category buttons has changed slightly from those on the Point A banner before you went online. The Product Support button is no longer there, and there are two new buttons, Project Center and Industry Centers.

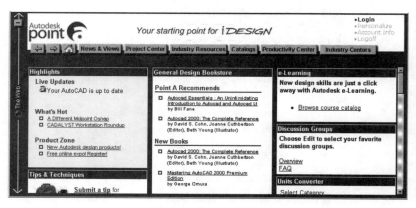

FIGURE 15.13: The Point A home page

2. Move the cursor up to the buttons and slowly go over the buttons without clicking. A large tooltip explains the category as your mouse hovers over it.

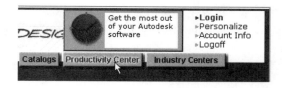

3. Notice the word "Login" in the upper-right corner. This is where you sign up with Point A and answer questions about your interests. This will personalize the Point A display to your specialty. There's no charge and the information is easily edited and updated. You are not required to log on. It's only for your convenience.

4. To see an example of a category, click the News & Views button. The home page changes to the News & Views page (Figure 15.14).

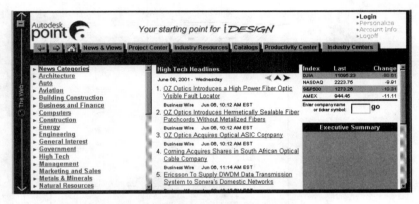

FIGURE 15.14: The News & Views page of Point A

If you have logged in and personalized Point A, some of the category buttons may not be available. Also, in News & Views, the news categories will be trimmed down to those related to your specified interests.

This finishes our tour of AutoCAD Today. Let's move on to a few other Internet features that AutoCAD 2002 offers.

eTransmit

If you use e-mail, you can attach AutoCAD files to your messages. eTransmit is a utility that bundles AutoCAD drawings and their relevant auxiliary files in preparation for e-mail attachment. It saves you the trouble of identifying and collecting these auxiliary files, and organizes them according to various options.

To see how eTransmit works, let's use a file we have developed in this book. When you make a .dwg file the current file, eTransmit will set up the transmission for this file.

1. Open the Site14a drawing (Figure 15.15). This is the drawing of the site plan with three auxiliary views of the externally referenced Cabin12a.dwg file. This Xref'd file should be included in the bundle we are sending.

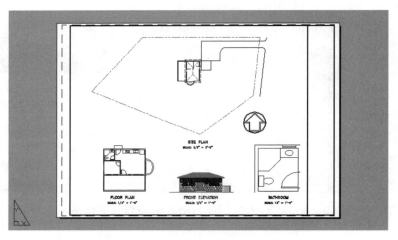

FIGURE 15.15: The Site14a drawing

2. Click the eTransmit button on the Standard toolbar. This brings up the Create Transmittal dialog box.

3. Click the Files tab to bring it to the front (Figure 15.16). The view shown here is the Tree View. It displays the two .dwg files and the 11 associated files that need to be included in the transmission, in a hierarchical tree form.

4. Click the General tab to make it active (Figure 15.17). The Notes text box at the top is a place for you to write a message that will be sent with the transmittal report.

An alternate view, the List View, can be accessed by clicking the left button at the top of the display window on the Files tab in the Create Transmittal dialog box.

FIGURE 15.16: The Create Transmittal dialog box with the Files tab in front

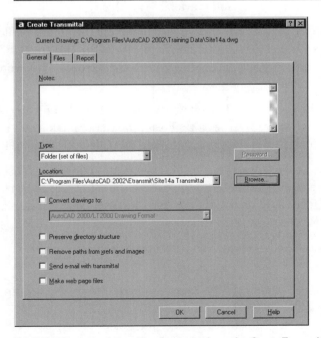

FIGURE 15.17: The General tab on the Create Transmittal dialog box

5. Open the Type drop-down list. There are three options for the format in which the set of associated files are grouped and sent. Note the Password button to the right.

Each option has its own characteristics.

▶ Folder (set of files): Bundles the files into a folder that you designate, uncompressed, and saves the folder on your hard disk. Then you can use a file compression utility to create a compressed file and attach this file to an e-mail. The password option is not available for this type.

▶ Self-extracting executable (*.exe): Creates a self-extracting .exe file titled with the name of the current drawing (such as Site14a .exe) and saves it in the folder you designate. When the receiver downloads and double-clicks this file, the bundled files are extracted. The password option is available for this type.

▶ Zip (*.zip): Creates a .zip file containing the bundle of files. When the receiver downloads and double-clicks this file, the WinZip application is started and the files can be extracted. The password option is available.

6. Click the Report tab. It displays the contents, including any text you may have entered in the Notes box of the General tab, of a .txt file that accompanies the transmittal bundle. Click the General tab again.

7. Below the Type drop-down list is the Location drop-down list and a Browse button, for determining where the set of files to be transmitted will be saved on your computer. The drop-down list displays locations of previous transmittals.

8. Below the Location drop-down list are five check boxes for further options:

▶ Convert Drawings To: Saves the .dwg files being sent in R14 format.

▶ Preserve Directory Structure: When this box is checked, AutoCAD creates a set of folders matching those that the files being sent were in, to be part of the bundle. For the Site14a.dwg, the folders would look like Figure 15.18. The .dwg files are in the C:\ProgramFiles\AutoCAD 2002\Training Data folder. When unchecked, all files are put in one folder.

FIGURE 15.18: The folder structure for transmittal of Site14a

▶ Remove Paths from Xrefs and Images: When checked, the current paths of accompanying .dwg files or image files that are attached to the current drawing (or nested) are deleted.

▶ Send E-mail with Transmittal: When checked, the transmittal will be attached to an e-mail.

▶ Make Web Page Files: Posts the transmittal to a Web page.

9. When all options have been set, click OK. The transmittal is created and saved in the designated folder on your hard disk.

Meet Now

Meet Now is an AutoCAD feature based on Microsoft's Net Meeting software. With Meet Now, you set up a meeting on the Internet where participants can view and modify an AutoCAD drawing. As the host, you control the meeting by choosing participants, selecting the .dwg file to be viewed, and deciding whether and for how long to allow the other participants to use AutoCAD to make changes to your drawing.

Meet Now supports an interactive chat window in which participants enter and view each other's comments in text in real time, and an electronic whiteboard on which participants collectively draw and view each other's drawings, also in real time. If microphones and video cameras are available, Meet Now will support this input as well. For Meet Now to work smoothly, high-speed Internet access is a must.

We'll go through the steps required to set up a meeting.

1. Bring up an AutoCAD drawing that will be the subject of the online meeting. (We'll use Cabin11a.dwg for our example.)

2. Click the Meet Now button on the Standard toolbar. For the first use of Meet Now, you will have to enter personal information, answer some questions about configuration settings and preferences, and, if you are using microphones, perform some sound calibration tests. For the server preference, choose meetnow.autodesk.com. Tell your Meet Now participants to log on to this server through either Net Meeting or, if they have AutoCAD, Meet Now. When this is completed, AutoCAD uses your default Internet service provider to connect and brings up the Online Meeting toolbar in the drawing area (Figure 15.19).

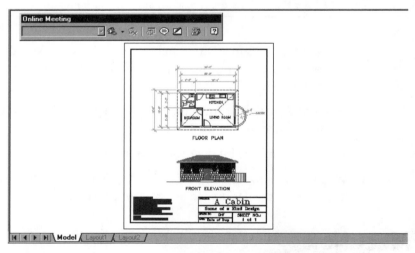

FIGURE 15.19: The drawing area with the Meet Now toolbar and Cabin11a.dwg

3. Click the down arrow on the right side of the Participants button on the Online Meeting toolbar. This opens up the two choices for determining meeting participants, Use Directory Server or Call Someone Direct.

▶ If you choose Use Directory Server, and have selected `meetnow`
`.autodesk.com` as your server, open the Find Someone window.
This displays the list of people currently logged on to the server
(Figure 15.20) and should include the participants scheduled to
join your meeting.

N O T E **Autodesk makes the** `meetnow.autodesk.com` **server site
available to anyone using AutoCAD 2002.**

▶ Call Someone Direct brings up a dialog box where you can key in
the e-mail address of an individual who might not be listed with
your standard server.

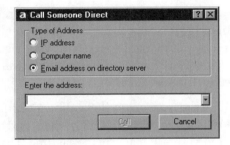

Participants in the meeting need to be online when you call them.
They don't have to have AutoCAD or Meet Now on their computers,
but they must have Net Meeting running and be logged on to the
`meetnow.autodesk.com` server.

4. If you use the directory, highlight the first participant's name and
click Call. If you use the Call Someone Direct dialog box, enter a participant's Internet address in the Enter The Address drop-down list,
or pick it from the list, and click Call. When connected, the participants' screen names will appear in the drop-down list on the Online
Meeting toolbar.

5. Close the Find Someone window or the Call Someone Direct dialog
box. Your screen will look like Figure 15.19 with the difference that
all icons on the Online Meeting toolbar are now available and the
drop-down list will display the participants' names.

6. Click the Display Chat Window icon on the Online Meeting toolbar.
The resizable Chat window appears. Conversations are recorded here,

can be saved as .htm files, and printed. Chat will keep a record of each comment, who made it, and when.

 7. Type a message in the Message text box and click the Send Message Now button. The message will appear in the upper text box of the Chat window and on the participant's screen. (If you have microphones for all participants, this feature is superfluous, so you can close the Chat window.)

 8. Click the Display Whiteboard icon on the Online Meeting toolbar. This brings up the Whiteboard (Figure 15.20) where participants can draw (or use other tools) simultaneously in real time. The results can be printed or saved as .wht files. One file can contain several screens and they can be prepared offline, so a Meet Now participant could set up a series of screens and present them.

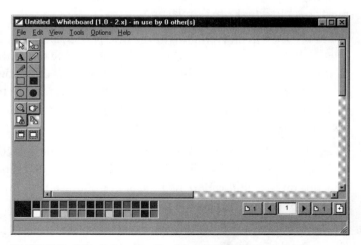

FIGURE 15.20: The Meet Now Whiteboard window

9. Close the Whiteboard and click the Allow Others to Edit icon on the Online Meeting toolbar. This is an on/off toggle, and the button stays depressed when the feature is active. Now a participant can control the AutoCAD screen and modify the current drawing. The meeting host can regain control of AutoCAD at any time by pressing Esc or by clicking the Allow Others to Edit button.

10. To remove a participant, the host selects that person's name on the Online Meeting toolbar drop-down list, then clicks the Remove Participants icon. Others can quit the meeting by using the hang-up tool in Net Meeting.

11. To end the meeting, the host clicks the End Meeting icon on the Online Meeting toolbar.

Other Internet Features

AutoCAD 2002 has several other Internet-related features. They are outside the scope of this book, but we can mention them in passing.

Publish to Web

Publish to Web is a utility for publishing your AutoCAD drawings on the Web. When you click on the Publish to Web icon on the Standard toolbar, the Publish to Web wizard comes up.

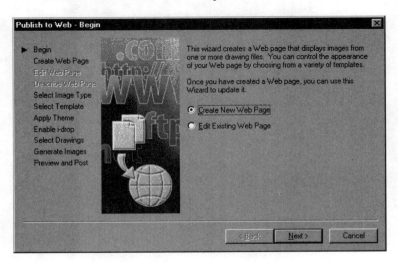

A series of screens with helpful descriptions walk you through the utility's features. They let you:

► Name the Web page, specify its location, and enter a description.

► Select an image type and, depending on the type you choose, size. One of the three choices is an AutoCAD type, .dwf, which has no size option.

► Choose among four format styles, or templates. Your drawings can be thumbnail sketches or listed by name with a viewing box.

► Choose a color scheme from seven options (Theme).

► Decide whether to include a drag-and-drop tool called i-drop.

► Choose which drawings to regenerate as they are captured (Figure 15.21).

The wizard generates the Web page and offers you a preview (Figure 15.22). You can click on the filenames and see the various drawings. Then close the preview and click Post to post the page to a Web site. The same procedure is used to edit an existing Web page.

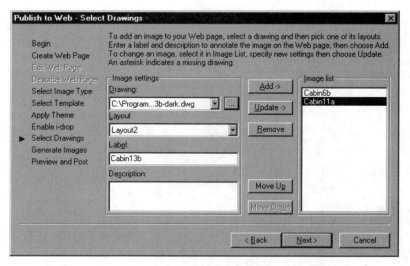

FIGURE 15.21: The Select Drawings page of the Publish to Web wizard

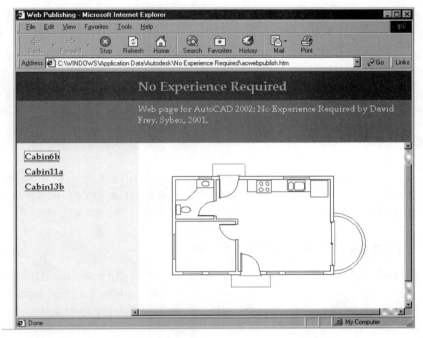

FIGURE 15.22: Preview of new Web page with AutoCAD drawings

Hyperlinks

A hyperlink is a mechanism that links an object in an AutoCAD drawing to something else. For example, it can link a block in a drawing to an Internet Web site, another drawing, or a Word document.

Click the Insert Hyperlink icon on the Standard toolbar to create a new link. After you select objects, the Insert Hyperlink dialog box comes up. Specify the file or click the Web Page button to go onto the Internet and find a site to link to. Once a hyperlink has been created, the object with the link acts like a hot button. When you move the cursor to that object, AutoCAD displays the hyperlink icon and a tooltip.

Select the object, then right-click to bring up a shortcut menu. Select Hyperlink at the bottom of the menu. A submenu is displayed that includes the Web site or the file location of the document that the AutoCAD object is linked to.

In this example, the word BALCONY in the AutoCAD drawing is linked to the main Autodesk Web site, so the Web site is displayed on the submenu. When you click on it, you are taken onto the Internet and connected to the Web site.

Buzzsaw and RedSpark

These features are secure commercial Web sites that can be accessed from AutoCAD. RedSpark is set up to provide services to professionals in the manufacturing industry, and Buzzsaw does the same thing for the design and construction industry. As mentioned in the earlier section on AutoCAD Today, you can access RedSpark or Buzzsaw from the Select File dialog box. Both services offer free 30-day trials, so you can sign on and see whether one of them is right for your business (Figure 15.23).

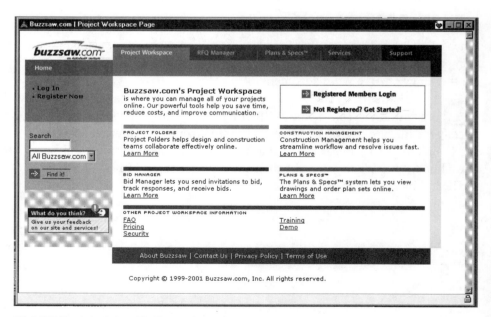

FIGURE 15.23: The Buzzsaw.com home page

Some of the Internet features mentioned in this chapter, such as meeting online and posting .dwg files to the Web, are offered by Buzzsaw. If you are working on a project in which you have a need to distribute or share documents between associated companies, consider using Buzzsaw or RedSpark. Check them out at www.buzzsaw.com and www.redspark.com.

Summary

I encourage you to experiment with the Internet tools offered by AutoCAD. Some readers may be beginners at AutoCAD but quite savvy on the Internet. If so, you may already know about tools like those described in this chapter.

The appendices that follow contain tutorials and discussion about drawing in 3D and using Attributes. You will also find a glossary of terms related to Auto-CAD, building construction, and design, that have been mentioned in the book. I hope you have found the book useful in learning AutoCAD 2002.

Are You Experienced?

Now you can...

- ☑ navigate through AutoCAD Today and Point A
- ☑ send AutoCAD drawings with e-mail through eTransmit
- ☑ use Meet Now for online meetings
- ☑ publish an AutoCAD drawing to the Web
- ☑ link an AutoCAD drawing to a Web site
- ☑ find commercial Web sites that are linked to AutoCAD

A Look at Drawing in 3D

Nothing in CAD is quite so fascinating as drawing in 3D. Compared to a traditional 3D rendering of a building on a drafting board that uses vanishing points and projection planes, a true 3D computerized model of a building that can be rotated and viewed from any angle, as well as from the inside, is a world of difference. Many architectural firms still use the drafting board to create 3D presentation drawings, even though they may use AutoCAD for their construction drawings. But more and more of them are using AutoCAD's 3D features to create either perspective drawings or simple 3D models that are then traced over by hand in the process of creating the final presentation drawing. So it's useful to acquire some skills in working in 3D. It's also a lot of fun.

Constructing a 3D model of a building requires many of the tools you have been using throughout this book, and some new ones that you will be introduced to in this appendix. Your competence in using the basic drawing, editing, and display commands is critical to your successful study of 3D for two reasons. First, drawing in 3D is more complex and difficult than drawing in 2D, and it can be very frustrating. If you aren't familiar with the basic commands, you will become that much more frustrated. Second, accuracy is critical in 3D drawing. The effect of errors is compounded, so you must be in the habit of using tools, like the Osnap modes, to maximize your precision.

Don't feel discouraged, just be warned. Drawing in 3D is a fascinating and enjoyable process, and the results you get can be astounding. I sincerely encourage you to make the effort to learn some of the basic 3D skills presented here.

There are many 3D software packages on the market today, and some are better for drawing buildings than others. Many times, because of the precision that AutoCAD provides, a 3D .dwg file will be exported to one of these specialized 3D packages for further work, after being laid out in AutoCAD. Other drawings will be created in 2D, converted to 3D, and then refined into a shaded, colored, and textured rendering with specific lights and shadows. In this book, we will look at the basic techniques of *solid modeling* and touch on a couple of tools used in *surface modeling.* In the process, you will learn some techniques for viewing a 3D model. At the end of the appendix, we will introduce the processes of setting up and rendering a 3D model.

3D Modeling

We will begin by building a 3D model of the cabin, using several techniques for creating 3D *solids* and *surfaces*. When using solid modeling tools, the objects you create are solid, like lumps of clay. They can be added together or subtracted from one another to form more complex shapes. By contrast, 3D surfaces are a composite of two-dimensional planes that stretch over a frame of lines the way a tent surface stretches over the frame inside.

As you construct these 3D objects, you will get more familiar with the User Coordinate System, learn how it is used with 3D, and begin using the basic methods of viewing a 3D model.

Viewing a Drawing in 3D

Let's start with Cabin07b. This version of the cabin has all the basic components of the floor plan on their respective layers, with no blocks or hatch patterns, and no front elevation or title block. If you haven't been following through the whole book and saving your work progressively, you can download this file from Sybex's Web page, www.sybex.com. You can still follow along if you have another floor plan to use for the exercise that isn't too much more complex than that of the cabin.

1. Open Cabin07b. When the floor plan comes up, make the Walls layer current and turn off all other layers. Your drawing will look like Figure A.1. Try to start thinking of it in three dimensions. The entire drawing is on a flat plane parallel to the monitor screen. When you add elements in the third dimension, they will project straight out of the screen toward you if they have a positive dimension, and straight through the screen if they have a negative dimension. The line of direction is perpendicular to the plane of the screen and is called the z-axis. You are familiar with the x and y axes, which run left and right and up and down, respectively. Think of the z-axis for a moment as running in and out of the screen. At the end of the appendix, we will introduce the processes of setting up and rendering a 3D model.

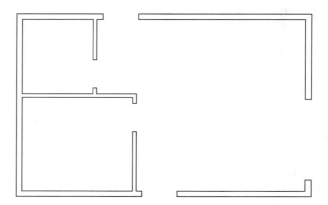

FIGURE A.1: Cabin07b **with all layers turned off except Walls**

2. If the User Coordinate System icon is not visible on your screen, choose View ➢ Display ➢ UCS Icon ➢ On, to place a check mark next to On. The UCS Icon appears again. We turned it off in Chapter 5, *Gaining Drawing Strategies: Part 2*, then used it in Chapter 8, *Generating Elevations*, to help construct some of the elevations, and we'll be using it again in a moment. For now, just keep an eye on it as the drawing changes. Remember that the icon's arrows indicate the positive direction for the *x, y,* and—in 3D—the *z*-axes.

3. Now you'll change the view from a plan view of the drawing—looking straight down at it—to one in which you are looking down at it from an angle. Choose View ➢ 3D Views ➢ SW Isometric. ("SW" means from the southwest.) The view changes to look like Figure A.2. Notice how the UCS icon has changed with the change of view. The *X* and *Y* arrows still run parallel to the left side and bottom of the cabin. But the icon and the floor plan are now at an angle to the screen. And the *Z*-axis is visible.

4. Zoom out and pan down to give yourself some room to put the walls in 3D.

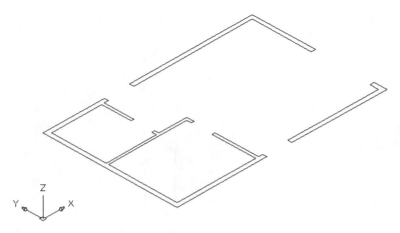

FIGURE A.2:   The walls as seen from the SW Isometric view

Making the Walls

The main task ahead is to create what is called a *3D model* of the cabin. We will be using solid elements for the cabin's walls, doors, windows, floor, and steps. You will learn several ways of viewing your work as you progress. To make the walls, we'll start with a solid box and then, like a sculptor, remove from the box everything that is not an interior or exterior wall. The elements to be removed will be the spaces of the rooms and the openings for the doors and windows.

1. Set the Endpoint Osnap to be running, and be sure Polar and Ortho are turned off. Create a new layer called 3D-Walls, assign it color 22, and make it current.

2. Choose Draw ➢ Solids ➢ Box. Click the lowest corner of the walls, then click the uppermost corner. At the Specify height: prompt, type 9' ↵. A box is drawn over the entire floor plan, and AutoCAD displays it as a *wireframe* (Figure A.3a). Wireframes are 3D drawings in which the lines represent the intersection of walls or other planes. What you are viewing is actually a solid block, a fact that will become apparent as we move along.

    ◄
    For the various heights of the windows, doors, roof, etc., see Figure 8.1 in Chapter 8.

3. Restart the Box command and repeat step 2 to make another 9'-high box in the living room. Pick the inside corner to the left of the front door and the inside corner where the refrigerator stands (Figure A.3b).

4. Repeat step 2 again and create a third box in the remaining part of the living room that wasn't included in the second box (Figure A.3c).

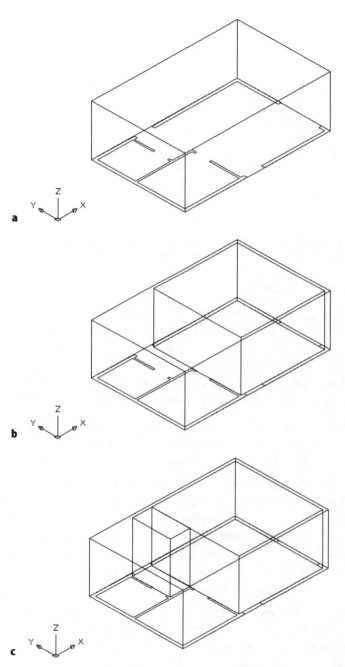

FIGURE A.3: The first box covers the floor plan (a), a box fills most of the living room (b), and a third box fills the rest of the living room (c).

5. Repeat step 2 twice more to create 9' boxes at the interior corners of the bedroom and bathroom (Figure A.4).

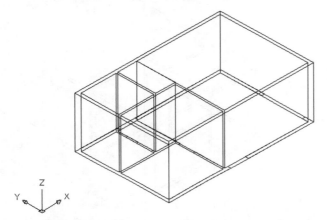

FIGURE A.4: The interior spaces of the cabin are filled with boxes.

Notice that the empty spaces between the boxes' vertical faces are the exterior and interior walls. Because all five boxes are solid, we can subtract the four inside boxes from the larger outside box and be left with the walls.

6. Choose Modify ➢ Solids Editing ➢ Subtract. Pick the large outside box, then press ↵. Pick the four smaller inside boxes and press ↵. The smaller volumes are subtracted from the larger volume, creating our walls (Figure A.5a).

7. You need a better view to really see what has happened. Choose View ➢ Hide. Hidden lines are removed and you can see solid walls (Figure A.5b). The walls are one object, consisting of the large box after the smaller boxes were subtracted away from it.

8. Choose View ➢ Regen to restore the hidden lines. We'll use a similar procedure to put in the doorway openings.

When you choose View ➢ Regen, Auto-CAD recalculates all the geometry of the drawing as if you were just opening it. It's called a *regeneration*. Choosing View ➢ Redraw merely refreshes the screen.

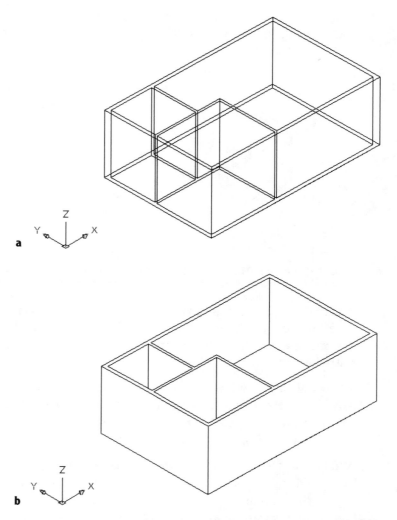

FIGURE A.5: The solid after subtracting the interior boxes (a) and the view after using the Hide command (b)

Cutting Doorway Openings

The five doorway openings vary in width but have the same height. We can make boxes where the openings should be and then subtract them from the wall solid object.

1. Create a new layer called 3D-Doors and make it current. Leave its color as the default (white or black).

2. Freeze the 3D-Walls layer. Make a zoom window that includes just the five openings in the floor plan of the walls. Be sure Endpoint Osnap is running.

3. Bring up the Solids toolbar to the screen and dock it on the right side of the drawing area, next to the Object Snap toolbar. Click the Box icon to start the Box command.

4. Make a box for the front, bedroom, and balcony door openings. Click opposite corners of each opening, then enter 7'6 ⏎ at the Specify height: prompt. Copy the front door box to the back door opening, and the bedroom one to the bath opening.

5. Zoom Previous (Figure A.6a).

6. Thaw the 3D-Walls layer.

7. Choose Modify ➢ Solids Editing ➢ Subtract. Click the wall solid, then press ⏎.

8. Click the five boxes that are serving as openings, and press ⏎ (Figure A.6b).

9. Choose View ➢ Hide (Figure A.6c). The doorway openings have been cut.

10. Choose View ➢ Regen. The window openings can be made in the same way, after a modification to the floor plan.

> ◄
> **You can also start the Box command by choosing Draw ➢ Solids ➢ Box or by typing box ⏎.**

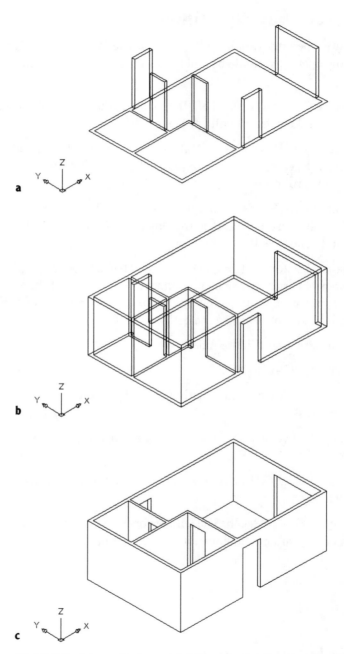

FIGURE A.6: The boxes in all five openings (a), the wall solid after sub-tracting the boxes (b), and the view after a Hide (c)

Subtracting Window Openings

As you might expect, the window openings will be cut out of the walls just as the doorway openings were. The only difference is that the bottoms of the window openings sit above the 2D floor plan.

1. Create a new layer called 3D-Windows and make it current. Let it take on the default color. Before you leave the Layer Properties Manager, turn off the Walls layer, turn on the Windows layer, and freeze the 3D-Walls layer. There should be only window blocks visible (Figure A.7). If the screen doesn't display what is illustrated in the book, or what you expect, choose View ➤ Regen.

> ◄ When you want to make 2D layers invisible, it doesn't matter whether you freeze them or turn them off. But when working with 3D layers, it is best to freeze them. When they are frozen, they won't interfere with the appearance of the 3D model during a Hide.

FIGURE A.7: The cabin drawing in 3D with only the Windows layer visible

2. Zoom into a closer view like you did for the doorway openings.

3. Use the Box command to create six box solids that are 3'-6" high at each of the windows except the 2'-wide one in the front wall of the living room, then Zoom Previous (Figure A.8a). The 2' window in the living room is a round window and will be dealt with separately.

4. Start the Move command. Select the six boxes, then press ↵. Click any point on the screen, then type @0,0,4' ↵. The window boxes are moved up 4'.

5. Thaw the 3D-Walls layer and zoom out if necessary. The drawing should look like Figure A.8b.

6. Choose Modify ➤ Solids Editing ➤ Subtract. Click the wall solid, then press ↵.

7. Pick the six window boxes, then press ↵. The window openings are cut out of the walls. After hiding, the drawing looks like Figure A.8c.

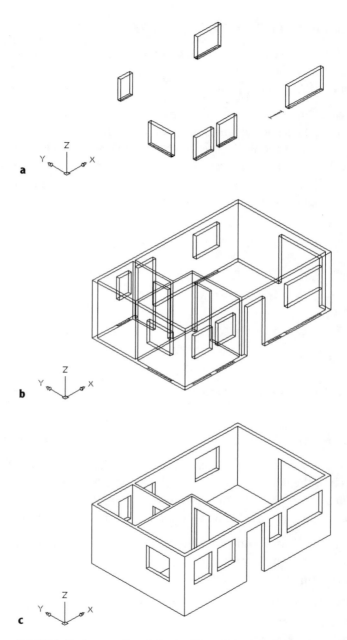

FIGURE A.8: The window solid boxes that were created on the floor plan (a), the wall solid and the window boxes after being raised (b), and the view after a Hide (c)

Now we need to create a circular window opening for the front wall. We'll use a second basic solid shape, or *primitive*, to cut this circular hole. AutoCAD has six primitive shapes that are solids. When you choose Draw ➢ Solids, the top of the cascading menu displays them.

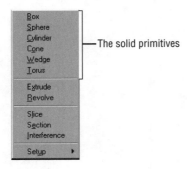
The solid primitives

On the Solids toolbar, the primitives have icons that illustrate their basic shapes.

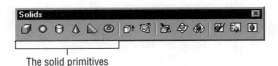

The solid primitives

So far, we've used only the box. For the circular window, we'll use the cylinder.

1. Zoom in close to a view of the front wall, like Figure A.9a. We will need to change the UCS icon to make the cylinder.

2. Type ucs ↵ x ↵ -90. The UCS icon rotates such that the plane defined by the *x* and *y* axes is parallel to the front wall and the *z* axis points away from us (and is therefore dashed) (Figure A9.b).

3. Click the Cylinder icon on the Solids toolbar.

4. Use Insert Osnap to locate the center point for the base of the cylinder at the insertion point of the 2' window.

5. Specify the radius for the base of the cylinder by using Endpoint Osnap and clicking the point where one of the window jamb lines meets the front wall.

6. Specify the height of the cylinder by typing 6 ↵. The cylinder is placed (Figure A.9c). It has an abbreviated, almost abstract form.

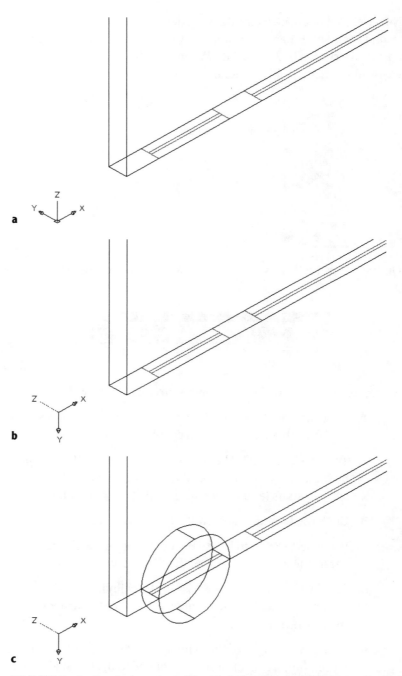

FIGURE A.9: A close view of the 2' window (a), the UCS after reorientation (b), and the cylinder placed in the wall (c)

7. Zoom Previous. Use the Move command, Polar Tracking, and Direct Distance entry to move the cylinder up 6'.

8. Type **ucs** ↵ ↵ to return the UCS icon to the World Coordinate System orientation.

9. Choose Modify ➤ Solids Editing ➤ Subtract. Click the walls solid, press ↵, then click the round window and press ↵ again.

10. Choose View ➤ Hide. The shell of the cabin walls is complete (Figure A.10).

You are still looking at one object, the walls solid. Solids that represented doorway and window openings and spaces in rooms have been subtracted from it.

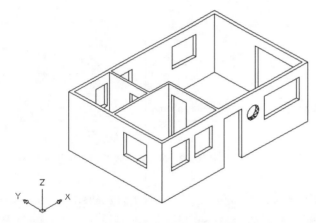

FIGURE A.10: The finished cabin walls solid, after a Hide

Creating a Floor for the Cabin

In designing our cabin, we didn't draw a floor, but one was implied. The three exterior doorway openings have thresholds that indicated a change in level from the cabin floor down to the steps and the balcony. We'll now use those thresholds to make a 3D solid for the floor.

1. Continuing from the previous set of steps, click the Layers icon on the Object Properties toolbar and do the following:

   ▶ Freeze the 3D-Walls and 3D-Windows layers, and turn off the Windows layers.

▶ Turn on the Walls and Steps layers.

▶ Create a new layer called 3D-Floor, assign it a brownish color, and make it current.

The drawing will look like Figure A.11. If lines are missing, choose View ➤ Regen to regenerate all the lines. We're going to create a series of solid primitives with the Box command that will represent parts of the floor. Then we'll combine them.

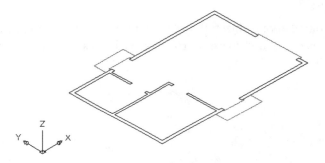

FIGURE A.11: The walls and steps in 2D

2. Use the Zoom Window tool to set up a view of the front door opening and its threshold.

3. Start the Box command and create a box that sits in the opening, between the jamb lines. Give it a height of 2". Then make a second box, also 2" high, that sits on the threshold overhang (Figure A.12).

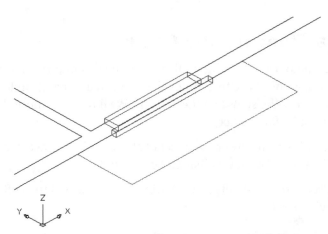

FIGURE A.12: The front door opening with two solid boxes

4. Repeat step 3 for the back door and the sliding glass door openings. Then make similar boxes that fit in the bedroom and bathroom door openings.

5. Finally, make 2"-high boxes for the three rooms, using the inside corners and Endpoint Osnap. There will be two boxes for the living room. You will end up with 12 boxes (Figure A.13).

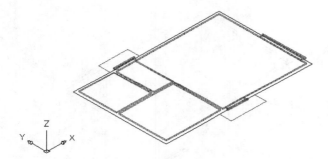

FIGURE A.13 : The full floor with 12 solid boxes

6. Turn off the Walls and Steps layers. Choose Modify ➤ Solids Editing ➤ Union, then use a selection window to select all the boxes. Press ↵. The 12 boxes unite to form a 2"-thick floor solid (Figure A.14).

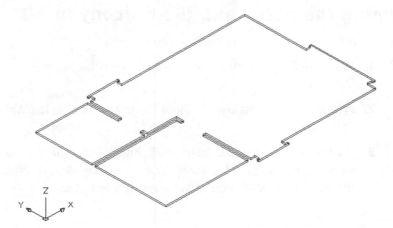

FIGURE A.14 : The 12 boxes unite to form a new floor solid object.

7. Start the Move command, select the floor and press ↵.

8. Click any blank location on the drawing area, then type @0,0,10 ↵. The floor will be moved up 10".

9. Thaw the 3D-Walls layer. Choose View ➤ 3D Views ➤ SE Isometric.

10. Choose View ➤ Hide. The drawing should look like Figure A.15.

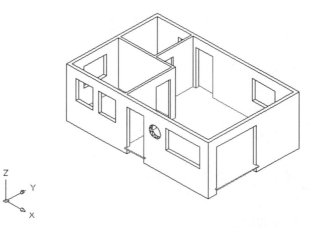

FIGURE A.15: The 3D walls and floor after a Hide

Forming the Steps and the Balcony in 3D

The steps require only a new layer and two boxes.

1. Make a new layer called 3D-Steps, assign it color number 8, and make it current.

2. Freeze the 3D-Walls and 3D-Floor layers and turn on the Walls and Steps layers.

3. Use the Box command to make a 10"-high box for the front and back steps (Figure A.16). If the screen doesn't display what is illustrated in the book, or what you expect, choose View ➤ Regen.

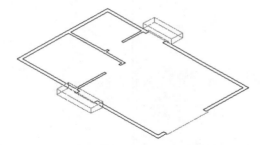

FIGURE A.16: The front and back steps as 3D solids

For the balcony, we'll use the cylinder primitive and the Subtract Solids editing command.

1. Make another new layer called 3D-Balcony, assign it color number 24, and make it current. Zoom into the area around the balcony, leaving a little extra room for the 3D view. Turn on the Balcony layer.

2. Choose the Cylinder tool to create a cylinder solid for the floor of the balcony. Use Center Osnap to locate the center at the center point of the arcs that represent the balcony walls. Select a radius of 4'-6" and a height of 3'-2".

3. Move this cylinder up 10" (Figure A.17a).

4. Draw a second cylinder using the same center point, with a radius of 5' and a height of 4'.

5. Choose Modify ➢ Solids Editing ➢ Subtract. Select the larger cylinder, press ↵, then select the smaller cylinder and press ↵. A shape is created that looks like a bowl or hot tub (Figure A.17b).

6. Click the Slice button on the Solids toolbar, then select the balcony and press ↵.

7. At the first prompt, type yz ↵. This defines the plane that we'll use to slice the balcony.

8. At the second prompt, pick the bottom corner of the cabin wall, where the bottom of the balcony meets the corner.

9. At the third prompt, click a blank spot below and to the right of the balcony. The shape is cut in half and the balcony is complete (Figure A.17c).

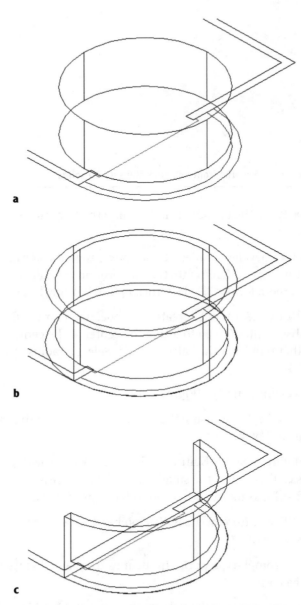

FIGURE A.17: The first cylinder of the balcony (a), the balcony solid after subtraction (b), and the finished balcony after using the Slice tool (c)

10. Zoom Previous, then turn off the Balcony, Walls, and Steps layers, and thaw the 3D-Walls and 3D-Floor layers. Then choose View ➤ Hide (Figure A.18a). Note the series of flat, triangular surfaces that compose the curved surface of the balcony.

11. Choose View ➤ Shade ➤ Gourard Shaded, Edges On. This type of shading blends the shades of two adjacent surfaces that define a curve at their adjoining edges, and creates a realistic appearance (Figure A.18b).

12. Click the 3D Orbit button on the standard toolbar. A green circle called an *arcball* is superimposed over your 3D model. There are smaller circles at the quadrant points of the larger circle. This is a viewing tool in which the view of the 3D model is controlled by the movement of the cursor. Depending on whether you click and drag inside or outside the big circle, or within one of the small circles, the cabin will move in 3D space in different ways.

13. Place the cursor inside the circle, then click and hold down the left mouse button. As you move the cursor, the model turns in space. Release the mouse button to fix a view (Figure A.18c). Play around with this feature for a bit.

14. When finished, press Esc to end 3D Orbit. Choose View ➤ Shade ➤ 2D Wireframe to restore the view to that of the wireframe.

15. Choose View ➤ 3D Views ➤ SE Isometric to restore the view you had after step 10.

The 3D model is taking shape. To finish it, we will add doors, windows, and the roof.

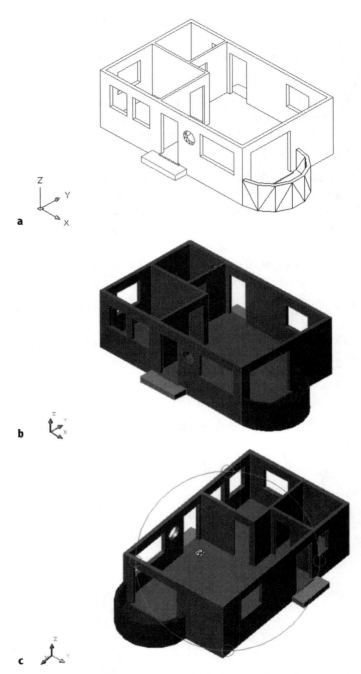

FIGURE A.18: The balcony, walls, and floor after a Hide (a), after using the Shade command (b), and while using 3D Orbit (c)

Finishing Up the 3D Model

The 3D solids of the swinging doors are constructed with the box primitive that we have been using. There is no need for any step-by-step instructions here. Just follow the same procedure that you did for creating the floor, steps, and balcony. You can use the 3D-Doors layer that you created earlier for the openings, but change its color to No. 34. Construct the swinging doors over the 2D doors on the Door layer, with a height of 6'-5½". Then move them up 12½". Use the Shade command and 3D Orbit tool to check your work.

The sliding glass door and the windows are similar in construction. They both have a frame and a piece of glass held in the frame. Once we do the sliding glass door, you can apply the same method to the windows. Our strategy will be to create a frame by subtracting a smaller box from a larger one. Refer back to Chapter 4, *Gaining Drawing Strategies: Part 1*, for the dimensions of the opening. The frames are 2" wide and 1½" thick.

1. Set the view to SE Isometric (choose View ➢ 3D Views).

2. Turn on the Doors layer and freeze all 3D layers except 3D-Walls and the current layer, 3D-Doors.

3. Zoom into the sliding glass door panel that is closest to the corner (Figure A.19a).

4. Use the Box tool to make a solid box that sits on the outside corners of the door panel frame, with a height of 6'-6".

5. Make a second box that sits inside the frame. To do this, snap to the opposite inside corners of the little rectangles that represent the frame. Give this box a height of 6'-2" (Figure A.19b).

6. Move the smaller box up 2" (in the positive Z direction).

7. Subtract the smaller box from the larger one.

8. Create a new layer called 3D-Glass, assign it color 151, and make it current.

9. Choose Draw ➢ Surfaces ➢ 3D Face.

Remember: To make 3D layers invisible, freeze them.

A *3D Face* is a three- or four-sided two-dimensional surface object that turns opaque in a Hide.

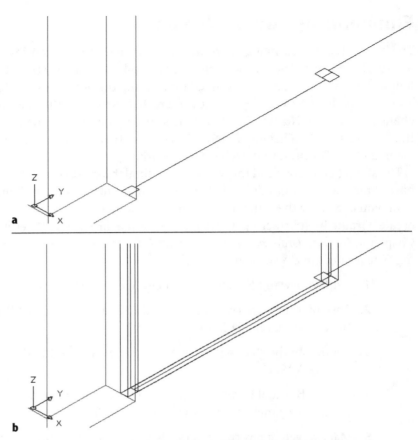

FIGURE A.19: A close view of one sliding glass door panel (a) and two new box solids on the 2D view of the panel (b)

10. Set Midpoint to be the only running Osnap, then click on the midpoints of the lines representing the lower inside corners of the frame (Figure A.20a).

11. Pan up and pick the midpoints of the upper inside corners of the frame in a circular fashion to complete the 3D face (Figure A.20b).

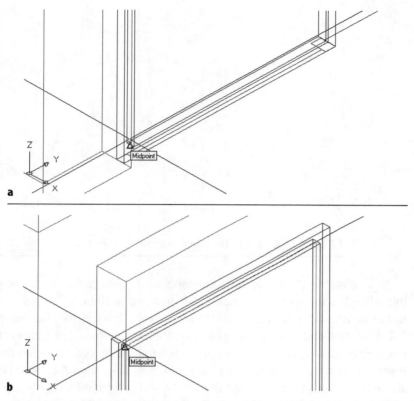

FIGURE A.20: Beginning the 3D face at the bottom of the frame (a) and finishing it at the top of the frame (b)

12. Zoom Previous until you are back at the view of the bottom of the frame. Make Endpoint the only running Osnap, and copy the frame and glass to the other sliding glass door panel.

13. Zoom out to a view of the whole opening, then move the two doors with their glass up 12".

14. Turn off the Doors layer, and thaw all 3D layers except 3D-Balcony. Use Hide to get a view of the completed sliding glass door in 3D (Figure A.21).

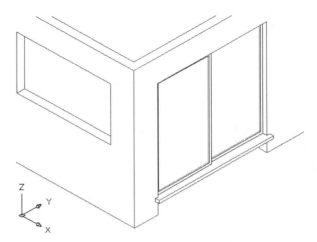

FIGURE A.21: The completed sliding glass door

By keeping the glass as a separate object on its own layer, we can make it invisible while leaving the frame unchanged, to allow us to look through the window. Either panel can be moved to give the appearance that the door has been slid open.

This same technique can be used to create the windows. The frames can be constructed in place (in the window openings), and the glass installed in the frames. If you use two frames, as you did for the sliding glass door (but in this case, one above the other), they will look like double-hung windows. If only one panel is used, the window will appear to be fixed in place. Figure A.22 shows a partial view of the cabin. The front living room window is fixed in place and the bathroom window is double hung. The bathroom window has the addition of a sill at the bottom of the opening.

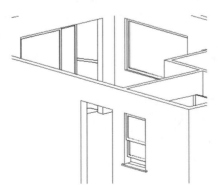

FIGURE A.22: A partial view that shows two windows and the sliding glass door

Putting a Roof on the Cabin

We'll finish the 3D model of the cabin by constructing a roof. The edge of the roof will be a different color than the roof surface, so we'll make them as two separate objects, each on its own layer. The edge will be a solid and the sloping part will be a set of surfaces.

1. Create two new layers: 3D-Roof_Edge with color 32, and 3D-Roof with color 114. Make 3D-Roof_Edge current.

2. Freeze all 3D layers except the two new ones, and turn all other layers off except Roof. Choose View ➤ 3D Views ➤ SE Isometric. Just the roof will be visible. (If it's not, the Roof layer may be frozen, so thaw it.)

3. Use the Box icon on the Solids toolbar to make a box that is 6" high and sits on the four corners of the roof (Figure A.23a).

4. Move the box up 9'. Then copy the ridge line and hip lines of the roof up to the top edge of the box.

5. Use Properties to change these copied lines to the 3D-Roof_Edge layer. Then turn off the Roof layer (Figure A.23b).

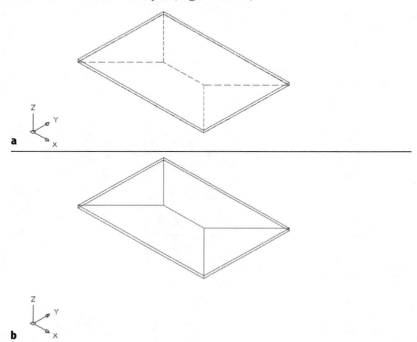

FIGURE A.23: The solid box is made (a) and the copied roof lines are moved to the 3D-Roof_Edge layer (b)

6. Start the Stretch command (on the Modify toolbar) and use a crossing window to select just the ridge line and the ends of the four hip lines that touch the ridge line.

7. Press ↵. Click a blank part of the drawing area for the base point, then type @0,0,3' ↵. The roof is stretched up 3' (Figure A.24a).

8. Make the 3D-Roof layer current, then choose Draw ➤ Surfaces ➤ 3D Face.

9. With Endpoint Osnap, start at the leftmost corner of the sloping planes and pick the four corners of the front plane of the roof. Then, at the `Specify third point or [Invisible] <exit>:` prompt, move to the rightmost corner and click this point twice. Follow the diagram in Figure A.24b. Press ↵ to end the 3D Face command.

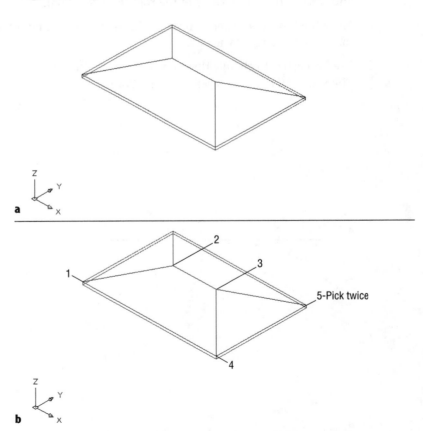

FIGURE A.24: The ridge and hip lines are stretched up (a) and the sequence of picks for the first two 3D Faces (b)

10. Repeat steps 8 and 9 for the back and left surfaces of the roof.

11. Momentarily turn off the 3D-Roof layer, erase the ridge and hip lines, then turn the 3D-Roof layer back on again and thaw all 3D layers except the 3D-Glass layer.

12. Choose View ➤ Hide to view the cabin (Figure A.25).

13. Use the Shade options and 3D Orbit to view the model in color and at different angles.

14. Save this file as CabinA1.

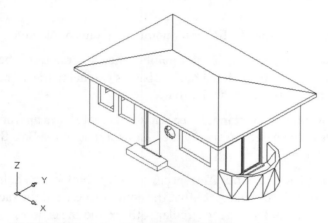

FIGURE A.25: The completed cabin after a Hide

Further Directions in 3D

Covering 3D in real depth is beyond the scope of this book, but we can mention a few other tools and features that you may enjoy investigating. First we will summarize a few of the solids and surface modeling tools that we didn't cover in the tutorial on the cabin. Then we will take a quick look at the rendering process as it is approached in AutoCAD.

Other Solids Modeling Tools

We used the Box and Cylinder primitive solid tools to build up the model of the cabin. There are four other primitive shapes, all found on the Solids toolbar:

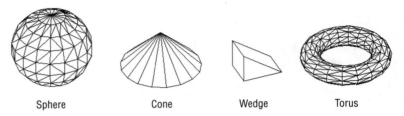

Sphere   Cone   Wedge   Torus

► **Sphere:** You specify the center point and radius or diameter.

► **Cone:** You specify the center point of the base, radius of the base, and height of the pointed tip. The base is parallel to the *XY* plane and the height is perpendicular to it.

► **Wedge:** It has a rectangular base and a lid that slopes up from one edge of the base. You specify the base as you do in the Box, then enter the height.

► **Torus:** This is a donut. You specify a center point for the hole, the radius of the circular path that the donut makes, and the radius of the tube that follows the circular path around the center point.

Two other tools exist for creating solids by moving 2D shapes in the third dimension:

► **Extrude:** Select a closed 2D shape like a rectangle or circle. Then specify a height of the extrusion or a path to extrude along. If the extrusion is straight up, you enter an angle to taper the edges away from the vertical.

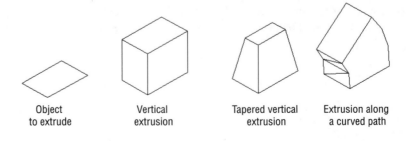

Object   Vertical   Tapered vertical   Extrusion along
to extrude   extrusion   extrusion   a curved path

▶ Revolve: Select a closed 2D shape, then define the axis and the angle of rotation.

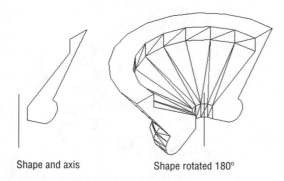

Shape and axis   Shape rotated 180°

There are many tools for modifying solids. When we formed the cabin walls, floor, and balcony, we used Union and Subtract, as well as Slice. Another solids editing tool called *Intersect* finds the volume that two solids have in common when they partially occupy the same space. It's at the top of the Modify ➤ Solids Editing menu, with Union and Subtract. Click on the solids that are "colliding" and AutoCAD creates a solid from their intersection.

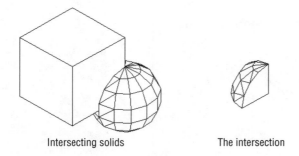

Intersecting solids   The intersection

These are only a few of the many tools for creating and modifying solids, but should be enough to get you started.

Surface Modeling Tools

Surface modeling has its own set of tools, some of which are similar to those for solid modeling. When you choose Draw ➤ Surfaces > 3D Surfaces, the 3D Objects dialog box comes up.

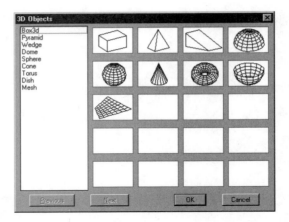

Most of these shapes are the same as, or vary slightly from, the six primitive solid shapes. But 3D Surface objects can't be joined using the Union, Subtract, and Intersection tools. Here is a brief description of a few of the other tools on the Surfaces menu.

1. In the 3D Objects dialog box:

   ▶ **Mesh:** Creates a rectangular three-dimensional surface mesh when you pick four points in 3D space and specify the number of divisions of faces.

2. On the Draw ➤ Surfaces menu:

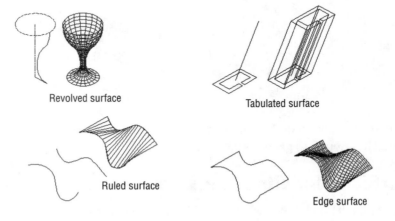

Revolved surface

Tabulated surface

Ruled surface

Edge surface

   ▶ **Revolved surface:** Creates a 3D surface mesh by rotating a 2D curved line around an axis of revolution.

- ▶ **Tabulated surface:** Creates a 3D surface mesh by extruding a 2D object in a direction determined by the endpoints of a line, arc, or polyline.

- ▶ **Ruled surface:** Creates a 3D surface mesh between two selected shapes.

- ▶ **Edge surface:** Creates a 3D surface mesh among four lines that are connected at their endpoints. Each line can be in 2D or 3D, and the original shape must be a boundary of a shape that does not cross or conflict with itself.

Most 3D models today use the solid modeling tools for their basic shapes because the tools for adding, subtracting, slicing, and so forth are easy to use and allow complex shapes to be fabricated quickly. Still, surface modeling has its uses, and sometimes a shape will lend itself to surface over solid modeling. Any serious 3D modeler will be familiar with both sets of tools.

Rendering with AutoCAD

The next step after developing a 3D model is to render it. This process has several parts:

- ▶ Setting up a 3D view of the scene to be rendered

- ▶ Creating a lighting scheme

- ▶ Enabling and controlling shadow effects

- ▶ Assigning material textures to surfaces

- ▶ Possibly choosing a background view

- ▶ Putting in auxiliary objects such as people and trees

- ▶ Saving setup views and lights as restorable Scenes

- ▶ Outputting a rendering to a file

In this book, we will just give you a quick tour of some of the rendering steps listed above, as we set up a view of the cabin and render it. Developing a full rendering takes time and patience, but touching on a few of the many steps involved will give you a feel for the process. You have put in a lot of time working your way through this book, and you deserve to have a rendered 3D view of your cabin, however simple, to complete the process.

Setting Up a 3D View to Render

1. Type ucs, then press ↵ twice to return to the World Coordinate System, if you weren't already there.

2. Choose View ➤ 3D Views ➤ Plan View ➤ World UCS to return to a plan view of your drawing. Turn off the UCS icon.

3. Create a new layer called 3D-Land, assign it color 74, and make it current.

4. Zoom out and create a rectangle around the cabin that is 160' wide × 140' high. To be sure the rectangle is created at "ground level." Don't snap to any parts of the cabin.

5. Move that rectangle to a position relative to the cabin approximately as in Figure A.26. Again, don't snap to any parts of the cabin yet.

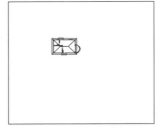

FIGURE A.26: A plan view with the rectangle around the cabin

6. Choose Draw ➤ Region, then select the rectangle and press ↵. This creates a 2D object called a *region* that behaves like a 3D object. It turns opaque in a Hide, Shade, or Render, and holes can be cut out of it.

7. Choose View ➤ 3D Views ➤ SE Isometric. This is one of the standard 3D views we used to construct the 3D model of the cabin. Now we'll modify it slightly.

8. Choose View ➤ 3D Views ➤ Viewpoint Presets. The Viewpoints Presets dialog box comes up. Here you can fine-tune the rotation of the

view in the *xy* plane and the angle of the view relative to the *xy* plane. The rotation is all right, but we will make the angle flatter.

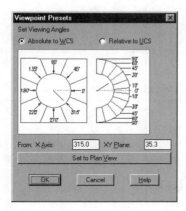

9. On the right, in the *XY* Plane text box, change 35.3 to 5, then click OK.

10. Use a Zoom Window to bring the cabin in closer, like in Figure A.27.

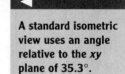

A standard isometric view uses an angle relative to the *xy* plane of 35.3°.

FIGURE A.27: A close view of the cabin after zooming in

11. Pan the view down so only the back lines of the rectangular region are visible.

12. Be sure all 3D layers are thawed and turned on.

13. Start 3D Orbit. Right-click in the drawing area, and choose Projection ➤ Perspective. Exit 3D Orbit. This completes the view setup for the render (Figure A.28).

FIGURE A.28: The view ready to be rendered

Creating a Light Source

Here are AutoCAD's three kinds of lighting and their equivalents:

- ▶ Point Light: a hanging light bulb
- ▶ Distant Light: the sun
- ▶ Spotlight: a floodlight

Each has unique setup parameters. We'll set up a Distant light, which will light the cabin as the sun would. To do this, we have to march through a series of dialog boxes.

 1. Bring up the Render toolbar and let it float in the drawing area. On this new toolbar, click the Lights button. This brings up the Lights dialog box (Figure A.29).

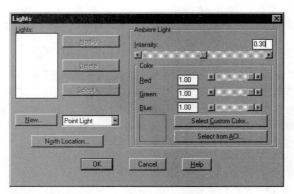

FIGURE A.29: The Lights dialog box

2. On the left side, next to the New button, open the drop-down list and select Distant Light. Then click the New button. The New Distant Light dialog box comes up (Figure A.30).

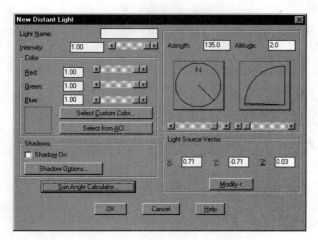

FIGURE A.30: The New Distant Light dialog box

3. Choose Sunlight for the Light Name, then click the Sun Angle Calculator button. This brings up the Sun Angle Calculator dialog box (Figure A.31).

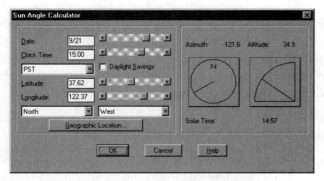

FIGURE A.31: The Sun Angle Calculator dialog box

4. Change the date to 9/8 and the time to 11:00, then click the Geographic Location button. This brings up the Geographic Location dialog box (Figure A.32).

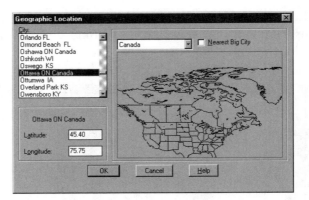

FIGURE A.32: The Geographic Location dialog box

5. In the drop-down list above the map, select North America. Then scroll down the list of cities on the left, and select San Francisco, CA. Click OK to close this dialog box.

6. Click OK twice more to get back to the Lights dialog box (see Figure A.29). In the Ambient Light area, change the intensity from .30 to .50. You can change the Intensity setting by using the scroll bar or by typing it in. Then click OK to return to your drawing.

Enabling Shadows

To control shadows, you have to make a few choices and adjust several settings. Shadows can be soft- or hard-edged, and are calculated by a couple of different methods. This part of the rendering process is too technical to go into in this book, but you can follow along and end up with at least one setup for shadows that will enhance the rendering of the cabin.

1. Click the Lights button on the Rendering toolbar to bring back the Lights dialog box.

2. With Sunlight highlighted, click the Modify button. This brings up the Modify Distant Light dialog box. It's almost identical to the New Distant Light dialog box in Figure A.30.

3. In the Shadows area, put a check mark in the Shadow On box. Then click the Shadow Options button. This brings up the Shadow Options dialog box (Figure A.33).

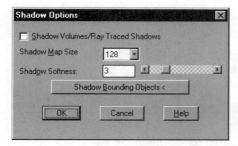

FIGURE A.33: The Shadow Options dialog box

4. Put a check mark in the Shadow Volumes/Ray Traced Shadows box, then click OK. This will give the shadows harder edges.

5. Click OK to return to the Lights dialog box. Then click OK again to return to the drawing. When we start to render, we will have a few more changes to make for the shadows.

The First Render

Let's make the adjustments for shadows and then make a preliminary render. Then we'll add a background and try again. First, we need to check our layers to be sure they are colors that render well. Below are listed the 3D layers and the colors that I have found work well with a white background in the drawing area for the rendering that we are setting up here.

Layer	Color	Layer	Color
3D-Balcony	24	3D-Roof	250
3D-Doors	34	3D-Roof-Edge	32
3D-Floor	42	3D-Steps	8
3D-Glass	132	3D-Walls	40
3D-Land	76	3D-Windows	22

These colors don't all match the colors that I instructed you to assign to these layers as we were building the 3D model earlier in the chapter. You can save the current assignments by using the Save State button in the Layer Properties Manager. Then, for the rendering, change the colors to match the table.

1. Click the Render button on the Render toolbar. This brings up the Render dialog box (Figure A.34).

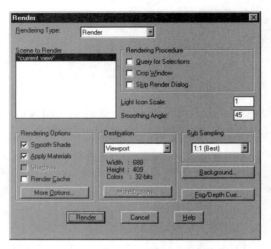

FIGURE A.34: The Render dialog box

2. At the top, be sure the Rendering Type drop-down list displays Photo Raytrace.

3. In the Rendering Options area, put a check mark in the Shadows box.

4. Click the Render button. After a few moments, the rendering appears (Figure A.35).

The building looks fine, but it would be nice to have something in the background other than the blank screen.

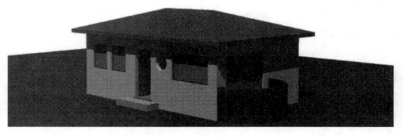

FIGURE A.35: The preliminary render

Controlling the Background of the Rendering

Some of the options in choosing a background for the rendering are:

▶ **The AutoCAD background:** That is what we used for the preliminary rendering.

▶ **Another solid color:** You use slide bars to choose it.

▶ **A gradient:** Varying colors (usually light to dark) blended together.

▶ **An image:** A bitmap image that you supply or choose.

We'll choose the last option and use a file that is supplied with AutoCAD.

 1. Click the Background button on the Render toolbar. This brings up the Background dialog box (Figure A.36).

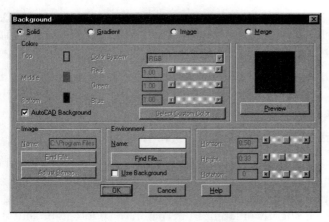

FIGURE A.36: The Background dialog box

2. The four radio buttons across the top determine the kind of background. Click the Image radio button; then, in the Image area, click the Find File button. This brings up the Background Image dialog box (Figure A.37). It's a Select File type of dialog box.

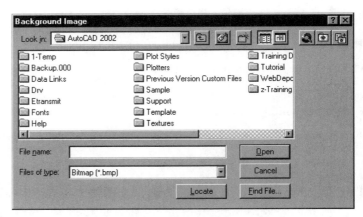

F I G U R E   A . 3 7 :   The Background Image dialog box

3. Navigate to the Textures subfolder of the AutoCAD 2002 folder. Open the Files of Type drop-down list and select the *.tga type. There are quite a few .tga files listed.

4. Find valley_1.tga and select it, then click Open. Back in the Background dialog box, the file and its path will be displayed in the Name text box in the Image area.

5. Click OK to close the Background dialog box.

6. Click the Render button on the Render toolbar, then click the Render button in the Render dialog box. Your rendering now has a photographic scene as a background (Figure A.38). The lighting on the cabin is slightly different from that in the photograph, but the overall effect works well enough.

Now you need to save this view and this rendering.

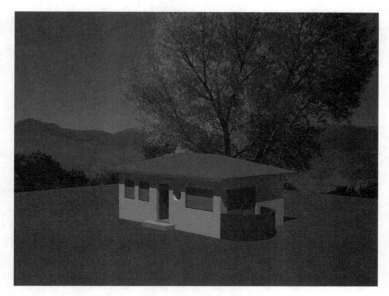

FIGURE A.38: The complete rendered scene

Saving a Rendering Setup

Two things need to be saved in order to recreate this rendering at a later time: the view that was set, and the light or lights that were used for the rendering. First we'll save the view, then we'll save the view and distant light as a *scene*.

1. Choose View ➤ Named Views to bring up the Views dialog box.

2. Click the New button. In the New View dialog box, enter **Render1** for the view name. Click the radio button for Current Display, then click OK. The view is saved and now displayed in the list of views. Click OK again to close the Views dialog box.

3. Click the Scenes button on the Render toolbar. The Scenes dialog box comes up. Click the New button. This brings up the New Scene dialog box. In the left box, views are listed; in the right, the one light we have set up (Figure A.39).

FIGURE A.39: The New Scene dialog box

4. Enter Scene_A in the Scene Name box. Then select Render1 under Views and Sunlight under Lights, then click OK. You are returned to the Scenes dialog box. Scene_A is now on the list (Figure A.40). Click OK.

Now you can change the view and add new lights to create a second scene.

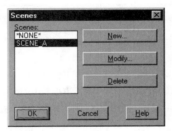

FIGURE A.40: The Scenes dialog box with Scene_A listed

Rendering to a File

The Render feature creates a rendering on the drawing area. The picture itself can't be saved (except by a screen grab), but we can re-render the scene to a file. Then it is saved and can be viewed by various applications.

1. Click the Render button on the Render toolbar. In the Render dialog box, go to the Destination area, open the drop-down list, and select File. Then click the More Options button that is in the same area. This brings up the File Output Configuration dialog box (Figure A.41).

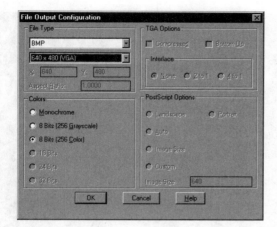

FIGURE A.41: The File Output Configuration dialog box

2. Set your preference for the file type, pixel size, color, etc., then click OK.

3. Back in the Render dialog box, click the Render button. This will bring up the Rendering File dialog box.

4. Designate a folder and a name, then click Open and Save. The Scene is rendered and saved to the chosen folder.

Try Another View

Let's finish by changing our view and turning off a layer to see a slightly different result.

1. Freeze the 3D-Glass layer.

2. Click the 3D Orbit button on the Standard toolbar.

3. Change the view of the cabin so that it's a little flatter and you can see through windows and doors into the cabin and out to the background scene.

4. Right-click and choose Projection ➢ Perspective. (It may already be selected.)

5. Right-click again and select Exit.

6. Click the Render button on the Render toolbar.

7. In the Destination area of the Render dialog box, open the drop-down list and select Viewport. Then click the Render button in the dialog box. AutoCAD renders this scene (Figure A.42).

FIGURE A.42: The second rendered scene

8. If the view or lighting needs modification, you can now change them and try another render. If you like the results, re-render the scene to a file. Save the view as a named view, and then save the view and lights as a Scene.

This has been a very brief introduction into the world of 3D and rendering in AutoCAD, but you should now be oriented to the general way of doing things and have enough tools to experiment further. For a more in-depth discussion of the entire process, including rendering, see *Mastering AutoCAD 2002* (Sybex, 2001) by George Omura.

Summary

This appendix is a brief introduction to 3D drawing and its concepts. The main features we've covered here are:

▶ Three methods of viewing a 3D model: Standard Isometric, Viewpoint Presets, and 3D Orbit

▶ A few of the basic solid modeling and surface modeling operations

▶ A summary of other solid and surface modeling techniques

▶ The User Coordinate System (UCS)

▶ Basic rendering operations

An Introduction to Attributes

ttributes are a special type of AutoCAD object made up of text that resides inside a block. Many architectural firms use the attribute feature for setting up title blocks, grids, and symbols. Since the content of attributes can be data, people involved in facilities management and interior design often use them when generating specifications for office partitions and furniture. Attributes are different from text in several ways, including these:

▶ The text content of attribute text can be extracted from an AutoCAD drawing and manipulated as data in a database, spreadsheet, or word processor.

▶ Attributes must be part of a block definition in order to function.

▶ Regular text that is part of a block has the same content for all instances of the block, whereas attribute text can be different in content for each instance of the block.

Attributes attach information in text form to blocks. Each time a block containing attributes is inserted, the user is prompted to enter data in the categories that have been set up with attributes in the block definition. In the AutoCAD drawing, each instance of the inserted block can contain data specific to that block.

Because attributes exist as part of a block, they have several applications in CAD drawings. They are frequently used to attach information to geometric objects that are blocked. Information that you would normally find in a door or window schedule can be stored with the individual doors or windows in the floor plan.

 N O T E A *schedule* is a chart in a drawing that contains logically organized information about a particular building component, such as doors, windows, or room finishes. Each of these would have its own schedule. Information in a door schedule, for example, might include size, material, finish, location, and type of jamb.

In fact, the information in schedules can be generated from the attributes in the drawing. Number or letter symbols in column grids are easier to set up and update with attributes than with the regular text you used when you created a structural grid for the cabin floor plan in Chapter 10, *Controlling Text in a Drawing*. Title blocks can be easily standardized for a project so that the text that is the same on each sheet uses regular text, and the text that might be different from sheet to sheet, such as sheet title, page number, date, scale, etc., will use attributes.

In this appendix, you'll have a chance to set up attributes for the grid you created in Chapter 10. Then you'll go through a set of exercises to learn a basic application for attributes, and you'll extract the information contained in the attributes that you create for the drawing.

Using Attributes for a Grid

The grid lines for a building usually are located at the centerlines of structural components, such as walls or columns. Columns in buildings can then be identified by the letter and number identifying the two grid lines intersecting at their location. In the Cabin drawing, we used grid lines to indicate the outside edge of exterior walls and the center lines of interior walls. Grids generally have a circle or hexagon with a number or letter in it at the end of each grid line, with the numbers running in one direction (horizontal or vertical) and letters in the other.

A very simple but handy use of attributes is to make the letter or number in the circle an attribute, then make a block out of the attribute and circle. By redoing the grid symbols in the cabin drawing, you will learn how attributes are set up.

1. Open Cabin10a. The drawing consists of the floor plan with a structural grid and the front elevation. Be sure the Grid layer is current.

2. Zoom into the floor plan, keeping the grid visible. In this case, the letters run horizontally across the top, and the numbers run vertically along the side.

3. Erase all the circles, letters, and numbers in the grid except those for *A* and *1*. Leave the grid lines intact (Figure B.1).

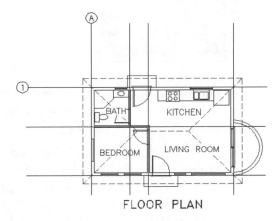

FIGURE B.1: The floor plan of Cabin10a with all but two grid symbols erased

4. Type li ↵ to start the List command. Select the letter *A*, then press ↵. The text window displays information about the text. You need to know the text style and height: Label and 1'-0".

5. Press F2 to return to the drawing, then erase the letters *A* and *1*, but not the circles.

6. Start the Scale command. Select the circle on the top and press ↵.

7. Use Endpoint Osnap and pick the endpoint of the grid line where it meets the circle. Type **1.25** ↵. The circle is enlarged.

8. Repeat steps 6 and 7 for the circle on the left side.

9. Choose Draw ➢ Block ➢ Define Attributes. The Attribute Definition dialog box appears. In the Attribute area, there are three text boxes: Tag, Prompt, and Value. The cursor is flashing in the Tag text box. Think of the letter in the grid circle. It's a grid letter: that's a *tag*.

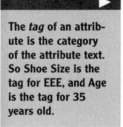

The *tag* of an attribute is the category of the attribute text. So Shoe Size is the tag for EEE, and Age is the tag for 35 years old.

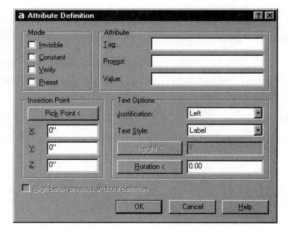

10. Type **grid_letter**. Don't press ↵. Press the Tab key to move to the Prompt text box. Here you enter a prompt for the future user who will be setting up a grid.

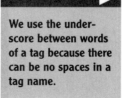

We use the underscore between words of a tag because there can be no spaces in a tag name.

11. Type **Enter grid letter**. Press Tab to move to the Value prompt. Here you enter a default or sample value to help the future user. You want it capitalized in this case, so enter **A**. This sets up the attribute so that the drafter setting up the grid will be prompted to enter the grid letter, and will be given a default of *A*. The *A* will let the user know it should be an uppercase letter.

12. The lower portion of the dialog box is where you set up parameters for the attribute text: location in the drawing, justification, text style, height, and rotation. Click the Justification drop-down list and select Middle.

13. Be sure Label is in the Text Style list box. If not, open the drop-down list and select Label. Since the Label text style has a height set to 12", the height text box in the Attribute Definition dialog box is faded out.

14. In the Insertion Point area, click the Pick Point button. This returns you to the drawing to pick an insertion point. Back in the drawing, use Center Osnap and click the circle at the top of the grid. You are returned to the dialog box.

15. Back in the Attribute Definition dialog box, click OK. GRID_LETTER is centered in the circle (Figure B.2).

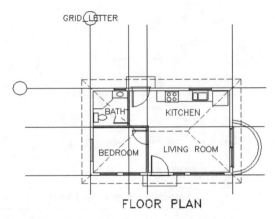

FIGURE B.2: The first attribute definition placed in the grid circle

The text in the circle is called the *attribute definition* and has a similar function in AutoCAD as a block definition. When you made the Win-1 block for the windows, the definition was a 12"-long window with an insertion point. When the Win-1 block was inserted, you could use the original block definition to make windows of various sizes. The same is true for the attribute definition. When it becomes part of a block that's inserted, the attribute can be any letter you like. You'll see that happen in just a minute. First, make a similar attribute definition for the numbered grid symbol.

1. Type att ↵ to start the Attribute definition command. The Attribute definition dialog box appears again.

2. Repeat steps 10 through 15 above, using the following guidelines:

   A. Enter grid_number for the Tag.

   B. Type **Enter grid number** for the prompt.

   C. Enter 1 for the value.

   D. Select Middle justification.

   E. Click the Pick Point button, use Center Osnap, and click the grid circle on the left.

   F. Click OK in the Attribute Definition dialog box.

The second attribute definition will be centered in the circle on the left side (Figure B.3).

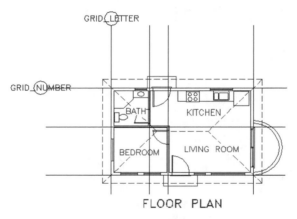

FIGURE B.3: The second attribute definition is placed.

You now have two attribute definitions and are ready to make each of them part of a block that will include the circle they are presently centered in.

Defining Blocks with Attributes

We have to define two blocks for the grid symbols and their attributes. The block used for the top of the grid will need its insertion point to be at the lowest point of the circle. The one for the left side will need its insertion point to be at the point on the circle furthest to the right.

1. Click the Make Block button on the Draw toolbar to start the block command. The Block Definition dialog box comes up.

2. In the Name drop-down list, enter **grid-v** (for vertical), then click the Pick Point button in the Base Point area.

3. In the drawing, use Endpoint Osnap and select the grid line that ends at the circle on top.

4. In the Block Definition dialog box, click the Select Objects button.

5. In the drawing, select the circle and attribute definition on the top. Press ↵.

6. In the Block Definition dialog box, be sure the Delete button is selected in the Objects area and click OK. The block is defined and includes the attribute definition. In the drawing, the top circle and attribute definition have been deleted.

7. Start the Block command again. Repeat steps 2 through 6 to define a second block for the circle and attribute definition on the left side. Use the following guidelines:

    A. Enter **grid-h** in the Block Name text box.

    B. Click Pick Point. Use Endpoint Osnap and pick the horizontal grid line that ends at the rightmost point of the grid circle on the left of the floor plan.

    C. When selecting objects, select the circle on the left and its block definition.

When you complete the command, you will have a second block definition that includes an attribute definition. Your drawing will look like Figure B.4.

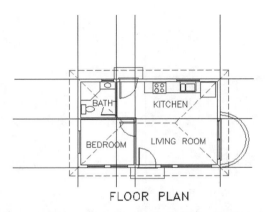

FLOOR PLAN

FIGURE B.4: The floor plan with grid circles and attribute definitions erased

Inserting Blocks with Attributes

Let's insert these blocks (which are now grid symbols) at the endpoints of the grid lines. As you insert them, we will assign them the appropriate letter or number.

1. Be sure the Endpoint Osnap is set to be running, then type **attdia** ↵.

2. If the value in the angle brackets is set to 0, press ↵. Otherwise, type 0 ↵.

3. In the Insert dialog box, open the Name drop-down list and select grid-v.

4. Be sure the Specify Onscreen box for Insertion point is checked, but not for Scale and Rotation. Click OK.

5. Click the leftmost vertical grid line in the drawing. Now look at the bottom line in the command window.

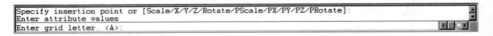

```
Specify insertion point or [Scale/X/Y/Z/Rotate/PScale/PX/PY/PZ/PRotate]:
Enter attribute values
Enter grid letter. <A>:
```

This is the text you entered in the Attribute Definition dialog box for the Prompt. *A* is the text you entered as the default value. To accept the default value for this grid line, press ↵.

6. The grid symbol is inserted at the endpoint of the leftmost vertical grid line (Figure B.5).

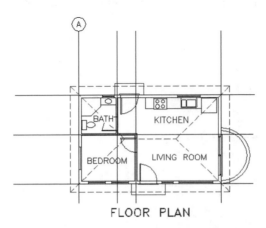

FLOOR PLAN

FIGURE B.5: The first grid symbol block is inserted.

7. Press ↵ to restart the Insert command. Click OK to accept grid-v as the current block to be inserted.

8. Click the grid line to the right of the one you just selected above.

9. At the `Enter grid letter <A>:` prompt, type **B** ↵. The second grid symbol is inserted on a grid line and the letter *B* is located in the circle.

10. Repeat steps 7 through 9 to insert the other two grid symbols across the top of the floor plan.

11. Keep repeating steps 7 through 9, but select the grid-h block for the three grid symbols that run down the left side of the floor plan. The results should look like Figure B.6.

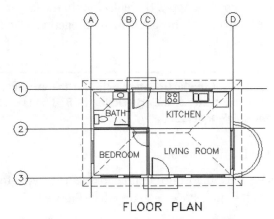

FIGURE B.6: The grid with all symbols inserted

Editing Attribute Text

To illustrate how attribute text can be edited, let's assume we decided to change the C grid symbol to B1. The D symbol will then have to be changed to C.

1. Double-click the C grid symbol. This starts the Ddatte command.

2. The Enhanced Attribute Editor dialog box appears. There are several things we can change here, but we want to change only the value.

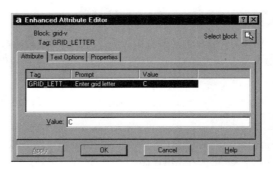

3. Be sure the Attribute tag is in front, then highlight C in the Value text box and type **B1**, then click Apply. B1 replaces C in the larger window where the tag, prompt, and value are displayed together. Click OK to close the dialog box.

 N O T E   Because you set the justification point for the attribute text to Middle and located it at the center of the grid circle, the B1 text is centered in the circle just like the single letters.

4. Double-click the D grid symbol.

5. In the Enhanced Attribute Editor dialog box, repeat step 3 to change the D to C. The attributes have been updated (Figure B.7).

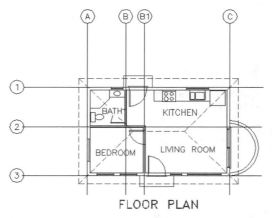

F I G U R E   B . 7 : The grid symbols after being updated

The above exercises have illustrated the basic procedure for defining, inserting, and changing attributes. You can apply these same procedures to the process of setting up a title block in which attributes are used for text that will change from one sheet to the next. You can download a supplemental section that shows how to use attributes in a title block at Sybex's Web site, www.sybex.com. Use the Catalog or Search tool to find this book, then click on Downloads. We can now move to a more complex application of the attribute feature to see its full power.

Setting Up Multiple Attributes in a Block

In the cabin, we have three rooms and a balcony, with the kitchen and living room sharing a room. Each room has a different area and floor covering. This information, along with the room name, can be stored in the drawing as attributes. We will set up a block that consists of three attributes (name, area, and covering). Then we'll insert the block back into the floor plan. If you remember, the text style for the room labels is LABEL. We'll use that for the attributes.

We have to erase the room labels for now, but it would be nice if we could mark where their justification points are. That way we can insert the attribute exactly where the label text is now.

1. With the Grid layer current, choose Format ➢ Point Style on the pull-down menus. This brings up the Point Style dialog box.

2. Click the fourth point style example in the second row down. It's the one with the circle and the ×. Then click OK to close the dialog box.

3. Set Insertion Osnap to be running, then click the Point button on the Draw toolbar. Place the cursor on the LIVING ROOM text. When the Insertion symbol appears at the lower-left corner, click. Don't end the command yet.

4. Repeat this for the BEDROOM and BATH labels. We don't need one for the KITCHEN because it will remain as is and have no attributes. The balcony doesn't have text in this drawing, so we can place the attribute anywhere we want. Click Esc to end the Point command.

5. Erase the Living Room, Bedroom, and Bath labels. The drawing should look like Figure B.8.

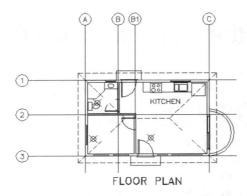

F I G U R E B . 8 : The floor plan with markers for insertion points and three room labels erased

6. Make the 0 layer current. Choose Draw ➤ Block ➤ Define Attributes. The Ddattdef command starts and the Attribute Definition dialog box appears.

7. For the tag, enter **rm_name**. For the prompt, type **Room name**. For the value, enter **LIVING ROOM**. (This default value will remind the user to use all uppercase letters.)

8. In the bottom half of the dialog box where the settings for the text are, everything is going to stay the same, so go to the Insertion Point area and click Pick Point.

9. In the drawing, use Endpoint Osnap and click the right end of the grid line that has the number *1* in the circle. In the dialog box, click OK. The first attribute definition is placed in the drawing (Figure B.9). Since we're going to make a block out of it and reinsert it into the rooms, we don't have to place the attribute definition where the room labels are; any place on the edge of the drawing is fine.

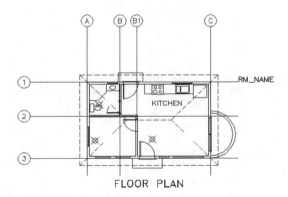

FIGURE B.9: The room name attribute definition placed in the drawing

10. Press ↵ to restart the Ddattdef command. For this attribute, in the Tag text box, enter **rm_area**. For the prompt, type **Area of room**, and for the value, enter **10.00 Sq. Ft.** This will show the user the proper format for the area.

11. In the Mode area, click to activate Invisible. The Invisible mode will make the attribute values invisible in the drawing, but they are still stored there.

12. In the lower-left corner of the dialog box, click the check box next to Align Below Previous Attribute Definition. All the text options fade out. The style will be the same as the first attribute, and this attribute definition will be placed right below the first one.

13. Click OK. The second attribute definition is placed in the drawing below the first one.

14. Repeat steps 10 through 13 to define the third attribute. For the tag, enter **rm_floor**. For the prompt, type **Floor Material**. For the value, enter **Wood Parquet**. Be sure the Invisible mode is still checked, and put a check mark in the Align Below Previous Attribute Definition box, if one isn't already there. Click OK. All three attribute definitions are now in the drawing (Figure B.10).

Now we will make a block out of the three attributes.

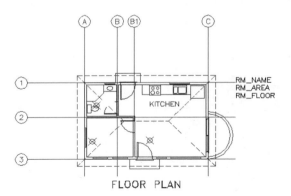

FIGURE B.10: The floor plan with all three attribute definitions

Defining a Block with Multiple Attributes

A block with attributes usually includes lines or other geometrical objects along with the attribute definitions, but it doesn't have to. In this case, the three attribute definitions are the sole content of the block, and the block's insertion point will be the justification point for the first attribute, the room label text.

1. Start the Block command.

2. In the Block Definition dialog box, enter **room_info** for the Name.

3. Click the Pick Point button. In the drawing, use Insertion Osnap and choose the first attribute definition. This aligns the justification point of this attribute with the insertion point of the block.

4. Back in the Block Definition dialog box, click the Select Objects button. In the drawing, pick each attribute definition in the order you created them. By selecting them in this order, they will be listed in the Enter Attributes dialog box in the same order. Press ↵ after selecting them, then click OK in the dialog box. The Room_Info block is defined, and the attribute definitions are deleted from the drawing.

You are almost ready to insert the Room_Info block in each of the three rooms and near the balcony. But first you need to calculate the area of each room.

Calculating Areas

You can calculate areas in a drawing by using the *Area command*. Because area calculations are made over and over again in design and construction, the Area command is an important tool. You can calculate an overall area and then subtract sub-areas from it, or you can add sub-areas together to make a total. For this exercise, you will use the command to simply calculate the areas of the four floor spaces in the floor plan. You will need to write down the areas after you make the calculations.

1. Type **undo** ↵, then type **m** ↵. This places a marker at the end of the sequence of steps you have been following up to now. After the next series of steps, you will undo the results until your drawing returns to the state it's in right now.

2. Make the Walls layer current. Turn off all the other layers, except Balcony and Walls. Your drawing should look like Figure B.11.

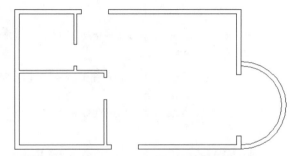

FIGURE B.11: The floor plan with all layers turned off except Walls and Balcony

3. Set the Osnaps so that Endpoint is the only one running.

4. Right-click any toolbar button. Select Inquiry from the toolbar menu. This brings up the Inquiry toolbar. Move it to a blank portion of the drawing area.

5. Click the Area button on the Inquiry toolbar. Be careful—it looks like the Region/Mass Properties button. At the Specify first corner point or [.tif][Object /Add /Subtract]: prompt, click the four inside corners of the bathroom, moving around the perimeter, then press ↵. The command line will display the results of your calculation: Area = 5616.00 square in. (39.0000 square ft.), Perimeter = 25'-0".

6. Write down the area in square feet. Press ⏎ to restart the Area command and click the four inside corners of the bedroom. (It might be helpful to zoom in closer to pick the corners.) Press ⏎. The command line displays the area and perimeter. The area should be 76.2222 square feet. Write this number down (you can shorten it to two decimal places).

7. Repeat this for the living room, where you will have to pick six points. The area should be 236.6667 square feet. Write down 236.67.

8. Restart the Area command. Type o ⏎ to select the Object option of the Area command, then click the inside arc of the balcony. You will get this message in the Command window: `Selected object does not have an area`. The arc must be converted to a polyline to have its area calculated.

9. Press Esc to cancel the Area command. Choose Modify ➤ Object ➤ Polyline to start the Pedit command.

10. Click the inside arc of the balcony. The prompt now reads `Object selected is not a polyline Do you want to turn it into one? <Y>`. Press ⏎ to accept the default of Yes. Then type x ⏎ to exit the Pedit command.

11. Now you can click the Area button on the Inquiry toolbar to restart the Area command.

12. Type o ⏎ to use the Object option, then click the inside arc again. You will get a calculation this time of 31.8086 square feet. Write down 31.81.

13. Type undo ⏎, then type b ⏎. The drawing is restored to the state it was in back at step 1.

14. Click the × box in the corner of the Inquiry toolbar to close it.

The area of polyline arcs will be calculated as if a straight line were drawn across the open side between endpoints of the arc.

N O T E   The Add and Subtract options in the Area command prompt allow you to add areas together that you have calculated, and to subtract areas from each other. If you are going to add or subtract areas, type A ⏎ after you start the command. Then, after each calculation you make, you will be given the Add and Subtract options. If you don't enter an *A* at the beginning, you can make only one calculation at a time.

Inserting the Room_Info Block

You have four areas calculated and recorded, and are ready to insert the room_info block. When we inserted the grid symbols as blocks with attributes earlier in this appendix, the prompts for the attribute text were displayed in the Command window. With multiple attributes in a block, it is more convenient to display all the prompts in a dialog box. Let's change the setting that makes the dialog box replace the command prompts.

1. Make the Text1 layer current. Then type **attdia** ⏎. At the prompt, type 1 ⏎. This will enable the dialog box containing the prompts.

2. Select Insert ➤ Block. In the Insert dialog box, select room_info from the Name drop-down list. Click OK. Set Node Osnap to be the only one running. Select the point that marks the justification point for the Living Room label text. This brings up the Enter Attributes dialog box.

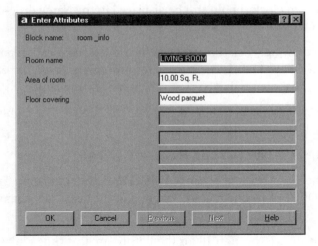

3. In the Enter Attributes dialog box, the only change that needs to be made is the value for Room Area. The defaults are correct for the other two.

4. Press the Tab key to highlight the Area of Room box and type **236.67** Sq. Ft. Click OK.

5. The room_info block is inserted into the drawing in the living room. The room label is the only visible attribute (Figure B.12). We set the other two to be invisible.

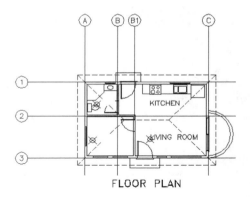

FLOOR PLAN

FIGURE B.12: The first room_info block is inserted.

6. Press ↵ to restart the Insert command. In the Insert dialog box, the room_info block should still be displayed in the Name drop-down list. Click OK.

7. In the drawing, click the point that marks the justification point of the BEDROOM text label. The same three prompts as before appear in the Enter Attributes dialog box with the same default values.

8. LIVING ROOM is highlighted. Type **BEDROOM** ↵. The highlight bar drops down to the next prompt.

9. For the area, type **76.22 Sq. Ft.** ↵.

10. For the Floor Material, change Wood Parquet to **Linoleum Tile**, then click OK. The second block is inserted in the bedroom. Again, only the room label text is visible.

11. Repeat steps 6 through 10 for the Bathroom, this time replacing the existing text with **BATH, 39.00 Sq. Ft.,** and **Ceramic Tile.**

12. Repeat steps 6 through 10 for the Balcony, this time using **BALCONY, 31.81 Sq. Ft.,** and **Wood Plank.** For the Specify insertion point prompt, place the Balcony label outside the balcony, a little above the midpoint of the arcs.

13. Erase the points you used to locate the insertion points. Your drawing will look like Figure B.13.

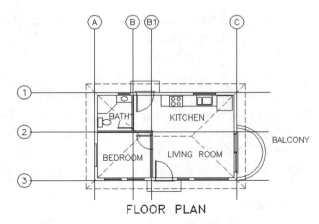

FIGURE B.13: All Room_Info blocks inserted

Controlling the Visibility of Attributes

The floor plan looks the same as it did at the beginning of this exercise, except for the addition of the balcony label. But there's more in it than meets the eye. What was regular text is now an attribute, and your drawing is "smarter" than it was before.

1. Choose View ➤ Display ➤ Attribute Display ➤ On. The invisible attributes are displayed with the room labels (Figure B.14).

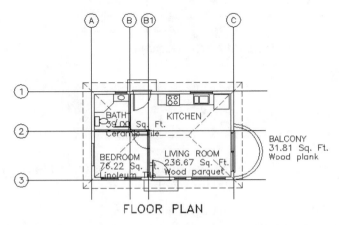

FIGURE B.14: The floor plan with all attributes displayed

2. Press ↵ to restart the Attdisp command, then type **off** ↵. All attributes disappear, including the room labels and the letters and numbers in the grid symbols.

3. Press ↵. Type **n** ↵ to change the setting back to Normal. Along with the room labels, the grid numbers and letters reappear. On and Off settings make all attributes visible or invisible, regardless of what was set for the visible/invisible mode in the attribute definition. The Normal setting allows attributes to be displayed only if the visible/invisible mode was set to visible in their definition.

Editing Attributes

Once attributes have been defined and inserted as blocks, you can easily edit any value using the same method you used at the beginning of this appendix to modify a grid number.

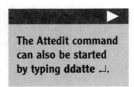

The Attedit command can also be started by typing ddatte ↵.

1. Choose Modify ➢ Object ➢ Attribute ➢ Single to start the Attedit command. Select the Living Room label. The Enhanced Attribute Editor dialog box appears, displaying both the visible and invisible attributes' values for the living room, along with their tags and prompts. You can now change any of the values. When you highlight an attribute, its value is displayed in the Value text box, where you can edit it.

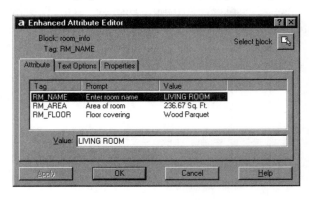

2. We won't make any changes right now. Press Cancel to cancel the Attedit command and return to the drawing.

3. Save this drawing in your training folder as CabinB1.

You can also edit more than one attribute at a time by using the –Attedit command. (The dash in front indicates that this is an older version of the Attedit command.) Start the command by choosing Modify ➢ Attribute ➢ Global, or by typing **atte** ↵. The prompt will read Edit attributes one at a time? [Yes/No] <Y>. If you accept the default of Yes, you will be taken through a series of options for selecting attributes to edit. Select the attributes to edit. A large × will appear at the insertion point of one of the selected attributes. At this point, you get the following prompt: Enter an option [Value/Position/Height/Angle/Style/ Layer/Color/ Next] <N>:, allowing you to modify any of the characteristics listed in the prompt above for the attribute with the ×. Press ↵ to move to the next selected attribute.

If you respond to the first prompt with No, you will be taken through a similar set of selection options. Then you are asked to enter a current value to be changed, and to enter the new value after the change. Values of attributes can be changed globally by using the –Attedit command in this way.

If you double-click an attribute definition, a dialog box appears that lets you modify the tag, prompt, and default value of the definition. The Properties dialog box can be used to edit all the properties of an attribute definition before it has become part of a block definition. Use the Block Attribute Manager (choose Modify ➤ Object ➤ Attribute ➤ Block Attribute Manager) to modify properties of attributes that are already part of a block definition.

In the last section, you will go through an exercise that will demonstrate how the information that attributes hold can be extracted from an AutoCAD drawing and used in other applications. The room information from this drawing will be extracted to a text file.

Extracting Data from an AutoCAD Drawing

The extraction process allows you to copy attribute data from a drawing and put it into a text file, from which it can be inserted into a database, word processor, spreadsheet, or even another AutoCAD drawing. You have to set up a template file to control the form in which the data is placed when it comes out of the drawing. If you are familiar with databases, think of the attribute tag as the column or field of a database, and the values as records or rows. The template file sets up the columns by allowing them to be a certain width, and controls whether the data in the rows is considered numerical data or not.

We need to set up a template file for the four attributes that have information about the rooms. We will end up with a text file that has three columns, one for each attribute, and four rows, one for each room that has attribute data. This text file will be based on the template file, which we will create first.

Creating a Template File for Data Extraction

1. Minimize AutoCAD and open the Notepad program that comes with your Windows operating system. (It can be found in the Accessories folder when you choose Start ➤ Programs.) Notepad opens with a blank page and a flashing cursor.

2. Type **RM_NAME C015000** ↵ **RM_AREA C020000** ↵ **RM_FLOOR C020000** ↵. That's it. Be sure to press ↵ once, and only once, after typing the last line. You should have three lines of text.

3. Choose File ➤ Save As and save this file as Room-1 in your training folder. It will be saved as Room-1.txt.

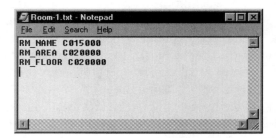

Take a moment to look at the new template file. Each line of text contains an attribute tag and a code. The code has three parts: the letter, the first three numbers, and the last three. The letter has to be a *C* or an *N*. This means the value of the attribute is treated either as a character or as a number. In this exercise, we will consider all values for the three attributes as characters, whether they are numbers or letters.

Attribute values that are numbers can be treated in the extraction process as either characters or numbers. If they are considered numerical, they could be added together in a database or spreadsheet program. But since we included the words *Sq. Ft.*, we need to treat them as characters.

The first three spaces following the *C* are where you enter the width you need for this field in the table, from 0 to 999 characters. Our columns will be 15, 20, and 20 characters wide.

The last three spaces are where you enter the number of decimal places a numerical value can have, from 0 to 999. Since we have no numerical data, we leave this at 0.

Extracting Attribute Data

The next step is to perform the actual extraction.

1. Minimize Notepad and return to AutoCAD.

2. Type attext ↵. The Attribute Extraction dialog box appears.

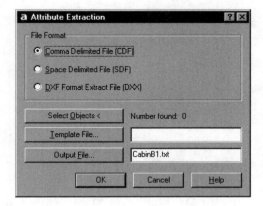

You will accomplish five tasks with this dialog box:

▶ Choose one of the three extraction file formats.

▶ Select the template file you just made.

▶ Select an output file name and folder.

▶ Select objects in the drawing for the extraction to operate on.

▶ Execute the extraction.

3. Select the Space Delimited File (SDF) radio button. This mode will separate the columns of data with spaces.

4. Click the Template File button. Find the Room-1.txt file and click Open. The file will be displayed in the text box next to the Template File button.

5. By default, the Output File will be a .txt file with the same name as the current drawing file, in this case, CabinB1.txt. You will have to direct AutoCAD to save this file to your training folder, so click the Output File button and do that. Click Save.

6. Click the Select Objects button. In your drawing, window the floor plan (Include the BALCONY text, but do not select the grid numbers and letters.) and press ↵. The Attribute Extraction dialog box will look like this:

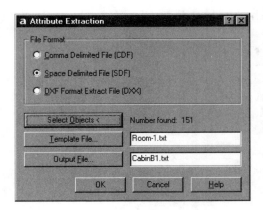

The `Number Found:` listing will vary, depending on how much of your drawing you selected.

7. Click OK. The Command window will say, for example, `4 records in extract file`. This tells you that the extraction was a success.

8. Minimize AutoCAD and bring up Notepad again. Choose File ➤ Open, then find and open `CabinB1.txt`. It will look like this:

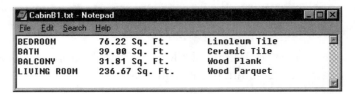

There are four rows of text. Each row contains the three pieces of information about a room: name, area, and covering. In this format, you can use Windows copy-and-paste tools to insert this as a schedule in the AutoCAD drawing or as a table in a word processor. Any text inserted into AutoCAD is placed as multiline text. Then it can be exploded into single-line text and moved around. As easy as this is to do, it is difficult to line up the columns of data using this method. Use the process described next to link an Excel spreadsheet of extracted data back into an AutoCAD drawing.

To insert extracted data into a database or spreadsheet application, use the Comma Delimited File format in the Attribute Extraction dialog box. This will give you output like this:

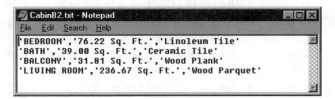

There are four rows of data. The three pieces of data in each row are separated by commas and are in quotes. This format works well for databases and spreadsheets, though it is obviously difficult to read and would not make a good schedule or table in this form. Once imported into Excel, however, the data can be made visible in an AutoCAD drawing as a schedule, through a linking process known as OLE (Object Linking and Embedding). The data can then be updated in Excel, and the changes will show up in the AutoCAD drawing.

Summary

This has been a quick tour of the various features of attributes and the commands used to set them up, modify them, and extract the data they contain. As well as being used for grid symbols and room, window, and door schedules, attributes are widely used in standardized title blocks. One of the most frequent uses of attributes is in facilities management and interior design. Every piece of office furniture in a building can be specified with attributes. The data can then be extracted and sent to a furniture specifier who will input the data into their databases and complete the order. The big office furniture manufacturers sell their own proprietary software that works with AutoCAD and automatically sets up attributes when you insert their blocks of the furniture, which they have pre-drawn and included in the software package.

Attributes are also being used more and more in maps drawn in AutoCAD, which are then imported into Geographical Information System (GIS) software, a powerful analysis and presentation tool. When map features, such as buildings, are blocks containing an attribute, such as a building number, they are transformed in the GIS program in such a way that linkages can be set up between the map features (buildings) and database tables that contain information about the map features. In this way, analyses can be performed on the database tables and the results are automatically displayed graphically on the map. (For example, you could quickly locate all buildings that have a total area greater than a specified square footage.)

In this appendix, you were introduced to the AutoCAD tools used for setting up and modifying attributes, and saw several ways they can be used in an AutoCAD drawing. You also looked at an advanced application for attributes—data extraction—and reviewed a couple of possible uses for that process. Finally, you learned how this feature is used in mapping and facility management. If you continue to work with attributes, you will find them to be a powerful tool and a way to link information in your AutoCAD drawing to other applications.

GLOSSARY

3D mesh

A set of adjacent flat surfaces that together form a geometrical depiction of a three-dimensional curved surface.

3D model

An AutoCAD drawing file containing Auto-CAD *objects* that occupy 3D space and represent building components or geometrical objects in the real world.

A

Absolute coordinates

Values for locating a point in space that describe its distance and direction from the *origin* (0,0,0) point of the drawing.

Alias

A shortcut for starting commands. It is a set of one or two letters that can be entered at the *command line* instead of the full command.

Aligned dimension

A linear dimension measuring the distance between two points. The dimension line for an aligned dimension is parallel to a line between the two points.

Angular dimension

A dimension that measures the angle between two lines or the angle inscribed by an arc segment.

Angular unit

The unit in which angle values are displayed. The choices are decimal degrees, degrees-minutes-seconds, grads, radians, or surveyor's units.

Associative dimension

A dimension that updates automatically when the object being dimensioned changes size.

Associative hatch pattern

A hatch pattern that updates automatically when the shape of the hatched area is modified.

Attribute

An *object* inside a *block* that contains text data. The value of an attribute (*attribute value*) is specified when the block is inserted.

Attribute definition

A special AutoCAD *object* that is included in a *block definition* so that varying text information can be included in the *block reference* when a block is inserted in a drawing.

Attribute extraction file

A text file in which extracted attribute data is stored.

Attribute extraction template file

A text file (.txt) that is used to organize the data in an *attribute extraction file*.

Attribute prompt

The part of the *attribute definition* that instructs the user what to enter at the *command line* or in a dialog box when they are entering *attribute values*.

Attribute tag

A part of the *attribute definition* that represents the field of the table into which attribute data is extracted.

Attribute value

The data that is the content of an attribute. It is always text and appears in the record or rows of the table into which attribute data is extracted.

AutoCAD object

See *Object*.

AutoSnap

A feature of AutoCAD that works with the Object Snap tools by displaying a symbol on the places in the drawing that can be snapped to. Each of these *Object Snap modes* has a different *AutoSnap* symbol. The symbol appears when the cursor is near a location where the active Object Snap can be used.

B

Baseline dimension

A dimensioning option that allows you to do multiple measurements from a designated baseline.

Base point

1. The initial point of reference for a number of modify commands, including Copy, Move, Rotate, Stretch, and Scale. 2. The insertion point for a drawing, as designated by the Base command.

Bearings

See *Surveyor's units*.

Blip marks

Small crosses which, when enabled, mark points in the *drawing area* that have been picked or specified, and where objects have been selected.

Block

See *Block reference*.

Block definition

The description of a grouping of AutoCAD objects that is stored with the drawing file and includes a name, an *insertion point*, and a listing of objects in the grouping.

Block reference

An instance of a grouping of objects that is inserted into a drawing and is based on the block definition for that grouping. Casually called a *block*.

Bylayer

A property that can be assigned to colors and linetypes so that objects will receive their color and linetype properties according to the layer they are on.

C

Cartesian coordinate system

A 2D system of locating points on a plane. It uses a horizontal (x) and a vertical (y) component to locate a point relative to the 0,0 point, or origin.

Command line

A text window at the bottom of the screen that displays command prompts. This is where you see what you are entering through the keyboard. Also called the *command window*.

Command: prompt

The prompt at the *command line*, when no commands are currently running.

Command window

See *Command line*.

Continued dimension

A dimensioning option that allows you to place sequential dimensions that are adjacent to each other so that the dimension lines are aligned.

Context menu

A menu that appears on the drawing area and contains options relevant to what the user is doing at that moment. Also called a *shortcut menu* or a *right-click menu*.

Crosshair cursor

A form of the *cursor* that consists of a horizontal line and a vertical line intersecting at their midpoints, resembling the crosshair in a sighting device.

Crossing window

A selection tool that selects an area defined by two points acting as opposite corners of a rectangle. All objects within or crossing the rectangle are selected.

Current UCS

The User Coordinate System that is active in a drawing. It determines the positive *x*, *y*, and *z* directions. See also *User Coordinate System*.

Cursor

The pointing symbol on the computer monitor that is moved by moving the mouse. It can appear as, among other things, an arrow, a *pickbox*, and a *crosshair*.

Cutting edge

The role certain objects can be temporarily assigned to play in a trimming operation. If an object is designated as a cutting edge, lines or other objects being trimmed will be trimmed back to the point where they intersect the cutting edge.

Cycling

A procedure for selecting a particular line when it coincides with one or more lines. It's done by holding down the Ctrl key and selecting the lines over and over until the one you want is selected.

D

Default

A value or option in a command that will be used unless you designate otherwise. In AutoCAD, default values and options are enclosed in angle brackets (< >).

Dimension style

A collection of settings for *dimension variables* that is saved in a drawing under a specified name. Dimensions placed in the drawing will follow the settings of the current dimension style.

Dimension text

The text in a dimension. It expresses the measurement that the dimension is displaying.

Dimension variables

A group of settings and values that control the appearance of dimensions in AutoCAD.

Direct Entry

An option for specifying the next point in a series of points, by using the cursor to indicate direction and the keyboard to enter the distance from the last point.

Docking

Relocating a toolbar or a window to a place outside the *drawing area* so it won't interfere with the AutoCAD drawing or other items on the screen.

Donut

A command on the Draw menu that draws filled rings, like the donut pastry. If you specify an inside diameter of 0, it draws a filled circle.

Drawing area

The portion of the monitor screen where you draw objects and view your drawing.

Drawing extents

The minimum rectangular area with the same proportions as your *drawing area* that will enclose all visible objects in your drawing. When you *Zoom* to Extents, the rectangular area fills the drawing area.

Drawing limits

The area in a drawing that is covered by the *grid*. It can be defined by the user. It is stored as the coordinates of the lower-left and upper-right corners of the rectangular area covered by the *grid*.

Drawing units

The intervals of linear and angular measurements chosen for use in a drawing.

Dwg

The file extension and format for the standard AutoCAD drawing.

E

Edge

1. The side of a *3D face* or a *3D mesh*. 2. A command for controlling the visibility of the edges of 3D faces.

Elevation view

A view of a building that viewers get when they look at it horizontally, perpendicular to an interior or exterior wall.

Entity

See *Object*.

Explode

A command to undo a grouping of objects. It can be used on blocks, *multiline text, polylines*, and dimensions. Exploded multiline text becomes single-line text. Exploded polylines become lines. Exploded blocks become the individual objects that make up the block.

External reference

A drawing file that has been temporarily attached to another drawing for read-only purposes. Also called an Xref.

External reference host file

The drawing file to which *external references* have been attached.

Extrusion

1. A 2D object that has been given *thickness*. 2. A 3D solid object created with the Extrude command, by sliding a closed 2D shape along a path that is usually perpendicular to the 2D shape. If you use the Path option of the Extrude command, the extrusion need not be perpendicular to the 2D shape.

F

Face

A triangular or four-sided flat surface that is the basic unit of a 3D surface.

Fill

A display mode that can be set to on or off. When it is set to on, it displays a solid color for shapes made with wide *polylines*, 2D solids, *donuts*, and *hatch patterns* using the Solid pattern. When it is set to off, the solid color area is invisible and only the boundary of the fill is displayed.

Floating toolbar

A toolbar that is located in the drawing area. It can be moved around by dragging its title bar.

Floating viewports

Rectangular windows created in the *Paper space* of a drawing that allows you to view a drawing in *Model space*.

Font

A group of letters, numbers, and other symbols all sharing common features of design and appearance.

Freeze

The Off portion of a setting called Freeze/Thaw that controls the visibility of objects on *layers* and determines whether AutoCAD calculates the geometry of these objects during a *regeneration*.

G

Ghosting

The fuzzy or hazy appearance that a line or other object takes on when it's been selected.

Graphical User Interface

See *Graphics window*.

Graphics window

The appearance of your screen when Auto-CAD is running. It consists of the *drawing area* and surrounding *toolbars*, *menu bars*, *command window*, and *status bar*. Also called the *Graphical User Interface*.

Grid

1. A drawing aid that consists of a regularly spaced set of dots in the *drawing area*. 2. A series of horizontal and vertical lines in a floor plan or section that locate the main structural elements of a building, such as columns and walls. Also called a *column grid* or a *structural grid*.

Grips

An editing tool that allows you to perform five modify commands on selected objects without having to start the commands themselves. When grips are enabled, small squares appear on selected objects. By clicking a square, you activate the first of the available commands. You can cycle through the rest of the commands by pressing the spacebar.

H

Hatch patterns

Patterns of lines, dots, and other shapes that fill in a closed area.

Host file

See *External reference host file*.

Hyperlink

An electronic connection between an Auto-CAD object and any of several places, including: another drawing, a Word document, a Web site, etc.

I

Icon

One of a set of small pictures on a toolbar. When the cursor rolls across an icon, it takes on the appearance of being a picture on a button.

Insertion point

A reference point that is part of a *block* and is used to locate the block when it is inserted into a drawing. It is attached to the cursor while a block is being inserted. Once a block has been inserted, use the Insertion *Osnap* to snap to the insertion point of the block.

Isometric view

A view of a 3D object in which all lines that are parallel on the object appear parallel in the view. See also *Perspective view*.

J

Jamb

A surface that forms the side or top of an opening for a door or window in a wall.

Justification Point

A reference point on a line of single-line text, or a body of multiline text, that acts like the *insertion point* for blocks.

L

Layer

An organizing tool that operates like an electronic version of transparent overlays on a drawing board. Layers can be assigned color and *linetype*, and their visibility can be controlled.

Layout

An optional interface that serves as an aid to the user in setting up a drawing for printing. It rests "on top of" the *Model space* in which the drawing of the building resides. It contains the title block, notes, scale, and other information. Users view a drawing through openings in the layout called *viewports*. A single drawing file may have multiple layouts, one for each print to be made from the file. The layout interface is sometimes referred to as *Paper space*.

Layout tab

A tab at the lower-left corner of the drawing area that is used to switch from a *Model space* view of the drawing to a Layout view.

Limits

See *Drawing limits*.

Linetype

The style of appearance of a line. AutoCAD styles include continuous, dashed, dash-dot, etc.

Linetype scale

A numerical value for non-continuous linetypes that controls the size of dashes and spaces between dashes and dots. In an Auto-CAD drawing, a global linetype scale controls all non-continuous linetypes in the drawing, and an individual linetype scale can be applied to one or more selected lines.

Lineweight

The value of a line's width. AutoCAD offers 24 lineweights in a range from 0.00" to 0.083".

M

Menu bar

The set of drop-down menus at the top of the AutoCAD graphics window.

Mirror

This command makes a copy of selected objects and flips it around a specified line to produce a mirror image of those objects.

Mirror line

An imaginary line about which an object is flipped by the Mirror command.

Model space

The portion of an AutoCAD drawing that contains the lines representing the building or object being designed, as opposed to the notes and title block information, which are kept on a *Layout*.

Mtext

See *Multiline text*.

Multiline text

A type of text in which an entire body of text is grouped together as one object. Casually called *Mtext*, it can be edited with word-processing techniques. Individual characters or words in the Mtext can have different heights, fonts, and colors from the main body of Mtext. *Dimension text* is Mtext. When *exploded*, Mtext becomes *single-line text*.

N

Named view

A view of your drawing that is saved and given a name so that it can be restored later.

O

Object

A basic AutoCAD graphical element that is created and manipulated as part of the drawing, such as a line, arc, dimension, block, or text. Also called an *entity*.

Object Snap mode

Any of a set of tools for precisely picking strategic points on an *object*, including Endpoint, Midpoint, Center, etc. It is casually called *Osnap*.

Object Snap Tracking

See *Tracking*.

Origin

The point with the coordinates 0,0,0, where the x, y, and z axes all meet.

Orthogonal drawing

A system of creating views in which each view shows a different side of a building or object, such as top, front, left side, right side, etc.

Ortho mode

An on/off setting that, when on, forces lines to be drawn and objects to be moved in a horizontal or vertical direction only.

Osnap

See *Object Snap mode*.

Otrack

See *Tracking*.

P

Pan

A command that slides the current drawing around on the drawing area without changing the magnification of the view.

Paper space

A term sometimes used to refer to the interface for a drawing that contains *Layouts*.

Path

The hierarchy of drive, folder, and sub-folders where a file is stored, along with the file's name, such as C:\AutoCAD2002\Training\Cabin8a.dwg.

Perspective view

A view of a 3D object in which parallel lines that are not parallel to the plane of the screen appear to converge as they move further away from the viewer, similar to the way objects appear in the real world, such as railroad tracks in the distance. See also *Isometric view*.

Pickbox

A form of the cursor as a small square that occurs when AutoCAD is in *selection mode*.

Pick button

The button on the mouse (usually the left one) that is used to pick points, buttons, or menu items, as well as select objects in the drawing area.

Plan view

A view of a drawing in which the viewer is looking straight at the *xy plane* in a direction parallel to the *z* axis.

Plot style

A group of settings that are assigned to a layer, color, or object. The settings determine how that layer, color, or object is printed.

Plot style table

A set of plot styles that control the way in which a Layout or drawing is printed.

Point filters

A set of tools that allow you to specify a point in the drawing by using some of the *x*, *y*, and *z* coordinates from another point or points to generate the coordinates for the point you are specifying.

Polar tracking

A tool for temporarily aligning the cursor movement to preset angles while drawing. See also *Tracking*.

Polyline

A special type of line that (a) treats multiple segments as one object, (b) can include arcs, (c) can be smoothed into a curved line, and (d) can have width in 2D applications.

Precision of units

The decree of accuracy in which linear and angular units are displayed in dialog boxes, at the command line, or in dimensions.

Prompt

The text at the command line that asks questions or tells you what action is necessary to continue the execution of a command. The Command: prompt tells you that no command is presently running.

R

Redraw

A command to refresh the *drawing area* or a particular *viewport*, thereby ridding it of any *blip marks* or graphic distortions, that show up on the monitor while you're drawing.

Regeneration

A process in which the geometry for the objects in the current drawing file is recalculated.

Regular window

A selection tool that selects an area defined by two points acting as opposite corners of a rectangle. All objects completely within the rectangle are selected. See also *Crossing window*.

Relative coordinates

Values for locating a point in space that describe its distance and direction from the last point picked in the drawing rather than from the *origin*.

Right-click menu

See *Context menu*.

Rubberbanding

The effect of a line extending between the last point picked and the crosshair cursor, stretching like a rubber band as the cursor is moved.

Running Object Snap

An *Object Snap mode* that has been set to be continually activated until turned off.

S

Scale factor

The number that expresses the *true ratio* of a scale. For example, 48 is the scale factor for quarter-inch scale (¼" = 1'-0").

Selection mode

The phase of a command that requires the user to select objects, and thereby build up a *selection set* of objects, to be modified by or otherwise used in the function of the command.

Selection set

Any object or group of objects that have been selected for modification, or have been selected to be used in a modification process.

Selection window

A tool for selecting objects whereby the user creates a rectangular window in the *drawing area* and objects are selected in two ways, depending on whether the selection window is a *crossing window* or a *regular window*.

Shortcut menu

See *Context menu*.

Single-line text

A type of text *object* in AutoCAD in which each line of text is treated as a single object, with its own *justification point*, whether it be a sentence, word, or letter.

Snap mode

An on/off setting that locks the cursor onto a spatial grid, which is usually aligned with the *grid*, allowing you to draw to distances that are multiples of the grid spacing. When the grid spacing is set to 0, the grid aligns with the snap spacing.

Soffit

The underside of the roof overhang that extends from the outside edge of the roof, back to the wall.

Stud

A vertical piece of lumber or metal used in framing walls. It is usually 2" × 4" or 2" × 6" in cross dimension and extends the height of the wall.

Surveyor's units

An angular unit of direction in which the value is the angle that the direction deviates away–or "bears"–from true north or south, toward the east or west.

T

Template drawing

A drawing that has been set up to serve as a format for a new drawing. This allows the user to begin a new drawing with certain parameters already set up, because various settings have been predetermined.

Text style

A collection of settings that controls the appearance of text and is saved in a drawing under a specified name. Text placed in the drawing will follow the settings of the current text style.

Thaw

The On portion of a setting called Freeze/ Thaw that controls the visibility of objects on *layers* and determines whether AutoCAD calculates the geometry of these objects during a *regeneration*.

Thickness

The distance a 2D object is *extruded* in a direction perpendicular to the plane in which it was originally drawn, resulting in a 3D object. For a floor plan of a building, wall lines can be extruded to a thickness that is the wall's actual height.

Tracking

The process by which the user sets up temporary points or angles as guides for the cursor, used to locate desired points in the process of drawing. *Object Snap Tracking* (or *Otrack*) creates the temporary points, and *Polar Tracking* sets the angles.

Tracking points

The temporary points that are set up for use in Object Snap Tracking. See also *Tracking*.

Transparent command

A command that can be executed while another command is running, without interfering with the running command. Display commands, such as Zoom and Pan, are transparent.

True ratio

An expression of two numbers that defines the actual size differentiation in a scale, i.e., the number of units represented by a single unit. See also *Scale factor*.

U

UCS

See *User Coordinate System*.

UCS icon

The double-arrow icon in the lower-left corner of the *drawing area* that indicates the positive directions of the x and y axes for the current *User Coordinate System*. In 3D views, the z axis is also represented in the icon.

User Coordinate System (UCS)

A definition for the orientation of the x, y, and z axes in space relative to 3D objects in the drawing or to the *World Coordinate System*. UCSs can be named, saved, and restored.

V

View

A picture of the current drawing from a particular user-defined perspective that is displayed on the screen or in a *viewport*. Views may be named, saved, and restored.

Viewport

A rectangular window through which the user can view their drawing or a portion of it. There are two kinds of viewports: *tiled viewports* (used in *Model space*) and *floating viewports* (used in *Layouts*).

W

Wireframe

The representation of a 3D object with lines that represent the intersections of planes or the corners of walls and other building components.

World Coordinate System

The default *User Coordinate System* for all new drawing files, in which the positive directions for the x and y axes are to the right and upwards, respectively, and in which the positive direction for the z axis is toward the user and perpendicular to the plane of the screen.

Wysiwyg

An acronym for "what you see is what you get." It's a description applied to preview features that show you exactly what a screen will look like when printed.

X

XY plane

The 2D flat surface, defined by the x and y axes, which is parallel to the monitor screen in a new AutoCAD drawing file.

Z

Zoom

The name of a command with several options, all of which allow the user to increase or decrease the magnification of the *view* of the current drawing in the *drawing area* or in a *viewport*.

INDEX

Note to the Reader: Throughout this index **boldfaced** page numbers indicate primary discussions of a topic. *Italicized* page numbers indicate illustrations.

A

a command
    for arcs, 101
    for selections, 185
abbreviations for commands, 124
Above dimension option, 381
absolute coordinates, 32, 634
acad.ctb file, 529
Acad.dwt file, 54
Acad_ISO linetype family, 175
acad.stb file, 532
access roads, 421, 424, *425*
accuracy
    in 3D drawings, 562
    in Architectural units, 55–56
    in dimensions, 383
    of units, 641
Add-a-Plot Style Table Wizard, 528
Add Layers command, 251
Add option for Area, 622
Add Profile dialog box, 20, *21*
Advanced tab, 324
Advanced Wizard, 70
alias keys
    defined, 634
    modifying, 22
Align Below Previous Attribute Definition option, 619
Align button, 403
Aligned command, 403
Aligned with Dimension Line button, 381
aligning
    dimensions, 381, **402–404**, *403*, 634
    viewports, **471–472**, *472*
alignment paths
    temporary, 128
    tooltips for, 128–129, 133, *134*
Allow Others to Edit icon, 555
Alt key for hotkeys, 124

Alternate Units tab, 384
Ambient Light area, 598
American Institute of Architects, 171
American National Standards Institute (ANSI), 302–303
Angle setting, 70
Angle Direction setting, 70
Angle Measure setting, 70
angles
    Advanced Wizard, 70
    arcs, 101, 108
    dimension orientation, 397
    hatches, 300
    isometric views, 595
    leader lines, 402
    polar coordinates, 34, *34*
    Polar Tracking, 198, *199*
    rotation
        blocks, 215, 230
        doors, 100
        external references, 428
    sun, 228, 597, *597*
    surveyor units, 421
Angular button, 403
Angular command, 403
angular dimensions, **402–404**, *403*, 634
Angular Dimensions area, 382–383
angular units, 54, 57, 634
ANSI (American National Standards Institute), 302–303
ANSI patterns, 302
ANSI tab, 299–300, *300*
ANSI31 pattern, 299, *300*, 321
appearance
    of external references, **430–432**, *431*
    of windows, 228
AR-PARQ1 pattern, 319, *319*
AR-RROOF pattern, 300, 303
AR-RSHKE pattern, 306, 324
Arc command and arcs
    grips for, 177–178, *177*
    options for, **101–102**

L

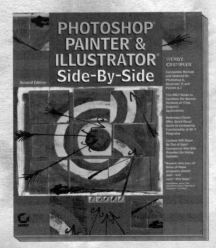

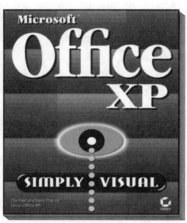
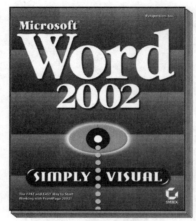